Advance Praise for

AFRICAN AMERICAN STUDENTS IN URBAN SCHOOLS

"If you ever thought student achievement would improve if schools would 'just let the teachers teach,' then this book is for you. There are so many issues affecting students, especially African American students, which have to be dealt with in order for teachers to be able to do just that. This book has opened my eyes by providing a holistic view of just what those challenges are and then goes a step further to offer solutions to those challenges. I highly recommend this book to all who are committed to eliminating the achievement gap."

—*Vanessa Benton, Director of Academic Services,*
Charlotte-Mecklenburg Schools, Charlotte, North Carolina

"The many issues affecting education in urban areas, across the country, have seemingly provided extreme situations for our urban youth. Students of color in those areas, particularly African American youth, must be provided with better opportunities, where education is concerned, to address societal issues of economic status, joblessness, and unfortunately, incarceration. I applaud Drs. James L. Moore III and Chance W. Lewis' efforts at identifying and providing opportunities for thought provoking action in this regard. Until we as a nation make and take every opportunity to improve educational circumstances for all youth, we run the risk of falling further and further behind the rest of the world."

—*Isaac C. Carrier, Principal, WJ Plummer Middle School,*
Aldine Independent School District, Houston, Texas

AFRICAN AMERICAN STUDENTS
IN URBAN SCHOOLS

Educational
PSYCHOLOGY

Critical Pedagogical Perspectives

Greg S. Goodman, *General Editor*

Vol. 4

The Educational Psychology series is part of the Peter Lang Education list.
Every volume is peer reviewed and meets
the highest quality standards for content and production.

PETER LANG
New York • Washington, D.C./Baltimore • Bern
Frankfurt • Berlin • Brussels • Vienna • Oxford

AFRICAN AMERICAN STUDENTS IN URBAN SCHOOLS

Critical Issues and Solutions for Achievement

Edited by James L. Moore III & Chance W. Lewis

PETER LANG
New York • Washington, D.C./Baltimore • Bern
Frankfurt • Berlin • Brussels • Vienna • Oxford

Library of Congress Cataloging-in-Publication Data

African American students in urban schools: critical issues and
solutions for achievement / edited by James L. Moore III, Chance W. Lewis.
p. cm. — (Educational psychology: critical pedagogical perspectives; vol. 4)
Includes bibliographical references.
1. African Americans—Education. 2. Education, Urban—United States.
I. Moore III, James L. II. Lewis, Chance W. III. Title.
LC2717.M66   371.829'96073—dc23   2012010519
ISBN 978-1-4331-0687-3 (hardcover)
ISBN 978-1-4331-0686-6 (paperback)
ISBN 978-1-4539-0812-9 (e-book)
ISSN 1943-8109

Bibliographic information published by Die Deutsche Nationalbibliothek.
Die Deutsche Nationalbibliothek lists this publication in the "Deutsche
Nationalbibliografie"; detailed bibliographic data is available
on the Internet at http://dnb.d-nb.de/.

The paper in this book meets the guidelines for permanence and durability
of the Committee on Production Guidelines for Book Longevity
of the Council of Library Resources.

© 2012 Peter Lang Publishing, Inc., New York
29 Broadway, 18th floor, New York, NY 10006
www.peterlang.com

Printed in the United States of America

This book is dedicated to my beloved mother, Edna Marie Moore, who passed away on April 26, 2011. She was a towering figure in my life as well as others. Her words of endearment, gestures of kindness, acts of courage, and expressions of hope will forever live in me. All that I am or hope to be is because of my mother. This book represents one of the many ways that I honor her commitment to humanity and her impact in my life. I am forever indebted to her. Thanks mama for always supporting and loving me!

—James L. Moore III

This book is dedicated to my wife, Mechael Lewis, and my two beautiful daughters, Myra and Sydney Lewis, who have all given their time and space for me to complete this monumental project. I thank you for being supportive. I love you!

—Chance W. Lewis

Table of Contents

Acknowledgments ix

Foreword: A Long-Needed and Refreshing Book xi
Donna Y. Ford

PART I: INTRODUCTION 1

Chapter One: Confronting the Dilemmas of Urban Education:
The Scope of the Book 3
James L. Moore III and Chance W. Lewis

Chapter Two: Urban Education in the 21st Century: An Overview of
Selected Issues That Impact African American Student Outcomes 11
Chance W. Lewis, Terah Venzant Chambers, and Bettie Ray Butler

PART II: PERSPECTIVES AND PATTERNS IN URBAN SCHOOL CONTEXTS 31

Chapter Three: Meeting the Academic and Social Needs of Urban
African American Students: Implications for School Counselors 33
Cheryl Holcomb-McCoy and Beverly Booker

Chapter Four: Nurturing Resiliency Among African American Adolescent
Males: A Focus on Writing 53
Alfred W. Tatum

Chapter Five: Special Education and Disciplinary Disproportionality of
African American Students 75
Gwendolyn Cartledge, Lenwood Gibson Jr., and Starr E. Keyes

Chapter Six: Trends and Patterns of Career and Technical Education for
Urban African American Students 95
Edward C. Fletcher Jr.

Chapter Seven: Salient Factors Affecting Urban African American
Students' Achievement: Recommendations for Teachers, School
Counselors, and School Psychologists 113
Desireé Vega, James L. Moore III, Caroline A. Baker, Nikol V. Bowen,
Erik M. Hines, and Barbara O'Neal

PART III: CULTURALLY RELEVANT PEDAGOGY IN URBAN CLASSROOMS.....................141

Chapter Eight: Developing Culturally Relevant Classrooms for Urban
    African American Students 143
    H. Richard Milner IV

Chapter Nine: Using Culturally Relevant Pedagogy and Social Justice to
    Understand Mathematics Instructional Quality in an Urban Context 161
    Robert Q. Berry III and Temple A. Walkowiak

Chapter Ten: Bridging the Culture of Urban Students to the Culture
    of Science: The Roles of Culturally Relevant Pedagogy, Discursive
    Identity, and Conceptual Continuities in the Promotion
    of Scientific Literacy..185
    Bryan A. Brown, Matthew Kloser, and J. Bryan Henderson

PART IV: URBAN SCHOOL LEADERSHIP AND OUTREACH 205

Chapter Eleven: Urban School Administrators: A Grassroots Approach
    to No Child Left Behind Mandates...207
    Christopher Dunbar Jr. and Laura McNeal

Chapter Twelve: The Fast and the Serious: Exploring the Notion
    of Culturally Relevant Leadership 231
    Floyd D. Beachum and Carlos R. McCray

Chapter Thirteen: Reaching Out: Partnering With the Families and
    Communities of African American Urban Youth 249
    Mavis G. Sanders, Gilda Martinez-Alda, and Michelle D. White

PART V: PERSPECTIVES AND INSIGHTS IN POSTSECONDARY CONTEXTS 269

Chapter Fourteen: Inside Information on High-Achieving African
    American Male College Students 271
    Fred A. Bonner II and John W. Murry Jr.

Chapter Fifteen: In the Pursuit of Excellence: Examining the Effects
    of Racial Identity on African American College Students'
    Academic Orientations 289
    LaTrelle D. Jackson, W. Max Parker, and Lamont A. Flowers

About the Editors..315
About the Authors...319

Acknowledgments

First, I wish to acknowledge my precious wife, Stephanie, and our three outstanding children, James IV, Sienna Ava, and Savanna Marie-Ann, for allocating consistent space and time for me to complete this book project. Without their love and support, completing this book would have been impossible. Second, I wish to thank my brother, Marcus T. Moore, and my sister, Dr. S. Rochelle Sullivan, for their unwavering support and encouragement throughout my life. Third, I want to express my sincere appreciation to my extended family and close friends, especially my Aunt Frances and Uncle WC Anderson. Both my family and friends have enriched my thinking about education and its importance in American society.

Fourth, I want to thank my former teachers, coaches, and professors for investing their time and talents in me. Fifth, I offer special thanks to my staff at the Todd Anthony Bell National Resource Center on the African American Male, as well as my colleagues, students, and staff who have supported me in both the Office of Diversity and Inclusion and the College of Education and Human Ecology at The Ohio State University. Sixth, I wish to thank my series editor for selecting this book to be a part of the publications of Peter Lang Publishers. Seventh and above all, I thank my Creator for the many blessings bestowed to me.

—James L. Moore III

I wish to thank my mother, Brenda Clem Davis, for sharing her love for teaching and her knowledge of how a teacher can have a major impact on the world. Words cannot adequately express my gratitude to her. I also want to acknowledge my dear grandparents, Dr. William W. Clem, K. Frances Thomas, Lloyd O. Lewis, Sr., and Peggy Lewis, who planted seeds of greatness in me. Although they are no longer here with me, I constantly feel their presence as I navigate this life. Last, I want to express my sincere gratitude to my students who have taken my courses over the years and implemented the knowledge learned from these experiences in both their professional and personal life. My students have certainly enriched my work as a professor. I have learned just as much from them as they have learned from me.

—Chance W. Lewis

Foreword: A Long-Needed and Refreshing Book

DONNA Y. FORD

For over 20 years, I have endeavored to add to the compassion, action, and knowledge base on education in terms of what is right with urban schools and what is wrong with them. Like a seesaw, the discussion is seldom balanced—what is wrong tends to outweigh what is right, what is not successful tends to overshadow what is successful, and those students who fail tend to be more emphasized than those who thrive. Simply put, the poor achievement of urban students, particularly African American ones, has reached epidemic portions, with little hope for change in sight based on current treatments, which frequently represent Band-Aids.

Generally speaking, the achievement gap is prevalent in virtually every school district, school building, and classroom, where African American students, on average, fail to achieve at the levels of their White and Asian classmates. The data consistently show that African Americans enter school an average of one year behind White kindergarteners, and it is equally clear that the gap widens *significantly* during the school years. Interpretations abound, as does finger pointing. Educators, policy makers, and families rarely take responsibility for the problems of urban education, including the persistent achievement gaps. Wallowing in this unceasing debate are African American students, many of whom are aware that expectations for them are low and that they are viewed as expendable in a nation that professes to place a premium on equality, equity, excellence, and being first globally in education (as well as in everything else). It is not surprising that apathy runs deep in school hallways and in the minds and hearts of urban African American students. Apathy is also evident among many of the teachers, too few of whom have been adequately trained or retrained to work effectively and proactively with African American students in urban school contexts. At their respective universities and colleges, urban educators often have not been equipped with the knowledge, skills, and dispositions to teach African American students. Even worse, the professional development—extended to the educators in their respective school systems—seems to not be comprehensive and systemic, which further intensifies teacher quality problems. These problems contribute to personnel burn-out and poor teacher-retention rates.

In urban school settings, morale is frequently low among school personnel. Teachers, administrators, and other school staff (e.g., school counselors, school psychologists, etc.) are often faced with school and nonschool challenges that hamper their ability to effectively educate and academically challenge African American students. What differentiates urban school systems from those of suburban and rural schools is that the school challenges are frequently more pronounced. Further, the school factors—combined with the nonschool factors—challenge teachers, administrators, and other school personnel to be culturally responsive to the interests and needs of their African American students.

It is important to note that teacher quality alone does not contribute to all of the shortcomings of urban school systems involving African American students. Decision makers and policy makers, such as politicians, state-level education administrators, and district-level leaders, must take their share of the blame and witness how schools are funded, how resources are allocated, where quality teachers are assigned, and the like. Many of these groups' decisions, or lack of decisions, have contributed to the demise of urban school systems. The challenges in urban school systems are some of America's most pressing social justice and civil rights issues.

Recently, I was privy to a discussion about the research being produced about urban education ad infinitum and ad nauseam. I and other participants in the discussion were on research overload, often questioning the purpose and utility of many recent studies. Scholars seem to be grappling in desperation for something, anything, to write about. In particular, I experience dread, frustration, and anger frequently when another study comes out pertaining to urban education—*now*, what is the complaint and stereotype that is being posed here, I question?

This impending doom I think is just as relevant when a new book comes out on urban education and our students. And I use "new" loosely. Much of what is being published on urban education is a rehash of what is already known, thought to be known, and published; there are too few new or refreshing insights and alternative treatises and explanations. Likewise, much of this regurgitation continues (unfortunately and unnecessarily) to be loaded with deficit thinking, often exonerating educators from even partial responsibility and accountability for the omnibus issue of the achievement gap in all its forms—gifted education and advanced placement (AP) underrepresentation; special education overrepresentation; disproportionality in discipline, suspension, and expulsion; and so much more.

This edited volume, under the leadership and visionary thinking of Drs. James L. Moore III and Chance W. Lewis, is a breath of fresh air. The editors and authors address real students, real issues, and real solutions in urban education. They highlight the issues, while still focusing on the future of urban education, which is currently bleak. The contributors naturally kvetched about the subject; however, they still offered hope by offering strategies to improve education outcomes for African American students. The authors explore and untangle issues of low achievement and underachievement in its myriad of forms. Their treatment is comprehensive, addressing many critical topics. I appreciate the comprehensiveness of the collection of chapters, with its focus on both K–12 and college settings. The urban school problems do not end with formal schooling or after college. It is unfortunate that it is a perpetual cycle.

Education factors are the book's foundation, but the editors and authors remind readers and decision makers to not forget about factors that do not involve education. Yes, we can and must focus on the education factors, but it is negligent to ignore or relegate to second-class status the non-education issues and needs of African American students, particularly in urban schools.

Both necessary and unique in this edited volume are chapters that focus specifically on African American males. In schools all across America, this group is often overrepresented in special education and underrepresented in gifted and AP classes. The students are routinely the recipients of disciplinary practices, such as school suspension and expulsion. At an early age, African American males experience school differently from their student counterparts, which sometimes places them on a pathway to crime, drugs, and prison. Those who deny seeing this destructive social and educational pattern have buried their heads in the proverbial sand. Readers will glean information from the chapters, which focus specifically on African American males and how to improve education outcomes for these students. Further, I hope that the readers will understand the social and economic consequences of not improving our urban schools. Chapters in the book demonstrate with clarity that African American students will continue to lose edge in life, if society does not drastically overhaul and reform its urban schools.

This edited volume covers some extremely important topics, such as career and technical education, racial identity development, resiliency, culturally responsive education, and postsecondary education. These topics, as well as the others, are timely, thorough, and essential. I applaud the editors for putting this book together and for assembling a diverse group of urban education scholars. Readers will benefit from this edited volume. Just as important, the African American students will also benefit.

It is so very long overdue for the nation to get angry, compassionate, and proactive about change. None of us can afford to be bystanders. We are a nation of one—no exceptions. A sense of co-destiny must guide all of our work as professionals and, more important, as citizens of the United States. Without question, as readers will learn from this book, if African American students fail, America fails. If they succeed, the entire country succeeds.

INTRODUCTION

CHAPTER ONE

Confronting THE Dilemmas OF Urban Education: The Scope OF THE Book

EDITORS: JAMES L. MOORE III AND CHANCE W. LEWIS

Access to a quality education is not only the foundation of a democratic society; it is also a characteristic of a productive nation. Education and the economy are inextricably linked. The future of the United States rests in its education system. Globalization has spurred the need for more skilled workers. Those countries who are able to "produce the most important new products and services can capture a premium in world markets that will enable them to pay high wages to their citizens. In many industries, producing the most important new products and services depends on maintaining the worldwide technological lead, year in and year out, in that industry and in the new industries that new technologies generate" (National Center on Education and the Economy, 2007, p. xviii); therefore, strong preparation in education is vital in today's global market.

Globalization, over time, has taken a toll on the United States. An important occurrence is that the United States can no longer boast about having the most *skilled* and *educated* workforce in the world, because other countries have drastically improved their education systems. One country after another has begun to surpass the United States in the proportion of workers entering the workforce with the equivalent of a high school diploma or higher (National Center on Education and the Economy, 2007). These countries, increasingly, no longer have to recruit skilled workers from other places in the world. Improvements to their education systems have made it easier for countries to recruit more highly skilled workers among their own citizens and at cheaper costs (National Center on Education and the Economy, 2007).

A disheartening reality is that too many Americans are not benefiting from the U.S. public education system. A closer examination of the system, as a whole, reveals some distressing patterns. There are huge disparities in education outcomes among certain demographic groups and school contexts. For example, go visit any large urban school system in the United States, and you will find some of America's most vulnerable students (Lewis & Moore, 2008a, 2008b). At every point of the education continuum, you will witness a large number of students who are academically unprepared or underprepared. It is sad to observe that a disproportionate number of these students are *African American* and *poor* (Cartledge & Lo, 2006). Many of them start their school experiences behind other students because early childhood programs are not available to them (Tsoi-A-Fatt, 2010). Stated in a different way, Kozol (2005) asserts:

> More commonly in urban neighborhoods, large numbers of children received no preschool education and they come into their kindergarten year without the minimal social skills that children need in order to participate in class activities and without even such very modest early-learning skills as knowing how to hold a pencil, identify perhaps a couple of shapes or colors, or recognize that printed pages go from left to right (pp. 52–53).

Nevertheless, today's urban school systems are confronted with a number of harsh realities, beyond curricula. Wilson (1996) writes that urban African American youth "grow up in neighborhoods with devastating rates of joblessness, which trigger a whole series of other problems that are not conducive to healthy child development or intellectual growth. Included among these are broken families, antisocial behavior, social networks that do not extend beyond the confines of the ghetto environment, and a lack of informal social control over the behavior and activities of children and adults in the neighborhood" (pp. xv–xvi).

It is widely recognized that the communities where these school systems are situated are often strapped for resources and opportunities. They are commonly based in low-income segregated neighborhoods. In these communities, the schools are often funded at lower levels than suburban schools (Shaffer, Ortman, & Denbo, 2002). Thus, it becomes the responsibility of urban school systems to respond to the growing demands associated with poverty, such as insufficient medical care, lack of basic needs, and amplified crime rates (Ockerman, 2006). They are nevertheless expected to educate all their students, as well as prepare them for different postsecondary opportunities (e.g., college, military, or the workplace).

In spite of the challenges, some urban school systems still have been able to achieve success in educating African American students. There are many notable success stories in urban schools (Reid & Moore, 2008; Sanders, 1997). But the dilemmas of urban school systems remain widespread for African American students (Lewis, James, Hancock, & Hill-Jackson, 2008; Lewis & Moore, 2008a, 2008b). Failure is still characteristically seen in these settings (Neckerman, 2007). Even when this is not the case, prevailing *negative* perceptions seem to obscure any successes.

Similar to suburban and rural school districts, urban school systems are significant social institutions in American society. Because the United States wants to thrive in the global market now and in the future, there is a strong need to fix urban schools across the country. Recent education reforms and funding initiatives at the federal and state levels are a strong indication of this point. In virtually every urban school system around the country, there are education reform efforts being implemented. They range from smaller classroom sizes and longer class time to new curricula and teacher-training modules to more assessments and testing. Despite the reform efforts, urban African American students still constitute a population at risk (Jackson & Moore, 2006, 2008; Noguera, 2008). This is reflected in current popular and social science literature (Lewis & Moore, 2008a, 2008b; Neckerman, 2007; Shaffer, Ortman, & Denbo, 2002).

Over the last decade, a plethora of publications has been devoted to African American students in urban contexts. Some of this literature base has provided rich information on the education experiences and outcomes of urban African American students, as well as the shortcomings of urban school systems that they attend. What is most often missing from these publications is depth and breadth, which is very difficult to accomplish in a single journal article, policy brief, or book chapter. This edited volume, *African American Students in Urban Schools: Critical Issues and Solutions for Achievement,* seeks to offer readers a critical yet comprehensive examination of the issues confronting the education experiences of African American students and affecting their achievement in urban school systems and beyond. A number of the ideas presented in this edited volume are not new, but few books have attempted to present a complete picture. Across education disciplines (e.g., general teacher education, school counseling, school psychology, gifted education, career and technical education, higher education, etc.), this collection of chapters aims to achieve this goal by presenting theoretical, conceptual, and research-based evidence of the unique challenges facing urban African American students and illustrating what can be done to reduce, if not diminish, these challenges. This edited volume, hopefully, will help readers better understand some of the complex and multifaceted dilemmas faced by today's urban school systems. An equal hope for this publication is that it will motivate readers to make a commitment to improving urban schools for the betterment of African American students.

This volume is organized into 5 parts, comprising 15 chapters. What follows is a brief overview of the chapters in these five sections:

Part I: Introduction

Part I of this volume comprises two chapters. It begins with this one. In Chapter 2, our coauthors Chance W. Lewis, Terah Venzant Chambers, and Bettie Ray Butler present snapshots of selected issues (e.g., teacher stability, dropout rates, funding, resegregation, urban district leadership, etc.) that have been found to influence African American student outcomes in urban schools. The content from this chapter is rich and descriptive.

Part II: Perspectives and Patterns in Urban School Contexts

Part II comprises five chapters. The authors are concerned with factors that commonly affect education outcomes for urban African American students. Although there are some overlaps, each chapter makes its own individual contribution to the edited volume. In Chapter 3, our coauthors, Cheryl Holcombe-McCoy and Beverly Booker, present a framework on how school counselors can make a significant impact on the emotional and academic development of urban African American students. The framework includes five areas of focus, including counseling, parent and teacher consultation, data usage, school culture, and rigorous course enrollment. In the summer of 2009, Alfred W. Tatum engaged 12 African American adolescent males in texts that involved reading and writing to examine the sociocultural benefits of writing. In Chapter 4, Tatum presents a qualitative case study, highlighting his work with these adolescent African American males. He concludes that there may be a need to (re)theorize writing for adolescent African American males. In urban schools around the country, special education is a topic of major concern. In Chapter 5, our coauthors, Gwendolyn Cartledge, Lenwood Gibson Jr., and Starr E. Keyes, focus on the inequities that take place in special education for African American students in urban settings. The authors highlight trends in special education, such as disproportionality. They also pinpoint the factors that contribute to the overrepresentation of African American students in special education. Chapter 6 focuses exclusively on urban African American students in career and technical education. Edward C. Fletcher Jr. presents national data to illustrate the trends and patterns for African American students in career and technical education programs. He also highlights best practices and policies for infusing career and technical education in urban school contexts. In Chapter 7, our coauthors, Desireé Vega, James L. Moore III, Caroline A. Baker, Nikol V. Bowen, Erik M. Hines, and

Barbara O'Neal, focus on the factors that *most* commonly affect urban African American students' education outcomes. The authors categorize these factors into three broad topical areas: school, social-cultural, and psychological. The authors conclude with specific recommendations for teachers, school counselors, and school psychologists.

Part III: Culturally Relevant Pedagogy in Urban Classrooms

Part III includes three chapters. The work in this section focuses on culturally relevant pedagogy. The various authors make a case for culturally relevant pedagogy and explain how it could be used to reach, connect, and teach African American students in urban classroom spaces. In Chapter 8, H. Richard (Rich) Milner IV explains what culturally relevant pedagogy is and how urban educators can create classroom spaces grounded in the cultural experiences of African American students. He concludes with useful teacher implications. In Chapter 9, coauthors, Robert Q. Berry III and Temple A. Walkowiak, focus on the factors that most impact the instructional quality of mathematics and African American students' experiences related to mathematics in urban school contexts. They also provide descriptions and examples of culturally relevant pedagogy and teaching mathematics for social justice. They conclude with recommendations for mathematics teachers. In Chapter 10, coauthors, Bryan A. Brown, Matthew Kloser, and J. Bryan Henderson, illustrate the importance of building bridges with urban African American students in science classrooms. Further, they suggest that science educators should possess the proper pedagogical skills to build bridges between students and science.

Part IV: Urban School Leadership and Outreach

Part IV includes three chapters. The contributors in this section highlight the importance of school leadership and partnering with families and communities. In Chapter 11, coauthors, Christopher Dunbar Jr. and Laura McNeal, present a qualitative analysis of how urban school principals from two urban school districts and one Urban Charter school in Michigan were able to achieve the standard of Adequate Yearly Progress (AYP) on No Child Left Behind (NCLB), despite being out of compliance with their mandates. In Chapter 12, coauthors, Floyd D. Beachum and Carlos R. McCray, address the issue of relationships in K–12 schools and offer a broader vision of urban school leadership. The authors also encourage ethical action on behalf of students. In Chapter 13, coauthors, Mavis G. Sanders, Gilda Martinez-Alda, and Michelle D. White, define school, family, and community partnerships and highlight the different types of involvement within the context of effective outreach to urban families and communities. The authors additionally highlight evidence that supports the school, family, and community success of African American urban youth.

Part V: Perspectives and Insights in Postsecondary Contexts

Part V includes two chapters. The work in this section focuses on higher education issues that African American students often experience in college. In Chapter 14, coauthors, Fred A. Bonner II and John W. Murry Jr., pinpoint the factors that positively impact academic outcomes for high-achieving African American male college students who attended urban public schools. The two authors conclude their chapter by offering recommendations directed at academic/college advisors and student affairs professionals at the college level. In Chapter 15, using survey data, coauthors, LaTrelle D. Jackson, W. Max Parker, and Lamont A. Flowers, investigate African American students' attitudes that are based on racial identity development regarding their learning orientations and academic outlooks in college. Multivariate analyses indicate that students' racial identity development significantly impacts their perceptions of academic achievement and intellectual engagement.

This edited volume does not represent the complete range of topics that affect school outcomes for African American students in urban school contexts; however, it is more comprehensive than a single journal article, policy brief, or book chapter. We believe that the authors of these chapters do address important topics that affect urban African American students, as well as the urban educators who serve them (e.g., teachers, school counselors, school psychologists, principals, etc.). Thus, there are still a lot of topics that need to be researched. In closing, we hope that the readers will join us in trying to make a difference in urban school systems to improve education outcomes for African American students.

REFERENCES

Cartledge, G., & Lo, Y. Y. (2006). *Teaching urban learners: Culturally responsive strategies for developing academic and behavioral competence.* Champaign, IL: Research Press.

Jackson, J. F. L., & Moore, J. L., III. (2006). African American males in education: Endangered or ignored? *Teachers College Record, 108*(2), 201–205.

Jackson, J. F. L., & Moore, J. L., III. (2008). The African American male crisis in education: A popular media infatuation or needed public policy response? *American Behavioral Scientist, 51*(7), 847–853.

Kozol, J. (2005). *The shame of the nation: The restoration of apartheid schooling in America.* New York, NY: Crown.

Lewis, C. W., James, M., Hancock, S., & Hill-Jackson, V. (2008). Framing African American students' success and failure in urban settings: A typology for change. *Urban Education, 43*(2), 127–153.

Lewis, C. W., & Moore, J. L., III. (2008a). African American students in K–12 urban educational settings. *Urban Education, 43*(2), 123–126.

Lewis, C. W., & Moore, J. L., III. (2008b). Urban public schools for African American students: Critical issues for educational stakeholders. *The Journal of Educational Foundations, 22*(1–2), 3–10.

National Center on Education and the Economy (2007). *Tough choices or tough time: The report of the new commission on the skills of the American workforce.* Hoboken, NJ: Jossey-Bass.

Neckerman, K. M. (2007). *Schools betrayed: Roots of failure in inner-city education.* Chicago, IL: University of Chicago.

Noguera, P. A. (2008). *The trouble with black boys: . . . And other reflections on race, equity, and the future of public education.* San Francisco, CA: Jossey-Bass.

Ockerman, M. (2006). *Urban students' school experiences and their perceptions of the Ohio State Counseling and Wellness Center* (Unpublished dissertation, The Ohio State University).

Reid, M. J., & Moore, J. L. III. (2008). College readiness and academic preparation for postsecondary education: Oral histories of first-generation urban college students. *Urban Education, 43*(2), 240–261.

Sanders, M. G. (1997). Overcoming obstacles: Academic achievement as a response to racism and discrimination. *Journal of Negro Education, 66*(1), 83–93.

Shaffer, S., Ortman, P. E., & Denbo, S. J. (2002). The effects of racism, socioeconomic class, and gender on the academic achievement of African American students. In S. J. Denbo & L. Moore Beaulieu (Eds.), *Improving schools for African American students: A reader for educational leaders* (pp. 19–29). Springfield, IL: Charles C. Thomas.

Tsoi-A-Fatt, R. (2010). *We dream a world: The 2025 vision for black men and boys.* Washington, DC: Center for Law and Social Policy.

Wilson, W. J. (1996). *When work disappears: The world of the new urban poor.* New York, NY: Alfred A. Knopf.

CHAPTER TWO

Urban Education IN THE 21st Century: An Overview OF Selected Issues That Impact African American Student Outcomes

CHANCE W. LEWIS, TERAH VENZANT CHAMBERS, AND
BETTIE RAY BUTLER

In the 21st century, K–12 schools in urban settings continue to face a variety of complex issues that have a direct impact on student outcomes (i.e., course grades, standardized test scores, discipline occurrences, high school graduation rates, etc.), particularly for African American students. Many of these complex issues have been clearly documented in the scholarly literature, but others are still yet to be adequately examined. These complex issues, in many cases, impact African American student outcomes even though they are beyond the control of these students. As a result, African American students, when compared to their counterparts in other ethnic groups, are at or near the bottom of every major academic barometer (Lewis, 2009). Even more disturbing is that many researchers and practitioners still do not view this as a crisis but as a normal level of achievement for African American students (Landsman & Lewis, 2006; Lewis, 2009; Lewis & Moore, 2008a, 2008b).

Based on the extant literature, we have come to learn that this level of performance by African American students does not happen solely according to their individual aptitude but according to a tangled web of issues that currently plague our urban schools. Many scholars have noted that issues in urban schools are not the same as issues in suburban and rural communities (Strizek, Pittsonberger, Riordan, Lyter, & Gruber, 2006). However, sometimes overlooked in this argument is that these current and future generations of African American students will not be prepared to be productive members in a society that demands that its citizens have the increasing levels of intellectual capacities and educational training needed to achieve financial prosperity. Given the multidimensional nature of this issue and the lack of appropriate attention in previous research to the implications of this situation, the overall goal of this chapter is to organize a set of core issues at the national, school district/community, and student levels that have an impact on African American student outcomes. We realize that one book chapter is inadequate to address every issue that exists; however, we provide an overview of selected issues that have an impact on African American student achievement in urban schools.

NATIONAL ISSUES

Teacher Stability

In urban schools across the United States, one issue that all education stakeholders agree has an impact on African American achievement is teacher stability in urban schools and its impact on academic outcomes for African American students (Darling-Hammond & Bransford, 2005; Kunjufu, 2002). According to the scholarly literature, we still find an overwhelming percentage of teachers in all schools, particularly urban schools, who are White and female (Landsman & Lewis, 2006). The literature also informs us that larger percentages of teachers of color usually gravitate toward urban schools. As an example, "Black teachers comprise 15 percent of teachers in urban schools, which is twice their share of the entire public teaching force" (Frankenburg, 2009, p. 264). One trend that overwhelmingly impacts African American student outcomes is the instability of the teaching force in these same urban schools.

Teachers, particularly White teachers, in urban schools are more likely to transfer from schools with high percentages of African American and Hispanic students (Freeman, Scafidi, & Sjoquist, 2005; Hanushek, Kain, & Rivkin, 2004; Lankford, Loeb, & Wykoff, 2002; Loeb & Reininger, 2004). Thus, the challenge for urban schools is to keep a stable quality teaching force for all students, particularly African American students, from year to year to improve academic achievement. It is unfortunate that this is a rare occurrence, based on data from the most recent School and Staffing Survey (SASS; National Center for Education

Statistics, 2009), which reports that urban schools have the highest percentage of novice teachers (who have been teaching from zero to three years): 18.3%. Given this trend, African American students in our nation's urban schools are exposed to many novice teachers, who, in many situations, are "trying to find their way" in negotiating the classroom (Milner, 2006). As a result of the instability of the teaching force in urban schools, African American student outcomes are, in most cases, compromised because of a very important variable they have no control over—the teacher in the classroom. The long-term ramification is that African American students are then placed at a severe disadvantage for the rest of their lives, because they have missed out on the quality instruction that scholars have documented to be a critical ingredient to the future success of this population (Kunjufu, 2002; Landsman, 2008; Thompson, 2004).

Dropout Rates

Another issue that impacts student outcomes for African American students is the dropout rates of this population. Even though many constituents agree that this issue impacts student outcomes, finding reliable data on the impact for African American students is a major task, because of the lack of consistency of the term "dropout" and the trouble in defining it. The source of this obscurity stems from what many educational researchers and practitioners believe to be intentionally skewed dropout data from state education agencies, school districts, and schools (Fossey, 1996). In consequence, the research community cannot accurately determine if in fact there is decline or growth in the reported number of all students, particularly urban African American students, who exit school prior to completion. Another complexity in examining this issue is the fact that there is not a common definition or consistent reporting mechanism used across all states, districts, and schools. This type of inconsistency makes it difficult to accurately track the number of African American students that could be considered "dropouts" across these same states, districts, and schools.

In an attempt to inform this issue, the federal government utilizes multiple sources of data to determine the national dropout rate (Kaufman, 2004). One source is the Current Population Survey (CPS). This survey collects information on degree attainment and enrollment status for both the current year and prior year to identify dropouts. CPS data is collected by the U.S. Census Bureau and is recognized as the only source of national time series data on dropout rates (Laird, Cataldi, KewalRamani, & Chapman, 2008). Another source is the Common Core of Data (CCD). This national database reports public school dropout rates from 50 state-level education agencies, the District of Columbia, and other outlying areas (Kaufman, 2004).

The information reported by CCD is updated annually by the National Center for Education Statistics (NCES). The most common dropout statistics reported by CPS and CCD is the *annual*, or *event*, *dropout rate*, which measures the proportion of students who drop out within a single year without obtaining a high school credential (Thurlow, Sinclair, & Johnson, 2002). The Longitudinal Studies Program generally reports a very different dropout rate than those of CPS and CCD. This source reports the *cohort*, or *longitudinal*, *dropout rate*, which measures what happens to a single group of students (i.e., a cohort) over a specified length of time (Thurlow et al., 2002). Dropout data from these databases, High School and Beyond (HS&B) and the National Education Longitudinal Studies of 1988 (NELS: 88), are obtained by surveying students every year for an extended period of time (Planty, Hussar, Snyder, Kena, KewalRamani, Kemp, Bianco, & Dinkes, 2009). The most frequently used source of data within the most recent years is the U.S. Census Bureau's American Community Survey (ACS). Of all the data sources mentioned, this survey provides the most detailed comparison of *status dropout rates*—the percentage of 16- through 24-year-olds who are not enrolled in school and have not earned a high school credential—by race/ethnicity, nativity, and gender (Planty et al., 2009). The most current estimates by ACS reveal that, in general, African American dropout rates declined between 1980 and 2007 (Planty et al., 2009). Approximately 19% of all 16- through 24-year-old African Americans were reported to have dropped out of school and discontinued attempts to earn a high school diploma or the equivalent in 1980; in 2007, this rate dropped to 8%, contributing to a total decline of nearly 11 percentage points.

If taken at face value, this decrease in dropout rates suggests that today more African Americans are staying in school and earning their high school credential in comparison to two decades ago. Yet, because of the ambiguity in how dropout data is collected, no one can be entirely certain that this decline is as authentic as these statistics would allow one to believe. For this reason, it is necessary to conduct further assessments of this phenomenon for comparative purposes and in an effort to fully understand the magnitude of the national dropout rate.

Funding

The issue of school funding is perhaps the most important one for schools in general, and urban schools in specific due to its direct impact on so many other issues with which schools contend. Although schools receive a significant portion of their funding from federal sources (approximately 10%), the majority of school funds are generated at the state (45%) and local (45%) levels through property taxes, although the proportions vary slightly in each state (Cohen & Johnson, 2004).

Federal funding. Because, under the U.S. Constitution, education has historically been the responsibility of the states, the federal government has largely played a supplemental role. The 1965 Elementary and Secondary Education Act (ESEA), reauthorized in 2001 as the No Child Left Behind Act (NCLB), is the federal government's first major contribution to education. Today, the federal government's contributions lie primarily in two programs: (a) Title I, which provides monetary assistance under ESEA to economically disadvantaged students, and (b) the Individuals with Disabilities Education Act (IDEA), which provides assistance to children with disabilities.

State funding. The most significant decisions about school operations lie at the state level. Not only do most states provide a large portion of the money for educational expenditures, they also retain the organizational and administrative power—through state departments of education, or similarly titled entities. However, although a significant amount of school funding comes from the state level, there remains a significant amount of variability *between* states with respect to the amount of money provided. For example, the average per-pupil spending across the nation in the 2006–2007 school year was close to $10,000, but New York spent almost $16,000 per student, whereas Idaho and Utah each spent less than $7,000 (U.S. Census Bureau, 2009). This also does not mean that those funds are distributed equally. According to a report by the Education Trust, a respected national education think tank, 26 states provide less money to the poorest school districts than to the richest (as much as $1,000 less per pupil in some states). Further, 28 states also provide more funding to the lowest minority districts than to the higher minority districts (Education Trust, 2006).

Local funding. Another significant source of funding for schools comes at the local level, primarily through the collection of property taxes. In accordance, communities with a higher tax base collect more funds and can do so with a lower tax rate. Many urban communities have a lower tax base and are therefore often unable to collect the same amount of money, even if they impose a much higher tax rate (which they often do). As a result, there continue to be disparities in the way funds at the district level are distributed, with high-poverty schools receiving fewer district dollars for teacher salaries and unrestricted funds (Education Trust, 2006).

The issue of school funding affects urban education in that schools in cities consistently get less money by every measure—their teachers are paid less and often live in areas with lower property tax bases, which give them less money to allocate to teaching; the states give urban schools less money than other wealthier districts in the same state; and the federal government does not adequately address or compensate for these disparities. Without urban schools having adequate funds to hire the best teachers, acquire high-quality instructional materials, and maintain good working order, how can we expect the African American children who attend them to fairly compete with students who attend more affluent schools?

Resegregation

In gaining an understanding of the various variables that affect urban education in the 21st century, we see that resegregation is a major issue that has impacted African American student outcomes. This may be due to the fact that school segregation is widely thought to be something that was addressed many years ago and is believed to have very little connection to these current issues. Despite what many may imagine, issues of resegregation are now and have long been a pressing national concern, beginning with the 1954 *Brown v. Board of Education of Topeka* decision and continuing through the recent 2007 *Parents v. Seattle District* case. In large part as a response to diligent efforts by researchers at the UCLA Civil Rights Project (previously conducted at Harvard University), we have detailed comprehensive information about the legacy and implications of racial segregation in our schools today. The rapid resegregation now occurring throughout the United States is important to urban education because of the effect of de-segregation on all students, particularly students of color. For these reasons, resegregation should be considered to be a critical issue affecting African American student outcomes, particularly in urban educational settings.

Resegregation trends in the United States. The 1954 *Brown* decision ended the era of schools that were legally segregated by race, but it was not until the 1960s that the enforcement power necessary to uphold that ruling was available through the 1964 Civil Rights Act, the 1965 Voting Rights Act, and the 1965 Elementary and Secondary Education Act (ESEA). Armed with the full enforcement power of the federal government, widespread de-segregation was achieved throughout the nation, but particularly in the South. In fact, by 1981, there was not one school district in the nation that was more segregated than it was before de-segregation orders were implemented (Frankenberg, Lee, & Orfield, 2003). Improvement in de-segregation occurred through that decade until three separate Supreme Court decisions in the 1990s (e.g., *Board of Education of Oklahoma City v. Dowell* [1991], *Freeman v. Pitts* [1992], and *Missouri v. Jenkins* [1995]) reversed that progress almost overnight. At the current time, schools are more racially segregated in many areas than they were before the implementation of widespread de-segregation reform in the 1960s and 1970s (Orfield, 2001; Frankenberg et al., 2003). The return to segregation continues to occur even as our current national student body is more diverse than any previous time in U.S. history (Orfield, 2001). The most recent

Supreme Court case relating to de-segregation was the 2007 *Seattle* case, where the Court found even the voluntary efforts that schools in cities like Seattle and Louisville were employing to achieve de-segregation were unconstitutional (Orfield & Lee, 2007).

Positive effects of de-segregation. Many positive benefits can be seen in students who attend integrated school environments. For example, those who attended integrated schools are more comfortable living and working among people with diverse backgrounds and are better prepared to work among diverse communities (Orfield & Lee, 2005). Evidence of the business community's support of employees with diverse school experience can be found in the many amicus curiae briefs filed by prominent corporations in the *Seattle* case supporting the continuation of voluntary de-segregation plans. Other positive benefits of de-segregated environments include: (a) enhanced learning, (b) higher educational and occupational aspirations, (c) positive social interaction among members of different racial and ethnic backgrounds, (d) increased racial comfort, (e) increased minority high school graduation rates, (f) narrowed test score gaps, (g) increased college attendance rates, (h) higher rates of employment, and (i) the propensity to live in integrated settings as adults (Frankenberg et al., 2003; Orfield, 2001). In addition, a study of Black law students found that the majority had attended integrated college environments (Orfield, 2001).

Negative effects of segregation. Students attending segregated schools are often at a significant disadvantage in their learning, and they may experience positive benefits from de-segregated school environments (Orfield & Lee, 2005). African American and Latino students are more likely to attend urban schools that are highly segregated. These schools have much higher numbers of drop-outs, are more likely to be classified as "failing" under NCLB, and have a much more difficult time recruiting and retaining highly qualified teachers (Orfield & Lee, 2005). These schools often deal with the double- and triple-level effects according to segregation by race, class, and language, being that many of these schools have high concentrations of poverty and English Language Learners (ELLs).

This continues to be an issue of concern for urban education, because urban schools continue to be the most segregated, with African American students remaining among the most racially segregated group. Although it is not the case that White students themselves improve the learning of African American students (i.e., there is nothing "magical" about White students being in the classroom with African American students), it is often believed that positive educational benefits tend to follow these White students. Therefore, urban schools will continue to suffer the negative effects of resegregation until we decide to change their situation.

SCHOOL DISTRICT / COMMUNITY ISSUES

Urban Education District Leadership

According to the Council of Great City Schools (2009), superintendents in urban school districts have one of the most challenging jobs in the United States. Urban superintendents in this era of accountability and standards are "charged with making visible and rapid improvements on the academic achievement of the nation's most vulnerable children" (p. 1). In a review of the 100 largest urban districts in the United States, researchers find that, in many instances, some of the most vulnerable children are urban African American students. Given that district leadership is of critical importance to the academic outcomes of African American students, it is imperative for us to stress that there are major leadership challenges in urban schools, particularly in terms of the tenure of its superintendents.

The Council of Great City Schools notes that the average tenure of superintendents in urban schools was 3.5 years in 2009, which is an increase from 3.1 years in 2006. A closer look at the data reveals that, as of 2009, 18% of urban superintendents had been in office for five or more years, and 33% of urban superintendents had been in office for one year or less, the same percentage as in 2006 (Council of Great City Schools, 2009). As a result of this trend, African American students in urban schools can have on the average four to five superintendents before they complete grades K–12. This type of transition in a key leadership position that is ultimately responsible for the academic achievement of students in urban schools is another great injustice that African American students have no control over but nevertheless has a great impact on their lives.

The unfortunate scenario is that, in this era of high salaries and financial incentives, little has been done to increase the tenure of these superintendents. For example, the average salary for superintendents in the nation's 100 largest urban districts was $228,000, in 2008, plus an average benefit package of $58,000. In 1998, the average superintendent's salary was $191,000, with a benefits package of $42,000 (Council of Great City Schools, 2009). However, what we learn is that the increase in urban superintendent salary has had little corresponding influence on tenure in urban school districts. This is unfortunate for African American students. Because with the instability of the superintendency in urban schools, African American students do not have stable leadership in these positions, which ultimately impacts their academic outcomes. This is another issue that the African American student has no control over but has a major impact on her future.

Discipline Disproportionality

Over the past three decades, there has been a burgeoning interest in *discipline disproportionality;* the type of interest that has consequently stimulated a plethora of studies that attempt to understand why the phenomenon exists, whom it most likely impacts, and what kind of consequences it has on academic performance for students in urban settings (Butler, Joubert, & Lewis, 2010; Fenning & Rose, 2007; Ferguson, 2000; Gonzalez, & Szecsy, 2004; Monroe, 2005; Raffaele Mendez & Knoff, 2003; Skiba, Michael, Nardo, & Peterson, 2002; Skiba & Rausch, 2006). Discipline disproportionality, as it is understood in the context of classroom management, is a concept that is used to reference the overrepresentation of a group of pupils for in-school behavioral referrals. Research has often identified students of color (Bennett & Harris, 1982; Children's Defense Fund, 1975), low socioeconomic status (SES) populations (Bowditch, 1993), and the learning disabled (Balfanz, Spirikakis, Neild, & Legters, 2003; Morrison & D'Incau, 1997) as those most susceptible to disciplinary consequences. The racial disproportionality found in school discipline practices, however, has received the most extensive coverage within both the administrative (i.e., among practitioners) and academic (i.e., among scholars) sectors.

With heightened attention to the disproportional representation of students of color—namely inner-city African American males—for disciplinary action, some have argued that school-based discipline policies (e.g., zero tolerance) can be racially discriminatory (Lawson, 2003). Allegations, such as these, have led to a widespread investigation by researchers of cross-racial differences of the treatment of the male subjects that exclusionary discipline sanctions are imposed on (e.g., regarding suspensions and expulsions). In their study of out-of-school suspensions in a large, ethnically diverse school district in Florida (the 12th largest district in the nation and second largest district in Florida), Raffaele Mendez and Knoff (2003) find that African Americans accounted for 17% of the student population, yet they constituted approximately 33% of all suspensions (see also Education Trust, 1998). Gregory and Weinstein (2008) observe similar dynamics in the district they assessed; their study reveals that although African American students constituted only 30% of the total student enrollment, they made up 58% of student referrals for defiance-related infractions. In contrast, their Anglo peers made up roughly 37% of the total student enrollment, and yet they comprised just 5% of the total number of student referrals for defiance-related infractions (Gregory & Weinstein, 2008). In alignment with the previous research, Wallace, Goodkind, Wallace, and Bachman (2008) conclude in their longitudinal analysis (1991–2005) of school discipline trends among high school students in the United States that African Americans males represented a staggering 330% of the total number of suspensions and expulsions over the duration of the specified 14 years, which is roughly 3.3 times higher than the rate at which their same-gendered Anglo peers were suspended and expelled over the same span of time. As evidenced by these reports, African Americans, particularly males, undoubtedly had the highest reported suspension rates of any of their counterparts (Skiba et al., 2002).

As a result of these findings, one thing is certain: A conscious effort must be made to reduce the overall percentage of exclusionary sanctions for African American students and additionally to make discipline consequences more equitable. To do this, it is vital that the root—or rather, the source—of discipline disproportionality be uncovered. Albeit, many education theorists have speculated that the overrepresentation of African American males for disciplinary action is the product of these students' failure to behave appropriately and follow rules and instructions; others contend that such disproportionality is possibly the function of cultural and/or social misunderstandings, lack of teacher training, and classroom and/or social climate, or worse, discrimination (Raffaele Mendez & Knoff, 2003). The truth of the matter is that no one is completely sure about why discipline disproportionality exists. However, despite this uncertainty, the need to identify its source is no less important. As a result, educators, particularly those in urban settings, have the potential to not only improve classroom management but student productivity as well. As the logic concerning this improvement stands, if a student is suspended or expelled, he is not in school; hence, every day the student is not in school, he is not learning. If one can effectively reduce the percent of exclusionary sanctions imposed, it is likely that she will positively impact academic performance by simply increasing the opportunity to learn. Urban educators should not forget that these opportunities are afforded to those who have access to education; without access to an academic learning environment, the opportunity to learn is drastically minimized.

Disparities in Special and Gifted Education

In considering the many influences on the school outcomes of African American students, one school-level factor that cannot be neglected is the implications of disproportionate special education and gifted education placements. African American students are vastly overrepresented in the special education spectrum of our education system and underrepresented in gifted classes (Losen & Orfield, 2002). Considering the long-term implications of such placements on the academic outcomes of African American students, these disparities must remain a part of any exploration into issues concerning urban education.

Special education. The obvious overrepresentation of African American students in special education and the disparities between populations have been extensively documented (see Bellanca & Swartz 1993; Losen & Orfield, 2002; Wheelock, 1992, 1994). Indeed, students of color are overrepresented in almost every special education category in which records are kept (Losen & Orfield, 2002). However, statistics regarding special education placement are not consistent across the nation, states, or, indeed, even across school districts. They vary in interesting ways and in patterns that suggest that an unfair, biased intervention is at play. For example, African American children living in Connecticut, Mississippi, North Carolina, Nebraska, and South Carolina were found to have a four times higher chance of being labeled as mentally retarded as African American students in other states (Parrish, 2002). It is clear that students in these states are not so different from those in neighboring states as to account for such significant differences. It has been suggested that the way special education is funded in these states may incentivize them to overidentify students in need of special education services. However, although the disparities may seem quite large in some states in particular, this is a widespread and general problem, with African American children being overidentified in some special education categories in at least 45 states (Parrish, 2002). The disproportionate identification occurs specifically in high-incidence categories, such as mental retardation, emotional and behavioral disorders, and learning disabilities, which are more subjective in diagnosis. However, in low-incidence categories, such as severe or multiple disabilities, deafness, and blindness, which are more often diagnosed by medical personnel and have clearer eligibility criteria, the racial disparity all but disappears (Blanchett, 2006).

Gifted education. The numbers for the participation of different populations in gifted and talented (G/T) programs are not as readily available as they are for special education. This results, in large part, from the fact that schools are not required to keep track of statistics regarding the demographics of their G/T populations to the same extent that they are for special education. In accordance, educators do not have as clear a picture of the issue of underrepresentation of African American students in G/T programs. Much work in this area has focused on the lack of recruitment of students to these programs. It has also been found that there is a significant challenge in retaining these students once they are in these programs (Bonner, Lewis, Bowman-Perrott, Hill-Jackson, & James, 2009; Moore, Ford, & Milner, 2005). Other research has suggested additional variables that may impact the number of students of color in gifted education include a lack of other students of color (the problem of being the "only one"), a lack of teacher support, and a lack of culturally appropriate teaching materials and strategies, among others (Blanchett, 2006; Ford, 1996; Moore et al., 2005).

Social Capital

Social capital is a concept that is very distinctive from all other *capital*-isms. It is not to be confused with *cultural capital* (with reference to forms of knowledge), *physical capital* (with reference to physical objects), or *human capital* (with reference to properties of individuals). Coleman (1988) suggests that social capital is defined by its function (e.g., the ability to make connections among individuals) and is best understood by how well certain outcomes can be achieved (e.g., academic achievement) that would otherwise not be possible in its absence (Dika & Singh, 2002). Social capital, here, is represented by the amount, or density, of positive interaction found between the student and her environment (i.e., family, friends, community, school, etc.; Teachman, Paasch, & Carver, 1996).

The concept of social capital, in itself, has evoked much discussion and has found a place in conversations—among urban educators—about the influence of social networks on student performance, particularly in the case of African American students (Bourdieu, 1985, Coleman, 1988; Putnam, 2000). Social scientists have long suggested that this type of connectedness—a combination of social relationships and social involvement found between the student and his environment—has the potential to translate into higher academic achievement. This maxim, although easy to argue, is rather difficult to analyze since the concept is still being developed and measured; hence, the wide speculation concerning the value of social capital.

The inability of researchers to agree upon a measurable indicator of social capital ultimately makes it that much harder to prove that the lack thereof—or the deficit of social capital—is problematic. Herein lies the real issue: As Putnam (2000) puts it, bad things—with respect to a student's opportunities and choices, behavior, and/or development—tend to happen to kids who live and learn in areas where there is a deficit of social capital. These areas are typically situated in large, diverse, impoverished communities (Orr, 1999; Monconduit, 2007).

Notwithstanding the skepticism surrounding social capital, many theorists seemingly remain optimistic about its potential benefits for African American students (Noguera, 2001; Orr, 1999; Putnam, 2000). Increasing concerns regarding the quality of education forces educators—and those alike—to look for answers to why these problematic situations occur; and it is in the evaluation of the statistical findings of the effects of social capital that many seek refuge. In essence, these proponents flesh out the positive implications of social capital from research studies in an attempt to support their claim that there is indeed value in encouraging students to build social networks.

Using the Social Capital Index (SCI), Putnam (2000) finds that social capital is the single-most important explanatory factor in students' scores on standardized tests and the rate at which they remain in school. This finding suggests that communities with increased levels of social capital, irrespective of their affluence, generally have higher SAT scores and lower dropout rates (Putnam, 2000; Orr, 1999). A similar finding, by Perna and Titus (2005), shows that social capital is positively related to higher education enrollment. This is of particular importance for students of color, who attend college at rates significantly lower than those of their Anglo peers—as evidenced by recent reports from the U.S. Department of Education (American Council on Education, 2007).

Arguments about the potential power of social capital are not just intuitive; they are empirically sound. The rationale that sociability (i.e., the involvement or participation in groups) fosters or facilitates positive outcomes for students is—as Portes (1998) suggests—"a staple notion" (p. 2). Thus, the lack thereof, or the deficit of social capital, is expected to produce less desirable effects for students (e.g., poor academic performance, an increased probability of attrition, etc.; Coleman, 1988; McGraw, 1992). With this decline in social capital permeating mainly marginalized communities located in economically depressed areas, urban schools tend to offer a critical site for building social capital (Noguera, 2001). Further investigation of the value of social capital in these institutions is warranted.

STUDENT-LEVEL ISSUES

Test Score Gap

One of the frequent "buzzwords" in the field of education, specifically in urban education, is the standardized "test score" gap between African American students and their ethnic group counterparts, in specific, White students. Although many researchers in the field of education know that a gap in test scores exists, few, if any, actually take the time to research the extent of the gap and its potential impact. Further, with so much data at the local, school, district, state, and national levels, researchers are finding many of these data sources are skewed for a variety of reasons. As a result, we examine the most reliable database—the National Assessment of Educational Progress (NAEP) from the National Center for Education Statistics at the U.S. Department of Education. The NAEP suggests that it makes "the only nationally representative and continuing assessment of what America's students know and can do in various subject areas . . . NAEP results serve as a common metric for all states and selected urban districts" (2009, p. 1). As a result, we provide a brief snapshot of the test score gap between African American students and their White counterparts; the group to which African American students are so often compared.

Mathematics at Grade 4 for African American Students in Urban Settings

An examination of the documentation in Table 1 of NAEP's data from the Trial Urban District Assessment (TUDA, 2007) for mathematics illustrates that each of a sample of the largest urban school districts under examination (e.g., Atlanta, Boston, Chicago, Los Angeles, and New York City) has over 80% of their African American students that are not considered "proficient" in mathematics at grade four. New York City experienced the "best-of-the-worst" achievement rates among urban educational learners, with exactly 80% of African American fourth graders that scored below the "at proficient" category. Further, none of these urban school districts has 20% of the African American fourth-grade math students rank in the "at proficient" or the "at advanced" categories. This is particularly troubling given that the national average of urban school districts in the United States is 30% of students scoring in the "at proficient" category in grade-four math (TUDA, 2007). In comparison, the national average for White students is 40% in the "at proficient" category and 12% for African American students; this difference of 28 percentage points is so significant that the systemic causes should be considered.

Mathematics at Grade 8 for African American Students in Urban Settings

Likewise, in Table 1, each of the five urban educational settings under examination has at least 49% of their African American students in the "below basic" category.

Table 1. Percentage of African American Students at Each Achievement Level on NAEP Assessments in Grade 4 and Grade 8 Mathematics in Selected Urban School Districts for 2007

Urban District	Race	Grade 4				Grade 8			
		Below Basic	At Basic	At Proficient	At Advanced	Below Basic	At Basic	At Proficient	At Advanced
Atlanta	Black	45	44	10	—	62	30	7	1
	White	1	18	59	22	*	*	*	*
Boston	Black	29	53	17	1	49	39	12	1
	White	7	41	43	9	11	31	36	22
Chicago	Black	52	40	8	—	65	29	5	1
	White	16	37	39	8	21	44	28	7
Los Angeles	Black	46	41	12	1	72	21	7	—
	White	10	40	41	8	27	33	30	12
New York City	Black	28	52	19	1	55	36	9	1
	White	9	38	45	8	23	37	27	13

Note. — = not enough students to equal 1 percent; * = did not meet NAEP sample requirements. Adapted from U.S. Department of Education, Institute of Education Sciences, National Center for Education Statistics, National Assessment of Educational Progress, 2007 Trial Urban District Assessment—Mathematics.

It is unfortunate that 49% to 72% of the African American students are in the "below basic" category. When examining the total percentage of African American students in the "below basic" and "at basic" categories (which is still below "at proficient"), the following results in these large urban school systems are revealed: (a) in Atlanta, 92% are below the "at proficient" category; (b) in Boston, 88% are below the "at proficient" category; (c) in Chicago, 94% are below the "at proficient" category; (d) in Los Angeles, 93% are below the "at proficient" category; and (j) in New York City, 91% are below the "at proficient" category. For the sake of comparison, the national average of students in grade eight who reached the "at proficient" status is 23%. Also, the national mathematics average for White students who rated "at proficient" is 30%, in comparison to the dismal 8% proficiency rate for African American students at this grade level. Again, the national mathematics achievement gap for eighth graders in urban classrooms is so markedly divergent from the national average that institutional causes (i.e., racism) should be considered.

Reading at Grade 4 for African American Students in Urban Educational Settings

In these same five urban educational systems (e.g., Atlanta, Boston, Chicago, Los Angeles, and New York City), the results on the reading assessment for fourth graders that documents NAEP data from TUDA (2005) reveal an equally grim record. Further, in Table 2, 58% of African American fourth graders tested at the

Table 2. Percentage of African American Students at Each Achievement Level on NAEP Assessments for Grade 4 and Grade 8 Reading in Selected Urban School Districts for 2007

Urban District	Race	Grade 4				Grade 8			
		Below Basic	At Basic	At Proficient	At Advanced	Below Basic	At Basic	At Proficient	At Advanced
Atlanta	Black	60	30	9	1	50	41	9	—
	White	5	24	42	29	*	*	*	*
Boston	Black	52	34	12	1	40	44	16	—
	White	24	34	32	10	20	32	38	10
Chicago	Black	66	24	9	1	50	41	9	—
	White	26	34	28	12	23	39	34	4
Los Angeles	Black	63	24	11	2	62	32	6	—
	White	21	42	30	7	19	40	36	5
New York City	Black	49	36	13	2	50	39	11	—
	White	23	32	32	2	20	39	36	5

Note. — = not enough students to equal 1 percent; * = did not meet NAEP sample requirements. Adapted from U.S. Department of Education, Institute of Education Sciences, National Center for Education Statistics, National Assessment of Educational Progress, 2005 Trial Urban District Assessment—Reading.

"below basic" category in reading (an average among the five urban districts). Even more disturbing, four of the five urban school districts have numbers higher than 50% of their African American students in the "below basic." Overall, reviewing the data in Table 2, 85% to 90% of the African American fourth graders at the five urban school districts scored at the below basic or at basic levels in reading. Once again, it is interesting to note that the national average for U.S. students in the "at proficient" category in grade-four reading is 23% (TUDA, 2005). More specifically, the national reading average for White students is 30% scoring at the "at proficient" standard in this category, whereas only 11% of African American students meet the "at proficient" standard. In a dreaded but expected conclusion, urban African American fourth graders around the country contend with a disparate achievement gap in reading in comparison to their White counterparts.

Reading at Grade 8

An examination of reading data at grade eight reveals similar patterns of performance among African American students in these five large urban educational settings. In Table 2, we combine the percentage of African American students in the "below basic" and "at basic" categories to yield the total percentage of grade-eight African American students testing below the "at proficient" status in reading, with the following results for each of these cities: (a) in Atlanta, 91% tested below the "at proficient" status; (b) in, Boston, 84%; (c) in Chicago, 91%; (d) in Los Angeles, 84%; and (e) in New York City, 89%. This is especially troubling given that the national average for U.S. students in the "at proficient" category in grade-eight reading was 26%. More specifically, the national average for White students was 34% in the "at proficient" category in comparison to an 11% at-proficiency rate for African American students.

The national and urban achievement NCES, NAEP, and TUDA data shared for African American fourth and eighth graders in mathematics and reading are deplorable. Only 12% of fourth graders (the national average being 30%) and 8% of eighth graders (the national average being 30%) are at the "at proficient" level in math. It is still alarming that 11% of African American fourth graders (the national average being 23%) and 11% of African American eighth graders (the national average being 26%) are "at proficient" in reading (TUDA, 2005). Given the totality of the data presented, these statistics clearly underscore the importance of this book.

CONCLUSION

In this chapter, we have attempted to overview a sampling of selected issues (i.e., teacher stability, dropout rates, funding, resegregation, urban district leadership, discipline disproportionality, disparities in special and gifted education, social capital, and the standardized test score gap) that have direct and indirect impact on African American student outcomes in urban schools. We acknowledge that one chapter cannot fully explain every issue that has potential implications for African American student outcomes. However, to frame the essence of this monumental book, the field of education, particularly urban education, should be aware that student effort is not the sole criterion that has impact on African American students; there are a plethora of issues at a variety of levels that impact the achievement outcomes of African American students. As scholars and practitioners seek solutions for the education of this population, it is imperative that they understand the aforementioned complex web of issues as they seek to answer the most pressing questions for African American students in urban schools.

REFERENCES

American Council on Education. (2007). *Gaps persist in college participation rate of students of color and Whites, according to ACE's annual report on minorities in higher education.* Washington, DC: Author.

Balfanz, R., Spirikakis, K., Neild, R. C., & Legters, N. (2003). High-poverty secondary schools and the juvenile justice system: How neither helps the other and how that could change. In J. Wald & D. J. Losen (Eds.), *New directions for youth development: Deconstructing the school-to-prison pipeline* (pp. 71–89). San Francisco, CA: Jossey-Bass.

Bellanca, J., & Swartz, E. (Eds.). (1993). The *challenge of detracking: A collection*. Palatine, IL: IRI/Skylight.

Bennett, C., & Harris, J. J., III. (1982). Suspensions and expulsions of male and black students: A study of the causes of disproportionality. *Urban Education, 16*(4), 399–423.

Blanchett, W. J. (2006). Disproportionate representation of African American students in special education: Acknowledging the role of White privilege and racism. *Educational Researcher, 35*(6), 24–28.

Bonner, F. A., II, Lewis, C. W., Bowman-Perrott, L., Hill-Jackson, V., & James, M. (2009). Definition, identification, identity and culture: A unique alchemy impacting the success of gifted African American males in school. *Journal for the Education of the Gifted, 33*(2), 176–202.

Bourdieu, P. (1985). The forms of capital. In J. G. Richardson (Ed.), *Handbook of theory and research for the sociology of education* (pp. 241–258). New York, NY: Greenwood.

Bowditch, C. (1993). Getting rid of troublemakers: High school disciplinary procedures and the production of dropouts. *Social Problems, 40*(4), 493–509.

Butler, B. R., Joubert, M., & Lewis, C. W. (2010). Who's really disrupting the classroom? An examination of African American male students and their disciplinary roles. *The National Journal of Urban Education & Practice 31*(1), 1–12.

Children's Defense Fund. (1975). *School suspensions: Are they helping children?* Cambridge, MA: Washington Research Project.

Cohen, C., & Johnson, F. (2004). *Revenues and expenditures for public elementary and secondary education: School year 2001–2002* (Report No. NCES 2004-317). National Center for Education Statistics, U.S. Department of Education, Institute of Education Science. Retrieved from National Center for Education Statistics Web site: http://nces.ed.gov/pubs2004/2004341.pdf

Coleman, J. S. (1988). Social capital in the creation of human capital [Supplement]. *American Journal of Sociology, 94,* S95–S120.

Council of Great City Schools. (2009). *Urban school superintendents: Characteristics, tenure and salary sixth survey and report.* Washington, DC: Author.

Darling-Hammond, L., & Bransford, J. (2005). *Preparing teachers for a changing world: What teachers should learn and be able to do.* San Francisco, CA: Jossey-Bass.

Dika, S. L., & Singh, K. (2002). Applications of social capital in educational literature: A critical synthesis. *Review of Educational Research, 72*(1), 31–60.

Education Trust. (1998). *Education Watch 1998: State and national data book, Vol. II.* Washington, DC: Author.

Education Trust. (2006). *Funding gaps 2006.* Washington, DC: Author.

Fenning, P., & Rose, J. (2007). Overrepresentation of African American students in exclusionary discipline: The role of school policy. *Urban Education, 42,* 536–559.

Ferguson, A. A. (2000). *Bad boys: Public schools in the making of black masculinity.* Ann Arbor: University of Michigan Press.

Ford, D. Y. (1996). *Reversing underachievement among gifted black students: Promising practices and programs.* New York, NY: Teachers College Press.

Fossey, R. (1996). School dropout rates: Are we sure they are going down? *Phi Delta Kappan, 78,* 140–145.

Frankenberg, E., Lee, C., & Orfield, G. (2003). *A multiracial society with segregated schools: Are we losing the dream?* Retrieved from http://civilrightsproject.ucla.edu/research/k-12-education/integration-and-diversity/a-multiracial-society-with-segregated-schools-are-we-losingthe-dream

Frankenburg, E. (2009). The demographic context of urban schools and districts. *Equity & Excellence in Education, 42*(3), 255–271.

Freeman, C., Scafidi, B., & Sjoquist, D. (2005). Racial segregation in Georgia public schools, 1994–2001: Trends, causes and impact on teacher quality. In J. C. Boger & G. Orfield (Eds.), *School resegregation: Must the South turn back?* (pp. 148–163). Chapel Hill: University of North Carolina Press.

Gonzalez, J. M., & Szecsy, E. M. (2004). *The condition of minority access and participation in Arizona: 2004.* Retrieved from http://epsl.asu.edu/aepi/EPSL-0405-108-AEPI.pdf

Gregory, A., & Weinstein, R. (2008). The discipline gap and African Americans: Defiance or cooperation in the high school classroom. *Journal of School Psychology, 46*(4), 455–475.

Hanushek, E., Kain, J., & Rivkin, S. (2004). Why public schools lose teachers. *Journal of Human Resources, 39*(2), 326–354.

Kaufman, P. (2004). The national dropout data collection system: History and the search for consistency. In G. Orfield (Ed.), *Dropouts in America: Confronting the graduation crisis* (pp. 107–130). Cambridge, MA: Harvard Education Press.

Kunjufu, J. (2002). *Black students: Middle class teachers.* Chicago, IL: African American Images.

Laird, J., Cataldi, E. F., KewalRamani, A., & Chapman, C. (2008). *Dropout and completion rates in the United States: 2006* (Report No. NCES 2008-053). Washington, DC: National Center for Education Statistics. Retrieved from http://nces.ed.gov/pubs2008/2008053.pdf

Landsman, J. (2008). *Growing up White: A veteran teacher reflects on racism.* Lanham, MD: Rowman & Littlefield.

Landsman, J., & Lewis, C. (2006). *White teachers/diverse classrooms: A guide for building inclusive schools, promoting high expectations and eliminating racism.* Sterling, VA: Stylus.

Lankford, H., Loeb, S., & Wykoff, J. (2002). Teacher sorting and the plight of urban schools: A descriptive analysis. *Educational Evaluation and Policy Analysis, 24*(1), 37–62.

Lawson, E. (2003). Re-assessing safety and discipline in our schools: Opportunities for growth, opportunities for change. *Orbit, 33*(3), 23–25.

Lewis, C. W. (2009). *An educator's guide to working with African American students.* West Conshocken, PA: Infinity.

Lewis, C. W., & Moore, J. L., III. (2008a). African American students in K–12 urban educational settings. Urban Education, *43*(2), 123–126.

Lewis, C. W., & Moore, J. L., III. (2008b). Urban public schools for African American students: Critical issues for educational stakeholders. The Journal of Educational Foundations, *22*(1–2), 3–10.

Loeb, S., & Reininger, M. (2004). *Public policy and teacher labor markets: What we know and why it matters.* East Lansing, MI: The Education Policy Center at Michigan State University.

Losen, D., & Orfield, G. (Eds.). (2002). *Racial inequity in special education.* Cambridge, MA: Harvard University Press.

McGraw, L. (1992). Social capital: A new concept for explaining failure to achieve. *Journal of Educational and Psychological Consultation, 3*(4), 367–373.

Milner, H. R., IV, (2006). But good intentions are not enough: Theoretical and philosophical relevance in teaching students of color. In J. Landsman & C. Lewis (Eds.), *White teachers/diverse classrooms: A guide for building inclusive schools, promoting high expectations and eliminating racism* (pp. 79–90). Sterling, VA: Stylus.

Monconduit, C. A. (2007). *Identifiable variables which measure the impact of social capital within schools* (Doctoral dissertation). Available from ProQuest Digital Dissertations (AAT 3293449).

Monroe, C. (2005). Why are "bad boys" always black? Causes of disproportionality in school discipline and recommendations for change. *Clearing House: A Journal of Educational Strategies, Issues and Ideas, 79*(1), 45–50.

Moore, J. L., III, Ford, D. Y., Milner, H. R. (2005). Recruitment is not enough: Retaining African American students in gifted education. *Gifted Child Quarterly, 49*(1), 51–67.

Morrison, G. M., & D'Incau, B. (1997). The web of zero-tolerance: Characteristics of students who are recommended for expulsion from school. *Education and Treatment of Children, 20,* 316–335.

National Center for Education Statistics. (2009). *School and staffing survey.* Washington, DC: Author.

Noguera, P. A. (2001). Transforming urban schools through investment in the social capital of parents. In S. Saegert, J. P. Thompson, & M. R. Warren (Eds.), *Social capital and poor communities* (pp. 189–212). New York, NY: Russell Sage.

Orfield, G. (2001). *Schools more separate: Consequences of a decade of resegregation.* Retrieved from http://civilrightsproject.ucla.edu/research/k-12-education/integration-and-diversity/schools-more-separate-consequences-of-a-decade-ofresegregation/?searchterm=resegregation

Orfield, G., & Lee, C. (2005). *Why segregation matters: poverty and educational inequality.* Retrieved from http://www.civilrightsproject.ucla.edu/research/deseg/Why_Segreg_Matters.pdf

Orfield, G., & Lee, C. (2007). *Historic reversals, accelerating resegregation, and the need for new integration strategies.* Retrieved from http://www.civilrightsproject.ucla.edu/research/deseg/reversals_reseg_need.pdf

Orr, M. (1999). *Black social capital: The politics of school reform in Baltimore, 1986–1998.* Lawrence: University of Kansas Press.

Parrish, T. (2002). Racial disparities in the identification, funding and provision of special education. In D. Losen and G. Orfield (Eds.), *Racial inequity in special education* (pp.15–38). Cambridge, MA: Harvard University Press.

Perna, L. W., & Titus, M. A. (2005). The relationship between parental involvement as social capital and college enrollment: An examination of racial/ethnic group differences. *The Journal of Higher Education, 76*(5), 486–518. doi: 10.1353/jhe.2005.0036

Planty, M., Hussar, W., Snyder, T., Kena, G., KewalRamani, A., Kemp, J., Bianco, K., & Dinkes, R. (2009). *The condition of education: 2009* (Report No. NCES 2009-081). Washington, DC: National Center for Education Statistics.

Portes, A. (1998). Social capital: Its origins and applications in modern sociology. *Annual Review of Sociology, 24*, 1–24.

Putnam, R. (2000). *Bowling alone: The collapse and revival of the American community.* New York, NY: Simon & Schuster.

Raffaele Mendez, L. M., & Knoff, H. M. (2003). Who gets suspended from school and why: A demographic analysis of schools and disciplinary infractions in a large school district. *Education and Treatment of Children, 26*(1), 30–51.

Rubinson, F. (2004). Urban dropouts: Why so many and what can be done. In S. R. Steinberg & J. L. Kincheloe (Ed.), *19 urban questions: Teaching in the city* (pp. 53–67). New York, NY: Peter Lang.

Skiba, R., Michael, R., Nardo, A., & Peterson, R. (2002). The color of discipline: Sources of racial and gender disproportionality in school punishment. *The Urban Review, 34*, 317–342.

Skiba, R., & Rausch, M. K. (2006). Zero tolerance, suspension, and expulsion: Questions of equity and effectiveness. In C. M. Evertson & C. S. Weinstein (Eds.), *Handbook of classroom management: Research, practice, and contemporary issues* (pp. 1063–1092). Mahwah, NJ: Lawrence Erlbaum.

Strizek, G. A., Pittsonberger, J. L., Riordan, K. E., Lyter, D. M., & Gruber, K. (2006). *Characteristics of schools, districts, teachers, principals and school libraries in the United States, 2003–04* (Report No. NCES 2006-313 Revised). Washington, DC: National Center for Education Statistics. Retrieved from http://nces.ed.gov/pubs2006/2006313.pdf

Teachman, J. D., Paasch, K., & Carver, K. (1996). Social capital and dropping out of school early. *Journal of Marriage and Family, 58*(3), 773–783.

Thompson, G. (2004). *Through ebony eyes: What teachers need to know but are afraid to ask about African American students.* San Francisco, CA: John Wiley.

Thurlow, M. L., Sinclair, M. F., & Johnson, D. R. (2002). *Students with disabilities who drop out of school: Implications for policy and practice.* Minneapolis, MN: National Center on Secondary Education and Transition.

United States Census Bureau. Population Finder. Washington, D.C.: US Census Bureau (2009). Available from: http://factfinder.census.gov/servlet/SAFFPopulation?_submenuId=population_0&_sse=on

Viadero, D. (2001). The dropout dilemma. *Education Week, 20*, 26–29.

Wallace, J., Goodkind, S., Wallace, C., & Bachman, J. (2008). Racial, ethnic, and gender differences in school discipline among U.S. high school students: 1991–2005. *Negro Educational Review, 59*(1/2), 47–62.

Wheelock, A. (1992). *Crossing the tracks: How "untracking" can save America's schools.* New York, NY: The News Press.

Wheelock, A. (1994). *Alternatives to tracking and ability grouping.* Thousand Oaks, CA: American Association of School Administrators.

PART TWO

PERSPECTIVES AND PATTERNS IN URBAN SCHOOL CONTEXTS

Meeting THE Academic AND Social Needs OF Urban African American Students: Implications FOR School Counselors

CHERYL HOLCOMB-MCCOY AND BEVERLY BOOKER

One of the greatest challenges confronting education reform lies within urban metropolitan areas, where large numbers of students of color attend underfunded and low-performing schools with low standardized test scores and high dropout rates (Council of Great City Schools, 2006). From increased standardization, privatization, and testing to a growing number of students who are not ready for college or the workforce, urban public schools face many daunting tasks. Growing poverty and social stratification along racial and class lines has impacted the access that low-income urban youth, particularly African American students, have to a quality education, decent jobs, housing, and health care (Noguera, 2004).

Students from the largest ethnic minority groups, mainly African Americans and Latinos, form a major portion of the population of urban schools in the United States. According to the Council of the Great City Schools (2010), 36% of students attending 66 of the largest city school districts are African American in 2010–2011 and 35% are of Hispanic/Latino descent. The U.S. Bureau of the Census (2008) reports, on the other hand, that 76% of students attending inner city or urban schools in the United States between grades 1 and 12 are African American.

Even more important, although the general rate of poverty in the United States for children under 18 is 19% for 2007, the rate for African American children is 34%, with four out of five impoverished African American families living in urban communities (U.S. Bureau of the Census).

The educational needs of urban African American students are disproportionately affected by the problems associated with urban public schools. Many studies have indicated that most students in urban public schools fail to perform at the basic level of educational achievement, and many of these students drop below grade level starting in elementary school and continue to decline each school year thereafter (Jencks & Phillips, 1998; Orr, 2003; Phillips, 2000; Viteritti, 1999). In the research literature, it has also been well documented that urban students who attend schools that have higher levels of poverty are more likely to have lower achievement scores, higher absenteeism and suspension rates, and less qualified teachers (Obidah & Howard, 2005). Equally documented is the fact that many school professionals, including school counselors, avoid working in urban, high-poverty schools, predominately those made up mainly of African American students, because of the prospect of having large, high-needs, student caseloads (Bakari, 2003; Bondy & Ross, 1998; Holcomb-McCoy & Johnston, 2008).

Given the increasingly dire academic and social needs of students of color in urban communities, the work of school counselors in these school settings has never been more important than it is today. Nevertheless, very little has been written on urban school counselors' influence or role in urban education. Julius Menacker's 1974 book, *Vitalizing Guidance in Urban Schools*, describes the work of school counselors in urban settings. In this classic text, Menacker encourages urban school counselors to act more as advocates and challengers of the status quo in urban schools. He believes that urban counselors should have a thorough understanding of large urban school bureaucracies and, more important, that they need the skills to navigate and work effectively within these large districts. Menacker also encourages urban school counselors to practice not only advocacy for students and parents but also community activism. He stresses that school counselors should build on students' and families' strengths, given these groups' experiences with environmental stressors (e.g., poverty, crime, overcrowding). Although Menacker wrote about urban schools over 30 years ago, many of the same themes of advocacy, resilience, systemic change, and empowering urban youth are found in today's education literature.

After Menacker's book, only one special issue of the premier school-counseling professional journal, *Professional School Counseling*, has focused on urban education issues and challenges (e.g., Holcomb-McCoy & Lee, 2005). The American School Counselor Association (ASCA), The Education Trust, and the American Counseling Association (ACA) all cite roles of accountability as integral to the effectiveness of school counselors in impacting student achievement. If the school-counseling profession is to follow its historical role as the advocate for change in all types of schools, then it faces a formidable task in crafting practices and strategies for working with African American youth in urban school settings. We believe that school counselors can make a significant impact on the emotional and academic development of urban youth, particularly African American students, if five areas are focused on: (a) counseling, (b) parent and teacher consultation, (c) data usage, (d) school culture, and (e) rigorous course enrollment. The remainder of this chapter discusses each of these five areas.

COUNSELING

School counseling is a field of practice involving multiple roles and tasks, including advocacy, coordination, collaboration, coordination, and counseling. As expected, counseling has been the dominant task that school counselors perform. School counselors have the skills and knowledge to implement individual as well as group counseling. Given the social and emotional problems that students encounter on a daily basis, counseling is greatly needed in urban schools. However, there is far too much culturally unresponsive and inappropriate counseling occurring in schools. When working with African American urban students, school counselors should conduct counseling that is social justice-oriented and strengths-based. To this end, we believe that by using a social justice framework, school counselors are able to utilize strategies that enhance students' self-worth, academic and personal self-efficacy, and feelings of empowerment. The challenge for school counselors who work with African American urban students is to initiate counseling that involves an understanding of the environmental barriers that impede students' academic and social development, a keen understanding of equity and empowerment in the context of education, and the ability to build on students' strengths. What follows is a more detailed description of the five counseling modalities that may be most effective in urban school settings with African American students—empowerment-based, strengths-based, social justice-oriented, group-oriented, and solution-focused and brief.

Empowerment-Based Counseling

The concept of empowerment originated in the social sciences as early as the 1970s, although it is a relatively new concept in the field of education (Perkins & Zimmerman, 1995). Hipolito-Delgado and Lee (2007) define *empowerment-focused counseling* as based on a two-fold concept. It involves students' abilities to make grounded choices that recognize their critical consciousness of how issues of oppression may impact personal and community well-being along with educational, social, economic, political/civic, and health domains. It also involves students' acquisition of knowledge and skills to eradicate barriers and social injustices in their lives and communities. With these factors in mind, it is important to note that school counselors who utilize empowerment-focused counseling advocate for a student's self-empowerment rather than seeking to empower the student. McWhirter (1994) states that counselors utilizing empowerment-focused counseling highlight student's assets and strengths in relation to how those attributes can foster a greater locus of control in their personal lives.

Empowerment-focused counseling can be a powerful approach for school counselors to utilize with urban, African American students. This student population is often identified as a marginalized group. Throughout U.S. history, these students have experienced a high degree of oppression based on racism and prejudice. In various domains of society (e.g., education), African Americans have frequently been subjected to social and economic inequities. For example, national data indicate that there have been gatekeeping practices restricting African American students' access to rigorous academic courses, inhibiting high levels of achievement (Education Trust, 2003). The following are empowerment-focused counseling strategies that are suitable to use with African American students: (a) creating a counseling environment in which students can share their stories/experiences without hesitation or reluctance; (b) acknowledging the systemic oppression and marginalization that impact students of color, particularly those residing in urban contexts; (c) facilitating dialogue about students' desired choices or goals, with a critical awareness of how the "power" of social groups plays a role in oppression; and (d) exploring how students' assets and strengths can be used to access their own power to make choices and address barriers and injustices endured. Hipolito-Delgado and Lee (2007) recommend that school counselors reflect on their own attitudes, biases, assumptions, and belief systems about their students' ability to make choices in their own lives and communities, which they suggest is a precondition for them to be able to effectively advocate for students' empowerment. In addition, they suggest that school counselors should take time to reflect and process their views of the systemic oppression and marginalization of diverse groups of students within the educational system in which they work.

A final component of empowerment-focused counseling is for urban school counselors to have the knowledge of how race plays a significant role in the daily lives of African Americans. Introducing the topics of race, ethnicity, and culture is an integral factor in the effectiveness of empowerment-focused counseling with these students (Day-Vines et al., 2007). Day-Vines and colleagues constructed a continuum of broaching behavior, which is based on the counselor's ability to effectively keep racial and cultural contexts in consideration. The continuum has six levels, with one extreme being "the avoidant counselor" who does not acknowledge or address the idea that race, ethnicity, and culture may play a role in issues at hand. They suggest that counselors' lack of skill or refusal to broach racial topics can be attributed to early termination of counseling by former clients. The other end of the continuum is "the infusing counselor," who both integrates race within the counseling setting and advocates for clients' empowerment, in order to address the larger issue of social justice in collaboration with the clients.

Strengths-Based Counseling

Strengths-based counseling focuses on student assets and positive messages rather than weaknesses and negative messages (Galassi & Akos, 2007). School counselors view students as experts on their own lives as they explore their strengths and resiliency traits in the counseling process. Further, they encourage positive coping skills and gaining success in various areas of life. The approach attempts to achieve two goals: (a) problem prevention and reduction and (b) skill acquisition. In essence, the strengths-based approach emphasizes a developmental asset framework. Research has indicated a positive correlation between students' strengths, protective factors, and resources and academic achievement (Scales, 2005), which are the assets the framework is based on.

The developmental assets are aligned to actions school counselors can take to advocate for student success. Scales (2005) suggests that high expectations are also closely linked to developmental assets. As a result, this type of approach suggests that school counselors should promote rigorous curricula for all students by working to remove tracking and/or gatekeeping practices that have traditionally limited access for African American students to college preparatory programs and courses.

Social Justice-Focused School Counseling

Social justice counseling, according to the Counselors for Social Justice (CSJ) Division of ACA, represents a multifaceted approach to counseling in which counselors strive to simultaneously promote human development and the common good by addressing challenges related to both individual and distributive justice (Counselors for Social Justice, 2008). Social justice counseling involves empowerment of students, as well as enabling active confrontation of injustice and inequality, as they impact the students and the many other individuals in their urban context. Social justice counselors often direct their work efforts to the promotion of four critical principles: (a) equity, (b) access, (c) participation, and (d) harmony. Their work is often executed with a focus on the cultural, contextual, and individual needs of those served.

Within the context of school counseling, Holcomb-McCoy (2007) offers a social justice framework specifically for school counselors. It includes six key functions:

1. counseling
2. consultation
3. connecting schools, families, and communities
4. collecting and utilizing data
5. challenging bias
6. coordinating student services and support

The first key function, counseling, consists of school counselors being able to tailor their interventions to meet the needs of specific student populations. Holcomb-McCoy further suggests that cultural differences and cultural group membership can significantly influence the behaviors of school counselors and students. During counseling, cultural differences and expectations can influence how a school counselor perceives a student and how the student perceives a counselor. In many cases, school counselors think that, if they treat all students the same, they are being fair and culturally sensitive. Although the intent is right, this practice is problematic because all students are not the same, even if they are racially and/or culturally similar. Students have different needs, experiences, and perceptions. Therefore, students' cultural backgrounds are likely to determine the way in which they approach counseling, perceive their counselor, and react to the content of what the counselor says.

Holcomb-McCoy (2007) also stresses that school counselors should place an emphasis on students within their own environments and their interactions with others in their families and immediate communities. From a social justice perspective, counseling is ideally carried out by school counselors who are culturally competent, meaning that they are able to combine cultural awareness and sensitivity with counseling skills, which together bring about effective cross-cultural practices. School counselors may use the School Counselor Multicultural Counseling Competence Checklist (Holcomb-McCoy, 2004). It is used to assess school counselors' cultural knowledge, awareness, and ability to work with culturally diverse students. The checklist includes 51 competencies that were developed through a theme analysis of the literature pertaining to multicultural school counseling. Nine areas of competence are assessed: multicultural counseling, multicultural consultation, understanding racism and student resistance, multicultural assessment, understanding racial identity development, multicultural family counseling, social advocacy, developing school-family-community partnerships, and understanding cross-cultural interpersonal interactions.

When using a social justice approach to counsel urban African American students, it is thought to be critical for school counselors to consider the historical oppression and discrimination that African Americans have endured and currently endure in their communities. Getting past racism has been a challenge for most African American people. For years, African Americans have experienced acts of discrimination and prejudice. African American males, in particular, have been impacted by discriminatory policies and practices in schools (Tatum, 2004). As a result, many have drifted into dysfunctional and counterproductive behavior because they felt that they were not valued or respected (Boyd-Franklin & Franklin, 2000). School counselors, therefore, should not avoid or ignore the implications of race, when counseling African American students. Students who attend schools with a majority of African American students are frequently aware of race and the meaning of their racial background to other persons.

As a case example, Rahsaan, a 15-year-old high school student in an inner-city school made up primarily of ethnic minorities, reported to his African American counselor about his African American teacher: "Mr. Freeman doesn't like none of us. That's why I don't go to his class anymore. He calls us 'thugs', and I heard him tell the principal that us kids from the projects are no good." As another case example, Tina, a 10-year-old African American student, told her African American counselor about schools in the suburbs, "Those schools out there are not for us [African American students]." Social justice counseling would point out that both of these students' statements signify racial undertones and should be explored by the school counselor. It would also suggest that school counselors who want to build a relationship of trust and openness with students need to acknowledge the effects of prejudice and discrimination and approach the counseling relationship with mindfulness of the manifestations of racism and oppression on the lives of individuals and groups.

Group Counseling

Group counseling has been shown to be an effective means to work with urban youth at various developmental stages (Phillips & Phillips, 1992; Zinck & Littrell, 2000). Studies indicate that students who participate in group work show enhanced self-perception and improvement in school attitudes and behavior (e.g., Nelson, Dykeman, Powell, & Petty, 1996). Many school counseling professionals (e.g., Bailey, Getch, & Chen-Hayes, 2003; Bemak, Chung, & Murphy, 2003) even suggest that group counseling is often the primary mode of intervention for school counselors. Day-Vines, Patton, and Baytops (2003) highlight the fact that

African American students benefit from group counseling, because it provides an environment for them to share and process individual and shared experiences, learn and practice coping strategies, and establish a sense of belonging.

In 2005, Bemak, Chung, and Siroskey-Sabdo introduced an empowerment group approach for urban African American girls at-risk of dropping out of high school. The group consisted of an unstructured process approach in which group members rather than group leaders decided on the topics for group discussion. Although the approach has not been empirically studied, a follow-up survey with the group members one year later found that the girls expressed a greater ability to share their individual feelings and to more effectively resolve interpersonal problems. Another study, by Wyatt (2009), reveals positive outcomes in student grade-point-averages for an African American male mentoring group whose design is based on the needs of the group members. As a result of these positive results, Wyatt suggests a six-step action plan for developing a group for urban African American students:

1. Survey the student population regarding the needs of the counseling groups.
2. Seek professional development and consultation in the domain area of the topic for the group.
3. Create a mission and purpose for the group.
4. Create a creed or code of honor and/or set of expectations that represents the topic for the group. In order to create buy in, students should be a part of creating the mission, purpose, and code of honor for the group.
5. Recruit students who can benefit from the topical group.
6. Collaborate with students to identify goals and objectives that include activities and events for the topic group.

Another group counseling intervention that holds promise, although needing more research, is Afrocentric rites of passage programs (Banks, Hogue, Timberland, & Liddle, 1996; Lee, 2003). These culturally based programs help teach youth self-pride, family unity, community values, and personal responsibility. As a form of group work involving socialization, rites of passage programs can also be instrumental methods of intervention with urban African American youth. School counselors should explore the possibility of using such programs in the school setting. They can enlist support from trusted community members and even train school personnel to assist with these programs.

Solution-Focused Brief Counseling

Another promising counseling intervention is the use of solution-focused brief counseling with urban African American youth. Solution-focused counseling meets many counselors' practical needs, which involve numerous duties and functions. Outcome studies suggest that brief solution-focused counseling is comparable in effectiveness to long-term counseling (Bruce, 1995). DeShazer et al. (1986) report that 72% of the clients at the Brief Therapy Center, which enforces a 10-session limit, either met their goal for treatment or made significant improvement. The researchers also indicate that the average number of meetings per client declined from six to fewer than five. More recently, Newsome (2004) reports that 26 urban African American middle school students who participated in a solution-focused group intervention increased their GPAs at the end of the group, compared to 26 students who did not participate in the group.

Brief solution-focused therapy, which focuses on discussions about solutions rather than about problems, does not seek causal explanations for solving human problems (Kelly, Kim, & Franklin, 2008). Although the school counselor listens attentively with empathy, she quickly moves toward finding solutions. The key to brief counseling, as DeShazer and colleagues (1986) define it, is "utilizing what clients bring with them to help them meet their needs" (p. 208). Students are viewed as already having the knowledge and ability to solve their own problems. In particular, the school counselor's function is to help students construct a new use for the knowledge they already have. Specific techniques include finding exceptions to the problem, amplifying or expanding news of positive changes, and establishing concrete goals.

CONSULTATION

Consultation, unlike counseling, is an indirect service delivery approach and can be used to influence change in an entire classroom, school, or family. School counselors typically use consultation as a means to assist parents and/or teachers as they grapple with some type of student problem or difficulty. One of the most recent advances in the field of consultation concerns the increasingly apparent influence that culture and other environmental aspects have on the process of consultation (Ingraham, 2000, 2003; Tarver-Behring & Ingraham, 1998). Most of the literature written on multicultural issues in consultation has been published in school psychology journals and books, whereas little discussion of multicultural consultation can be found in the school-counseling literature. When school counselors consult with parents and teachers from culturally diverse backgrounds, they need to consider the impact of culture on not only the client (e.g., student) but also on the consultation process.

In a classic multicultural consultation article, Gibbs (1980) focuses on the differences in consultation processes between African American and White teachers.

She proposes a model that looks at the initial responses of African American and White teachers, or "consultees," to participating in consultations in inner-city school settings. Gibbs concludes that African American teachers, due to a combination of historical, cultural, and social patterns, respond minimally and indicate little interest in the initial stages of consultation. White teachers, on the other hand, were described as being much more attentive and asking questions related to the methods and goals of the project. Gibbs purports that the African American consultees prefer an interpersonal consultation style that focuses on trust and building rapport between the consultant and consultee. White teachers, according to Gibbs, prefer an instrumental consultant style that is task driven. As a result of her observations, Gibbs recommends that consultants be genuine, down to earth, and establish nonhierarchical relations with the African American teacher or parent. The research on Gibbs's conclusions, nevertheless, has contradicted her findings. For instance, Duncan and Pryzwansky (1993) find that African American teachers prefer the instrumental rather than the interpersonal style of consultation. The question of a preferred and effective consultation style for diverse groups of consultees, particularly parents, is an area of research that still warrants more extensive research.

It is important to note that, in many cases, school counselors/consultants may view cultural differences as the problem. Sheridan (2000) purports that status or demographic variables, such as race, class, or marital status, are often perceived as the source of a student's problem (e.g., a consultant believing that a child's problem is based on the mother's marital status). Davies (1993) finds that educators believe parents who are less educated, poor, and members of ethnic minorities are deficient in their ability to help their children with schoolwork and uninterested in their children's education. However, research has indicated that, in most instances, less educated, poor, and minority parents are interested in their children's education, want the best for them, and have the capacity to support their children's learning (Henderson, Mapp, Johnson, & Davies, 2007).

Regarding parent consultation, the strategies used can be roughly divided into two types: (a) those that focus on the presentation of new information or ideas as the primary change agent and (b) those that focus on the relationship between the consultee and the consultant as the source of change. Many consultants influenced by the "information as change agent perspective" view the consultant–parent relationship as important only to the extent that it facilitates the dissemination of knowledge regarding appropriate parenting practices and family functioning. Such consultants generally adhere to behavioral or cognitive-behavioral theories, and they typically subscribe to a psycho-educational approach to altering what are viewed as maladaptive patterns of behavior through the use of behavioral strategies. This approach can create several problems if cultural factors are not taken into account when consulting with parents of diverse backgrounds. Turner (1982), for instance, notes the problem African Americans may have with certain behavior modification techniques and terminology, such as aversive conditioning, behavior control, extinction, and stimulus-reward. From a cultural perspective, these techniques focus heavily on controlling or changing behavior, which is reminiscent of many groups' oppressive history. African American parents, therefore, may not be receptive to such conceptualizations of their children's behavior or to the use of what may appear to be intrusive treatment programs (Wayman, Lynch, & Hanson, 1991).

Consultation, based solely on education and imparting information, may also fail to consider the importance of psycho-social influences, such as family structure, cultural value systems, interactional patterns, and adaptive coping strategies, on behavior and functioning in culturally diverse families and may instead focus on factors that play a more important role in the lives of middle-income White American families (Boyd-Franklin, 2003). Consultants who use this approach would ignore the fact that African American families traditionally involve extended families, such as grandparents, in family decision making and child-rearing practices to a greater extent than many White families.

In addition to differences in family structure, consultation may be influenced by the adaptive coping strategies of African Americans. They have found such coping strategies as suspicion of outsiders and group unity to be necessary to deal with hostile environments. These strategies are often misdiagnosed as pathological if not examined within the appropriate cultural context. For instance, the literature is replete with evidence documenting the misclassification of African Americans as having behavior problems (Losen & Orfield, 2002). Thus, consultants should not assume that referred African American children have been accurately classified as problematic. Attempts to change what are assumed to be maladaptive behaviors through the use of consultation may lead to ineffective interventions that fail to address the true source of the difficulties, such as frustration with teachers' low expectations, anger associated with family situations, or inability to feel safe. These alternative sources of the problem, if not addressed, can result in resistance and hostility from parents.

African Americans have been reported to present passive resistance in therapeutic and helping alliances (Boyd-Franklin, 2003), in regard to their anticipation of racial prejudice and discrimination by White American therapists. This resistance often leads to early termination and discontent with the services provided. Therefore, one might expect the consultations with African American parents to involve passive behavior, early termination, and/or resistance to consulting services.

Parents' attitudes and actions toward consultants may also affect the working alliance or relationship in parent consultation. For example, Kalyanpur and Rao

(1991) identify three qualities that are related to low-income African American mothers' perceptions of outreach agency professionals. First, parents perceive that consultants have a lack of respect for them and thus do not trust them, which are cited as a significant barrier to fostering a collaborative relationship. Second, parents believe that professionals focus on children's deficits and ignore their strengths. The third factor involves parents' perceptions that consultants lack appreciation for the mothers' parenting styles and blames them for their children's behavior problems at school.

UTILIZING DATA

Data can provide a tremendous impetus for change in schools in which low expectations lead to low results for large numbers of students, particularly low-income urban African American students (Johnson, 2002). Urban schools should first examine data, such as high dropout rates, low standardized test scores, and low graduation rates, to absorb the troubling implications of status quo practices (e.g., tracking) that have worked "against" students rather than "in favor" of them. To this end, school counselors should lead these data discussions. They may occur in meetings with departmental teams, case management teams, school improvement teams, and school–community focus groups. Collaborative teaming between school and community stakeholders can involve analysis and dissemination of data. These practices can help increase awareness of data trends related to African American students' academic progress. For example, Montgomery County Public Schools in Maryland utilizes the Study Circles Program to foster dialogue on topics related to race, ethnicity, and barriers to student achievement and parental involvement. In this program, parents, teachers, administrators, and school counselors collaborate with trained facilitators to work on students' achievement-related issues (www.montgomeryschoolsmd.org/departments/studycircles). Therefore, school counselors are critical participants in these collaborative efforts, in that they can serve as advocates for students and their social/emotional issues.

Over the last decade, there have been several data templates developed to assist school counselors with utilizing data in their programs. For instance, Dahir and Stone (2003) offer a seven-step process called M.E.A.S.U.R.E., which assists school counselors in delivering a data-driven school counseling program that supports the accountability component of the ASCA National Model. M.E.A.S.U.R.E. is an acronym for Mission, Elements, Analyze, Stakeholders, Unite, Reanalyze, and Educate that helps school counselors to connect to the mission of their school, examine critical data elements that are part of their schools' report cards, analyze those critical data elements to see which elements their program can positively impact, identify internal and external stakeholders who can collaborate to impact the data, unite with these stakeholders to form partnerships and assign strategies, and reanalyze the data to determine which strategies should be replicated, redesigned, or discarded.

Ford and Whiting (2008) suggest that analyzing student achievement data should be conducted from a balanced viewpoint. They warn that education professionals will often review data solely through the "lens" of deficits. In other words, they see only students' shortcomings, not their strengths. This seems especially true in the case of urban African American students, particularly in the gifted identification process (Whiting, Ford, Grantham, & Moore, 2008).

SCHOOL CULTURE

School culture includes the values, beliefs, and norms that lay the foundation for a school's climate, programs, and practices. It is unfortunate that, in today's urban schools, school counselors and other school professionals believe that African American students come to school with cultural deficits (Abdul-Adil & Farmer, 2006; Conchas, 2006). This belief may be translated into assumptions about African American students' cognitive abilities and is reflected in common educational practices, such as assigning African American students to special education classes at disproportionately higher rates than their peers in other racial and ethnic groups. The school's negative perception of African American students as a racial group creates a climate of low expectations that can evolve into self-degrading feelings and low achievement (Denbo, 2002). To create nurturing urban school cultures that support the achievement of African American students, school counselors should utilize programs and practices that result in the elimination of harmful institutional practices; support the belief that African American students, like other students, can achieve high standards; and support the belief that the African American culture, like other cultures, is a valued one.

For more than a decade, numerous researchers (Bernard, 1991; Hawkins, Catalano, & Miller, 1992; Sadowski, 2001; Somers, Owens, & Piliawsky, 2008; Werner & Smith, 1992) have identified characteristics of schools that promote resilience and high academic achievement among African American students. They suggest that these types of schools tend to do the following: (a) promote close bonds among students; (b) value and encourage education; (c) use a high-warmth, low-criticism style of interaction; (d) set and enforce clear boundaries (e.g., rules, norms, and laws); (e) encourage supportive relationships with many caring others; (f) promote sharing of responsibilities and service to others; (g) provide access to resources for meeting the basic needs of housing, nutrition, employment, health care, and recreation; (h) establish high and realistic expectations for success; (i) encourage goal setting and mastery; (j) support the development of prosocial values (e.g., altruism) and life skills (e.g., cooperation); (k) provide opportunities for leadership, decision making, and other meaningful ways to participate; and (l) support the unique talents of each individual. School counselors can work with other professionals (e.g., teachers) to promote resiliency and academic achievement among urban African American students.

In an early study, Davidson (1996) illustrates that students' racial or ethnic identities are negotiated in school and classroom contexts. These settings are found to both support and not support the extent to which students perceive school as a part of or in opposition to their racial/ethnic identities. Further, Davidson finds that the features of schools that contribute to manifestations of disengagement and opposition for African American students include academic tracking, negative expectations, racial discrimination, bureaucratized relationships and practices, and barriers to information. An important factor for urban school counselors to understand is that the schooling practices that African American students are exposed to influence their academic outcomes and identities (Mehan, Villanueva, Hubbard, & Lintz, 2004; Shelton & Sellers, 2000).

An underexamined social and cultural feature of urban schools is the impact that student–adult relationships have on students' experiences in school. Despite the challenges associated with large urban high schools, personalized student–educator relationships can promote student engagement and achievement and mediate against dropping out (Bryk & Schneider, 2002). For example, these relationships have been found to be linked to learning (Nieto, 1999), especially when driven by care and respect (Rodriguez, 2003). On the other hand, negative student–adult relationships have been associated with dropping out and academic failure (Noddings, 1992).

Student–adult relationships are particularly significant for low-income African American students (Noguera, 2004). In describing some common characteristics of care among 13 teachers in his study, Brown (2003) reports that the teachers actually showed genuine interest in the students by explicitly stating expectations for appropriate student behavior and academic growth. Milner (2007) asserts that educators, such as teachers, can demonstrate their interest in students by offering students compliments, allowing them to do makeup work and extra credit, volunteering to serve as sponsors/advisers to clubs and organizations, and attending after school activities (e.g., basketball games). In regard to urban African American students, the demonstration of care is particularly important (Conchas, 2006).

Considering the human relations skills of school counselors, developing caring relationships with urban African American students and developing caring school cultures should be one of their major responsibilities. This suggests that urban school counselors should spend a significant portion of their time developing and sustaining caring and positive relationships with students to decrease school disengagement and poor academic achievement.

RIGOROUS COURSE ENROLLMENT

Twenty years ago, a national College Board report, *Changing the Odds: Factors Increasing Access to College* (Pelavin & Kane, 1990), examined the relationship between enrollment in college-level courses and college-going rates and whether African American, Latino, and White students participated equally in college preparation courses. The authors find that low-income African American and Latino students were less likely to enroll in geometry and foreign languages and had lower aspiration for obtaining a bachelor's degree than their White counterparts. However, when these students did enroll and complete geometry and foreign language courses, college enrollment increased and the gap between ethnic minority students and Whites decreased. A more recent College Board report (2001) finds that students who take challenging courses such as precalculus, calculus, and physics have significantly higher average Scholastic Achievement Test (SAT) scores than those students who do not engage in rigorous coursework. More data supporting the contention that higher level coursework improves academic achievement of all students were found by Gamoran and Hannigan (2000) in an analysis of data from more than 12,500 students in the National Assessment of Educational Progress Study.

In typical practice, school counselors develop a school's master schedule and individual students' schedules, and high school counselors, in particular, are often students' only resource for college counseling and advisements related to college readiness. Many school counselors also make decisions about who goes to college and who does not. And, all too often, low-income African American students are sent the message that they are not "college material" and are subsequently advised to take courses that do not prepare them for college admission.

In order to ensure that urban African American students have an opportunity to pursue a college degree, it is imperative that school counselors create a school culture in which students expect that college can be a reality in their future. Muhammed (2008) finds that school counselors' expectations for students' future education positively influence their college predisposition at a high magnitude. School counselors, frequently, hold a powerful position in the college admission process. For African American first-generation college students, school counselors are even more important and may be the key to whether or not a student will apply to college or take the courses that are necessary for college admission.

SUMMARY

Addressing the academic and social needs of urban African American students is imperative for urban educators. Given that these students will make up a major portion of the future workforce, our nation's schools can no longer fail to educate and graduate "college-ready" African American students. Creating urban schools that support the high achievement of African American students requires a cultural transformation, and school counselors can play a pivotal role in this transformation process. Urban school counselors should be able to provide culturally appropriate counseling and consultation, as well as use data to highlight inequities in the education and opportunities afforded urban students. Most importantly, school counselors should play an active role in creating new policies and practices that support the cognitive and affective development of African American students.

There is no doubt that school counselors can play a transformative role in urban schools. Urban education reform requires celebrating cultural diversity and recognizing cultural conflict, which are two skills that school counselors should possess to be effective in urban schools. The collective involvement of school counselors, teachers, administrators, and other school personnel must characterize school change so that goals for the entire school become greater than the personal goals of individuals within the school. Urban school counselors within this transformational context should assume leadership roles and challenge their assumptions about themselves as school counselors, their students, and their schools. These school counselors should help to create new learning communities where high achievement is universal and the norm. Further, we believe that the road to universal achievement for urban African American students consists of new innovative and diverse strategies for school counselors that promote opportunity equity and access. Most importantly, however, we believe that urban school counselors' major responsibility is to help African American students believe in themselves.

REFERENCES

Abdul-Adil, J. K., & Farmer, Jr., A. D. (2006). Inner-city African American parental involvement in elementary schools: Getting beyond urban legends of apathy. *School Psychology Quarterly, 21*(1), 1–12.

Bailey, D. F., Getch, Y. G., & Chen-Hayes, S. (2003). Professional school counselors as social and academic advocates. In B. T. Erford (Ed.), *Transforming the school counseling profession* (pp. 411–434). Upper Saddle River, NJ: Merrill Prentice Hall.

Bakari, R. (2003). Preservice teachers' attitudes toward teaching African American students. *Urban Education, 38*(6), 640–654.

Banks, R., Hogue, A., Timberland, T., & Liddle, H. (1996). An Afrocentric approach to group social skills training with inner-city. *Journal of Negro Education, 65*(4), 414–423.

Bemak, F., Chung, R. C. Y., & Murphy, C. (2003). A new perspective on counseling at risk youth. In B. T. Erford (Ed.), *Transforming the school counseling profession* (pp. 285–96). Upper Saddle River, NJ: Merrill Prentice Hall.

Bemak, F., Chung, R. C.-Y., & Siroskey-Sabdo, L. A. (2005). Empowerment groups for academic success: An innovative approach to prevent high school failure for at-risk, urban African American girls. *Professional School Counseling, 8*(5), 377–400.

Bernard, B. (1991). *Fostering resiliency in kids: Protective factors in the family, school, and community.* Portland, OR: Western Regional Center for Drug-Free Schools and Communities, Northwest Educational Laboratory.

Bondy, E., & Ross, D. (1998). Confronting myths about teaching black children: A challenge for teacher educators. *Teacher Education and Special Education, 21*(4), 251–254.

Boyd-Franklin, N. (2003). *Black families in therapy: Understanding the African American experience* (2nd ed.). New York, NY: Guilford.

Boyd-Franklin, N., & Franklin, A. J. (2000). *Boys into men: Raising our African American teenage sons.* New York, NY: Dutton.

Brown, D. F. (2003). Urban teachers' use of culturally responsive management strategies. *Theory into Practice, 42*(4), 277–282.

Bruce, M. A. (1995). Brief counseling: An effective model for change. *School Counselor, 42,* 353–363.

Bryk, A. S., & Schneider, B. (2002). *Trust in schools: A core resource for improvement.* New York, NY: Russell Sage Foundation.

College Board (2001). *Access to excellence: A Report to the Commission on the Future of the Advanced Placement Program.* New York, NY: College Entrance Examination Board.

Conchas, G. Q. (2006). *The color of school success: Race and high achieving urban youth.* New York, NY: Teachers College Press.

Council of Great City Schools. (2010). *Urban school statistics.* Retrieved from http://www.cgcs.org/site/default.aspx?pageid=75

Council of Great City Schools. (2006). *Critical trends in urban education.* Washington, DC: Author.

Counselors for Social Justice. (2008). *What is social justice counseling?* Retrieved from http://counselorsforsocialjustice.com/

Dahir, C. A., & Stone, C. B. (2003). Accountability: A M.E.A.S.U.R.E. of the impact school counselors have on achievement. *Professional School Counseling, 6*(3), 214–221.

Davidson, A. (1996). *Making and molding identities in schools: Student narratives on race, gender, and academic engagement.* Albany: State University of New York Press.

Davies, D. (1993). Benefits and barriers of parent involvement. In N. Chavkin (Ed.), *Families and schools in a pluralistic society* (pp. 205–216). Albany: State University of New York Press.

Day-Vines, N. L., Wood, S., Grothaus, T., Holman, A., Douglass, M., Craigen, L., & Dotson Blake, K. (2007). Broaching the subjects of race, ethnicity and culture during the counseling process. *Journal of Counseling and Development, 85*(4), 401–409.

Denbo, S. (2002). Institutional practices that support African American student achievement. In S. J. Denbo & L. M. Beaulieu (Eds.), *Improving schools for African American students* (pp. 55–70). Springfield, IL: Charles Thomas.

DeShazer, S., Berg, I. K., Lipchik, E., Nunnally, E., Molnar, A., Gingerich, W., & Weiner-Davis, M. (1986). Brief therapy: Focused solution development *Family Process, 25*(2), 207–221.

Duncan, C. F., & Pryzwansky, W. B. (1993). Effects of race, racial identity development, and orientation style on perceived consultant effectiveness. *Journal of Multicultural Counseling and Development, 21*(2), 88–96.

Education Trust. (2003). African American achievement in America. Retrieved from http://www.mnadvocates.org/sites/608a3887-dd53-4796-8904-997a0131ca54/uploads/AfAmer_Achivement_2.pdf

Ford, D. Y., & Whiting, G. W. (2008). Cultural competence: Preparing gifted students for a diverse society. *Roeper Review, 30*(2), 1–7.

Galassi, J. P., & Akos, P. (2007). *Strengths-based school counseling: Promoting student development and achievement.* New York, NY: Taylor & Francis/Lawrence Erlbaum.

Gamoran, A., & Hannigan, E. C. (2000). Algebra for everyone? Benefits of college-preparatory mathematics for students with diverse abilities in early secondary school. *Educational Evaluation and Policy Analysis, 22*(3), 241–254.

Gibbs, J. T. (1980). The interpersonal orientation in mental health consultation: Toward a model of ethnic variation in consultation. *Journal of Community Psychology, 8*(3), 195–207.

Hawkins, J. D., Catalano, R. F., & Miller, J. Y. (1992). Risk and protective factors for alcohol and other drug problems. *Psychological Bulletin, 112*(1), 64–105.

Henderson, A. T., Mapp, K. L., Johnson, V. R., & Davies, D. (2007). *Beyond the bake sale: The essential guide to family-school partnerships.* New York, NY: The New Press.

Hipolito-Delgado, C. P., & Lee, C. C. (2007). Empowerment Theory for the professional school counselor: A manifesto for what really matters. *Professional School Counseling, 10*(4), 327–332.

Holcomb-McCoy, C. (2004). Assessing the multicultural competence of school counselors: A checklist. *Professional School Counseling, 7*(3), 178–186.

Holcomb-McCoy, C. (2007). *School counseling to close the achievement gap: A framework for success.* Thousand Oaks, CA: Corwin Press.

Holcomb-McCoy, C., & Johnston, G. (2008). A content analysis of pre-service school counselors' evaluations of an urban practicum experience. *Journal of School Counseling, 6*(16). Retrieved from http://jsc.montana.edu/articles/v6n16.pdf

Holcomb-McCoy, C., & Lee, C. C. (Eds.). (2005). School counseling in urban settings [Special issue]. *Professional School Counseling, 8*(3).

Ingraham, C. L. (2000). Consultation through a multicultural lens: Multicultural and cross cultural consultation in schools. *School Psychology Review, 29*(3), 320–343.

Ingraham, C. L. (2003). Multicultural consultee-centered consultation: When novice consultants explore cultural hypotheses with experienced teacher consultees. *Journal of Educational and Psychological Consultation, 14*, 329–362.

Jamieson, A., Curry, A., & Martinez, G. (2001). *School enrollment in the United States—social and economic characteristics of students.* U.S. Census Bureau (Current Population Reports, Series P20-533). Washington, DC: Author.

Jencks, C., & Phillips, M. (1998). The black-white test score gap: An introduction. In C. Jencks & M. Phillips (Eds.), *The black-white test score gap: An introduction* (pp. 1–54). Washington, DC: Brookings Institution Press.

Johnson, R. (2002). *Using data to close the achievement gap: How to M.E.A.S.U.R.E. equity in our schools.* Thousand Oaks, CA: Corwin Press.

Kalyanpur, M., & Rao, S. S. (1991). Empowering low-income black families of handicapped children. *American Journal of Orthopsychiatry, 61*(4), 523–532. doi: 10.1037/h0079292

Kelly, M. S., Kim, J. S., & Franklin, C. (2008). *Solution-Focused Brief Therapy in schools: A 360 degree view of research and practice.* New York, NY: Oxford University Press.

Lee, C. C. (2003). *Empowering young black males-III: A systematic modular training program for Black male children & adolescents.* Greensboro, NC: Caps.

Losen, D. J., & Orfield, G. (2002). *Racial inequity in special education.* Cambridge, MA: Harvard Education.

McWhirter, E. (1994). *Counseling for empowerment.* Alexandria, VA: American Counseling Association.

Mehan, H., Villanueva, I., Hubbard, L., & Lintz, A. (2004). *Constructing school success.* New York, NY: Cambridge University Press.

Menacker, J. (1974). *Vitalizing guidance in urban schools.* New York, NY: Dodd, Mead, & Company.

Milner, H. R., IV. (2007). African American males in urban schools: No excuses—teach and empower. *Theory into Practice, 46*(3), 239–246.

Muhammed, C. G. (2008). African American students and college choice: A consideration of the role of school counselors. *NASSP Bulletin, 92*(2), 81–94.

Nelson, J. R., Dykeman, C., Powell, S., & Petty, D. (1996). The effects of a group counseling intervention on students with behavioral adjustment problems. *Elementary School Guidance & Counseling, 31*(1), 21–33.

Newsome, W. S. (2004). Solution-focused brief therapy groupwork with at-risk junior high school students: Enhancing the bottom line. *Research on Social Work Practice, 14*(5), 336–345.

Nieto, S. (1999). *The light in their eyes: Creating multicultural learning communities.* New York, NY: Teachers College Press.

Noddings, N. (1992). *The challenge to care in schools: An alternative approach to education.* New York, NY: Teachers College Press.

Noguera, P. A. (2004). Special topic/transforming high schools. *Educational Leadership, 61*(8), 26–31.

Obidah, J. E., and Howard, T. C. (2005). Preparing teachers for "Monday morning" in the urban school classroom: Reflecting on our pedagogies and practices as effective teacher educators, *Journal of Teacher Education, 56*(3), 248-255.

Orr, A. (2003). Black-white differences in achievement: The importance of wealth. *Sociology of Education, 76*(4), 281–304.

Pelavin, S. H., & Kane, M. (1990). *Changing the odds: Factors increasing access to college.* New York, NY: The College Board.

Perkins, D. D., & Zimmerman, M. A. (1995). Empowerment theory: Research and application. *American Journal of Community Psychology, 25*(5), 569–580.

Phillips, M. (2000). Understanding ethnic differences in academic achievement: Empirical lessons from national data. In D. Grissner & M. Ross (Eds.). *Analytic issues in assessment of student achievement.* Washington, DC: U.S. Department of Education.

Phillips, T. H., & Phillips, P. (1992). Structured groups for high school students: A case study of one district's program. *The School Counselor, 39*(5), 390–393.

Rodriguez, L. F. (2003). *Struggling to recognize their existence: Structure, power, and relationships in three urban high schools* (Unpublished manuscript, Harvard Graduate School of Education).

Sadowski, M. (2001). Closing the gap one school at a time. *Harvard Education Letter, 17*(3), 1–3.

Scales, R. C. (2005). Developmental assets and the middle school counselor. *Professional School Counseling, 9*(2), 104–111.

Shelton, J., & Sellers, R. (2000). Situated stability and variability in African American racial identity. *Journal of Black Psychology, 26*(1), 27–50.

Sheridan, S. M. (2000). Considerations of multiculturalism and diversity in behavioral consultation with parents and teachers. *School Psychology Review, 29*(3), 344–353.

Somers, C. L., Owens, D., & Piliawsky, M. (2008). Individual and social factors related to urban African American adolescents' school performance. *The High School Journal, 91*, 1–11.

Tarver-Behring, S., & Ingraham, C. L. (1998). Culture as a central component of consultation: A call to the field. *Journal of Educational and Psychological Consultation, 9*(1), 57–72

Tatum, A. W. (2004). *Teaching reading to black adolescent males: Closing the achievement gap.* Portland, ME: Stenhouse.

Turner, J. C. (1982). Toward a cognitive redefinition of the social group. In H. Tajfel (Ed.), *Social identity and intergroup behavior* (pp. 15–40). Cambridge, UK: Cambridge University Press.

U. S. Bureau of the Census. (2008). *Income, poverty, and health insurance: Coverage in the United States: 2008* (Report P60, Table B-2). Washington, DC: Author.

Viteritti, J. P. (1999). *Choosing equality: School choice, the constitution, and civil society.* Washington, DC: Brookings Institute.

Wayman, K. I., Lynch, E. W., & Hanson, M. J. (1991). Home-based early childhood services: Cultural sensitivity in a family systems approach. *Topics in Early Childhood Special Education, 10*(4), 56–75.

Whiting, G. W., Ford, D. Y., Grantham, T. C., & Moore, J. L., III. (2008). Multicultural issues: Considerations for conducting culturally responsive research in gifted education. *Gifted Child Today, 31*(3), 26–30.

Werner, E. E., & Smith, R. S. (1992). *Overcoming the odds: High risk children from birth to adulthood.* Ithaca, NY: Cornell University Press.

Wyatt, S. (2009). The brotherhood: Empowering adolescent African-American males toward excellence. *Professional School Counseling, 12*(6), 463–470.

Zinck, K., & Littrell, J. M. (2000). Action research shows group counseling effective with at risk adolescent girls. *Professional School Counseling, 4*(1), 50–59.

CHAPTER FOUR

Nurturing Resiliency Among African American Adolescent Males: A Focus on Writing

ALFRED W. TATUM

Adolescent African American males who struggle with reading and writing often encounter reading materials, writing assignments, and instructional contexts in schools that reinforce their perceptions of being struggling readers and writers (Darling-Hammond, 2001; Tatum, 2005, 2008; Thernstrom & Thernstrom, 2003). As adolescents, they often ignore their desire for self-definition. Poorly conceptualized literacy practices for these young males utlimately contribute to the degradation of their full humanity (Alexander, 2010; Holzman, 2005; National Association of State Boards of Education, 2006; Noguera, 2008; Swanson, Cunningham, & Spencer, 2003). Many of these young males become stifled by low-level literacy skills that often manifest into negative life trajectories or deleterious pathways.

In examining the history of texts and their influences on African American males, the positive impact of reading and writing on their lives cannot be underestimated. Throughout U.S. history, African Americans engaged in literacy practices in which reading and writing were collaborative acts involving a wide range of texts that held social, economic, personal, political, or spiritual significance (Belt-Beyan, 2004; Fisher, 2009). For example, Negro literary societies (also known as reading room and debating societies) were formed in nine states and the District of Columbia in the late 1800s. The societies were often gender specific. Book talks in these societies were referred to as "mental feasts" (Wesley, 1939), which were discussions that profoundly affected the young males. These societies had a wide range of purposes, including building up a collection of useful books for the benefit of their members, training youth in the habits of reading and reflection, and cultivating the mind and improving the heart.

Literacy was also a collaborative undertaking undertaken for the sake of African American males' meaningful and purposeful activism. For instance, African American "conductors" of the Underground Railroad carried out resistance activities using various forms of oral, written, and graphic communication. Many African American civil war troops also benefited from collaborative literacy events. These troops would carve out time to become literate together by reading from a spelling book, an elementary school text, or scriptures whenever they had a spare moment. Within a meaningful social context, the goal of such collaborative acts was to be regularly and purposefully engaged with print (Belt-Beyan, 2004). Thus, there is ample historical precedence to suggest that it is viable to reconceptualize literacy as a collaborative act with and among African American adolescent males who live complex lives.

Collaboration around texts—in formal and informal settings and inside and outside schools—as an approach to advance the literacy development of African American males has been abandoned (Fashola, 2005; Tatum, 2008, 2009). Little, if any, purposefully designed collaborations are taking place in middle and high schools around reading or writing that pay attention to the context of the lives of African American adolescent males. These young males often have no knowledge of their history of collaborating around texts, being part of a broader literacy community, or reading and writing texts as a way to address issues related to their extant circumstances.

Knowledge about how to engage African American adolescent males with texts, both reading and writing, is warranted. This is particularly true for those students who experience difficulty with school-based reading and writing. Research is needed to examine how literacy practices, instructional contexts, and texts can be used to nurture resiliency among adolescents who struggle with reading and writing or who live in communities of turmoil. This is paramount. Having underdeveloped literacy skills places African American adolescent males at-risk of quitting school before high school graduation (Alliance for Excellent Education, 2006; Biancarosa & Snow, 2006; Holzman, 2005; National Governors Association Center for Best Practices, 2005; Snow, Porche, Tabors, & Harris,

2007; Sen, 2006). This, in turn, severely limits their opportunities to fashion positive life outcomes.

Yet, literacy researchers have given little attention to these young males. The lack of research became evident as I searched the PsychInfo and ERIC databases in May 2008 for empirical studies that focus on teaching writing and reading to African American male adolescents published, over the past 30 years. I used the descriptors *boys, reading, writing, adolescent,* and *African American* in different combinations. The ERIC search yielded 693 results when the descriptors *boys* and *reading* were combined. The combination of *boys, reading,* and *adolescent* yielded 50 results. The combination of *boys, writing, adolescent,* and *African American/black* yielded no results.

The lack of reading and writing research involving African American adolescent males is a significant problem because many educators are failing to increase these young males' engagement with texts and, in turn, their reading and writing achievement. Also, specific texts and subjects in the texts regarding the selection of curricula to support the reading and writing development of African American adolescent males are strikingly absent (Tatum, 2006). In addition, there is an absence of research that informs educators about how to mediate reading and writing with these young males and how to shape instructional contexts to counter in-school and out-of-school variables that heighten the vulnerability level of many African American adolescent males.

In this chapter, I discuss how a summer literacy institute designed with a historical orientation of the roles of reading and writing in the lives of African American males affected several adolescent males. Interactions among African American adolescent males across age groups at the institute and the benefits it yielded for the participants are discussed. Implications for mediating texts with adolescent males are also offered. The chapter ends with a discussion of the roles of texts in nurturing the resiliency of adolescents and the need to legitimize responsive literacy practices.

A LITERACY COLLABORATIVE FOR AFRICAN AMERICAN ADOLESCENT MALES

During the summer of 2009, I designed a five-week African American Adolescent Male Summer Literacy Institute (AAAMSLI) at the University of Illinois at Chicago. One of the goals of the institute was to reconstruct a communal approach to give young adolescent males the opportunity and support to write about the multiple contexts informing their lives. They wrote poetry, short stories, children's stories, and the beginning of a novel. The young males met for 9 hours each week for a total of 54 hours. The meeting times were Tuesday though Thursday from 10:00 a.m. to 1:00 p.m. The institute's daily schedule is below:

10:00 a.m. Institute's preamble
10:05 a.m. Writing warm-up with explicit instruction
10:30 a.m. Mentor writer or visiting author
11:00 a.m. Raw writing and critiques from other participants
12:30 p.m. Blog postings and writer's chair
1:00 p.m. Institute's preamble

AAAMSLI participants were charged with anchoring their writings into four platforms: (a) defining self, (b) becoming resilient, (c) engaging others, and (d) building capacity. These platforms were selected based on historical roles of writing for African American males (Mullane, 1993), and they were used as the framing for the literacy collaborative. Each day, the students recited the institute's preamble to open and close each three-hour writing session, envisioned to nurture a cooperative and conversational community:

> We, the Brother Authors, will seek to use language to define who we are, become and nurture resilient beings, write for the benefit of others and ourselves and use language prudently and unapologetically to mark our times and mark our lives.

> This, we agree to, with a steadfast commitment to the ideas of justice, compassion, and a better humanity for all. To this end, we write!

RESEARCHING THE LITERACY COLLABORATIVE

Twelve African American adolescent males who were selected to participate in the AAAMSLI agreed to participate in a qualitative case study designed to answer two research questions: (a) What are the sociocultural benefits of writing for African American adolescent males? and (b) What are the sociocultural benefits of the writing environment for African American adolescent males? The data sources consisted of 35 hours of observations, 58 hours of semistructured interviews, and 90 samples of students' writings.

Theoretical Framing

The study was grounded in a theory of literacy in African American male's lives that brings attention to how purposeful reading, writing, and speaking encircle each other, and how reading, writing, and speaking are propelled by a desire for people to become independent and self-sufficient (Fisher, 2009; Tatum, 2009). The study was also informed by a critical sociocultural approach to literacy teaching that brings attention to students' identity, agency, and power (Lewis, Enciso, & Moje, 2007). Additionally, it was framed by communities of practices that pay attention to how human actions are mediated by language and other symbol systems within particular cultural contexts (Lave & Wenger, 1991; Wenger, 1998).

These theoretical frames were important because the ultimate goal of the institute was to nurture the next generation of socially conscious readers and writers. The young males were pushed to write for themselves and for others. They were also asked to use their pens prudently and unapologetically.

Study's Sample

AAAMSLI participants were referred to as Brother Authors. They ranged in age from 12 to 17. Eleven different elementary and high schools in Chicago and Chicago-land area also attended. They were of high, average, and low academic range, according to the self-reported descriptions they provided about the grades they earned during the previous school year.

Each young male was selected based on ideas communicated in a writing sample that was required as part of the AAAMSLI's application process. Several Brother Authors can be considered vulnerable, as indicated by their own words. These voices reflect the presence of gang activity in their lives; the prevalence of poverty-ridden conditions; the absence of fathers in their households; and feelings of race-, culture-, and poverty-based rejection. Below are sample quotes from the aforementioned applications.

Chart 1. Participants, Age Ranges, and Self-Reported Academic Descriptors

Participants	Age	Self-Reported Academic Descriptors
1. BA 1	12–13 range	A, B, and high C student
2. BA 2	14–17 range	Honor roll all the time
3. BA 3	14–17 range	A and B student
4. BA 4	14–17 range	Average student
5. BA 5	12–13 range	C and some Fs student
6. BA 6	12–13 range	A and B student
7. BA 7	12–13 range	C and D student
8. BA 8	14–17 range	C student
9. BA 9	12–13 range	B or C student
10. BA 10	14–17 range	C and D and one B student
11. BA 11	12–13 range	D and F student
12. BA 12	14–17 range	C, D, and F student

Applicant 1

When you walk down the street do you think about getting shot by a gang member? Those questions have wondered through my head. Me, I'm Art Royal (pseudonym) and I am a 14 year old African American male that lives on the west side of Chicago, and it's hard for a lot of people mostly me. My mother is worried about me and my brother's safety sense we live in the hood. My mom always tells me and my brother before we go to school or the store "Don't take anything that looks funny, smell, or moves funny." Things were great before until the big accident.

Applicant 2

Affiliation in gangs has always affected young black males and this rate is constantly grow-ing. I attend [an urban] public high school, and for the last couple of years the number of my fellow Chicago Public Schools (CPS) students' death toll has increased. This year about 30 students were killed this school year and most of these incidents occurred off school grounds and were gang related. Still, some of this falls back on these young men backgrounds, because most do not know any better, since it was the life to be brought into. These gang members often get sentenced to prison for selling narcotics, homicide, and having unlicensed weapons.

Applicant 3

All my life, I have never been anything more but a trouble making black boy. I was always the one that got in the most trouble throughout my family. In my entire life, I never had my time to shine. Everyone around me was happy and joyful but not me. I was by myself in a cold world. I always tried my best at everything but my best wasn't good enough. I know no one in the world liked me because every time I walked in a room people looked at me like I was wanted for murder. Most people tell me that I will be locked up with the real bad boys, but truly I would love that because most of the bad boys I talked to know how much it hurts to be left out or forgotten. They know it hurts to look in the eyes of their family and friends and teacher and they see fire and disappointment. For me, I never could look in someone's eyes and see happiness when they look at me. All I would see is my reflection fading away.

Applicant 4

If I were that child, I would have his father
I would share the inspiration to be just like my dad when I grow up
I would be able to run to his bedside when I have a frightening dream
I could be shown how to talk to a woman, or toss a ball
But I am not that child.
If I were that child I would be praised by my teachers for being the perfect student
I would be able to dream of a perfect life
I could be a strong influence
But I am not that child.
But since I'm not that child, I am able to overcome! I am not that child, I am not that child,
I am not that child! But, if I were that child . . .

It is clear from their voices that adolescent African American males encounter a wide range of difficulties impacted by personal and environmental factors. These factors suggest that an oversimplified approach to literacy teaching that focuses on skill and strategy development alone without considering the complexity of teaching potentially vulnerable students is conceptually thin. A more comprehensive approach to literacy instruction—to nurture resiliency among adolescents who struggle with literacy—is necessary (Tatum, 2008). This is why I began to examine the role of writing in the lives of adolescent African American males.

INTERACTIONS AMONG BROTHER AUTHORS
IN A LITERACY COLLABORATIVE

The African American novelist Percival Everett (2001) begins his novel, *Erasure*, with the following:

> My journal is a private affair, but as I cannot know the time of my coming death, and since I am not disposed, however unfortunately, to the serious consideration of self-termination, I am afraid that others will see these pages. Since however I will be dead, it should not matter much to me who sees what or when. My name is Thelonius Ellison. And I am a writer of fiction. This admission pains me only at the thought of my story being found and read, as I have always been severely put off by any story which has as it main character a writer. (p. 1)

Everett is part of a storied lineage of African American writers who

> for more than three hundred years, in the face of economic exploitation, peonage, lynching, prejudice, and denial of basic civil and human rights . . . have collectively created a remarkable body of work . . . that resonates powerfully today for all Americans. (Mullane, 1993, p. xxii)

Although the Brother Authors entered the institute as individuals, they were asked to read and write publicly, quickly moving beyond the idea that writing is a private affair. I greeted the Brother Authors with a preamble that introduced four platforms for writing and poetic broadsides (Reid, 2002), during the first week of the institute. On day three, I gave them the following directions for writing a last stand/call to action/deathbed broadside, a broadside they wanted others to remember them by:

> As week one of the institute comes to an end, we will write for the benefit of others and ourselves. To do this, I ask you to reflect on an experience that you can use to teach the rest of us a lesson. I offer a broadside below that captures the first time I was placed at gunpoint at age 11 (4015 days after I was born) in the Ida B. Wells housing projects. This experience and others, mostly positive, shaped my decision to become a teacher. We are the change agents we need. Things will not change until . . .

As an example, I shared my own personal broadside titled, "Until":

Four thousand and fifteen days from my first breath
Cornered by the brown brick fearing death
Invisible in broad daylight
The wide-opened eyes closed shut by dull beginnings
Could not see me/himself
Because of what he was (mis) taught
Confused
Distraught
Blood continues to drip
On the inner-city asphalt
Until . . .
Until . . .
Until . . .

All of the Brother Authors later responded with their own broadsides. Below are two examples titled, "Stop" and "Autumn Message":

Example 1

I can hear the flames
Burning the future of others
Gun violence
Gangs
All of this is killing our city
Stop the violence
Stop the flames
Stop everything

Example 2

Leaves float down wistfully unto me, eyes shuddering; I see blurs.
They look like people I've known . . .
In the crisp grass I rest, is how it should be
A field of play abandoned by all, I hear the birds call
They sound familiar like people I've known . . .
I can taste the fading light in the air as the sun goes in hiding
My body feels cooler by the second and while I inhale the color of the leaves
My own fades. I feel weightless as if this field of grass was a never-ending cloud in the sky.
My thoughts are becoming hazy as the wind blows more of my friends before my eyes
They all speak to me as they pass; I have to tell them something.
The trees that surround me in a tight ring lean over me, watching.
Oh wait, it's my family surrounding me, they've come to help me stand.
I don't have the strength.
I stroke the hair on my brother's head
It's grown a lot, I have to, and I'll tell him.

"Listen . . . if you believe . . . that . . . Caucasians are the reason you can't excel . . . that
they're stopping you . . . then . . . you . . . are a Caucasian."
Through strained breaths I state my final words, to no one, no one
But my friends and family and my little brother, with his black mask on.
Who just happens to look like leaves, trees and a raccoon.
I hope he heard me . . . in the autumn breeze.

As shown in Table 1, during our first week together, the Brother Authors collectively wrote numerous pieces across a wide range of topics. Most of their early
writings tackled issues of racial and ethnic identity, discrimination, resiliency,
violence, and injustice, similar to the pieces above. When asked what it is like writing among a group of African American male writers from different schools, the
themes of community support, reciprocity, and purposeful engagement emerged
from their voices.

These themes are reflected in several of the comments in Table 2.

Two of the Brother Authors, in particular, expressed how the instructional
contexts assisted them. For example, one stated:

> The environment is good. We are able to talk and relate and actually help each other with
> our writing and so far they think that I've been writing good things and they've been writing
> some good things as well. So I think we're able to communicate and really become friends
> in this program.

Another brother asserted:

> Well as the days and weeks go on, me and the other Brother Authors, we're starting to
> express our thoughts with each other because we're becoming more familiar. And it's pretty
> cool actually once we've gotten to know each other and start talking about our writing
> more together it's good that we get to share our ideas and our viewpoints. That helps a lot
> in our writing.

It is worth highlighting that the young males assessed the instructional context as dissimilar from school and a "good place to come to express [one's] feelings
and show potential" in an environment that made them feel "like actual Brothers."
The Brother Authors also suggested that the writing platforms were central to the
positive instructional contexts.

Telling It Straight UP

At the end of each week, the Brother Authors were asked to reflect on the four
writing platforms: defining self, nurturing resiliency, engaging others, and building capacity. They were also asked to focus on the AAAMSLI preamble. The
Brothers' words indicated that they embraced the platforms as a contract that

Table 1. Writings From the First Week of the AAAMSLI and Topic Areas

Writing Topics	BA#1	BA#2	BA#3	BA#4	BA#5	BA#6	BA#7	BA#8	BA#9	BA#10	BA#11	BA#12	TOTAL
1. Identity: Personal Characteristics	X				X		X	XX	X	X	X	X	8
2. Identity: Race or Ethnicity		XXXX	XX	XX	XXX	XX		XXX	X	X	XXX	XXX	24
3. Love				X						X		X	3
4. Family		X		X	X						X	X	5
5. School or Education						X		X		X	X		4
6. Africa					X							XXX	4
7. America			X	X	X							XXX	6
8. God or Religion					X	X						XXXXXX	8
9. Racial Discrimination		XX	X		X	X		XX	XX		XXX		12
10. Caucasian People				X	X	X	X		X	X	X	XX	9
11. Social Justice—Equality	X								X	X	X		4
12. Politics									X				1
13. Resiliency	X	XX	XXXX	X	XXX			XXX	XX	XX		XXXX	22
14. Violence	X	XX	XX		XX	XX	XX		X	X	XX	XXX	18
15. Injustice	XX	XXX		X		X			X	X	X	XXX	13
16. Role Models—Mentors		X	X		XX		X		X	X		XX	9
17. Writing or Power of Words								X				XXX	4
18. Power	X										X		2
19. Fatherhood													0
20. Inner Conflict													0

Table 2. Themes Emerging From the Writing of African American Adolescent Males

Community Support	"There's been a lot of ideas bouncing around—like we help each other write and we tell each other what's wrong or *give a different perspective on your own writing as someone whose been looking outside into your own writing, you can remove the haze from your mind basically about your own writing or whatever ego you have.* They can tell you that this is an outside perspective. And you don't always have to go with that because *there's more people to give you other perspectives so you can gain knowledge of how you can see your writing from the outside and use that to make your pieces better.*" "Because here I have people who can help me out and I can help them out. At home, it's like you make more mistakes when you're by yourself because you don't have anybody to critique it."
Community Support	"I think I'm the youngest I think . . . I'd have to say it's pretty good. *I like to be around people of different ages so I can learn something, let their maturity brush off on me. I can tell that there are strengths in their writing that brushes off* so I can become a great writer."
Reciprocity	"Because *here I have people who can help me out and I can help them out.* At home, it's like you make more mistakes when you're by yourself because you don't have anybody to critique it."
Reciprocity	I think it's a good experience for you to join up with African Americans that you don't even know and just criticize and talk about African Americans. And the way we see it and the way we write about it, **we're able to help each other on our view about the stuff that's happened with us lately so I think this is a good experience for all of us.**
Purposeful engagement	The benefits for that are that I'm able to see what other brother authors write about like what kind of message they're trying to send. And **I like to help them with it so that way the message will be more clear to other people to understand it.**
Purposeful engagement	"I'm like 'what!' I'm holding back tears. This is interesting. I'm like what did he say that I didn't or how can I say something and what emotion did he put in there to cause that reaction and why didn't it appeal to me as much as it appealed to him . . . So I wanted to do that as well too. I was going to start doing that but I really wanted to make people if not more sympathetic towards these kids, more aware. So that's when I started doing it from the kids point of view. And that's all about appealing to some of the audiences, like what the other BAs have taught me to do. *But, right now I'm trying to appeal to everybody's sense of humanity.* So that's what the BA do. They help me see how to get my point across in a different way."

cemented their purposes for writing. In particular, as one male explained the meaning of the preamble:

> To me it means writing to express how we feel about ourselves and how others might feel. How we're becoming better men as we write telling our story. And, the last paragraph I'd say—or the last part—is a contract part that we are signing.

As part of the contract, the Brother Authors found direction and new personal boldness that strengthened their relationships to their own writing and the writing of the other young males in the literacy collaborative. For example, one of the Brother Authors' mentioned, in reference to the platforms, that "we are part of a group or commitment or relationship to our work." In a similar sense, another one asserted that "it tells us to write in our own way . . . and we write with no regret and we write with full effort."

Throughout the program, reconceptualization in their writing to pay attention to the four platforms, which characterized the writing of African American males, became a source of cognitive stimulation for the AAAMSLI participants. These young Brother Authors' writings became purposeful. They felt, as if they had become reflective, resilient beings. Further, the writings that they experienced in relationship to the platforms and the preamble were reflected in the words they shared during some of the interviews. As an example, one Brother Author stated: "It makes me think about what I am writing about. Not just writing for fun but writing to define myself. Some of it goes back to the preamble." Another brother indicated the following: "It actually helps me understand what I'm writing about like what kind of message it sends to the people. I didn't really know about the platforms, but I'd just write and I would have my own message to it. But, these four platforms kind of help me understand the things I'm writing and what kind of things I've written about." A third brother stated:

> Well it has a lot of meanings to me—becoming resilient. Just writing like no matter what and using your language unapologetically. When you write, don't apologize. Explain your thoughts. I really like the preamble because I'm bringing these ideas out in my writing and I'm expressing the thought I have toward the preamble.

In a similar sense, a fourth brother highlighted the power of the preamble. For example, he stated: "Through my writing, it's getting me to think about some things that I haven't thought about. Like with the preamble—it's really showing me that these thoughts I'm having I can put it all on paper in my writing."

In the group, there were several young males who were underachieving or low achieving. One brother's writings, in particular, stood out: His words illustrate his strong desire to use his pen to mark his time and mark his life:

You can take my life and my mind too. You don't have to take my heart; I'm giving it to you. But *the one thing you will never get is my pen because without it I'm nothing. Writing is the only thing I have left* [italics added]. My mom don't like me, my family treat me like I was a person on the street. Most of my family never wants me by their kids. Isn't that something; I cannot go next to my cousins. So kill me, let me rollover and die, *but when I go don't let my writing go with me, let it stay with you* [italics added]. I know people are getting tired of reading about my blank life, because I am. I can't take it anymore. Someone kill me and get it over. I'd rather die and be remembered than live and be forgotten. *So, when I turn to dust don't let my writing turn to ashes* [italics added].

One of his Brother Authors, after reading his piece, shared, "Some of our writing makes us seem like resilient beings." Another Brother Author's words neatly encapsulate the role that the preamble embraced during the literacy collaborative. He explained the platforms and the preamble in the following way in his reflections on one of his pieces:

I think it basically means to tell our story without the sugar. I basically like to tell our story straight up, like what's been happening and why it's been happening. And just let people know what's been going on and also to write for others in a sense as to give them insight into someone else's feelings or someone else's experiences. And I think it's basically just to mark our time, mark our lives to show what we're doing. It is really about nurturing resilience, engaging others.

Benefits of the Institute

As a researcher and instructional leader of the AAAMSLI, I was interested in examining the benefits of writing in a literacy collaborative in which students' multiple identities (i.e., community, developmental, ethnic, gender, and personal) were centered. When I asked them to discuss what they believed they would take away from the institute, each of the Brother Authors shared their insights. Their remarks focused on identity shifts, changed perspectives, and self-awareness. These issues, both internal and external to the writers, suggest that they were becoming socially conscious writers. The following remarks indicate an internal shift for one of the Brother Authors: "I think I would see the world differently like with the writing. I would look at everything differently. Because when you're writing and you hear a lot of writing, you feel different. It's like your feelings change and how you think of writing." Comments from another brother illustrate an external shift and a changed perspective about African Americans:

From this institute, I think I will take that all Black people are talented and I could do more than I thought I could. I can take all this stuff that I know and take it to the next level and nobody can tell me nothing—I can already know what I'm able to do.

Through the different writing activities, the Brother Authors began reaching down into themselves in ways they had not imagined or anticipated prior to the institute. Many began to believe that "all writing is significant [depending] on how you write it." Having the opportunity to write in ways that they were not afforded inside of their classrooms, many of the Brothers found a different way to express themselves. As suggested by one of the Brothers, when he applied what he learned through the AAAMSLI writings in other instructional contexts: "Well it's allowed me to express myself in different ways that usually I wouldn't be able to do like outside this class or without a paper and pen in front of me." These remarks were similar to other Brother Authors. As one Brother stated:

> The benefit from my writing is insight into myself because when I write, I don't really think about it. I write and it just flows. Basically I write what I'm thinking without really knowing what I'm thinking. I write this and then I'm like "oh this is what I'm thinking." It's kind of like weird. It's kind of like I have two selves and the one whose writing is telling me "this is you, and I'm just the one out here with the pen." Whenever I'm writing, I look at my writing as a reflection of myself. It's not like I had this played out before I did it. It's after I did it that I find out that this is what I had planned out. If that made any sense at all, but that's how it works. . . . It helps us like reach down into, like look down into ourselves and find like the inner core of our writing instead of the outer core. Because the inner core is more sensitive to experiences. What the inner core is gonna have it's gonna have more feeling in it than the outer core.

Many Brother Authors described how they were able to write about topics that were often difficult to say on a daily basis and how writing affords the opportunity for them to make things better. The benefits they described receiving from writing ranged from "I feel that after each writing, it makes me a better person," to getting "to know myself a lot more personally and [learning] stuff about myself that I had not learned [in other] type of experiences," to "just becoming a better person period."

The Brother Authors also connected writing to their roles as African Americans, and in a more broad sense to universal humanity, as they used their pens to name themselves and their realities. When asked how writing affected them as a person, one Brother Authors shared: "It helps me to be more intelligent and fluent . . . and it makes people see that African Americans are not just you know dumb or nothing. [The AAAMSLI] taught me to write because of the people. . . . give me something to do . . . for a better humanity." Another one stated:

> As an African American male, we have a lot to work on and think beyond the moment like [name of another Brother Author] said we don't think beyond the moment. We don't think about the consequences. Like if it's. . . . I definitely want to start doing that. And I'm going to think about it first, think about it first definitely. And think beyond.

Reflecting on the types of writing anchored in the platforms, one brother said: "The benefits from the types of writing . . . I learned to broaden my perspective of things and write about other subjects and topics that I usually wouldn't write about or never thought of writing about." Another Brother Author posited:

> From this institute I will take that before I was just writing because it was fun, it was some-
> thing that I was comfortable with because I was . . . writing on paper, so I would take away
> that I am something more than just a black person that could write but someone who likes
> new possibilities and say like you can do this. So if I write it's like doing things you've never
> seen before, writing things you've never heard, doing things that people just can't imagine.
> I take away that you are something and that you have something to write.

These young males clearly benefited from participating in the literacy collab-orative, both personally and academically. Several times, throughout the research project, the young males echoed the following sentiments: "I think I'm smarter now; I definitely have a lot more knowledge" and "As a person I was affected education-wise. I feel this will help me going to high school. It will definitely help me in writing classes, like grammar, poetry classes and stuff." It is unfortunate that writing instruction for African American adolescent males in many schools is not conceptualized in ways that allow them to reap the wide range of benefits possible from writing about the multiple contexts that inform their lives. Writing about school-oriented topics, instead of writing about one's life, is the usual paths approach taken in many classrooms.

To find direction from the young males' words for moving beyond the usual paths approach, I asked the Brother Authors to provide recommendations to teachers based on their writing experiences in the institute. As a result, they offered the following suggestions:

1. "Let us speak our mind, not with our mouth, but with our pens."
2. "Allow us to choose what we want to write about."
3. "Be straightforward with us. Like if there's something going on in society, tell us please so we have something to write about and be able to put that in our writing."
4. "Allow us to write for ourselves. We're writing not just for us or to complain about stuff we did. We're writing just so that people in society will know like what others go through and not just for themselves."
5. "Provide more time for feedback in one-to-one sessions."
6. "Refuse to give up on students. You just have to keep working with them even though it seems hopeless, that's your job as a teacher. You can't just give up on your student."
7. "Find something that relates to us."

8. "Get to know your students."
9. "Let us express ourselves as a person instead of simply assigning an activity."
10. "Interact with the students instead of just sitting there looking over the class making sure that nobody's talking to each other."

The Brother Authors recognized the challenges teachers face when mediating writing with students. They accepted shared culpability for creating barriers for teachers who may want to provide responsive writing instruction. They also offered practical challenges. A 15-year-old Brother Author, who attends one of the urban public high schools in CPS, stated:

> I know this is not possible for all the teachers but I would like more one-on-one sessions. And young African American males such as myself, we don't listen a lot. We don't um, really, I have respect, but nowadays they don't have respect for anything. They don't really care honestly. So what you have to do is you have to make them care. Find something that relates to them. You can't just say this is the lesson; you don't get it. . . . What you have to do is you have to do, like I said, a one-on-one session. You can't teach somebody without knowing them. You can't just teach somebody something, because you have to know how [the students] will receive it, how they will get it and how they can use it. You have to know the methods and teach them so that they actually take in the information and are able to use it later. And it's a lot of things—these overcrowded classes in some public schools. . . . At my school you don't even want to go in there. [High school] used to be a wonderful school, but now I don't even want to go in there. It's just the school is old, it's dated, the books are torn, the library is not good or has a selection. We don't have AC, the walls are dirty. . . . We have bricks in our cafeteria. Our cafeteria walls are bricks. It makes me feel like I'm in prison. . . . Nobody wants to sit and write a paper in a prison cell. Nobody wants to sit at the bottom of the ditch with a bunch of rats crawling around and think about geometry. You basically have to put these kids in a clean, caring environment. You have to actually care. . . . So I recommend that [teachers] basically care more because if [they] don't then [the students are] not gonna care. And if they don't care then they don't have a future.

Writing as a Legitimate Pathway for Nurturing Resilience

Resiliency research brings attention to individuals' strengths and resources, often referred to as protective factors or protective resources (D'Imperio, Dobow, & Ippolito, 2000; Small & Memmo, 2004). Personal attributes, such as temperament, self-esteem, self-efficacy, social competence, autonomy, and meaningful purpose and goals, are individual characteristics that research has discovered among resilient urban youth. These characteristics are key personal attributes for urban, middle, and high school students. Therefore, efforts should be made to examine or honor each of these attributes and combine them with other resources to shape positive literacy and personal trajectories.

Writing plays an important role in adolescent literacy development, but school writing is often too rigid to accommodate their personal needs, not allowing them to write for different purposes and different audiences (Coker & Lewis, 2008). Studies of writing generally focus on learning to write or writing to learn. Using a sociocultural lens, my research activities focused on writing to live or writing for personal growth (Soven, 1999), by engaging African American males to anchor their writing into four platforms—defining self, becoming resilient, engaging others, and building capacity—in a collaborative writing environment that they assessed to be being both engaging and supportive. As a result, writing became a social act for the males participating in AAAMSLI. It also provided these Brothers with several critical supports. The adolescent males experienced a new kind of power through writing, as they moved toward a stronger sense of self. This is illustrated by the following quote: "It's a lot of power behind writing and that's something I want to continue. . . . Let our testimony be our pen." As another example of this, a Brother stated: "I kind of know myself a lot more personally. I've learned stuff about myself that I had not learned. . . . And, when I use 1st person, it kind of defines myself."

According to one young brother, his perception of the role of writing changed during our time together. For example, he shared:

> Before I was just writing because it was fun, it was something that I was comfortable with . . . [Now,] if I write, it's like doing things you've never seen before, writing things you've never heard, doing things that people just can't imagine. I take away that you are something and that you have something to write.

All of the males echoed the need to put their voices on record and that writing has the potential to reshape the image of African American males and others who experience internal conflicts. During individual interviews, Brother Authors of different ages and academic abilities unanimously mentioned that there was power in working together. Each suggested that the length of the institute should be extended. In addition, they *all* called for more time to read and write together. This suggested that they viewed the institute as a good use of their time and a legitimate form of education.

Hilliard (1998) characterizes a legitimate education as one in which teachers: (a) expect and demand excellence from students; (b) conceptualize education as an indispensable prerequisite for liberation; (c) engage students in a reawakening that focuses on deep thought; and (d) shape an agenda for transformation, self-acceptance, and self-determination. These historical orientations of a legitimate education stand in stark contrast to the modern-day iterations of education, particularly those that focus on efficiency characterized by meeting national norms or education standards devoid of cultural significance and meaning, iterations that can fail to nurture resiliency for students who enter our educational spaces feeling vulnerable.

Based on the data findings, I recommend several approaches for providing responsive writing instruction and shaping instructional contexts that most if not all urban African American males will find legitimate, thus providing them with human, material, and instructional resources to nurture their resiliency. These are similar to recommendations for providing responsive reading instruction (Tatum, 2005, 2008, 2009). My suggestions include, but are not limited to, the following:

1. Anchor writing instruction in clearly defined platforms and use the platforms as points for critical thought for identifying, selecting, and mediating texts in ways that pay attention to fair and equitable treatment.
2. Identify texts (e.g., literary and nonliterary, conventional, and nonconventional) that are fast moving, deeply penetrating, and will stimulate students' writings.
3. Provide writing models and engage students in discussions involving complex issues and that honor their voices.
4. Move urban African American males beyond writing texts that only stresses a victim mentality. Instead, have them use their pens as a way of building self-reliance, self-determination, and resiliency.
5. Structure literacy collaboratives between African American males and provide authentic opportunities for them to write with a purpose.

Based on the findings, there are many potential benefits of writing that extend beyond grade level and immediate context if different approaches for mediating writing and different instructional contexts are undertaken. The adolescent males participating in this project used their writing to elicit perplexing inquiries, offer different viewpoints, and get others engaged in moving on topics affecting their world (Tatum & Gue, 2010). Further, I observed an increased engagement with both reading and writing during the AAAMSLI. This was easily observed as adolescent African American males used their pens as tools of exploration for the benefit of others and themselves.

CONCLUDING THOUGHTS

Although literacy researchers and educators have given an increased amount of attention to culturally responsive instruction (Gay, 2000; Ladson-Billings, 1994; Lee, 2007; Murrell, 2002), very little attention within this body of research focuses on the roles of writing for African American males, who, in particular, are characterized as vulnerable as a result of their lives in their out-of-school contexts. Mahiri (1998), in a past ethnographic study of African American youth and culture, comes close when he identifies African American students' lack of affirming experiences with writing. The students in his study have to overcome writing phobias, a general lack of motivation to write, and a negative value attached to writing. As a way to reduce these psychological barriers, Mahiri created motivational strategies to help these students personalize early writing tasks and build on their lived experiences.

This chapter extends beyond Mahiri's study in several ways: Beyond the focus on youth culture, the research project at the institute uses a historical orientation for African American males' writing in collaborative environments that leads to the identification of four writing platforms. It was anchored in a theory of literacy in African American lives, communities of practices, and critical sociocultural theory. These theoretical orientations, although useful for reconceptualizing the roles of reading and writing in the lives of adolescent African American males, are ignored in educational and policy research.

Although renewed attention is being given to students' writing, such as in *Writing Next*, and the important roles writing plays in adolescent literacy development (Graham & Perin, 2007), I have some concerns that the focus of this commissioned document and other research documents can interrupt African American males' classroom access to writing to instead use it as a practice by which to grade their experiences of their times and their lives. The narrow foci on writing proficiency and bridging the gap between school and workplace writing are shaping how educators think about writing as a legitimate pathway for advancing students' literacies. I remain concerned that this efficiency-oriented approach will continue to create a wedge between urban and suburban adolescents and writing, particularly for those males who have yet to discover the power of writing in their own lives.

The findings from this project highlight the need to grant males opportunities to write about subjects that they find meaningful and significant. With four clearly defined platforms, explicit writing instruction, mentor writers, and opportunities for raw writing that they assessed as being both prudent and unapologetic, the adolescent males used their pens to carve out pathways that allowed them to experience a full measure of humanity. To be a part of this literacy collaborative amid the backdrop of violence that prematurely snuffs out the life of so many young African American adolescent males in the city where I teach and live, I was reminded of the words of W. E. B. Du Bois, who writes:

> When a human being becomes suddenly conscious of the tremendous powers lying latent within him . . . he rises to the powerful assertion of self, conscious of its might, then there is loosed upon the world possibilities of good or of evil that make men pause. (1973/2001, p. 24).

I experienced this type of tremendous power in the words of the African American adolescent participants, a community of Brother Authors, who used their writings to tap into the power lying latent within them. On the last day of the institute, a Brother Author shared:

> At the beginning of the institute, I was kind of—I wasn't really a big writer so I was kind of lost and I didn't really know what to write about. But now since [Dr. Tatum] showed me about other writers and other authors . . . I've researched some of them at home to sort of put my writing signature together.

The signature he is searching for can become part of a storied lineage of signatures created by African American male writers. It is critical that the educators of adolescent African American males garner the courage, compassion, and competence to help these students find their signatures as they learn to write their lives. To this end, writing can empower these students with culturally responsive approaches to literacy teaching that they can assess as being legitimate. As they do this, educators too can become empowered.

REFERENCES

Alexander, M. (2010). *The new Jim Crow: Mass incarceration in the age of colorblindness.* New York, NY: The New Press.

Alliance for Excellent Education. (2006). *Who's counted? Who's counting?: Understanding high school graduation rates.* Washington, DC: Author.

Belt-Beyan, P. (2004). *The emergence of African American literacy traditions.* Westport, CT: Praeger.

Biancarosa, C., & Snow, C. E. (2006). *Reading next: A vision for action and research in middle and high school literacy. A report to the Carnegie Corporation of New York* (2nd ed.). Washington, DC: Alliance for Excellent Education.

Coker, D., & Lewis, W. (2008). Beyond writing next: A discussion of writing research and instructional uncertainty. *Harvard Educational Review, 78*(1), 231–251.

Darling-Hammond, L. (2001). *The right to learn: A blueprint for creating schools that work.* San Francisco, CA: Jossey-Bass.

D'Imperio, R., Dubow, E., & Ippolito, M. (2000). Resilient and stress-affected adolescents in an urban setting. *Journal of Clinical Child Psychology, 29*(1), 129.

Du Bois, W. E. B. (2001). *The education of black people.* New York, NY: Monthly Review Press. Originally published in 1973.

Everett, P. (2001). *Erasure.* New York, NY: Hyperion.

Fashola, O. S. (Ed.). (2005). *Educating African American males: Voices from the field.* Thousand Oaks, CA: Corwin Press.

Fisher, M. (2009). *Black literate lives: Historical and contemporary perspectives.* New York, NY: Routledge.

Gay, G. (2000). *Culturally responsive teaching: Theory, research, & practice.* New York, NY: Teachers College Press.

Graham, S., & Perin, D. (2007). *Writing next: Effective strategies to improve the writing of adolescents in middle and high school.* Washington, DC: Alliance for Excellent Education.

Henderson, N., & Milstein, M. (2003). *Resiliency in schools: Making it happen for students and educators.* Thousand Oaks, CA: Corwin Press.

Hilliard, A. (1998). *SBA: The reawakening of the African mind.* Gainesville, FL: Makare.

Holzman, M. (2005). *Public education and black male students: The 2006 state report Card.* Cambridge, MA: The Schott Foundation for Public Education.

Ladson-Billings, G. (1994). *The dreamkeepers: Successful teachers of African American children.* San Francisco, CA: Jossey-Bass.

Lave, J., & Wenger, E. (1991). *Situated learning: Legitimate peripheral participation.* New York, NY: Cambridge University Press.

Lee, C. (2007). *Culture, literacy, and learning: Taking bloom in the midst of the whirlwind.* New York, NY: Teachers College Press.

Lewis, C., Enciso, P., and Moje, E. (2007). *Reframing sociocultural research on literacy: Identity, agency, and power.* Mahwah, NJ: Lawrence Erlbaum.

Mahiri, J. (1998). *Shooting for excellence: African American and youth culture in new century schools.* New York, NY: Teachers College Press.

Mullane, D. (1993). *Crossing the danger water: Three hundred years of African American writing.* New York, NY: Anchor Books.

Murrell, P. (2002). *African-centered pedagogy: Developing schools of achievement for African American children.* Albany, NY: SUNY Press.

National Association of State Boards of Education. (2006). *Reading at risk: The state response to the crisis in adolescent literacy. The report of the NASBE study group on middle and high school literacy.* Alexandria, VA: Author.

National Governors Association Center for Best Practices. (2005). *Reading to Achieve: A governor's guide to adolescent literacy.* Washington, DC: Author.

Noguera, P. (2008). *The trouble with black boys: And other reflections on race, equity and the future of public education.* San Francisco, CA: Jossey-Bass.

Reid, M. (2002). *Black protest poetry: Polemics from the Harlem Renaissance and the sixties.* New York, NY: Peter Lang.

Sen, R. (2006). *A positive future for black boys: Building the momentum.* Cambridge, MA: The Schott Foundation for Public Education.

Small, S., & Memmo, M. (2004). Contemporary models of youth development and problem prevention: Toward an integration of terms, concepts, and models. *Family Relations, 53*(1), 3–11.

Snow, C., Porche, M., Tabors, P., & Harris, S. (2007). *Is literacy enough? Pathways to academic success for adolescents.* Baltimore, MD: Brookes.

Soven, M. I. (1999). *Teaching writing in middle and secondary schools: Theory, research, and practice.* Boston, MA: Allyn & Bacon.

Swanson, D., Cunningham, M., & Spencer, M. B. (2003). Black males structural conditions, achievement patterns, normative needs, and "opportunities." *Urban Education, 38*(5), 608–633.

Tatum, A.W. (2005). *Teaching reading to black adolescent males: Closing the achievement gap.* Portland, ME: Stenhouse.

Tatum, A.W. (2006). Engaging African American males in reading. *Educational Leadership, 63*(5), 44–49.

Tatum, A.W. (2008). Toward a more anatomically complete model of literacy instruction: A focus on African American male adolescents and texts. *Harvard Educational Review, 78*(1), 155–180.

Tatum, A.W. (2009). *Reading for their life: (Re)building the textual lineage of African American adolescent males.* Portsmouth, NH: Heinemann.

Tatum, A.W., & Gue, V. (2010). Adolescents and texts: Raw writing—a critical support for adolescents. *English Journal, 99*(4), 90–93.

Thernstrom, A., & Thernstrom, S. (2003). *No excuses: Closing the racial gap in learning*. New York, NY: Simon & Schuster.

Wenger, E. (1998). *Communities of practice: Language power and social context*. New York, NY: Cambridge University Press.

Wesley, C. H. (1939). The Negroes of New York in the emancipation movement. *Journal of Negro History, 24*(1), 65–103

Special Education AND Disciplinary Disproportionality OF African American Students

GWENDOLYN CARTLEDGE, LENWOOD GIBSON JR.,
AND STARR E. KEYES

The latest authorization of the Individuals with Disabilities Education Act (IDEA) 2004 defines *disproportionality* as both overrepresentation and underrepresentation according to the racial/ethnic group. States are expected to collect data to determine if significant disproportionality based on race or ethnicity is occurring with respect to the following: (a) the identification of children as children with disabilities; (b) the identification of children as children with a particular disability; (c) the placement of children with disabilities in particular educational settings; and (d) the incidence, duration, and type of disciplinary actions, including suspensions and expulsions (Coordinated Early Intervening Services [CEIS] Guidance, n.d., p. 4). Data on overrepresentation are generally presented in two different ways, which are both valid and important. According to Artiles and colleagues (2002), the two ways are special education enrollment by (ethnic) group and the percent of (ethnic) group in special education. The Office for Civil Rights (OCR) pays particular attention to the former, but the latter is equally useful in determining overrepresentation of ethnicities by special education category. In a similar sense, Skiba, Poloni-Staudinger, Simmons, Feggins-Azziz, and Chung (2005) and Skiba et al. (2008) discuss measuring disproportionality of an ethnic group by assessing the composition index (CI), risk index (RI), and risk ratio (RR). The CI refers to the proportion of the ethnic group within special education versus the proportion of that same group in the population or enrollment in school. For example, although African Americans make up 14% of the school-aged students, they constitute 26.4% of students in programs for emotional behavioral disability (EBD). The combined RI and RR is used to assess the difference in which certain ethnic groups are found eligible for special education in comparison to other ethnic groups (see Skiba et al., 2008, for a complete explanation).

Rates according to race/ethnicity. As noted by Blanchett (2006), disproportionality exists when a certain (ethnic) group's enrollment in a particular special education category or program exceeds that of their proportion in the school's population. This can be extended to larger data sets, as when the special education rates in a state or the whole country are reviewed. Zhang and Katsiyannis (2002) reviewed three federal government publications and determined that African Americans are overrepresented in special education across the nation. In specific, there is a significant excess of African Americans in the mental retardation (MR) and emotional/behavioral disorder (EBD) categories, even when taking poverty into account. This evidence is also shown in the U.S. Department of Education (2009) data (see Table 5.1), which plainly reveals disproportionality for African Americans in the categories of MR and emotional disturbance (ED).

Rates according to gender. Males also tend to be overrepresented in special education populations in comparison to females. Sacks and Kern (2008) provide an example of this by citing a study in which students with and without EBDs were asked about their quality of life. The sample population in this study is 86 students; 67 being male and only 19 female. Rice, Merves, and Srsic (2008) point out that girls are an underidentified and understudied population for having EBDs. The authors also note that a possible reason for this is that girls tend to internalize more. Existing measurement and identification tools might not detect internalizing, and common gender role assumptions as far as how girls usually behave might impede educators from referring them for a diagnosis of an EBD.

Some researchers (e.g., Wehmeyer & Schwartz, 2001) contend that females are underserved, not receiving services unless they evidence disabilities more severe than are typically observed in males. Furthermore, Skiba, Michael, Nardo, and Peterson (2002) review numerous studies dating as far back as 1978 that provide evidence that boys are sent to the office, suspended, and receive a variety of disciplinary consequences significantly more than girls. Achilles and associates (2007) also find that males are more likely to be excluded (i.e., suspended) than females; being older also increases the odds. According to Townsend (2000), African American males experience devastating consequences as a result of being overrepresented in special education and in disciplinary procedures.

Table 5.1 Disability Distribution by Race/Ethnicity of Students Ages 6 Through 21, Served Under IDEA: Fall 2004

Disability	American Indian/Alaska Native	Asian/Pacific Islander	Black (not Hispanic)	Hispanic	White (not Hispanic)
Specific learning disabilities	53.3	38.4	44.8	56.6	44.1
Speech or language impairment	16.3	26.2	14.4	18.6	20.2
Mental retardation	7.4	8.6	14.9	7.6	7.9
Emotional disturbance	8.0	4.4	11.0	4.9	7.9
Multiple disabilities	2.0	2.7	2.2	1.7	2.3
Hearing impairments	1.0	2.8	0.9	1.5	1.1
Orthopedic impairments	0.7	1.6	0.8	1.2	1.1
Other health impairments	6.4	5.8	6.9	4.7	10.1
Visual impairments	0.3	0.8	0.4	0.5	0.4
Autism	1.3	6.6	2.0	1.7	3.1
Deaf blindness	*	0.1	*	*	*
Traumatic brain injury	0.4	0.4	0.3	0.3	0.4
Developmental delay	3.0	1.5	1.3	0.6	1.3
All disabilities[a]	100.0	100.0	100.0	100.0	100.0

Note. Total sum may not equal 100 because of rounding of numbers. Percentage is <0. Adapted from U.S. Department of Education, (2009) *28th Annual Report to Congress on the Implementation of the Individuals With Disabilities Education Act, 2006*; Office of Special Education and Rehabilitative Services, "Data Analysis System" (DANS), Table 1–7, Vol. 1, Washington, DCData are for the 50 states, District of Columbia, Bureau of Indian Affairs (BIA) schools, Puerto Rico, and the four outlying areas of the United States.

Rates according to special education category. Disproportionality also exists in terms of how children from various races are classified within special education. In general, African Americans, for example, are overrepresented in special education and are especially disproportionately represented in the categories of high-incidence disabilities such as MR and EBD (Cartledge & Dukes, 2009; Zhang & Katsiyannis, 2002). Losen (2002) notes that African Americans are almost three times more likely than Whites to be categorized as MR and almost twice as likely to be categorized as having an ED. In the U.S. Department of Education's recent *28th Annual Report to Congress* (2009), African American students are 2.83 and 2.24 times more likely to receive special education for MR and EBD, respectively. The department additionally suggests that this disproportionate risk also exists in the multiple disabilities (MD) category, as African American students are 1.5 times more likely than any other racial group to receive special education services based on being classified as having MD.

Many sociodemographic factors are noted in the research literature as risk markers for being a victim of disproportionality, including socioeconomics, family dynamics, racial bias, quality schooling, media, and so forth (Coutinho, Oswald, & Forness, 2002; Osher et al., 2004). We limit our discussion to the most researched and salient factors for African American students: poverty, school quality, and teacher bias.

Predictors of Disproportionality/Overidentification

Poverty. The effects of poverty can be quite devastating to a person's life. This is especially true when it comes to education. The possibility of being at risk for school failure and/or being placed in special education is impacted both directly and indirectly by living in poverty (Artiles et al., 2002). Some of the factors noted by Artiles and colleagues are poor medical care for expectant mothers and newborns; less accessibility to clinics/medical care facilities; and the effects on children's development (i.e., cognitive and biological). As noted in the following section, poor children are more likely to attend impoverished schools, particularly in urban environments with correspondingly inadequate instruction, placing them at increased risk for special learning problems (Blanchett, Mumford, & Beachum, 2005; Donovan & Cross, 2002; Skiba et al., 2008). Coutinho et al. (2002) also found a connection between poverty and identification for EBD, especially for African American males. Less of a poverty effect emerged for African American females with EBD.

Skiba et al. (2005) studied the links among poverty, race, and disproportionality in special education and found that African Americans are disproportionately represented in special education, regardless of income levels. These researchers also found a relationship between poverty and mild mental retardation (MMR), but, in contrast to the previously noted researchers, they do not find that poverty relates to moderate mental retardation or EBD for African American students. Furthermore, they found that the rates of learning disabilities (LD) declined as poverty increased for this population. Skiba et al. discovered that disproportionality relates most consistently to district suspension-expulsion rates, which supports the findings of Achilles, McLaughlin, and Croninger (2007), including that poverty correlates with the disciplinary exclusions of African American students with EBD and LD. Thus, the role of poverty in special education is ambiguous;

it varies, according to disability, and does not rule out the influence of race in affecting disproportionality.

Teacher and school quality. The quality of schools and the teachers in them has a profound effect on the overall education of its students. This is especially true for students from poor and minority backgrounds. Skiba et al. (2008) cite numerous researchers who have reported on the disparity in the quality and quantity of educational resources for this population. These issues include inadequate buildings, resources, and teacher preparation and unequal school funding. It is also well known that high-poverty schools, which are typically found in urban areas, have a predominantly minority population (Gardner & Miranda, 2001), who are likely to receive an inferior education (Skiba et al.).

Teacher quality is more likely to be an issue in high-poverty urban schools, in which teachers tend to have less experience and fewer professional credentials (Artiles et al., 2002; Blanchett et al., 2005). Indeed, Peske and Haycock (2006) note that poor and ethnic minority children who need the most experienced, most educated, and most skilled teachers often receive the very opposite. Although Artiles and associates (2002) propose that the link between teacher quality, demographics, and special education placement is complicated, it is possible that urban students are at substantial risk for being placed in special education due to lack of quality instruction.

There is hope, however. To help mitigate the problem of overrepresentation of African Americans in special education, school personnel need to address these issues during preservice preparation and in-service professional development. In specific, Artiles and colleagues (2002) state that teachers should be trained in multicultural education and diversity to decrease the generalizations and stereotypes of minority groups and their families. Peske and Haycock (2006) further suggest (a) using a "draft strategy" to put more talented teachers in high-poverty, struggling schools; (b) paying effective teachers and principals more for improved academic achievement; (c) evaluating teacher preparation programs to ensure that they are producing effective teachers; and (d) eliminating state-level funding gaps so that more money actually goes to the high-poverty districts in most need.

Assessment practices for placement in special education. Another controversial issue in disproportionality is the assessment process. This controversy often focuses on the validity of assessment tools used; however, there is limited research on "the role of norming, content, linguistic, and cultural biases and test result uses on minority placement in special education" (Artiles et al., 2002, p. 7). Skiba et al. (2008) report reviews of empirical literature indicating that research on test bias is equivocal. Some reviews indicate little or no bias, whereas others show a bias toward minorities. Skiba and associates mention that even if psychometric tests were free from bias, low minority scores would still result from the unequal education often provided to minorities and the economically disadvantaged, as typically found in urban settings. Unequal educational opportunities could lead to a greater likelihood of becoming eligible for special education.

Expectations and bias. The empirical reports on teacher expectations and bias indicate that teachers often give African American students, especially males, lower evaluations than are warranted (Cartledge, Gardner, & Ford, 2009; Cartledge & Kourea, 2008). They also suggest a possible racial overtone on the part of the teacher, indicating that there is bias in the type of behaviors punished, indicating that in comparison to nonminority students, African American students are more likely to be reprimanded for vague, more subjective behaviors, such as defiance (Day-Vines & Terriquez, 2008; Skiba, 2002). Other researchers note that teachers might view "overlapping" speech (or the failure to observe turn taking in communication) as disrespect, play fighting as authentic aggression, and ritualized humor as valid insults (Monroe, 2005). Such misrecognition often creates conflict cycles in which disciplinary problems escalate. Social perception is a reciprocal issue. Male students of color (e.g., African American males) often complain, with some justification, that teachers not only misperceive their behavior but also deliberately label and respond to their behavior more severely than they do to that of females and nonminority males (Day-Vines & Terriquez, 2008). Students frequently internalize these labels and embark on a cycle of increasingly poor academic performance or disruptive actions.

Understanding gender. The increasing number of White female school professionals and African American male students underscore the need for using content with a focus on male culture, particularly related to African American males. Some students speculate that teachers more readily remove African American and Latino males from the classroom because the students intimidate them (Day-Vines & Terriquez, 2008). Males are not only more likely to be referred than females (e.g., Lo & Cartledge, 2007) but also to be referred for milder infractions than girls (Farmer, Goforth, Clemmer, & Thompson, 2004). Ferguson (2001), in an ethnographic study of African American males in elementary school that analyzes the African American male school culture, posits that certain behaviors, such as fighting, classroom disruption, and male dominance, are central to asserting male power. He further suggests that this power is critical to African American males and that these youths are prepared to challenge authority, especially female authority, to achieve it. Analyses by Ferguson, as well as other researchers, point out ways in which schools are complicit in fostering this maladaptive behavior, including academic tracking, competitive environments, excessive punishment, monocultural curriculums, uncaring attitudes, and so forth. Because African American males are the number-one candidates for special education and disciplinary disproportionality, it is important that school personnel study the African American male culture in particular, using, for example, readings by Ferguson or Milner (2007). These authors underscore the social justice issues that often elude the education of these youths.

Ferguson, for instance, gives us insight into the formative years of young African American males, describing how the culture of school and that of youth converge to shape life patterns that may or may not align with the expectations of the larger society. Milner (2007), on the other hand, emphasizes the importance of infusing hope and possibility instead of destruction in the lives of Black males. More specifically, he states:

> We pay a huge price when we speak destruction into the lives of students. Black male students hear people talk about them in deficit terms. They hear the media classify them as *at risk*. They understand that they are often not supposed to be successful. (p. 243)

THE PROBLEM OF SPECIAL EDUCATION PLACEMENT

There are many poor outcomes that students in special education might experience both during and after leaving formal schooling. The outlook is especially bleak for African American students in special education in urban settings, in which the quality of education and educational options are more limited (Skiba et al., 2008). Relatively little of the disproportionality research has focused on the restrictiveness of the instructional setting (Skiba, Poloni-Staudinger, Gallini, Simmons, & Feggins-Azziz, 2006). Researchers need to address the "failure to return," which describes that students who have been labeled with a disability and placed in special education often do not return to the general education class or to a less restrictive environment (LRE; Cartledge, 2005).

With educators, parents, and policy makers advocating for inclusive practices, one might believe that all students with disabilities would be afforded the benefits of inclusion, or at least being instructed in the LRE. However, this has not been the case for minority students in special education. According to Bradley, Doolittle, and Bartolotta (2008), students with EBD generally participate in the general education curriculum less and are more likely to be attended to with other students with EBD. De Valenzuela, Copeland, Qi, and Park (2006) conducted a study in a high-poverty school district and find that there are more segregated instructional settings for African Americans, Hispanics, Native Americans, and English language learners (ELLs) than for Whites, Asian/Pacific Islanders, non-ELL students, and others. Data from the U.S. Department of Education (2009) also show a discrepancy among racial groups and the different educational environments in which they are served.

Only 41% of African American students are attended to in the general education class for most of the day, whereas in that same setting their White counterparts are most likely to be attended to (56.8%). Black students also have the highest percentage rates of being served in separate facilities (5.5%) and being educated outside of the general education class for more than 60% of the day (26.2%).

Skiba et al. (2006) evaluated the data for all special education students in Indiana from five different categories (ED, MMR, MoMR, LD, and SL) and the general education and separate class settings. Their results support other research in suggesting that African American students are significantly overrepresented in separate classes (for ED, MMR, MoMR, LD) and underrepresented in the general education class (for SL). The restrictiveness of the instructional setting poses a serious problem, in that special education enrollment tends to decline during high school and also because we know these students are not being encouraged to join the mainstream; rather they are dropping out of school and going through any host of possible poor outcomes that occur for minority students in special education (Cartledge, 2005). Sinclair, Christenson, and Thurlow (2005), for example, report from national data that only 28% of African American students with ED graduate from high school.

African Americans do not have as many positive in-school or postschool outcomes as do their White counterparts (Blanchett, 2006), and the schools' exclusionary practices that disproportionately affect African American students with disabilities have severe consequences. In addition to leaving school early (Arcia, 2006; Reschly & Christenson, 2006), these students are more likely to have poorer grades, poorer academic achievement (Bradley et al., 2008), fewer opportunities for employment (Zhang & Katsiyannis, 2002), and greater likelihood of criminality (Cartledge et al., 2009). These conditions are exacerbated in urban areas, where the graduation rates are much lower than the national averages (Grey, 2008). Furthermore, these conditions violate IDEA, which specifies greater access to the general curriculum, and the civil rights accorded to all students in our schools.

ADDRESSING DISPROPORTIONALITY

Culturally Responsive Academic and Behavioral Management

Problems in reading (Manset-Williamson, St. John, Hu, & Gordon, 2002) and behavior (Skiba et al., 2006) are associated with special education referral.

Thus, an important means for curbing disproportionality is through effective early reading and behavior interventions. Students learn quickly that, if they act out, they are likely to escape the aversiveness of difficult academic tasks by being referred to detention. Imagine the following scenario: A first-grade teacher directs the class to take out their reading books for group reading. Frank, a student who is having difficulty reading, begins to feel a wave of anxiety sweep over him as he looks at the words on the page. He realizes that he does not know any of the words. The teacher casually goes around the room from student to student, asking them to read where the last one left off. Frank knows it will be his turn soon and does not want to face the embarrassment of not being able to read. He thinks, "What will my friends say?" So, to avoid being embarrassed, Frank crumbles up a piece of paper and throws it at another student. His friends begin to laugh and his teacher yells at him. This is the third time he has disrupted the class this week, and he is sent to the office. Once there, the assistant principal tells him he will spend the next two hours in the detention room. Frank thinks to himself, "I would rather be there than in class during reading and math."

Although this is a hypothetical scenario, it occurs all too often for students like Frank. These students come to school unprepared for the challenges that they need to overcome to be successful academically. Students who encounter difficult academic material in school may be affected in several different ways: Successful students might find strategies to compensate for their deficits including seeking extra help, studying longer hours, and/or obtaining a tutor. Other less successful students may muddle their way through doing just enough to pass. The least successful students may begin to develop behaviors to avoid academic tasks and the classroom setting altogether.

These patterns of behavior are likely to develop over a period of time. In fact, students begin to fall behind as early as kindergarten (Yurick, Cartledge, Kourea, & Keyes, 2010) and if they do not catch up by third grade tend to remain behind their peers. It is more likely that these students will be identified for special education placement and potentially dropout of school altogether. The students at the highest risk for this scenario come to school already behind and unprepared for the tasks that are expected of them. Although the contributing factors are multidimensional, it is sufficient to state that many African American students are behind even before they enter formal schooling. This pattern is more prevalent in urban schools, compared to suburban districts. The numbers of impoverished students are greater, the resources fewer, the expectations lower, and the professional personnel more limited (Skiba et al., 2008). Urban schools need to anticipate these problems and provide intensive early interventions at the point of school entry (i.e., kindergarten or preschool).

Culturally Responsive Academic Management

Under the Individuals with Disabilities Education Improvement Act (IDEIA, 2004), the government specifies CEIS funds, which could be used by districts with significant racial or ethnic disproportionality. These services are provided to K–12 (particularly K–3) students who are not in special education but are need of additional academic/behavioral support to succeed in general education. Response-to-intervention (RTI) is one framework offered for this purpose, using either academic or behavioral interventions (Harris-Murri, King, & Rostenberg, 2006). RTI is a relatively new paradigm in the field of education (Fuchs & Fuchs, 2009). In the case of academic behaviors, validated treatments include specific curricula or teaching procedures that have been proven effective for increasing the targeted academic behaviors. These treatments are provided to the students using a multi- or three-tier system in which the intensity of the intervention increases as the tiers increase.

Tier-one intervention is typically an evidence-based core curriculum for an entire classroom or school. In the case of reading, a classroom teacher may adopt a universal approach that she implements with all of the students in her class. This approach typically involves whole-class instruction, and the teacher may lead the class through reading activities, such as reading out loud and doing comprehension work sheets. It is generally effective for most of the students in a class, but, depending on the class, a significant minority is likely to need more intensive instruction.

Tier-two intervention focuses on a more intensive, small-group approach. In this tier, students who struggle with the universal approach are placed into small groups based on their level of need. They are usually provided with supplemental instruction to increase specific skills, in addition to the regular curriculum. This supplemental instruction may occur during designated intervention periods and is typically made up of an additional 30 minutes of instruction. For many of the students who fail to respond during tier-one instruction, the supplemental instruction is enough to get them back on track with their peers. For students who continue to struggle, tier-three, the most intensive instruction, is necessary.

Tier-three involves the implementation of very intense, targeted instruction, which may or may not include special education. Students in tier-three are provided supplemental instruction using a one-on-one format. This intensive instruction is designed to target the specific skill deficits identified for each student. Like tier-two, students in the third tier are provided the supplemental intervention during specified periods of the school day. Although only a small percentage of students are likely to need this type of instruction, they have been identified at the highest risk for failure.

Sample Early Reading Intervention

C. J. West Community School is an elementary charter school within a large Midwestern city. It is located within a predominately African American community and approximately 220 students are enrolled. At the time of the study, African Americans comprised 97% of these students, and 94% of the student body were considered economically disadvantaged (i.e., they qualified for free or reduced lunch). Approximately 7% of the students were labeled with a disability. Class sizes averaged 15 students per class, which made for a low teacher-to-student ratio. C. J. West Community School used an evidence-based core instructional program for reading.

Although the majority of students were making satisfactory progress in their original reading assignment (i.e., within their classroom grouping), there was a small percentage who continued to struggle. These students were considered to be "at risk" for reading failure and recommended for supplementary instruction. Of this group, four first graders were selected to participate in a reading intervention that focused on increasing oral reading fluency.

These students received supplementary instruction consisting of a one-on-one computerized reading program supervised by a doctoral-level graduate student. They used the program for about 30 minutes three to four times per week. For each lesson, the students learned new vocabulary words, read the story along with the computer, and practiced reading the story independently, during which they were timed for a one-minute duration. The one-minute timings assessed the number of words the students read correctly and were recorded to determine if the students reached end-of-year benchmark goals. After reaching their goal on a specific passage, the students answered comprehension questions. The teacher subsequently verified students' reading goals.

This secondary instruction lasted 16 weeks, with evidence that all students made substantial fluency and comprehension gains (Gibson, 2009). The average baseline fluency for the target students was approximately 18 words per minute. Following the completion of the 16th week, the students' average fluency rate increased to over 70 correct words per minute. Students made gains in the percentage of comprehension questions they answered, from baseline to treatment averages. During baseline stories, students answered an average of 43% of the questions correctly, which increased to over 90% correct answers during the intervention sessions. The combined results on both the reading fluency and comprehension measures gave good evidence that the reading program was successful in improving the skills of these struggling readers. The researcher was able to improve fluency generalization to untrained passages by systematically increasing the goals the students were to attain with the training passages. Generalization increased from 16 correct words per minute during baseline to 30 correct words per minute during supplementary instruction. In addition, students decreased their risk status according to standardized measures. An important feature of this intervention was progress monitoring. By closely monitoring student performance, the teacher could assess progress daily and adjust the instruction as needed. These adjustments unquestionably contributed to each child's progress. Well-designed and -implemented interventions can help students develop critical academic skills, especially if implemented in the early grades where the returns are the greatest.

Once students have acquired critical-reading skills, the work and recommendations of Tatum (2006) are instructive. With a focus on secondary school-level African American males, Tatum recommends engaging students by using enabling texts, which move "beyond a sole cognitive focus such as skill and strategy development—to include a social, cultural, political, spiritual or economic focus" (p. 47). Tatum specifies that these books are intellectually exciting, challenging, mentoring, and enable students to apply literacy skills. Effective academic instruction is critical to disproportionality issues and student engagement. Overly punitive and unproductive school environments lead many African American students to decide at a relatively early age that the existing schooling does not enable them to achieve socially desired rewards (Noguera, 2003). Effective instruction that incorporates high pupil response rates increases academic performance and reduces disruptive behavior (Greenwood, Hart, Walker, & Risley, 1994; Heward, 1994; Lambert, Cartledge, Lo, & Heward, 2006). There is an extensive literature on effective instruction, and teachers who master many of these skills will find a corresponding improvement in academic and social behavior.

Culturally Responsive Behavior Management

Office disciplinary referrals and subsequent suspensions are probably the most common means teachers use in dealing with students' behavior problems. Because these referrals reflect teacher and pupil behavior, professional development is often warranted as an initial point of intervention. Suspensions have dramatically increased in recent years, largely affecting students of color (i.e., Native and African Americans) and suggesting greater not lesser inequality due to zero tolerance policies (Krezmien, Leone, & Achilles, 2006). The need for professional development is especially indicated, when the referrals appear to disproportionately affect one subset of the student population (e.g., African American males).

School professionals teaching African American children need to see themselves as agents of change (Nevarez & Wood, 2007) who engineer change in students' social and academic behaviors. School professionals need to design and implement disciplined culturally responsive school environments and to use culturally responsive strategies to teach and nurture desired social skills. School professionals also need to be able to employ tertiary interventions for students' resistant to lower-level strategies, to enable students to become confident learners, and to affirm students as they continuously progress.

Disciplined, culturally responsive environments. In contrast to the typical school application, discipline should not simply be a method of punishment but needs to focus on ways to help students develop desired social behaviors. It entails systematic planning, teaching, and evaluation. Disciplined culturally responsive schools/classrooms are those that evidence *caring, fairness, behavior management, affirmations, social skill instruction, and commitment* (Cartledge et al., 2009).

Several professional authorities contend that many nonminority teachers prefer not to teach students of color, tend to have indifferent attitudes toward these students, and are inclined to disrespect the culture of CLD learners (Nevarez & Wood, 2007). These teachers are likely to be hyper-critical and punitive. *Caring* teachers, on the other hand, are characterized by setting high standards and expectations for performance, respecting their students, and working to build positive and productive relationships with their students.

To be effective in creating disciplined environments for African American students, disciplinary actions need to be commensurate with the infractions and need to be administered fairly. That is, punishing consequences should not be excessive and students should not feel that they are being singled out because of their gender and race. Many of the exclusionary actions taken against African American students have been for low-level offenses (e.g., Lo & Cartledge, 2007; Putnam, Luiselli, Handler, & Jefferson, 2003). For example, in studying the high rates of referrals for African American and Latino males, Day-Vines and Terriquez (2008) observe that most of the referrals are given for "defiance of authority," which is poorly defined and subjective and has consequences unevenly administered. These conditions can lead to student resentment/resistance, psychological disengagement (Cartledge & Kourea, 2008) and further escalation of behavior problems. It is fortunate that, in the case presented by Day-Vines and Terriquez, a multiracial student leadership group expresses concern about the racial/gender disproportionality and takes the initiative to work with students and the administration to reduce suspensions by 75%. Some of the initiatives include students learning how to express concerns appropriately over unfair disciplinary actions, teachers and students jointly participating in workshops to create more positive school climates, classroom management in-service for targeted teachers, and identifying alternatives to suspensions for disciplinary actions.

It is equally important for teachers to be introspective about their actions, constantly assessing whether disciplinary actions reflect the situation and if they are fair and potentially therapeutic. Toward this end, teachers might participate in a critical reflection sequence, such as the following one adapted from Howard (2003) and presented by Cartledge and Kourea (2008):

1. What is the race/gender breakdown of the students that I typically send from my class for disciplinary actions?
2. How often do I send the same students for disciplinary actions?
3. What messages am I communicating to the students who are the recipients of these actions and to their observing peers?
4. Is the behavior of my students getting better? How do I know? If it is not getting better, why not?
5. Do I distinguish culturally specific behaviors from behavioral inadequacies?
6. Am I punishing students for my lack of skill in effective behavior management?

Behavior management is a staple in the teacher preparation curriculum for teachers in special education but receives little attention in general education teacher training. The key strategies are largely proactive (e.g., social skill instruction) or preventive (e.g., highly structured, well-organized classes). In-service teachers would benefit from basic instruction on behavior management. In addition, they need to be aware of important cultural issues, such as culturally diverse learners, especially males of color, need to know that teachers care. This is true for all age groups. With young children, this can be accomplished through smiles, compliments, and overt statements, such as, "I really care about you and want you to do well on this reading assignment." Older students also respond to affirmations if delivered skillfully and sincerely. Day-Vines and Day-Hairston (2005) present the stroked, stifled, and stroked (SSS) strategy to use with African American males. For example, when a student swears in class, the teacher would tell him how articulate he has been on a particular assignment that there is no need for him to use such language and that, because of his language talents, the teacher wants to encourage him to serve as a model for other students.

A key strategy for proactive interventions is for the teacher to teach the desired behavior through social skill instruction. In this type of instruction, the teacher employs a simple model, lead, test, or paradigm to show the student how to perform the behavior, give the student opportunities to practice the skill until competence is evident, and then evaluate pupil performance. To make the instruction culturally relevant, two components are recommended: (a) selecting skills that are culturally specific and socially valid to the learner and (b) using the learner's culture to inform the instruction. Verbal aggression, for example, is a behavior problem associated with some urban African American students (Feng & Cartledge, 1996), and, thus, an important social skill for them to learn would be to express anger or disapproval using nonaggressive or nonassertive words. One means for using the learner's culture is through African American literature. For example, the book from the Little Bill book series by Bill Cosby and Varnette P. Honeywood, *The Meanest Thing to Say*, could be used to provide a rationale for speaking nonaggressively. Other books written by authors, such as Walter Dean Myers, could also be used for this purpose (see Cartledge et al., 2009; Cartledge & Milburn, 1996, for other suggestions). Myers stories focus on African American males in urban settings. In addition, socially appropriate popular African American music, poetry, films, video clips, and so forth could be analyzed to derive examples of using assertive statements to address a concern. Youth who learn how to use socially appropriate strategies to achieve desired goals are empowered to be successful in school, as well as other environments.

CONCLUSIONS AND IMPLICATIONS

Disproportionality in special education and discipline are perhaps greatest for urban African American students, especially the males. The contributing factors are complex and not easily distinguished. Although some of the existing research literature indicates that African American students are at a greater risk of special education and disciplinary disproportionality in predominately White school districts (e.g., Coutinho et al., 2002), urban settings also present special challenges. The strongest predictors of special education/disciplinary overrepresentation are poverty, poor school quality, and teacher bias or low expectations. These conditions are pervasive within urban schools. Considering the relatively intractable nature of disproportionality, it needs to be addressed at the earliest possible point of the child's schooling, which ensures that the child develops the requisite academic and social skills that enable him or her to successfully continue in general education programs. The federal government has designated CEIS for this purpose. Instructional frameworks (e.g., RTI), as discussed in this chapter, enable professionals to design, implement, and evaluate interventions that will foster the success of urban African American students. In addition to gaining skill in managing academic and social behaviors, teachers and other school personnel need to become committed to becoming culturally competent and designing school environments that are caring, nurturing, and helpful in affirming urban African American learners. To this end, urban African American students need to see these classrooms as places where they acquire the tools and values that enable them to achieve success immediately and in later life. They also need to feel wanted and valued.

REFERENCES

Achilles, G. M., McLaughlin, M. J., & Croninger, R. G. (2007). Sociocultural correlates of disciplinary exclusion among students with emotional, behavioral, and learning disabilities in the SEELS national dataset. *Journal of Emotional and Behavioral Disorders, 15*(1), 33–45.

Arcia, E. (2006). Achievement and enrollment status of suspended students: Outcomes in a large, multicultural school district. *Education and Urban Society, 38*(3), 359–369.

Artiles, A. J., Harry, B., Reschly, D. J., & Chinn, P. C. (2002). Over-identification of students of color in special education: A critical overview. *Multicultural Perspectives, 41*, 3–10.

Blanchett, W. J., Mumford, V., & Beachum, F. (2005). Urban school failure and disproportionality in a post-brown era: Benign neglect of the constitutional rights of students of color. *Remedial and Special Education, 26*(2), 70–81.

Blanchett, W. J. (2006). Disproportionate representation of African American students in special education: Acknowledging the role of white privilege and racism. *Educational Researcher, 35*(6), 24–28.

Bradley, R., Doolittle, J., & Bartolotta, R. (2008). Building on the data and adding to the discussion: The experiences and outcomes of students with emotional disturbance. *Journal of Behavioral Education, 17*(1), 4–23.

Cartledge, G. (2005). Restrictiveness and race in special education: The failure to prevent or to return. *Learning Disabilities: A Contemporary Journal, 3*(1), 27–32.

Cartledge, G., & Dukes, C. (2009). Disproportionality of African American children in special education. In L. C. Tillman (Ed.), *Handbook of African American education* (pp. 383–398). Los Angeles, CA: Sage.

Cartledge, G., Gardner, R., & Ford, D. Y. (2009). *Diverse learners with exceptionalities: Culturally responsive teaching in the inclusive classroom.* Upper Saddle River, NJ: Merrill/Pearson.

Cartledge, G., & Kourea, L. (2008). Culturally responsive classrooms for culturally diverse students with and at risk for disabilities. *Exceptional Children, 74*(3), 351–371.

Cartledge, G., & Milburn, J. F. (1996). *Cultural diversity and social skills instruction: Understanding ethnic and gender differences.* Champaign, IL: Research Press.

Coutinho, M. J., Oswald, D. P., & Forness, S. R. (2002). Gender and sociodemographic factors and the disproportionate identification of culturally and linguistically diverse students with emotional disturbance. *Behavioral Disorders, 27*(2), 109–125.

Day-Vines, N. L., & Day-Hairston, B. O. (2005). Culturally congruent strategies for addressing the behavioral needs of urban, African American male adolescents, *Professional School Counseling, 8*(3), 236–244.

Day-Vines, N. L., & Terriquez, V. (2008). A strengths-based approach to promoting prosocial behavior among African American and Latino students. *Professional School Counseling, 12*(2), 170–175.

De Valenzuela, J. S., Copeland, S. R., Qi, C. H., & Park, M. (2006). Examining educational equity: Revisiting the disproportionate representation of minority students in special education. *Exceptional Children, 72*(4), 425–441.

Donovan, M. S., & Cross, C. T. (Eds.). (2002). *Minority students in special and gifted education.* Washington, DC: National Academy Press.

Dunn, L. M. (1968). Special education for the mildly retarded—Is much of it justifiable? *Exceptional Children, 35*, 5–22.

Farmer, T. W., Goforth, J. B., Clemmer, J. T., & Thompson, J. H. (2004). School discipline problems in rural African American early adolescents: Characteristics of students with major, minor, and no offenses. *Behavioral Disorders, 29*(4), 317–336.

Feng, H., & Cartledge, G. (1996). Social skill assessment of inner city Asian, African, and European American students. *School Psychology Review, 25*(2), 227–238.

Ferguson, A. A. (2001). *Bad boys: Public schools in the making of black masculinity.* Ann Arbor: The University of Michigan.

Fuchs, D., & Fuchs, L. (2009). Responsiveness to intervention: Multilevel assessment and instruction as early intervention and disability identification. *The Reading Teacher, 63*(3), 250–252.

Gardner, R., Ford, D. Y., & Miranda, A. H. (2001). Introduction and overview: The education of African American students: The struggle continues. *The Journal of Negro Education, 70*(4), 241–242.

Gardner, R., & Miranda, A. H. (2001). Improving outcomes for urban African American students. *The Journal of Negro Education, 70*, 255–263.

Gibson, L. (2009). *The effects of a computer assisted reading program on the oral reading fluency and comprehension of at-risk, urban first-grade students* (Unpublished doctoral dissertation). The Ohio State University.

Greenwood, C. R., Hart, B., Walker, D., & Risley, T. (1994). The opportunity to respond and academic performance revisited: A behavioral theory of developmental retardation and its prevention. In R. Gardner et al. (Eds.), *Behavior analysis in education: Focus on measurably superior instruction* (pp. 213–223). Pacific Grove, CA: Brooks/Cole.

Grey, B. (April 3, 2008). "High school drop-out rate in major US cities at nearly 50 percent." Retrieved from http://www.wsws.org/articles/2008/apr2008/scho-a03.shtml

Harris-Murri, N., King, K., & Rostenberg, D. (2006). Reducing disproportionate minority representation in special education programs for students with emotional disturbances: Toward a culturally responsive response to intervention model. *Education and Treatment of Children, 29*(4), 779–799.

Heward, W. L. (1994). Three "low-tech" strategies for increasing the frequency of active student response during group instruction. In R. Gardner et al. (Eds.), *Behavior analysis in education: Focus on measurably superior instruction* (pp. 283–320). Pacific Grove, CA: Brooks/Cole.

Hosp, J. L., & Reschly, D. J. (2004). Disproportionate representation of minority students in special education: Academic, demographic, and economic predictors. *Exceptional Children, 70*, 185–199.

Howard, T. C. (2003). Culturally relevant pedagogy: Ingredients for critical teacher reflection. *Theory into Practice, 42*(3), 195–202.

Kern, L., Hilt-Panahon, A., & Sokol, N. G. (2009). Further examining the triangle tip: Improving support for students with emotional and behavioral needs. *Psychology in the Schools, 46*(1), 18–32.

Krezmien, M. P., Leone, P. E., & Achilles, G. M. (2006). Suspension, race, and disability: Analysis of statewide practices and reporting. *Journal of Emotional and Behavioral Disorders, 14*(4), 217–226.

Lambert, M. C., Cartledge, G., Lo, Y., & Heward, W. L. (2006). Effects of response cards on disruptive behavior and academic responding during math lessons by fourth-grade students in an urban school. *Journal of Positive Behavior Interventions, 8*(2), 88–99.

Lo, Y., & Cartledge, G. (2007). Office disciplinary referrals in an urban elementary school. *Multicultural Learning and Teaching, 2*(1), 20–38.

Losen, D. J. (2002). Minority overrepresentation and underservicing in special education. *Principal, 81*(3), 45–46.

Manset-Williamson, G., St. John, E., Hu, S., & Gordon, D. (2002). Early literacy practices as predictors of reading related outcomes: Test scores, test passing rates and special education referral. *Exceptionality, 10*(1), 11–28.

Milner, H. R., IV. (2007). African American males in urban school: No excuses—Teach and empower. *Theory into Practice, 46*(3), 239–246.

Monroe, C. R. (2005). Why are "bad boys" always black? Causes of disproportionality in school discipline and recommendations for change. *The Clearing House, 79*(1), 45–50.

Nevarez, C., & Wood, J. L. (2007). Developing urban school leaders: Building on solutions 15 years after the Los Angeles riots. *Educational Studies, 42*(3), 266–280.

Noguera, P. A. (2003). Schools, prisons, and social implications of punishment: Rethinking disciplinary practices. *Theory Into Practice, 42*(4), 341–350.

O'Connor, C., & Fernandez, S. D. (2006). Race, class, and disproportionality: Re-evaluating the relationship between poverty and special education placement. *The Educational Researcher, 35*(6), 6–11.

Osher, D., Cartledge, G., Oswald, D., Sutherland, K. S., Artiles, A. J., & Coutinho, M. (2004). Cultural and linguistic competency and disproportionate representation. In R. B. Rutherford, Jr., M. M. Quinn, & S. R. Mathur (Eds.), *Handbook of research in emotional and behavioral disorders* (pp. 54–77). New York, NY: Guilford Press.

Peske, H. G., & Haycock, K. (2006). *Teaching inequality: How poor and minority students are shortchanged on teacher quality.* Retrieved from, http://www.edtrust.org/sites/edtrust.org/files/publications/files/TQReportJune2006.pdf

Putnam, R. F., Luiselli, J. K., Handler, M. W., & Jefferson, G. L. (2003). Evaluating student discipline practices in a public school through behavioral assessment of office referrals. *Behavior Modifications, 27*(4), 505–523.

Reschly, A. L., & Christenson, S. L. (2006). Prediction of dropout among students with mild disabilities: A case for the inclusion of student engagement variables. *Remedial and Special Education, 27*(5), 276–292

Rice, E. H., Merves, E., & Srsic, A. (2008). Perceptions of gender differences in the expression of emotional and behavioral disabilities. *Education and Treatment of Children, 31*(4), 549–565.

Sacks, G., & Kern, L. (2008). A comparison of quality of life variables for students with emotional and behavioral disorders and students without disabilities. *Journal of Behavioral Education, 17*(1), 111–127.

Sinclair, M. F., Christenson, S. L., & Thurlow, M. L. (2005). Promoting school completion of urban secondary youth with emotional or behavioral disabilities. *71*(4), 465–482.

Skiba, R. (2002). Special education and school discipline: A precarious balance. *Behavioral Disorders, 27*(2), 81–97.

Skiba, R. J., Michael, R. S., Nardo, A. C., & Peterson, R. L. (2002). The color of discipline: Sources of racial and gender disproportionality in school punishment. *The Urban Review, 34*(4), 317–342.

Skiba, R. J., Poloni-Staudinger, L., Gallini, S., Simmons, A. B., & Feggins-Azziz, R. (2006). Disparate access: The disproportionality of African American students with disabilities across educational environments. *Exceptional Children, 72*(4), 411–424.

Skiba, R. J., Poloni-Staudinger, L., Simmons, A. B., Feggins-Azziz, R., & Chung, C. G. (2005). Unproven links: Can poverty explain ethnic disproportionality in special education. *The Journal of Special Education, 39*(3), 130–144.

Skiba et al. (2008). Achieving equity in special education: History, status, and current challenges. *Exceptional Children, 74*, 264–288.

Tatum, A.W. (2006). Engaging African American males in reading. *Educational Leadership, 63*(5), 44–49.

Townsend, B. L. (2000). The disproportionate discipline of African American learners: Reducing school suspensions and expulsions. *Exceptional Children, 66*(3), 381–391.

U. S. Department of Education. (2008). Coordinated Early Intervening Services (CEIS) Guidance. Retrieved from http://www.ed.gov/print/policy/speced/guid/idea/ceis.html

U. S. Department of Education. (2009). *28th Annual Report to Congress on the implementation of the Individuals with Disabilities Education Act, 2006* (Vol. 1). Washington, DC: Author.

Wehmeyer, M. L., & Schwartz, M. (2001). Disproportionate representation of males in special education services: Biology behavior or bias? *Education and Treatment of Children, 24*(1), 28–45.

Wynn, M. (1992). *Empowering African-American males to succeed: A ten-step approach for parents and teachers.* Marietta, GA: Rising Sun.

Yurick, A., Cartledge, G., Kourea, L., & Keyes, S. (2010). Reducing reading failure for kindergarten urban students: A study of early literacy instruction, treatment quality, and treatment duration. *Remedial and Special Education.*

Zhang, D., & Katsiyannis, A. (2002). Minority representation in special education: A persistent challenge. *Remedial and Special Education, 23*(3), 180–187.

CHAPTER SIX

Trends and Patterns of Career and Technical Education for Urban African American Students

EDWARD C. FLETCHER JR.

Since the earliest times, parents have attempted to prepare their children for the responsibilities of the real world and to be independent. One of the earliest developments of more formal types of vocational education came in the form of apprenticeships in colonial America (Scott & Sarkees-Wircenski, 2008). However, the apprenticeships were not considered to be a component of the school curriculum. They were formal agreements between an employer and an employee that provided the employee with training and the employer with labor. It is important to note the two types of apprenticeship programs: One type was voluntary and the other was involuntary. The involuntary apprenticeships consisted primarily of economically disadvantaged children and orphans (Gordon, 2008).

CURRENT CONCEPTIONS OF CAREER AND TECHNICAL EDUCATION

Career and technical education (CTE) has long been a source of serious debate among educators, philosophers, and policy makers. Some see CTE as a critical component of the educational process for students, whereas others see it as a "dumping ground" for special-needs students and those students with no aspiration of attending college. Gregson articulates the varying conceptualization of CTE in the foreword for Gordon's (2008) book on the history of CTE. He states,

> What is the purpose of career and technical education? Is it a curriculum that is intended to prepare students for the world of work? Is it a pedagogical approach that contextualizes academics in a way that promotes academic achievement and student engagement? Is it a tool used to transition students from high school to postsecondary education? Is it a "tracking" mechanism used to prepare students for jobs based on social class, race/ethnicity, and/or gender? Is it all of the above? None of the above? (p. xiii)

Despite the ancient historical presence of vocational education, the vocational education that mirrors more of what is seen today was established in the late 19th century in the form of trade schools, private business schools, and some agriculture programs (Gordon, 2008). Contemporary CTE programs, formerly referred to as "vocational education," constitute a tremendously large educational system in the United States through which adolescents and adults explore career areas and learn valuable skills for the workforce and for further educational pursuits (Scott & Sarkees-Wircenski, 2008). CTE has a presence in K–12 schooling as well as in institutes of higher education, particularly within community/technical colleges. At the postsecondary and secondary education levels, CTE is known for coursework and cooperative educational experiences that often lead to industry-recognized credentials, certificates, or articulation agreements (enabling the transfer of secondary course credits to postsecondary education). Thus, participants of CTE in high schools may earn credits leading to associates' degrees through an initiative typically referred to as College Tech Prep (CTP).

The largest component of CTE is curriculum programs provided for students at the high school level. In fact, almost every student (96.6%) in the country has taken at least one CTE credit throughout their K–12 schooling experience (Silverberg, Warner, Fong, & Goodwin, 2004). Further, 11,000 high schools, which constitute two-thirds of high schools currently in the United States, offer at least one CTE program. Despite the large student enrollments in CTE coursework, CTE remains an option/elective for students. CTE program areas cover a vast array of occupational pathways, including disciplines such as agriculture education, business education, family and consumer sciences education (formerly called home economics), health occupations education, marketing education (formerly called distributive education), differentiated content areas in technical and industrial (T&I) education, and technical/communications education. According to Scott and Sarkees-Wircenski (2008), 50% of students participating in CTE are enrolled in a business course, and 33% take T&I classes.

CTE instruction at the secondary level is largely provided through comprehensive high schools, offering core academic subjects as well. However, other settings for CTE at the secondary level include CTE (also called vocational-technical) high schools and CTE centers. The CTE schools and centers usually offer half-day instruction for students who are bused from their home comprehensive high schools. However, some CTE schools and centers offer instruction for the entire school day. The likelihood of a student enrolling in a CTE school/center is predicated on its availability and approval by students' parents or guardians. Regardless of the CTE high school configuration, students take core academic classes in addition to their CTE coursework. More and more, students who participate in CTE are earning higher numbers of credits in core academic areas (Silverberg et al., 2004). Nonetheless, on average students earn more credits in CTE (4.0) than in math (3.4) or science (3.0).

A certain portion of the high school-student population chooses to take a coherent set of CTE courses, and some even declare a career major. Individuals earning three or more credits in CTE are considered CTE concentrators, which typically involves taking three year-long courses. Based on focus group interviews, Silverberg et al. (2004) note that students choose to participate in CTE courses for a variety of reasons, some of which are "to gain career exposure, to help them select or prepare for a college major, to use as a fallback if college or other career plans fail to materialize, to pursue a leisure interest, or to take courses that present less of an intellectual challenge than do other courses" (p. 29).

BACKGROUND OF THE PROBLEM

The Separation of CTE and Core Academic Curricula

In the latter 1800s, a great debate occurred regarding the type of education that should be provided for African American students. Schools were primarily focused on the core academic areas (i.e., math, science, English, etc.). However, many believed that vocational education was a way to establish more equality in the schools due to the few opportunities it afforded students to pursue postsecondary degrees. Two influential Black educational philosophers, Booker T. Washington, an African American male educated in the South, and W. E. B. Du Bois, an African American male educated in the North, debated the purposes of education, particularly for Blacks.

Washington believed in the pedagogical concept of learning by doing and in a more pragmatic vocational education curriculum (e.g., courses in personal care, home care, farming, and mechanical skills). In addition, he established industrial schools. His thinking was that studies in vocational education would provide African Americans with a better chance at increasing their economic status and that social acceptance would be an outcome.

On the contrary, Du Bois argued for a more rigorous academic education for Blacks to release them from the oppressive social and economic inequalities of pursuing a more vocationally focused education (Gordon, 2008). Washington supported the notion of segregated schools; he believed this to be the most beneficial way to educate African Americans. On the contrary, Du Bois wanted African Americans to be treated equally in their schooling experiences. Stated differently, he desired that they have educational parity with whites. According to Scott and Sarkees-Wircenski (2008),

> Du Bois would have nothing to do with any compromise and favored an education for African-Americans that would make them into leaders who could protect the social and political rights of the African-American community and could make them aware of the need for constant struggle until they were treated with equality. (p. 214)

According to Gordon (2008), "Washington and Du Bois were trailblazers for the pattern of philosophical distinction between vocational and academic education" (p. 25).

In the early 20th century, a newer philosophical approach was emerging that was concerned with students' interests. The philosophy of idealism was moving toward pragmatism and experimentalism. The educational leaders of this philosophy are Charles Prosser and John Dewey. The ideas of Charles Prosser were merged in the creation of the Smith-Hughes Vocational Educational Act of 1917. Similar to the debates between Washington and Du Bois, Prosser and Dewey also had distinct views of vocational and academic education. Prosser emphasized the need for students to gain practical experiences and have financial rewards. He also believed that the learning space should be highly similar to the workplace. Dewey, on the other hand, proclaimed that education should be democratic. He wanted education to include vocational exploration to assist students in gaining more practical knowledge. Thus, he supported the integration of vocational and academic content. He advocated for vocational education as a means for transforming the social inequalities that existed (Gordon, 2008).

Dewey's vision of academic and vocational integration was transcendental for its time. In fact, the Carl D. Perkins Vocational and Applied Technology Education Act of 1990 was the first time federal legislation stressed the need to integrate vocational and academic content (Fletcher, 2006; Fletcher & Zirkle, 2009). This legislation was transformational in setting out new objectives for vocational education, which include the charge for it to prepare students not only for the demands of the workplace but also to pursue postsecondary degrees. However, individuals' perspectives regarding the purposes and nature of vocational education have been difficult to change. The difficulty of transforming perspectives may be closely related to the historical perceptions of vocational education and its separation from the core academic curriculum that have been in place since the distinction was established by the Smith-Hughes National Vocational Act of 1917.

STATEMENT OF THE PROBLEM

Prior research findings have indicated that tracking has been associated with long-term negative outcomes—such as perpetuating the widening of the academic achievement gap between Caucasians and minorities, as well as creating disparities between college-preparatory and noncollege-preparatory students (Burris & Welner, 2005; Fletcher & Zirkle, 2010). In fact, research has indicated that tracking of high-ability students often involves much higher quality discourse than for their low-ability counterparts, which typically involves the emphasis of lower-order cognitive skills (Lee & Byrk, 1988).

Not looking at the negative long-term effects of tracking, which is defined as the separation of students into distinct curriculum tracks based on perceived or measured cognitive ability, the primary rationale for tracking in schools is pedagogical, suggesting that students vary greatly in their academic ambitions and prior knowledge, and the environment in which learning is optimal (Gamoran & Mare, 1989; Lucas & Berends, 2002; McPartland & Schneider, 1996). And proponents suggest that tracking provides teachers with an opportunity to tailor their instruction in order to meet the varied student learning needs (Gamoran, Nystrand, Berends, & LePore, 1995; Hallinan, 1991; Page, 1990).

TRACKING AND CURRICULAR DIFFERENTIATION

American high schools structure educational opportunities for students by providing them with differentiated curricular programs based on their purported interests and talents (Gamoran & Weinstein, 1998; Hallinan, 1994). This sorting process results in stratified learning opportunities for students within the same school. Thus, the learning opportunities and instruction that schools expose students to (i.e., advanced placement courses) often set the boundaries for student experiences and achievement (Gamoran & Nystrand, 1991).

A wealth of long-standing knowledge and research has taken shape within the last few decades based on the phenomenon of tracking in U.S. schools, which has been well documented in the literature (Lewis, 2007; Oakes & Guiton, 1995) and highly contentious (Hallinan, 1994) among educators, administrators, researchers, and parents. Tracking has been cited as providing students with an unequal education (Alvarez & Mehan, 2007; Hallinan, 1991, 1994; Rubin, 2006); long-term social inequalities (Arum & Shavit, 1995; Ayalon & Gamoran,

2000; Biafora, & Ansalone, 2008; Gamoran, 1989; Gamoran & Mare, 1989; Kelly, 2007; Page, 1990; Rojewski, 1997; Rubin, 2006); unequal status attainment (Ayalon & Gamoran, 2000; LeTendre, Hofer, & Shimizu, 2003; Lewis, 2007; Oakes & Guiton, 1995; Rubin, 2006); and lower self-esteem, motivation to learn, and academic status (Hallinan, 1994). Researchers have also indicated that ability (Alexander & McDill, 1976; Biafora & Ansalone, 2008; Gamoran & Mare, 1989; Hallinan, 1991; Kelly, 2007; Lee & Bryk, 1988), past performance/achievement (Gamoran, 1989; Rubin, 2006), teacher and counselor recommendations (Hallinan, 1991), college and career aspirations (Akos et al., 2007; Gamoran, 1989; Lee & Byrk, 1988; Rojewski, 1997), interests (Lee & Bryk, 1988), race/ethnicity (Akos et al., 2007; Alvarez & Mehan, 2007; Burris, & Welner, 2005; Hallinan, 1991; Kelly, 2007; Lee & Byrk, 1988; Lewis, 2007; Lewis & Cheng, 2006; Oakes & Guiton, 1995; Rubin, 2006; Welner & Oakes, 1996; Yonezawa et al., 2002), socioeconomic status (SES; Akos et al., 2007; Alvarez & Mehan, 2007; Gamoran, 1989; Kelly, 2007; Lee & Byrk, 1988; Lewis, 2007; Lewis & Cheng, 2006; Rojewski, 1997; Rubin, 2006; Yonezawa et al., 2002), structural/institutional constraints (Oakes & Guiton, 1995), and family backgrounds (Kelly, 2007) are all determinants in the placement of students in different curriculum tracks. Thus, research examining and explanations describing the antecedents and effects of tracking are quite complex (Oakes & Guiton, 1995).

The distinct curriculum tracks include: (a) a college preparatory curriculum, (b) a CTE curriculum, and (c) a general curriculum. However, recent initiatives have developed an integrated curriculum combining college preparatory and CTE coursework—the dual track. This new phenomenon has been referred to as the new vocationalism and includes programs such as CTP, career academies, and High Schools That Work (HSTW). These curriculum reform models have attempted to increase college-preparatory course work in CTE programs as well as provide pathways for participation in postsecondary education. In addition, tracking in schools may also take the form of differentiated levels of courses, such as "advanced placement, honors, regular, and basic" (Hallinan, 1994, p. 1). Thus, the conceptualization of separate tracks is widely varied among American schools (McPartland & Schneider, 1996).

Defining the Various High School Curriculum Tracks

In general, high school curriculum tracks are categorized as college preparatory, CTE, dual, and general. Following are definitions of the various tracks:

Career and Technical Education Track. This is a high school curriculum track in which students must earn three credits or more in a CTE occupational pathway (Silverberg et al., 2004).

College Preparatory Track. This is a high school curriculum track in which students must earn an appropriate amount of credits in math, science, English, and a foreign language that are consistent with college entrance requirements at private and public four-year institutes of higher education.

Dual Track. This is a high school curriculum track in which students must earn three or more credits in CTE and take appropriate course work aligned with a college-preparatory track.

General Track. This is a high school curriculum track in which students must take the minimum amount of state-mandated credits and courses required to graduate.

NATIONAL TRENDS

The pathways of CTE concentrators and college-preparatory concentrators are markedly different (Kulik, 1998). Kulik (1998) estimates that 75% of college-preparatory students do indeed continue on to pursue postsecondary educational opportunities; however, only 20% of CTE students decide to further their education subsequent to earning their high school diplomas. Some research has been conducted that focuses on the impact on postsecondary education (Rojewski, 1997); attainment (Silverberg et al., 2004); and degree completion (Esters, 2007). Fletcher (2009) examines postsecondary education participation rates, degree attainment, and occupational earnings of high school graduates in the differentiated tracks by using the National Longitudinal Survey of Youth 1997 (NLSY97) data set. The NLSY97 data set is comprised of a national random sample of 8,984 individuals born between the years of 1980 and 1984. Based on his findings, *African Americans constituted the largest percentage of students participating in the CTE track,* Hispanics were largely in the general track, and Caucasian students made up the largest group in the college-preparatory track.

Further, Fletcher finds that students who participated in the CTE track were not significantly more likely to earn associate, bachelor, or graduate degrees than their general-track counterparts. However, students participating in the college-preparatory track were significantly more likely to earn high school diplomas, associate, bachelor, and graduate degrees than those in the general track. Students in the dual track (those high school graduates that earned credits in the CTE and college preparatory tracks) were significantly more likely to earn high school diplomas, associate, and graduate degrees.

It is interesting that Fletcher (2009) finds that CTE students are more likely to have higher earnings (by $3,279) than their general counterparts and that those students in the dual- and college-preparatory tracks are also expected to have higher earnings (by $2,754 and $1,386, respectively). Fletcher recommends that guidance counselors, in particular, be informed of the overrepresentation of Blacks in CTE and dual tracks and Hispanics in general tracks. He also indicates that efforts should be extended to help Black and Hispanic students learn of the long-term benefits of participating in the college-preparatory track. He additionally suggests that guidance counselors should become more aware of possible biases or dispositions that may predispose them to advise higher percentages of Black students to pursue the CTE track and Hispanics to pursue the general track.

DIVERSITY OF STUDENT PARTICIPATION IN CTE

Student participation in CTE is highest in low-income schools (Silverberg et al., 2004). In addition, *African American students earn more credits (on average 4.3 credits) than any other ethnic group.* Asian students earn the least number of credits (on average 3.2 credits) of any ethnic group. In terms of the types of CTE courses African Americans enroll in, they typically concentrate in health, food service and hospitality, personal services (i.e., cosmetology), and business and are much less likely to enroll in agriculture courses. Further, CTE has the largest presence in rural communities; however, these schools tend to have less of the specialty CTE courses offered at suburban and urban schools and their students tend to enroll in agriculture courses.

THE LACK OF PARTICIPATION AMONG AFRICAN AMERICAN STUDENTS IN HIGH SCHOOL AGRICULTURE COURSES

Despite the prevalence of African American students in CTE courses, the agricultural area has historically not been successful at recruiting and retaining them (Jones, Bowen, & Rumberger, 1998) Explanations for their low enrollment in agricultural programs range from (a) low earning potential, to (b) less-than-ideal working conditions, to (c) relating agriculture to historical events such as slavery, to (d) the lack of minority role models as teachers and agriculturalists. According to Soloninka (2003),

> Unlike their rural counterparts, urban students do not have the agricultural background knowledge (cultural capital) of children raised on farms. Farm children see and encounter agricultural and scientific processes day-in and day-out; urban students do not have these types of opportunities. (p. 42)

In addition, the scope of agricultural courses available in rural schools is vastly different than in urban schools (Soloninka, 2003). Oftentimes, rural schools offer three- or four-year programs, whereas urban schools are often one- or two-year programs. Even with the disadvantages of urban agricultural programs, urban communities have greater opportunities for agricultural careers and exposure to job placement sites. Soloninka notes, "Greenhouse and garden shops, golf courses, veterinary clinics, animal research facilities, zoos, pet shops, and pet grooming salons are a few of the potential job placement sites that are available to graduates of urban agricultural education programs" (pp. 45–46).

Much of the literature regarding the lack of diversity in and implementation of urban agricultural programs discusses strategies to recruit diverse students and establish urban programs. Scott and Lavergne (2004) recommend inclusion of an early agriculture course for junior high school students, being that many students' perceptions of education in this area are formed by the time they enter the ninth grade. Jones et al. (1998) suggest that (a) agricultural organizations and teacher educators should implement more activities to motivate agricultural teachers to recruit minority students, (b) minority agricultural students should be engaged to assist in recruiting other minority students, (c) teacher educators should teach teacher candidates culturally relevant pedagogical approaches and techniques, and (d) more research should be conducted to examine these issues.

PROMISING PRACTICES IN CAREER AND TECHNICAL EDUCATION

Reducing the Dropout Rate

Students dropping out of high school are of great concern to policy makers, researchers, educators, administrators, the larger community, and society. In fact, Hampden-Thompson, Warkentien, and Daniel (2009) report that in 2002, 82% of tenth-grade students graduated from high school on time; 1% graduated early; 5% left high school without earning a diploma or its equivalency; 2% were still enrolled; and 1% received an alternative credential, left the country, or died. Reasons for students dropping out of high school are many and varied. According to Plank, DeLuca, and Estacion (2005), "The reasons for dropping out involve a web of sociological, psychological, economic, and institutional factors" (p. 3). Compared to their graduating counterparts, individuals who do not complete high school oftentimes have substantially lower earnings and higher rates of unemployment and are more likely to live in poverty and require public assistance, to have health issues, to engage in criminal activity, and to engage in risky behaviors. Thus, reducing dropout rates is essential for both individual and public vitality.

CTE has a long history of retaining students in school that would have otherwise dropped out and of helping students secure employment after graduating from high school (Cohen & Besharov, 2002; Kulik, 1998; Rasinski & Pedlow, 1998). In a review of research studies on CTE participators/concentrators and

CTE's impact on reducing the dropout rate, the overwhelming majority of studies indicate a modest reduction in the dropout rate as well as a modest improvement in labor market outcomes for these students. In addition, CTE has been known to help students with the preparation and experience they may need in choosing academic majors and being successful in college. According to Cohen and Besharov (2002), "CTE could encourage these students—disproportionally poor and minority—to complete high school, ensure that they are better prepared for their jobs when they graduate, and perhaps even increase their chances of entering college" (p. 4). The main reasons given for CTE's influence on students choosing not to drop out are the program's strong connection with contextual teaching and learning, its relevancy to real-world circumstances, its partnerships with employers, and the relationships students build with teachers (particularly with cooperative occupational education experiences and CTE student organizations).

High School Reform Initiatives

As indicated previously, dual-track students have had promising long-term outcomes in terms of degree attainment (Fletcher, 2009; Novel, 2009) and earning potential (Fletcher, 2009). As such, high school reform initiatives have been emerging with an innovative curriculum plan of providing students with opportunities to engage in college-preparatory curricula and a sequence of CTE curricula, with the advantage of selecting a career major in high school.

School reform initiatives have undoubtedly shaped the field and curriculum of CTE (Rojewski, 2002). The school reform CTP has its roots in the 1950s (Miller & Gray, 2002) and was established to encourage students taking the CTE course to matriculate into postsecondary education. This program consists of an articulation agreement between secondary schools and postsecondary institutions and business and industry that provides students with a nonduplicative program of study when transitioning into an institute of higher education from high school (Draeger, 2006; Ruhland, 2003; Waller & Waller, 2004). This educational pathway leads to an associate's degree or two-year certificate (DeLuca, Plank, & Estacion, 2006; Kistler, 2004). Furthermore, CTP students may earn dual (high school and postsecondary) credit when they take certain high school courses. Students participating in CTP take a hybrid of advanced academic and CTE courses, such as advanced mathematics, applied science, and technical courses in their chosen fields of study. These courses are typically taken in students' junior or senior years (Miller & Gray, 2002). Despite its existence in the 1950s as a 2 + 2 program, CTP was expanded in the 1990s as a means for broadening CTE's objectives, as noted in the Carl D. Perkins Vocational and Applied Technology Education Act of 1990, and in order to include the preparation of students for postsecondary education. However, with the passage of the new Carl D. Perkins Career and Technical Education Act of 2006, a new model of CTP is emerging that is referred to as "career pathways" (Bragg, 2007; Lewis, 2006). Career pathways has a career focus and aligns postsecondary and secondary education with occupational directions. It begins in the first grade.

A second school reform initiative backed by federal legislation is the HSTW model, which structures schools in a way that enables students to participate in a blended curriculum. The HSTW model organizes school content so that students engage in CTE coursework and college-preparatory courses to prepare them for the workforce as well as for postsecondary education (Dare, 2006). Students also designate a career or academic major by taking four credits in their defined area of study (Bottoms, 1997). The HSTW model was developed in 1985 by the Southern Region Educational Board (SREB) and has similar objectives to the CTP initiative (Flowers, 2000). Students in HSTW schools take four or more credits in English, three credits in mathematics and science, and three or more credits in social studies (Bottoms, 1997).

A third high school reform initiative that emphasizes the integration of academic and CTE courses is career academies. Career academies began over three decades ago and supports over 2,500 career academies in existence currently. Its primary objectives are to get students engaged in school and prepare them for successfully transitioning from high school to college and for increasing their chances at securing employment. According to Kemple and Scott-Clayton (2004), "Career Academies are organized as small learning communities, combine academic and technical curricula around a career theme, and establish partnerships with local employers to provide work-based learning opportunities" (p. 1). Findings from Kemple and Scott-Clayton indicate that career academies are not more effective than noncareer academies in contributing to students' postsecondary attainment; however, career academies positively influence labor market outcomes (wages, hours worked, and employment stability) for young male graduates, as well as for those individuals that are at high risk for dropping out of high school.

Contextual Teaching and Learning

Many students taking courses in the traditional academic areas, such as mathematics, science, and English, are challenged by the abstract nature in which they learn concepts that seem to have little application to their existing understandings and circumstances. CTE, among other disciplines, utilizes the principles of contextual teaching and learning by bridging the gap between theory and practice. CTE provides students with opportunities to utilize what is learned in traditional academic areas into a more real-world context embedded with a career focus.

This mutually supportive relationship is the primary underpinning of contextual teaching and learning and is used as a pedagogical tool to maximize student learning and retention (Granello, 2000).

The concept of contextual teaching and learning was promulgated by John Dewey in 1916 in articulating a strong need for schools to provide students with meaningful and purposeful activities that have real-world application (Granello, 2000). The common thread throughout the vast majority of CTE courses is the way in which students learn. Learning environments in CTE classrooms facilitate a hands-on approach to learning in which students are constantly integrating traditional academic content within applied technical settings. In addition, CTE's work-based learning programs enable students to transfer concepts learned in the classroom to a real job setting.

SOCIAL JUSTICE ISSUES ASSOCIATED WITH TRACKING

Equality of Opportunities and Outcomes for All Students

Students in high school are faced with an array of pathways that, often unbeknown to them, strongly contribute to their long-term trajectories. Higher education, according to societal views, has historically been conceptualized as a high priority for individuals (Swail, Perna, & Redd, 2003; Venezia & Kirst, 2005) and as a vehicle for socioeconomic mobility (Kulik, 1998) and social stability (Corazzini, Dugan, & Grabowski, 1972). Furthermore, higher education has also been known to decrease the large inequities that exist in earning potential between ethnic minorities and Caucasians (Bailey, Kienzl, & Marcotte, 2004b). At the current time, 70% of the approximately 2.5 million public high school graduates in the United States pursue postsecondary education within a two-year span of graduation (Venezia & Kirst, 2005). Further, 50% aspire to earn a bachelor's degree.

Most individuals would agree that *all* students *should* have access to a rigorous and quality education. However, this is far from reality in today's schools. As indicated previously, students are tracked in high school, resulting in large disparities in the type, quality, and rigor of educational curricula students are exposed to, as well as contributing to the academic achievement gap between Caucasian and minority students. Research findings have indicated that those in the general and CTE tracks are less likely to earn postsecondary degrees (Fletcher, 2009; Kulik, 1998). Further, research has suggested that those in the college-preparatory and dual tracks are much more likely than their general and CTE counterparts to earn postsecondary degrees, more so for the college-preparatory track students.

It is also important to note that, in reality, not all students have the aspirations for pursuing postsecondary education. If this is the case, these students may be better suited for the CTE track (particularly in relation to the general track) to pursue their passions and interests. CTE students are more likely to be ready for the workforce. In fact, research studies have indicated that students participating in the CTE track are much more likely to benefit from higher earnings (Fletcher, 2009; Mane, 1999; Meer, 2007). Nonetheless, these students would also benefit from a rigorous set of CTE courses, with high-quality teachers and teaching as students concentrating in core academic subjects.

In fact, despite the acknowledgment that obtaining a bachelor's degree has many benefits and provides access to increased opportunities, according to the Bureau of Labor Statistics data, projections of job opportunities for individuals without a bachelor's degree indicate that approximately 42 million positions would be available between 2002 and 2012 (Moncarz & Crosby, 2004). This projection outweighs the number of expected positions available for those with bachelor's degrees three-fold.

CONCLUSION AND IMPLICATIONS

Qualitative studies about Black students' perceptions of the reasons why they were placed in the CTE track seem warranted. Prior research on tracking has suggested that Blacks are often funneled into the CTE track, resulting in a further widening of the achievement gap and exacerbating long-term social inequalities. Hence, exploring the lived experiences of Blacks in CTE tracks as well as the reasons why they participate may be quite telling.

Educational policy makers may also consider ensuring fair and equitable representation of all groups of individuals in the various high school curriculum tracks. Schools could include written documentation on how they are ensuring the diversity of classes, with equitable representation of minorities, females, and those individuals with disabilities, in the college-preparatory, CTE, and dual tracks. In addition, funding may be considered for teachers and guidance counselors to undertake professional development opportunities that seek to gain a better understanding of the effects of tracking students and how their dispositions may affect participation rates in the various high school curriculum tracks.

Prior research has indicated that students may be better suited to participate in the college-preparatory, CTE, or dual tracks. Educational legislation such as the No Child Left Behind Act (NCLB) may be made more effective by including provisions that mandate that all students take courses that are consistent with four-year institutions' requirements, earn career-oriented credits in CTE, or enroll in a combination of both types of courses. The phenomenon of abandoning the general track has already occurred in some school districts and school reform models. Thus, research findings presented in this chapter might explain the emergence of schools abandoning the general track.

This chapter is also pertinent to school counselors, parents, teacher education, teachers, and students. Guidance counselors, in particular, should be informed of the overrepresentation of Blacks in CTE and dual tracks and Hispanics in general tracks. Efforts should be extended to help Black and Hispanic students learn of the long-term benefits of participating in the various tracks. Guidance counselors should be more aware of possible biases or dispositions that may predispose them to advise higher percentages of Black students to pursue the CTE track and Hispanics to pursue the general track. Students and parents should be informed of the likely long-term outcomes that are predicted for students' futures in regard to degree attainment and occupational earnings. Teachers should also be aware of this. School administrators might consider attempting to better establish collaborative relationships with core academic and CTE teachers to develop interdisciplinary lessons and integrative planning time. Further, students, parents, and teachers should all be cognizant of the contemporary demands of employees in the workforce and the current expectations for students in terms of degree attainment and skill acquisition.

REFERENCES

Akos, P., Lambie, G., Milsom, A., & Gilbert, K. (2007). Early adolescents' aspirations and academic tracking: An exploratory investigation. *Professional School Counseling, 11*(1), 57–64.

Alexander, K. L., & McDill, E. L. (1976). Selection and allocation within schools: Some causes and consequences of curriculum placement. *American Sociological Review, 41*, 963–980.

Alvarez, D., & Mehan, H. (2007). Whole school detracking: A strategy for equity and excellence. *Theory Into Practice, 45*(1), 82–89.

Arum, R., & Shavit, Y. (1995). Secondary vocational education and the transition from school to work. *Sociology of Education, 68*(3), 187–204.

Ayalon, H., & Gamoran, A. (2000). Stratification in academic secondary programs and educational inequality in Israel and the United States. *Comparative Education Review, 44*(1), 54–80.

Bailey, T., Kienzl, G., & Marcotte, D. (2004b). *The return to a sub-baccalaureate education: The effects of schooling, credentials, and program of study on economic outcomes.* Washington, DC: U.S. Department of Education.

Biafora, F., & Ansalone, G. (2008). Perceptions and attitudes of school principals towards school tracking: Structural considerations of personal beliefs. *Education, 128*(4), 588–602.

Bottoms, G. (1997). Replacing high-school's general track. *Education Digest, 63*(2), 20–25.

Bragg, D. (2007). Teacher pipelines: Career pathways extending from high school to community college to university. *Community College Review, 35*(1), 10–29.

Burris, C., & Welner, K. (2005). Closing the achievement gap by detracking. *The Phi Delta Kappan, 86*(8), 594–598.

Cohen, M., & Besharov, D. (2002, March). *The role of career and technical education: Implications for the federal government*. Paper presented at the Preparing America's Future: The High School Symposium, Washington, DC.

Corbett, C., & Welner, K. (2008). Closing the achievement gap by detracking. In L. Abbeduto & F. Symons (Eds.), *Taking sides: Clashing views in educational psychology* (pp. 102–107). New York, NY: McGraw-Hill.

Corazzini, A., Dugan, D., & Grabowski, H. (1972). Determinants and distributional aspects of enrollment in U.S. higher education. *Journal of Human Resources, 7*(1), 26–38.

Dare, D. (2006). The role of career and technical education in facilitating student transitions to postsecondary education. *New Directions for Community Colleges, 135*, 73–80.

DeLuca, S., Plank, S., & Estacion, A. (2006). *Does career and technical education affect college enrollment?* Columbus, OH: National Dissemination Center for Career and Technical Education.

Draeger, M. (2006). How students benefit from high-tech, high-wage career pathways. *New Directions for Community Colleges, 2006*(135), 81–89.

Esters, L. T. (2007). Factors influencing postsecondary education enrollment behaviors of urban agricultural education students. *Journal Career and Technical Education Research, 32*(2), 79–98.

Fletcher, E. (2006). No curriculum left behind: The effects of the No Child Left Behind legislation on career and technical education. *Career and Technical Education Research, 31*(3), 157–174.

Fletcher, E. (2009). *The relationship of high school curriculum tracks to degree attainment and occupational earnings* (Unpublished doctoral dissertation). The Ohio State University, Columbus, Ohio.

Fletcher, E., & Zirkle, C. (2009). Career and technical education in light of the No Child Left Behind legislation. In V. Wang (Ed.), *Handbook of research on e-learning applications for career and technical education: Technologies for vocational training* (pp. 495–507). Hershey, PA: Information Science Reference.

Fletcher, E., & Zirkle, C. (2010). Examining the impact of tracking on long-term student outcomes. In V. C. X. Wang (Ed.), *Definitive readings in the history, philosophy, practice, and theories of career and technical education* (pp. 191–213). Hershey, PA: Information Science Reference.

Flowers, J. (2000). High Schools That Work and tech prep: Improving student performance in basic skills. *Journal of Vocational Education Research, 25*(3), 333–345.

Gamoran, A. (1989). Measuring curriculum differentiation. *American Journal of Education, 97*(1), 129–143.

Gamoran, A., & Mare, R. (1989). Secondary school tracking and educational inequality: Compensation, reinforcement, or neutrality. *American Journal of Sociology, 94*(5), 1146–1183.

Gamoran, A., & Nystrand, M. (1991). Background and instructional effects on achievement in eighth-grade English and social studies. *Journal on Research on Adolescence, 1*(3), 277–300.

Gamoran, A., Nystrand, M., Berends, M., & LePore, P. (1995). An organizational analysis of the effects of ability grouping. *American Educational Research Journal, 32*(4), 687–715.

Gamoran, A., & Weinstein, M. (1998). Differentiation and opportunity in restructured schools. *American Journal of Education, 106*(3), 385–415.

Gordon, H. (2008). *The history and growth of career and technical education in America* (3rd ed.) Long Grove, IL: Waveland Press.

Granello, D. (2000). Contextual teaching and learning in counselor education. *Counselor Education and Supervision, 39*(4), 270–283.

Hallinan, M. (1991). School differences in tracking structures and track assignments. *Journal of Research and Adolescence, 1*(3), 251–275.

Hallinan, M. (1994). School differences in tracking effects on achievement. *Social Forces, 72*(3), 799–821.

Hampden-Thompson, G., Warkentien, S, & Daniel, B. (2009). *Course credit accrual and dropping out of high school, by student characteristics* (Publication No. NCES 2009-035). Washington, DC: National Center for Education Statistics.

Harnish, D., & Lynch, R. L. (2009). Secondary to postsecondary technical education transitions: An exploratory study of dual enrollment in Georgia. *Journal Career and Technical Education Research, 30*(3), 169–188.

Jones, K., Bowen, B., & Rumberger, L. (1998). A qualitative assessment of teacher and school influences on African American enrollments in secondary agricultural science courses. *Journal of Agricultural Education, 39*(2), 19–29.

Kelly, S. (2007). The contours of tracking in North Carolina. *The High School Journal, 90*(4), 15–31.

Kemple, J., (with Scott-Clayton, J). (2004). Career academies: Impacts on labor market outcomes and educational attainment. *Manpower Demonstration Research Corporation.* Retrieved from http://www.mdrc.org/publications/366/overview.html

Kistler, L. (2004). *The essential elements of tech prep models that impacted graduation rates and student satisfaction in six Ohio tech prep consortia* (Unpublished doctoral dissertation). University of Cincinnati, Ohio.

Kulik, J. (1998). Curricular tracks and high school vocational education. In A. Gamoran & H. Himmelfarb (Eds.). *The quality of vocational education: Background paper from the 1994 national assessment of vocational education.* Washington, DC: U.S. Department of Education. Retrieved from http://www.ed.gov/pubs/VoEd/Chapter3/Part2.html

Lee, V., & Byrk, S. (1988). Curriculum tracking as mediating the social distribution of high school achievement. *Sociology of Education, 61*(2), 78–94.

LeTendre, G., Hofer, B., & Shimizu, H. (2003). What is tracking? Cultural expectations in the United States, Germany, and Japan. *American Educational Research Journal, 40*(1), 43–89.

Lewis, A. (2006). Career pathways. *Tech Directions, 66,* 5–6.

Lewis, T. (2007). Social inequality in education: A constraint on an American high-skills future. *Curriculum Inquiry, 37*(4), 329–349.

Lewis, T., & Cheng, S. (2006). Tracking, expectations, and the transformation of vocational education. *American Journal of Education, 113*(1), 67–99.

Lucas, S., & Berends, M. (2002). Sociodemographic diversity, correlated achievement, and de facto tracking. *Sociology of Education, 75*(4), 306–327.

Mane, F. (1999). Trends in the payoff to academic and occupation-specific skills: The short and medium run returns to academic and vocational high school courses for non-college-bound students. *Economics of Education Review, 18*(4), 417–437.

McPartland, J. M., & Schneider, B. (1996). Opportunities to learn and student diversity: Prospects and pitfalls of a common core curriculum [Extra issue]. *Sociology of Education, 69,* 66–81.

Meer, J. (2007). Evidence on the returns to secondary vocational education. *Economics of Education Review, 26*(5), 559–573.

Miller, D., & Gray, K. (2002). Tech prep persistence in comprehensive high schools: An exploratory study. *Journal of Industrial Teacher Education, 39*(4), 26–35.

Moncarz, R., & Crosby, O. (2004). Job outlook for people who don't have a bachelor's degree. *Occupational Outlook Quarterly, 48,* 3–13.

Novel, J. (2009) *Implementation of the Carl D. Perkins Career and Technical Education reforms of the 1990s: Postsecondary education outcomes of students taking an enhanced vocational curriculum* (Unpublished doctoral dissertation). The Ohio State University, Ohio.

Oakes, J., & Guiton, G. (1995). Matchmaking: The dynamics of high school tracking decisions. *American Educational Research Journal, 32*(1), 3–33.

Page, R. (1990). Games of chance: The lower-track curriculum in a college-preparatory high school. *Curriculum Inquiry, 20*(3), 249–281.

Plank, S., DeLuca, S., & Estacion, A. (2005). *Dropping out of high school and the place of career and technical education: A survival analysis of surviving high school*. St. Paul, MN: National Research Center.

Rasinski, K. A., & Pedlow, S. (1998) The effect of high school vocational education on academic achievement gain and high school persistence: Evidence from NELS:88. In A. Gamoran & H. Himmelfarb (Eds.), *The quality of vocational education: Background paper from the 1994 national assessment of vocational education*. Washington, DC: U.S. Department of Education. Retrieved from http://www.ed.gov/pubs/VoEd/Chapter5/index.html.

Rojewski, J. (1997). Effects of economic disadvantaged status and secondary vocational education on adolescent work experience and postsecondary aspirations. *Journal of Vocational and Technical Education, 14*. Retrieved from http://scholar.lib.vt.edu/ejournals/JVTE/v14n1/JVTE-4.html

Rojewski, J. (2002). Preparing the workforce of tomorrow: A conceptual framework for career and technical education. *Journal of Vocational Education Research, 27*(1), 7–35.

Rubin, B. (2006). Tracking and de-tracking: Debates, evidence, and best practices for a heterogeneous world. *Theory into Practice, 45*(1), 4–14.

Ruhland, S. (2003). Evaluating tech prep education programs: Implications for reporting program and student outcomes. *Journal of Vocational Education Research, 28*(1), 35–57.

Scott, F. L., & Lavergne, D. (2004). Perceptions of agriculture students regarding the image of agriculture and barriers to enrolling in an agriculture education class. *Journal of Southern Agricultural Education Research, 54*, 48–59.

Scott, J., & Sarkees-Wircenski, M. (2008). *Overview of career and technical education* (4th ed.). Homewood, IL: American Technical.

Silverberg, M., Warner, E., Fong, M., & Goodwin, D. (2004). *National assessment of vocational education: Final report to Congress*. Washington, DC: U.S. Department of Education.

Soloninka, J. (2003). *Accommodation in an urban agricultural education program in Ohio: A case study*. (Unpublished doctoral dissertation). The Ohio State University, Ohio.

Swail, W., Perna, L., & Redd, K. (2003). Retaining minority students in higher education: A framework for success. *ASHE-ERIC Higher Education Report, 30*(2), 1–172.

Venezia, A., & Kirst, M. (2005). Inequitable opportunities: How current education systems and policies undermine the chances for student persistence and success in college. *Educational Policy, 19*(2), 283–307.

Waller, S., & Waller, L. (2004). Texas tech prep environmental scan of partner opinions: An assessment of effectiveness. *Community College Journal of Research and Practice, 28*(7), 625–635.

CHAPTER SEVEN

Salient Factors Affecting Urban African American Students' Achievement: Recommendations FOR Teachers, School Counselors, AND School Psychologists

DESIREÉ VEGA, JAMES L. MOORE III, CAROLINE A. BAKER,
NIKOL V. BOWEN, ERIK M. HINES, AND BARBARA O'NEAL

Meager educational opportunities often lead to uneven life chances (Levin, Belfield, Muennig, & Rouse, 2007). Access to a quality education is increasingly becoming a requisite for achieving social and economic mobility (Jackson & Moore, 2006). More and more, education has become important to the citizens of the United States and abroad. The future of America is inextricably linked to its educational system. Increased globalization, technological advancements, and demographic shifts have spurred the need for workforce talent among nontraditional populations (e.g., women, immigrants, and ethnic minorities; Henfield, Owens, & Moore, 2008; Moore, 2006).

To respond to this necessity, public schools need to do a better job educating American students. "The security and social and economic well-being of our nation now and in the future depends on the collective ability of all people to thrive" (Tsoi-A-Fratt, 2010, p. 3). When large segments of the population are unable to thrive, the whole country suffers. It is sad that too many African American students are not reaping the benefits of a public education (Jackson & Moore, 2006, 2008; Moore & Owens, 2008). Around the country, many school systems are failing large numbers of African American students.

A disproportionate number of these students attend urban public schools, which are frequently underresourced, underfunded, and understaffed (Kozol, 1991; Lewis & Moore, 2008). Urban schools are commonly staffed by the least qualified teachers and administrators, and these schools frequently experience high teacher turnover (Ford & Moore, 2004; Moore & Owens, 2008). Farkas (2003) notes that in these urban education settings, students of color, such as African Americans, tend to attend schools that are racially isolated and low performing at the elementary levels. The researcher also notes that these education beginnings set them up for enrolling in lower track courses at low-performing schools at both the middle and high school levels. He further suggests that a number of factors contribute to the education outcomes of urban African American students.

In this chapter, we focus on the factors that *most* commonly affect urban African American students' education outcomes. Stated in a different way, we highlight the factors in the literature that account for the most consistent effects in education among urban African American students. Drawing from popular and social science literature, we place these salient in the following broad categories: (a) school, (b) psychological, and (c) social-cultural. There are some slight overlaps with the Lewis, Chambers, and Butler chapter in this edited volume; however, in this chapter, we place more attention on the most salient factors and on the recommendations offered to urban teachers, school counselors, and school psychologists.

SCHOOL FACTORS

The vast body of literature gives numerous explications as to why urban African American students are not achieving academically. One prevalent explanation is related to school factors. Like many other American social institutions, urban schools tend to have their own norms, values, and customs (Moore & Owen, 2008), which are frequently reflective of students' backgrounds and educators' beliefs and expectations of these students. It is widely recognized that school factors, such as the school environment, can both positively and negatively affect student outcomes (Flowers, Milner, & Moore, 2003). To this end, it is critical that urban educators—teachers, school counselors, and school psychologists—are cognizant of the school factors that most influence students' achievement as well as understand how to address them. In the following sections, we highlight some of these common school factors.

Tracking

Mickelson and Velasco (2006) find several reasons for the underenrollment in rigorous courses among urban African Americans adolescents, including personal beliefs, peer culture, parental expectations, the opportunity structure at school, and the fear of being labeled as acting White. The tracking structure of the schools makes students aware that the advanced courses are considered White courses, whereas African American students are thought to enroll in regular courses. However, the high-achieving African American students in the study, all of whom were enrolled in advanced courses, challenged this structure. The segregation within schools resulting from the tracking system creates the resentment Tyson, Darity, and Castellino (2005) explain in their study. Students begin to associate tracking levels with race and academic ability, which, in turn, shapes peer interactions. When Black students enroll in courses known as "White courses," they become the target of accusations among Black students not enrolled in these advanced courses. Nevertheless, Mickelson and Velasco find that the reason for these students' underachievement is not such accusations, as is the case for the students in Tyson et al. (2005).

Tyson (2006) also argues that schools create and sustain structures that construct racial boundaries. As African American students reach adolescence, they increasingly become aware of the lack of ethnic minority students in challenging courses, such as advanced placement (AP) and honors courses. This awareness is insulting to African Americans as they make sense of why students who look like themselves are not in rigorous courses. Tyson urges researchers and educators to evaluate students' early school experiences and examine how they may influence later school attitudes and behaviors. Students may become cognizant of tracking structures early in their academic career, which potentially affects how they interpret their schooling experiences as they progress through it.

Nasir, McLaughlin, and Jones (2009) similarly find that school context plays a large role in how African American adolescents make sense of their racial and academic identities. They find two identities that exist within the same school systems: a "street savvy" African American identity and a "school-oriented and socially conscious" African American identity. The former represents an identity characterized by a connection to the street or the "block"; it includes representations of African Americans as drug dealers, pimps, and gangsters; uneducated; and indifferent toward the law and their futures. The students in the study who personify this identity describe school as a place for social interaction rather than academic development; they also discuss their involvement in selling drugs, gang banging, and fighting in school.

The Discipline Gap

The overrepresentation of urban African American youth receiving harsh disciplinary consequences has been well documented throughout the literature for more than 30 years (Fenning & Rose, 2007). Schools, including urban ones, most frequently punish the students with the greatest academic, social, economic, and emotional needs (Johnson, Boyden, & Pittz, 2001). Skiba, Michael, Nardo, and Peterson (2002) find that African Americans receive harsher punishments than do their White peers and oftentimes for less serious or more subjective reasons. For instance, they find that teachers commonly refer White students to the office for offenses such as smoking, vandalism, and obscene language, whereas African American students receive office referrals for behavior such as excessive noise, disrespect, and loitering. Furthermore, differences in cultural learning styles lead teachers to misinterpret the behavior of African Americans as inappropriate, when the behaviors are not intended to be that way (Weinstein, Curran, & Tomlinson-Clarke, 2003). This cultural mismatch increases the chances of disciplinary action among urban African American youth.

Although schools react to the behavior of African American students, they neglect to respond to the unmet needs at the root of their problematic behavior (Noguera, 2003). Disciplinary practices, such as suspension and expulsion, contribute to the marginalization of these students, while removing them from school and ignoring the source of the problem. The need for control within urban schools appears to take precedence over meeting the academic needs of students. In addition, the adoption of zero tolerance policies has led to the significant increase in the number of children suspended and expelled from schools (Skiba & Rausch, 2006, 2008). To this end, it is critical that urban school systems reexamine these failing school disciplinary policies.

These disciplinary practices rid schools of the so-called "bad" students but leave these urban students with little options for a successful future. As a result, many of these students turn to criminal behaviors, which have large costs to society (Levin et al., 2007). The research literature has consistently demonstrated a direct link between these exclusionary disciplinary practices and entrance into the criminal justice system, referred as the "school-to-prison pipeline" (Fenning & Rose, 2007).

Casella (2003) examines how schools use preventive detention to punish students who appear to be dangerous. In most cases, these students are African American and Latino males. The researcher finds that preventive detention, the assignment of students to school out-placement programs, the increased presence of school police officers, and the adoption of zero tolerance policies, restricts and isolates students. The researcher also finds a correlation between the aforementioned practices and the criminal justice system. School officials explain that they feel pressured to maintain control in their schools due to highly publicized school shootings and they feel compelled to participate in out-placements provided by the district (Casella, 2003). This explanation is interesting, as many school shootings have occurred in suburban schools rather than urban settings.

Furthermore, Casella (2003) finds that, once students are suspended or expelled, readmission into school is often extremely difficult. For example, school officials report that placing students into out-placement programs, such as vocational programs, adult education, general education diploma (GED) programs, or, even worse, into settings such as boot camp or lockdown facilities, further marginalizes troubled urban youth and clearly puts them on the pipeline into prison. In addition, Casella reports that many schools do not take responsibility for their role in the criminalization of urban African American students. Rather than addressing their academic and emotional needs, these urban school systems place students into programs and/or classes that fail to meet their needs. As a result, students often disengage, literally and figuratively, from school and consequently engage in criminal behaviors.

For students who fail to abide by rules that enforce the schools' inherent need for control, the consequences are suspension and/or expulsion. Oftentimes, these students experience disciplinary action, and they learn that school is not a rewarding place and find little incentive to comply, being that their academic, social, and/or emotional needs are not being met. Noguera (2003) suggests that suspension does not improve student behavior; instead, it leads to the cycle of punishment within the criminal justice system. The disproportionate amount of African American youth suspended and expelled clearly demonstrates the ineffectiveness of such policies. In these cases, urban school systems deprive the neediest students of an education, as suspension and expulsion warrant student removal from the classroom; therefore, they miss out on much-needed learning opportunities (Noguera, 2003). School officials do not examine why the problem behaviors occur or attempt to solve them; instead, they take the simpler step of removing the student from the environment.

Monroe and Obidah (2004) examine how cultural synchronization, or a cultural match between teachers and students, results in a positive, engaging classroom environment. For example, the authors explore an African American teacher's disciplinary practices with students of the same race. They find that the teacher infused culturally based strategies into her disciplinary methods; for instance, she drew on referents (e.g., speech patterns, voice tones, facial expressions, and word choices) that conveyed her behavioral expectations to students in ways that were meaningful to them. The methods used in her classroom led to fewer disciplinary referrals. Therefore, teachers should examine how culture relates to effective classroom management techniques for African American students in urban schools. The lack of synchronicity causes teachers to focus more on discipline and takes away valuable opportunities for students to learn. Bridging the cultural gap between students and teachers is important in changing the negative experiences minority students face in urban schools.

Few studies have examined how teachers perceive discipline issues within their schools, considering they are the ones referring students for disciplinary action; it is an area that warrants examination. Gregory and Mosely (2004) find that teachers often attribute disciplinary problems to the school, adolescent, and community and that the majority of them hold color-blind approaches to the problem that fail to examine the intersection between race and discipline. For instance, the teachers in this study explain that because adolescence is a time in which youth rebel against all authority figures, students cope with academic problems through misbehavior. Teachers also attribute poverty, lack of school organization, and poor classroom management to the discipline issues within the school. These factors imply a consistent distribution of disciplinary practices across race throughout the school; however, this is not the case for African American students who are overrepresented in suspension (Gregory & Mosely, 2004).

Only two teachers in the study reflect on the relationship between race and discipline. One African American teacher discusses how school personnel perceive African American males in a negative sense and how she wishes her colleagues would set aside their stereotypes and get to know their students as individuals. A White female teacher discusses how, over the years, she learned to change her disciplinary practices because she "figured out that some of those issues, turns out they're not discipline issues, they're just different ways of participating" (p. 25). These teachers understand the implications of cultural differences and believe in getting to know African American students rather than judging them based on stereotypes or deficit perspectives. Urban school systems need to take strides to ensure cultural competence among teachers and employ culturally responsive discipline strategies to facilitate academic achievement among African American youth, as the teacher in Monroe and Obidah (2004) utilizes.

Teacher Expectations

Interactions between African American students and teachers influence the students' academic outcomes. In many urban schools, teachers hold low academic expectations and negative perceptions about the academic ability of African

American youth. Wiggan (2008) finds that teacher practices have the most significant impact of all the factors on school success. High-achieving African American students describe teachers who deliver high-quality instruction, care about students, and emphasize teamwork and self-direction as characteristics of engaging pedagogies. Tenenbaum and Ruck (2007) conducted meta-analysis comparing teacher expectations for European American, African American, Asian American, and Latino students. They find that teachers hold the highest expectations for Asian American students and hold more positive expectations for Whites than for Latino and African American students. These studies underscore the relevance of positive teacher–student relationships for the academic success of students of color (e.g., African Americans), in showing that when teachers demonstrate an investment in their students and remove deficit perspectives from their pedagogies, academic outcomes increase. Around the country, many urban school systems are predominantly African American, yet their teachers are not; this difference draws attention to the need for cultural competence and parity to provide equitable learning opportunities.

Long-standing deficit perspectives that place the blame on African American students, their families, and their socioeconomic status are commonplace in society. Rather than engage African American students in learning, many urban teachers assume that these students are incapable of learning and, in consequence, allow them to low achieve or underachieve. Rolon-Dow (2007) examines school engagement among girls of color in an urban public school and finds that low demands from teachers permitted students to pass time in class without actually engaging in learning. Further, the researcher finds that one teacher conducted class at a fast pace and those students who could not keep up academically ended up doing poorly. Rather than scaffolding instruction to meet the needs of the urban learners, the teacher disregarded the students who needed the most assistance. Aligned with this point, the teacher clarifies, "There are kids who will get it and there will be kids that no matter how long I spend on it, they will not get it. Because they don't take the time to pay attention or concentrate and focus on it for a while" (p. 359). In essence, the teacher fails to take responsibility for her students' inability to grasp material and to attempt to understand why students could not "get it." Instead, she blames the students for failing to pay attention.

Deficit-oriented teacher attitudes often depict urban students who underachieve as failures. As a result, many of these urban students disengage from learning (Ford, Whiting, & Moore, 2009). The students in Rolon-Dow's (2007) study give the appearance of being engaged in class by conforming to their teachers' values and expectations in the classroom, such as by sitting at their desks quietly completing worksheets and complying with teachers' requests. It seems that compliance took precedence over actual learning, because the teachers in the study did not attempt to actively engage their students in classroom activities or demand critical thinking, rather they required minimal amounts of work.

These kinds of teaching strategies often limit students' educational opportunities and capacity to learn, especially those students from urban communities. Allowing students to pass time without high academic requirements limits their competitiveness and chances to pass upper-level coursework dominated by Whites (Rolon-Dow, 2007). These deficit-oriented perspectives are inherent within many school systems, including urban ones, as educators generalize these beliefs as applying to all African American students. Teachers judge African American students as incompetent without knowing their actual capabilities, which is heightened when the student is *Black, male, and poor* (Jackson & Moore, 2006, 2008). These students construct the belief that school is an unwelcoming place that contributes to their perceived negative academic experiences.

Barajas and Ronnkvist (2007) examine school racialization and its resulting differential outcomes across racial lines. The racialization of school spaces demonstrates an investment in Whiteness as the norm and standard for achievement. These researchers find evidence of racialization in schools by looking at the effects of external markers of race, such as skin color. The educators in the study held perceptions that the students were unable to cope with normative academic standards based on their appearance, without knowledge of the students' actual academic ability. On the other hand, students become cognizant of these inaccurate views and disengage, both psychologically and emotionally, from school, as evidenced in Rolon-Dow's (2007) study.

A study by Barajas and Ronnkvist (2007) demonstrates how the inherent structure of the public school system positions students of color as inferior and makes them aware of their status through invalid assumptions about their ability. When urban African American students do not feel welcomed or supported in their school environment, many underachieve or low achieve. Through forming positive relationships with adult role models, they can instead develop an academic identity in which they see themselves as an important part of their educational experience (Cammarota, 2004). In order for this to occur, school personnel—teachers, school counselors, and school psychologists—need to work to rectify their deficit-oriented views and provide students with an opportunity to display and enhance their achievement levels.

School Belonging

In contrast to miscalculated teacher expectations and deficit-oriented views, school belonging—a feeling of relatedness or connection to others (Booker, 2007)—plays a significant role in student achievement. An urban school that is psychologically welcoming and supportive of African American students is likely to produce academically engaged urban learners who demonstrate higher levels of achievement. To this end, school disidentification is a strong predictor of academic disengagement (Osborne & Walker, 2006). Chronic negative interactions and experiences with teachers can prevent a genuine feeling of belonging at school. Both teachers and peers often influence perceptions of belonging among African American students. Students in the Booker (2007) study report that warmth and encouragement from their teachers and peers are important factors of belonging.

In a similar sense, Sánchez, Colón, and Esparza (2005) find that a sense of school belonging significantly predicts academic outcomes, including academic motivation, effort, and absenteeism among students of color. Close and Solberg (2008) also find that the students of color who report feeling connected to their teachers and schools describe higher levels of autonomous motivation for attending school. These same students also indicate performing better in school and feeling more confident in their academic ability. The aforementioned studies highlight the important role school climate plays in academic outcomes for students of color, including African American students; therefore, educators should develop culturally appropriate strategies to bridge the gap between themselves and their urban African American students to increase opportunities for academic success.

Resegregation

The resegregation of urban public schools has continued to intensify after the Supreme Court struck down voluntary desegregation plans. In 2007, the Supreme Court ruled in *Parents Involved in Community Schools v. Seattle School District No. 1* that schools could not assign or deny placement to individuals based on race even if the intent was to integrate schools (Orfield & Lee, 2007). In essence, this court decision reversed the *1954 Brown v. Board of Education of Topeka* ruling, which mandated the integration of schools or race-based assignment to schools. In a society where separate has never been equal and segregated schools have the poorest conditions, the school districts in Seattle and Louisville sought to remedy these issues by providing students with the opportunity to attend racially balanced schools; however, the Supreme Court deemed this remedy as unconstitutional.

According to the research literature, school segregation is strongly linked to inequalities in schooling opportunities, processes, and outcomes among African American students (Levin et al., 2007; Lewis & Moore, 2008). Many African American students attend inferior schools and live in poverty and in heavily segregated urban neighborhoods. Thus, their education struggles against overwhelming odds (Levin et al., 2007). The future of these students appears even more troubling, as schools throughout the country are instituting achievement tests as a requisite for grade promotion and graduation. Because a disproportionate number of urban youth attend poorly funded schools, with underqualified teachers that track them into remedial curricula, many urban school systems set them up for failure by providing them with inadequate preparation for these high-stakes exams.

SOCIAL-CULTURAL FACTORS

According to the research literature, there are a number of social-cultural factors that have been found to affect education outcomes for urban African American students. In urban contexts, African Americans often are confronted with many social-cultural realities (Henfield, Moore, et al., 2008; Henfield, Owens, et al., 2008; Moore & Owens, 2008). Moore and Owens (2008) assert: "Too often, life stressors experienced by African American students are a function of specific social ills in the African American community and society at-large, including poverty, discrimination, neglect and abuse, and drug and mental health problems" (p. 357). Ford (1996) posits that these same students sometimes experience social pressures that make them vulnerable to underachievement and low achievement.

Poverty

Disparities in income often reflect the apparent inequalities in society. It is widely recognized that many urban neighborhoods across the United States are not functioning optimally (Moore & Owens, 2008). In these communities, the poverty rate tends to be proportionate with that of the neighborhood population, and African Americans and Latinos are concentrated, most often, in these urban communities (Acevedo-Garcia, Rosenfeld, McArdle, & Osypuk, 2010). According to the research literature, there is a strong link between neighborhoods and schools (Khadduri, Schwartz, & Turnham, 2007). For example, at most elementary schools in the United States, student attendance is neighborhood based (Iceland, Weinberg, & Steinmetz, 2002). Stated in a different way, it is reasonable to believe that African American and Latino students from low-income families constitute the majority in urban schools. Research suggests that students from low-income communities tend to have harder times with education than those from affluent and middle-class communities (Berliner & Biddle, 1995). In addition, low-income students tend to have lower academic success but higher behavior problems, juvenile delinquency, and teenage pregnancies (Leventhal & Brooks-Gunn, 2000). In closing, poverty is an important variable in relation to student achievement.

Help-Seeking Behaviors

As urban African American children progress through adolescence and build their cognitive skills, they become more aware of their need for assistance. However, a problem arises when African American students need help and are aware of this need but do not seek out assistance (Ryan, Pintrich, & Midgley, 2001). In the research literature, several common explanations have been offered as to why African American students avoid seeking help. Such reasons include the feasibility of asking for help in a given situation (e.g., time constraints or the norms of a setting may prohibit help seeking). The perception that asking for assistance may serve as a threat to students' competence, the fact that there may not be a competent person to provide help or a desire for autonomy and self-reliance that may affect help-seeking behaviors (Ryan et al., 2001).

Students' competence concerns play a major role in seeking help from their teachers; they may feel as if their teachers and peers will make negative judgments regarding their intellectual ability (Ryan & Pintrich, 1997). It is critical that students understand that when they do not seek out needed assistance, they are putting themselves at a disadvantage by losing out on learning opportunities (Ryan et al., 2001). From their review of the literature, Ryan et al. (2001) find that, when teachers emphasize personal improvement and promote positive social connections, help-seeking concerns decrease. The researchers also find that low-achieving students are more likely to avoid seeking help. As discussed earlier, African American students may avoid help in the face of the fear of confirming negative intellectual stereotypes held by majority society concerning their racial group (Steele, 1997).

Thus, urban educators should understand the needs of their students and structure their classrooms in ways that foster an environment in which African American students feel comfortable asking for help. Moreover, urban educators should be in tune with the needs of their African American students and attend to those who clearly need help but are not seeking help. This may help in making urban African American students feel at ease of asking for help when they need it in the future.

Peer Influences

Peer influence is a major social factor in the lives of urban African American students (Henfield, Moore, et al., 2008). This influence has been found to both positively and negatively affect school outcomes for these students (Moore, Ford, & Milner, 2005a, 2005b). Gifted African American students, including urban ones, often encounter peer rejection (Henfield, Moore, et al., 2008; Lindstrom &

Van Sant, 1986). As a case study example, Ford (1998) presents the perceptions of Danisha, a gifted African American girl. Danisha moved from a low-income, predominately African American school to an affluent, predominately White school. According to Danisha, she had been in the gifted and talented program since fifth grade. In her new school, she was one of the few African American students in her gifted program. Danisha constantly felt torn between maintaining her grades in the gifted program and maintaining her friendships with her African American peers who were not in the gifted program. Because there were very few African American students in the gifted program, her nongifted African American friends often teased and accused her of "acting White." It is unfortunate that these students, such as Danisha, are not the exceptions to receiving these insults; however, many African American students across America are confronted with these harsh realities. Ford's work illustrates the negative effect peer relationships have on African American students.

Horvat and Lewis (2003) examine the role peer groups play in managing academic success among African American female adolescents. They found that these girls sometimes camouflaged their academic identities to downplay their school achievement among their less academically successful African American peers. They did this not to avoid being ostracized by their peers but, reportedly, to spare their peers' feelings. To this end, the avoidance methods assisted the academically successful students in maintaining their academic accomplishments and friendships with their lower achieving African American peers.

Fordham and Ogbu (1986) state, "One major reason black students do poorly in school is that they experience inordinate ambivalence and affective dissonance in regard to academic effort and success" (p. 177). It is believed that the historical experiences of African Americans and their relationship with Whites have contributed to the current problem of underachievement. Education was traditionally reserved for Whites during and after slavery; therefore, Whites relegated African Americans to a subordinate position in society. Generally speaking, some scholars think that this treatment contributed to the development of a fictive kinship or collective identity that current exists among African Americans (Ogbu, 2004).

It is widely accepted that slavery denied many African Americans basic human rights. During the era of slavery, African Americans were forbidden to speak their indigenous African languages and learn to read or write. Slave owners extended punishment for violation of rules to all slaves on the plantation. The collective experiences of oppression are thought to have caused African Americans to develop a sense of a Black community that embodied their collective racial identity (Ogbu, 2004). Toward this end, this collective identity served as a support system for all African Americans throughout difficult times.

Fordham and Ogbu (1986) argue that this collective identity is at the root of the underachievement of involuntary minorities, such as African Americans. Because these groups often reject White values, behaviors, and attitudes, including academic identification, they perform poorly in school. High-achieving students cope with the burden of "acting White" by sacrificing their racial identity to achieve success. In their study, the two researchers describe various strategies employed by students at Capital High to resolve the tension between the desire to do well and the desire to conform to their peer group's collective identity through activities like participating in athletics and group activities, camouflaging their academic effort by clowning around, associating with bullies, and not bragging about their success or bringing attention to themselves.

Fordham (1988) posits that high-achieving African Americans develop a race-less persona in order to be successful. The results of her study show that high-achieving African American students were unable to maintain a strong racial identity and achieve success at the same time; a Pyrrhic victory occurred in that their success came at the expense of a collective identity. In essence, a student with a race-less persona disidentifies from his own racial group and takes on attitudes, behaviors, and characteristics not typically attributed to African Americans (Fordham, 1988). This persona develops due to the tensions experienced by African American students as they try to define their dual relationship to their racial group and the individualistic culture of school and society. The incompatibility of the two identities, racial and academic, often leads to a race-less persona.

Since the time of these seminal studies (e.g., Fordham, 1988; Fordham & Ogbu, 1986), many researchers have examined the validity of the "acting White" thesis and the race-less persona theory (e.g., Bergin & Cooks, 2002; Horvat & Lewis, 2003; Spencer, Noll, Stoltzfus, & Harpalani, 2001; Tyson et al., 2005). The consensus among education researchers and social scientists is that the accusation of "acting White" does in fact exist; however, responses to this label vary. For example, Bergin and Cooks (2002) conducted a qualitative study on 38 relatively high-achieving African American and Mexican American students from various private and public schools. The researchers found that only 10 students reported receiving accusations of "acting White." Yet none of the students shunned academic achievement to avoid these accusations. This is evident by their fairly high grade point averages (GPAs) and statements of competing with their classmates for high grades.

In addition, these students did not report giving up their ethnic identity to do well. The accusations of "acting White" did bother some of these students; however, their academic achievement remained strong. For example, Joe, one of the study participants, states, "It made me feel bad because I had probably known more black history and had done more to delve into my history than most of them, and they had the nerve to see me as something that was trying to negate my heritage" (Bergin & Cooks, 2002, p. 128). Thus, these results nullify the existence of an oppositional culture or a race-less persona as students in the study continue to receive high grades in the face of taunts from their African American peers.

Familial Influences

Over the years, numerous studies have qualitatively explored the factors surrounding successful educational experiences among African American students. Both Hébert and Reis (1999) and Reis and Díaz (1999) published results from an ethnography conducted in an urban school system and found several factors contributing to the students' academic success, such as belief in themselves, supportive adults available to them, strong connections with high-achieving peers, participation in extracurricular activities, enrollment in challenging classes, motivation and resiliency in the face of urban community conditions, and family support. The supportive adults exist in educator roles, in the family, and in the community at large. The motivation and resiliency manifest through being able to ignore and avoid crime and violent activities in the community or on school grounds, such as gang activity. In the two studies, family support includes emotional reinforcement (e.g., encouragement) and concrete resources (e.g., study guides and enrichment materials), but direct involvement with the school is minimal.

Borland, Schnur, and Wright (2000) followed a group of high-achieving yet economically disadvantaged students through their early years of being identified as potentially gifted and moving to a school specifically designed to cater to the needs of gifted students. They employed a mixed-methods approach that includes observation and interaction as well as a review of test scores and survey completion. In their publication, the scholars make numerous assertions about the academic success factors of urban students related to the school environment, but, in respect to family involvement, their findings closely resemble previously mentioned studies. Parents of successful students value education and communicate this message to their children through positively socializing them in terms of ability and education. The aforementioned researchers also find that the students who achieve academic success are members of stable households similar to those of (White) middle-class families. Further, many of the parents ignore instances of racism or oppression when necessary for the benefit of their children and similarly broke out of a caste-like mentality. Likewise, Borland et al. (2000) find that parents of academically successful children take risks that enable their children to persist academically. These parents also recognize and nurture their children's educational talents.

The last finding juxtaposes assertions by Scott, Perou, Urbano, Hogan, and Gold (1992) in their study of White, Latino, and African American families, in which they find that African American and Latino parents are less likely to refer their children for gifted testing than are White parents.

Ford, Wright, Grantham, and Harris (1998) examine differences in academic achievement between single- and two-parent households. The researchers find that African American students coming from two-parent homes are more likely to be identified as gifted than those coming from single-parent homes. In addition, they note that the parents' ideology about education is reflected in the academic beliefs, attitudes, and behaviors of the students. The students, in other words, tended to have similar outlooks on education as their parents. On the converse, the researchers do not discover that the students perform any better based on coming from single- or two-parent homes; they are just simply more likely to be identified as gifted.

Past studies also confirm that authoritative parents in urban settings, as opposed to permissive and authoritarian parents, foster greater academic success in their children (Boveja, 1998). In other words, the children of the parents who set strict boundaries yet accept and show love toward them see the greatest educational success; a finding applicable to familial influences.

PSYCHOLOGICAL FACTORS

Similar to social-cultural factors, psychological factors have been found to affect education outcomes for urban African American students (Henfield, Moore, et al., 2008; Henfield, Owens, et al., 2008; Sanders, 1997). In many schools across America, urban African American students experience a host of psychological distress, such as racism, identity issues, and school disenchantment (Moore & Owens, 2008). Not in all instances but central to their experience, these students are frequently confronted with social issues that sometimes hamper them psychologically. In such cases, these students may disengage or disidentify with school. The following sections list some of the salient psychological factors that urban educators, such as teachers, school counselors, and school psychologists, need to be aware of.

Ethnic/Racial Identity Development

Adolescence is a transition period that is critical for establishing developmental trajectories relevant to psychological adjustment, coping, and identity development. For urban African American adolescents, the identity search includes the exploration of their racial/ethnic group membership in the context of White mainstream (Pahl & Way, 2006). Racial/ethnic identity development is a dynamic process that involves integrating both positive and negative perceptions of one's group (Oyserman, Gant, & Ager, 1995). Theories of ethnic identity development draw on both ego identity theory (Erikson, 1968) and social identity theory (Tajfel & Turner, 1986). Erikson (1968) asserts that the central crisis of development occurs in adolescence, when individuals have to resolve the conflict between identity versus confusion.

During this time of conflict, adolescents, including urban African American students, explore different roles before committing to an identity. Social identity theory, on the other hand, examines an individual's identification with social groups and the affective processes associated with group membership (Tajfel & Turner, 1986). In the case of urban African American students, identity development during adolescence involves the exploration of multiple social identities, including racial/ethnic identity (Pahl & Way, 2006). With this in mind, researchers in the past have proposed different models of racial/ethnic identity development (Cross, 1971; Cross & Vandiver, 2001; Helms, 1989; Phinney, 1989). For example, Phinney (1989) proposes a model of ethnic identity development for members of all ethnic groups in which individual's progress through three stages. In the first stage, *unexamined ethnic identity*, individuals have unexamined positive or negative views about their ethnic group. The second stage, *ethnic identity search*, involves beginning a search to understand what it means to be a member of one's own ethnic group. In the last stage, *achieved ethnic identity*, entails exploring one's ethnic group membership and the meaning ethnicity has in one's life.

Cross (1971) proposes a racial identity model that he calls "Nigrescence," which refers to becoming Black. Over the last three decades, his model has undergone numerous revisions. The most recently revised model (Cross & Vandiver, 2001) has eight identity types clustered into three major stages: *pre-encounter, immersion-emersion*, and *internalization*. Three identity types comprise the pre-encounter stage: *pre-encounter assimilation, pre-encounter miseducation*, and *pre-encounter racial self-hatred*. *Pre-encounter assimilation* involves a Black person who places little emphasis on racial group identity, affiliation, or salience and, as a result, is not engaged in the Black community and culture. *Pre-encounter miseducation* exemplifies a person who accepts the negative portrayal of Black people without question. This person often does not believe in the strength of the African American community and is hesitant to engage in working with it. The individual also frequently believes that she is different from other Black people and chooses to distance herself from them. The *pre-encounter racial self-hatred* type experiences deep negative feelings about being Black. Such feelings often limit the individual's positive engagement with Black problems and Black culture.

Two identity types characterize the immersion stage: *immersion-emersion anti-White* and *immersion-emersion intense Black involvement*. In *immersion-emersion anti-White*, the person is consumed with hatred toward White people and society. He or she engages in Black problems and culture but is full of fury and rage. In *immersion-emersion intense Black involvement*, the person holds a simplistic dedication to everything that is Black. Further, he or she engages in Blackness and holds a superior attitude toward others.

Three identity types comprise the final stage of internalization: *internalization nationalist*, *internalization biculturalist*, and *internalization multiculturalist*. *Internalization nationalists* stress an Afrocentric perspective about themselves, other African Americans, and the world. Without question, as compared to the pre-encounter miseducation type, these individuals engage much further with the Black community and its problems. *Internalization biculturalists* give equal importance to being an African American and an American. These individuals are able to celebrate and engage in both cultures without identity conflicts. *Internalization multiculturalists* are interested in resolving issues that address multiple cultural oppressions and are confident and comfortable in multiple groups.

Cross (1971) posits that, at any time, individuals can regress or stay at one stage. These models of racial/ethnic identity exemplify the heterogeneity of historically marginalized groups. Thus, not all African American students feel the same degree of affiliation toward their racial/ethnic group. The differences may explain why racial/ethnic identity can be a risk factor for achievement and psychological adjustment for some urban youth or a protective factor that facilitates success and positive adjustment for others. In closing, a strong racial/ethnic identity is associated with many positive benefits, including healthy psychological functioning; however, research also demonstrates its negative effects.

Over the years, several researchers have posited that having a strong racial identity places African Americans at risk for decreased academic engagement due to the increased awareness of the negative status of their racial group in society (e.g., Fordham, 1988; Fordham & Ogbu, 1986). However, other researchers suggest the opposite (e.g., Ford, 1996; Ford et al., 2006; Moore et al., 2005a, 2005b). Fordham and Ogbu (1986) present a cultural-ecological framework of ethnic minority achievement. The model illustrates that many involuntary minorities (e.g., African Americans) develop a collective identity that rejects ideals dominated by mainstream culture. In such cases, these students possess an oppositional view and reject the standard belief that they must be more like the dominant group (e.g., Whites) by doing well in school. Those individuals who achieve success are said to be "acting White" and face opposition from their peers for identifying with the mainstream (Fordham & Ogbu, 1986). As expected, this social exclusion can be detrimental to students' psyches and the degree to which they relate to their racial/ethnic group.

Other theories that perceive racial identity development as a threat to high academic achievement address coping strategies, such as a race-less persona, academic disidentification, stereotype threat, and cool pose theory. Fordham (1988) claims that African American students should develop a race-less persona by rejecting their own culture to be academically successful. In other words, the researcher suggests that a dual racial and academic identity is incompatible. Osborne (1997) finds that African American students disengage from school because to them academic success represents a social arena in which society regards their racial group negatively. The researcher presents results that indicate that African American students have higher self-esteem than Latino and White students but that their achievement grades drop over time, in specific between 10th and 12th grade.

In a similar viewpoint, stereotype threat theory (Steele, 1997) posits that out of fear of confirming the negative racial stereotypes related to their intellectual ability, African American students do not perform well academically. In consequence, they frequently identify and engage less with academics. Inadequate performance on an examination is not only personally damaging but also confirms the negative stereotype. Therefore, in order to protect their self-esteem, African American students sometimes devalue or reduce their identification with academics. To this end, it is important to note that Steele (1997) asserts that the stereotype threat tends only to affect academically identified students.

In order to escape this aversive situation, African American students commonly opt to disengage or withdraw from school. By disidentifying with school, these students no longer have to be concerned with how others evaluate them in terms of academics (Osborne, 1997). Withdrawal from school alleviates the worry by removing the student from the anxiety-provoking situation. Therefore, it is worth noting that academically identified students tend to be more at risk of dropping out or disidentifying from school due to the stereotype threat (Osborne & Walker, 2006).

Osborne and Walker (2006) examine the existence of the stereotype threat among a racially diverse sample of high school adolescents. The researchers find that for African American students, withdrawal is associated with higher identification with academics, whereas for Caucasian students, withdrawal is associated with lower identification with academics. These findings support Steele's (1997) stereotype threat theory and have significant implications concerning the importance of teaching coping strategies to prevent academic disidentification or withdrawal, not only for low-achieving urban African American students but also for those Black students who are highly academically identified.

Although the majority of research focuses on adolescents and adults, a study by McKown and Weinstein (2003) finds that children as young as age six become aware of others' stereotypes. More important, they find that this awareness increases dramatically with age. They also find that diagnostic testing of challenging cognitive tasks and self-reported effort lead to stereotype threat effects among academically diverse students. These findings directly contradict Steele's (1997) argument that only students strongly identified with school are affected by the stereotype threat, showing that it is a potential risk factor for all students. Nevertheless, children unaware of broadly held stereotypes do not show this pattern of performance.

Due to the importance of high-stakes testing, the finding that elementary school students' educational performance may be impaired as a result of stereotype threat is disturbing. This finding further demonstrates the impact stereotypes have on academic performance at such a young age. With this in mind, urban educators—teachers, school counselors, and school psychologists—require an awareness of the conditions that place African American students at risk for academic failure. They should develop prevention and intervention programs at the elementary school level to thwart the occurrence of academic disidentification.

Majors and Billson (1992) argue that some African American students, particularly the males, adopt a "cool pose," or the attitudes and behaviors that position them as calm, emotionless, and tough. A cool pose permits these students to cope in an environment of social oppression and racism, such as that which many urban youth experience in public schools. This persona—often thought to have been developed by African American males—buffers or masks the negative feelings caused by being a member of a stigmatized group. Although some of the coping mechanisms described protect students' self-concept, prevent the development of negative thoughts and feelings about themselves, and bar the negative psychological and emotional effects of racial discrimination, they are counterproductive in that academic outcomes suffer as a result. These strategies weaken the motivational attitudes and behaviors that lead to students' academic success. The theories discussed also underscore the belief that the only way African American students can have a positive academic identity is through disidentification with their culture (Smalls, White, Chavous, & Sellers, 2007).

Although these theories have identified a strong relationship between strong racial identity and poor academic performance, very little empirical evidence exists to support all of these assertions. Smalls et al. (2007) posit that few studies have directly assessed the relationship between racial identity attitudes and academic engagement in African American youth. For instance, Fordham and Ogbu's (1986) study does not ask students about their racial identity and its relation to their academic identity.

The low-achieving African American students in their study perceive behaviors, such as studying in the library, reading, and being on time, as inconsistent with their personal identities. Further, race is not discussed throughout the study.

RECOMMENDATIONS

It is evident that African American students, including urban ones, encounter many barriers throughout their educational journey. Educators need to be aware of their students' backgrounds; the effects these backgrounds have on their academic outcomes; and the knowledge of how to push their students past the school, psychological, and social-cultural barriers to achieve their full potential. In the following sections, we provide recommendations to urban teachers, school counselors, and school psychologists. In focusing our work on these education professionals, we believe that urban educators are key players in addressing the educational needs of urban African American youth.

Recommendations for Teachers

Teachers play a major role in the educational process for urban students; therefore, they need to make an assertive effort to establish genuine and caring relationships with their urban African American students (Kopetz, Lease, & Warren-Kring, 2006). Students often respond positively when they feel an adult is interested in who they are as individuals. It is widely accepted that student–teacher relationships can increase student engagement and classroom participation. Related to this point, Jenkins (2004) states that effective urban educators, including teachers, school counselors, and school psychologists, need to demonstrate high expectations, promote family involvement, not excuse student failure, and display patience for students' incremental success. Further, varied instruction is essential to engaging students in the learning environment.

Teachers who differentiate instruction in the classroom challenge students' thinking by promoting learning beyond their comfort zones; individualize study by accommodating their unique learning styles; involve all students in learning; and assess learning using a variety of evaluation methods (Burden, 2003). Instruction that utilizes visuals such as PowerPoint slides and videos, cooperative learning groups, parental involvement, building on previous student knowledge, and relevant lessons should be considered (Kopetz, Lease, & Warren-Kring, 2006). Cultural competence and the application of culturally relevant pedagogy also provide teachers the ability to better engage and teach African American students (Moore & Owens, 2008).

Henfield, Owens, et al. (2008) suggest that teachers should participate in professional development activities and trainings that increase their awareness of cultural biases and how they affect the learning environment. Low expectations for students perpetuate low academic performance as students become aware of how their teachers feel about them. Thus, teachers need to examine how their own perceptions and behaviors may impact their students' outcomes (Flowers et al., 2003; Moore & Owens, 2008).

Recommendations for School Counselors

School counselors are critical to students' success in high school, as well as college. They should work to promote social justice issues and equitable treatment of all students—throughout the school building—by maintaining the knowledge and skills necessary for working in urban schools. School counselors should also aim to develop positive relationships with their students and parents by creating an environment where they feel comfortable seeking out assistance (American School Counselor Association, 2006). In urban schools, school counselors should work with their principals to ensure that African American students have access to rigorous courses and curricula that will prepare them for college and future careers. As a part of students' academic plans, the school counselor's role includes providing them with information about careers and assisting in a selection of courses that will prepare them for attaining their career and postsecondary goals (Reid & Moore, 2008). In addition, urban school counselors should form an *ongoing* collaboration with students and their parents to assist with academic and career-planning decisions, as they may lack the social and cultural capital to make informed decisions. They can accomplish this goal by establishing and/or improving the relationships they have with the families of the students through innovative outreach and engagement activities (Henfield, Owens, et al., 2008). It is worth noting that forming close relationships with urban families can help school counselors become empowered as a proactive force in the educational success of their children (American School Counselor Association, 2009).

Urban school counselors should promote social justice by advocating for their students (Lee, 2005). They should also teach their students how to advocate for themselves, as well as how to navigate the education pipeline (i.e., at the elementary, secondary, and postsecondary levels). Because collaboration is a major component of school counselors' jobs, they should work to foster collaborative relationships with their colleagues (e.g., teachers and principals). Such collaborations can help increase their educational effectiveness, especially in social and structural school environments. Again, school counselors can be a major resource in an urban school building. Through their school-counseling graduate programs, they acquire a litany of skills, including the ability to develop and implement faculty development initiatives designed to increase awareness of the urban systemic factors that often impinge student development (American School Counselor Association, 2009).

Recommendations for School Psychologists

School psychologists are trained in various areas, such as assessment, consultation, counseling, and intervention. Therefore, they should collaborate with teachers, school counselors, and principals to determine how to best utilize the diversity of services that can be offered. Due to the multitude of barriers that often affect the achievement of urban African American youth, it is important for school psychologists to advocate for the use of evidence-based, culturally competent practice. For example, they could do this by helping their assigned schools change practices and policies that contribute to inequitable practices (National Association of School Psychologists, 2009). Similar to teachers and school counselors, school psychologists need to use their skills to ensure that students are given every opportunity to succeed. Further, school psychologists should act as instructional consultants for teachers, systems consultants for administrators, mental health practitioners, and advocates for students. Utilizing their consultant skills is an easy way to ensure that schools are responsive to the needs of their students.

As practitioners, school psychologists are trained to engage all relevant stakeholders, including students and families, in the academic or testing process from the onset. With this in mind, they should always work to develop positive and respectful relationships with their students and their families. In addition, they should work with their supervisors to ensure that they have the needed flexibility to fully engage in the process of assessment, intervention, consultation, and intervention (Sullivan & A'Vant, 2009). Not having this flexibility can easily compromise the services of students. Last, school psychologists should regularly initiate and provide professional development to their urban education colleagues. Due to the ethical standards mandated by the profession, school psychologists must receive ongoing continuous training. By receiving this, they often learn exemplary practices for the profession, which oftentimes they can translate to other professionals— like teachers, school counselors, and school psychologists. They could easily offer in-service presentations and trainings to their colleagues based on the professional development sessions that they attended.

CONCLUSION

As indicated in this chapter and others in this book, urban African American youth endure many challenges beyond the parameters of their schools. Urban schools and the staff that work in them must commit to educating their students with this in mind. Each school should develop an academic plan or road map that addresses the three broad factors mentioned in this chapter. The academic plan should outline the roles that education professionals, such as teachers, school counselors, and school psychologists, will play to ensure that the factors do not compromise their urban students' learning experiences and opportunities at their respective school(s). A strong commitment to educating urban African American youth is vital in assisting them in attaining success in school and beyond. It is essential that teachers, school counselors, and school psychologists understand the school and non-school experiences that urban African American youth bring to their education. Because the student issues go beyond the classroom, it is also critical that these professionals understand the importance of collaboration. Teachers, school counselors, and school psychologists all bring similar and unique skills to the table that need to be fully engaged to ensure academic success of urban African American students.

REFERENCES

Acevedo-Garcia, D., Rosenfeld, L. E., McArdle, N., & Osypuk, T. L. (2010). The geography of opportunity: A framework for child development. In C. Edley, Jr. & J. Ruiz de Valasco (Eds.), *Changing places: How communities will improve the health of boys of color* (pp. 358–406). Berkeley: University of California Press.

American School Counselor Association. (2006). *The professional school counselor and equity for all students*. Retrieved from http://asca2.timberlakepublishing.com//files/PS_Equity.pdf

American School Counselor Association (2009). *The professional school counselor and cultural diversity*. Retrieved from http://asca2.timberlakepublishing.com//files/CulturalDiversity.pdf

Barajas, H. L., & Ronnkvist, A. (2007). Racialized space: Framing Latino and Latina experience in public schools. *Teachers College Record, 109*(6), 1517–1538.

Bergin, D. A., & Cooks, H. C. (2002). High school students of color talk about accusations of "acting White." *The Urban Review, 34*(2), 113–134.

Berliner, D. C., & Biddle, B. J. (1995). *The manufactured crisis: Myths, fraud, and the attack on America's public schools*. Reading, MA: Addison-Wesley.

Booker, K. C. (2007). Likeness, comfort, and tolerance: Examining African American adolescents' sense of school belonging. *The Urban Review, 39*(3), 301–317.

Borland, J. H., Schnur, R., & Wright, L. (2000). Economically disadvantaged students in a school for the academically gifted: A postpositivist inquiry into individual and family adjustment. *Gifted Child Quarterly, 44*(1), 13–32.

Boveja, M. E. (1998). Parenting styles and adolescents' learning strategies in the urban community. *Journal of Multicultural Counseling and Development, 26*(2), 110–119.

Burden, P. R. (2003). *Classroom management: Creating a successful learning community* (2nd ed.). New York, NY: Wiley.

Cammarota, J. (2004). The gendered and racialized pathways of Latina and Latino youth: Different struggles, different resistances in the urban context. *Anthropology & Education Quarterly, 35*(1), 53–74.

Casella, R. (2003). Punishing dangerousness through preventive detention: Illustrating the institutional link between school and prison. In J. Wald & D. J. Losen (Eds.), *New directions for youth development: Deconstructing the school-to-prison pipeline* (pp. 55–70). San Francisco, CA: Jossey-Bass.

Close, W., & Solberg, S. (2008). Predicting achievement, distress, and retention among lower income Latino youth. *Journal of Vocational Behavior, 72*(1), 31–42.

Cross, W. E., Jr. (1971). The Negro-to-Black Conversion Experience. *Black World, 20*(9), 13–27.

Cross, W. E., Jr., & Vandiver, B. J. (2001). Nigrescence theory and measurement: Introducing the Cross Racial Identity Scale (CRIS). In J. G. Ponterotto, J. M. Casas, L. A. Suzuki, & C. M. Alexander (Eds.), *Handbook of multicultural counseling* (2nd ed.; pp. 371–393). Thousand Oaks, CA: Sage.

Erikson, E. H. (1968). *Identity: Youth and crisis.* New York, NY: Norton.

Farkas, G. (2003). Racial disparities and discrimination in education: What do we know, how do we know it, and what do we need to know? *Teachers College Record, 105*(6), 1119–1146.

Fenning, P., & Rose, J. (2007). Overrepresentation of African American students in exclusionary discipline: The role of school policy. *Urban Education, 42*, 536–559.

Flowers, L. A., Milner, H. R., & Moore, J. L., III. (2003). Effects of locus of control on African American high school seniors' educational aspirations: Implications for preservice and inservice high school teachers and counselors. *The High School Journal, 87*(1), 39–50.

Ford, D. Y. (1996). *Reversing underachievement among gifted black males: Promising practices and programs.* New York, NY: Teachers College Press.

Ford, D. Y. (1998). The underrepresentation of minority students in gifted education: Problems and promises in recruitment and retention. *Journal of Special Education, 32*(1), 4–14.

Ford, D. Y., & Harris, J. J., III. (1996). Perceptions and attitudes of Black students toward school, achievement, and other educational variables. *Child Development, 67*(3), 1141–1152.

Ford, D. Y., & Moore, J. L., III. (2004). The achievement gap and gifted students of color. *Understanding Our Gifted, 16*, 3–7.

Ford, D. Y., Whiting, G. W., & Moore, J. L., III. (2009). Gifts and talents denied: Under-representation of culturally and linguistically different students in gifted education. *Journal of Urban Education: Focus on Enrichment, 6*, 27–43.

Ford, D. Y., Wright, L. B., Grantham, T. C., Harris, J., III. (1998). Achievement levels, outcomes, and orientations of black students in single-and two-parent families. *Urban Education, 33*(3), 360–384.

Fordham, S. (1988). Racelessness as a factor in black students' school success: Pragmatic strategy or pyrrhic victory? *Harvard Educational Review, 58*(1), 54–84.

Fordham, S., & Ogbu, J. (1986). Black students' school success: Coping with the "burden of acting White." *Urban Review, 18*(3), 176–206.

Gregory, A., & Mosely, P. M. (2004). The discipline gap: Teachers' views on the overrepresentation of African American students in the discipline system. *Equity & Excellence in Education, 37*(1), 18–30.

Hébert, T. H., & Reis, S. M. (1999). Culturally diverse high-achieving students in an urban high school. *Urban Education, 34*(4), 428–457.

Helms, J. E. (1989). Considering some methodological issues in racial identity counseling research. *The Counseling Psychologist, 17*(2), 227–252.

Henfield, M. S., Moore, J. L., III, & Wood, C. (2008). Inside and outside gifted education programming: Hidden challenges for African American students. *Exceptional Children, 74*(4), 433–450.

Henfield, M. S., Owens, D., & Moore, J. L., III. (2008). Influences on young gifted African Americans' school success: Implications for elementary school counselors. *Elementary School Journal, 108*(5), 392–406.

Horvat, E. M., & Lewis, K. S. (2003). Reassessing the "burden of 'acting White": The importance of peer groups in managing academic success. *Sociology of Education, 76*(4), 265–280.

Iceland, J., Weinberg, D. H., & Steinmetz, E. (2002). *Racial and ethnic residential segregation in the United States: 1980–2000* (U.S. Census Bureau, Census Special Report, CENSR-3). Washington, DC: U.S. Government Printing Office.

Jackson, J. F. L., & Moore, J. L., III. (2006). African American males in education: Endangered or ignored? *Teachers College Record, 108*(2), 201–205.

Jackson, J. F. L., & Moore, J. L., III. (2008). The African American male crisis in education: A popular media infatuation or needed public policy response? *American Behavioral Scientist, 51*(7), 847–853.

Jenkins, W. L. (2004). *Understanding and educating African-American children* (12th rev. ed.). St. Louis, MO: William Jenkins.

Johnson, T., Boyden, J. E. & Pittz, W. J. (2001). *Racial profiling and punishment in U.S. public schools: How zero tolerance policies and high stakes testing subvert academic excellence and racial equity.* Oakland, CA: Appliked Research Center.

Khadduri, J., Schwartz, H., & Turnham, J. (2007). *Reconnecting schools and neighborhoods: An introduction to school-centered community revitalization.* Columbia, MD: Enterprise Community Partners.

Kopetz, P. B., Lease, A. J., & Warren-Kring, B. Z. (2006). *Comprehensive urban education.* Boston, MA: Pearson.

Kozol, J. (1991). *Savage Inequalities: Children in America's schools.* New York, NY: Crown.

Lee, C. C. (2005). Urban school counseling: Context, characteristics, and competencies. *Professional School Counseling, 8*(3), 184–188.

Leventhal, T., & Brooks-Gunn, J. (2000). The neighborhoods they live in: The effects of neighborhood residence upon child and adolescent outcomes. *Psychological Bulletin, 126*(2), 309–337.

Levin, H., Belfield, C., Muennig, P., & Rouse, C. (2007). The public returns to public educational investments in African American males. *Economics of Education Review, 26*, 699–708.

Lewis, C. W., & Moore, J. L., III. (2008). African American students in K-12 urban educational settings. *Urban Education, 43*(2), 123–126.

Lindstrom, R. R., & Van Sant, S. (1986). Special issues in working with gifted minority adolescents. *Journal of Counseling and Development, 64*(9), 583–586.

Majors, R., & Billson, J. M. (1992). *Cool pose: The dilemmas of Black manhood in America.* New York, NY: Lexington Books.

McKown, C., & Weinstein, R. S. (2003). The development and consequences of stereotype consciousness in middle childhood. *Child Development, 74*(2), 498–515.

Mickelson, R. A., & Velasco, A. E. (2006). Bring it on! Diverse responses to "acting White" among academically able Black adolescents. In E. M. Horvat & C. O'Connor (Eds.), *Beyond acting White: Reframing the debate on Black student achievement* (pp. 57–88). Lanham, MD: Rowman & Littlefield.

Monroe, C. R., & Obidah, J. E. (2004). The influence of cultural synchronization on a teacher's perception of disruption: A case study of an African American middle school classroom. *Journal of Teacher Education, 55*(3), 256–268.

Moore, J. L., III. (2006). A qualitative investigation of African American males' career trajectory in Engineering: Implications for teachers, school counselors, and parents. *Teachers College Record, 108*(2), 246–266.

Moore, J. L., III, Ford, D. Y., & Milner, H. R. (2005a). Recruitment is not enough: Retaining African-American students in gifted education. *Gifted Child Quarterly, 49*(1), 51–67.

Moore, J. L., III, Ford, D. Y., & Milner, H. R. (2005b). Underachievement among gifted students of color: Implications for educators. *Theory Into Practice, 44*(2), 167–177.

Moore, J. L., III, Henfield, M. S., & Owens, D. (2008). African American males in special education: Their attitudes and perceptions toward high school counselors and school counseling services. *American Behavioral Scientist, 51*(7), 907–927.

Moore, J. L., III, & Owens, D. (2008). Educating and counseling African American students: Recommendations for teachers and school counselors. In L. Tillman (Ed.), *The Sage Handbook of African American education* (pp. 351–366). Thousand Oaks, CA: Sage.

Nasir, N. S., McLaughlin, M. W., & Jones, A. (2009). What does it mean to be African American? Constructions of race and academic identity in an urban public high school. *American Educational Research Journal, 46*, 73–114.

National Association of School Psychologists. (2009). *Appropriate behavioral, social, and emotional supports to meet the needs of all students.* Bethesda, MD: Author. Retrieved from http://www. nasponline.org/about_nasp/positionpapers/appropriatebehavioralsupports.pdf

Noguera, P. A. (2003). Schools, prisons, and social implications of punishment: Rethinking disciplinary practices. *Theory into Practice, 42*(4), 341–350

Ogbu, J. (2004). Collective identity and the burden of "acting White" in Black history, community, and education. *The Urban Review, 36*, 1–35.

Orfield, G., & Lee, C. (2007). Historic reversals, accelerating resegregation, and the need for new integration strategies. Los Angeles, CA: The Civil Rights Project [Proyecto Derechos Civiles], UCLA.

Osborne, J. W. (1997). Race and academic disidentification. *Journal of Educational Psychology, 89*(4), 728–735.

Osborne, J. W., & Walker, C. (2006). Stereotype threat, identification with academics, and withdrawal from school: Why the most successful students of colour might be most likely to withdraw. *Educational Psychology, 26*(4), 563–577.

Oyserman, D., Gant, L., & Ager, J. (1995). A socially contextualized model of African American identity: Possible selves and school persistence. *Journal of Personality and Social Psychology, 69*(6), 1216–1232.

Pahl, K., & Way, N. (2006). Longitudinal trajectories of ethnic identity among urban black and Latino adolescents. *Child Development, 77*(5), 1403–1415.

Phinney, J. S. (1989). Stages of ethnic identity development in minority group adolescents. *Journal of Early Adolescence, 9*(1/2), 34–49.

Reid, M. J., & Moore, J. L., III. (2008). College readiness and academic preparation for postsecondary education: Oral histories of first-generation urban college students. *Urban Education, 43*, 240–261.

Reis, S. M., & Diaz, E. I. (1999). Economically disadvantaged urban female students who achieve in school. *The Urban Review, 31*(1), 31–54.

Rolon-Dow, R. (2007). Passing time: An exploration of school engagement among Puerto Rican girls. *The Urban Review, 39*(3), 49–72.

Ryan, A. M., & Pintrich, P. R. (1997). "Should I ask for help?" The role of motivation and attitudes in adolescents' help seeking in math class. *Journal of Educational Psychology, 89*(2), 329–341.

Ryan, A. M., Pintrich, P. R., & Midgley, C. (2001). Avoiding seeking help in the classroom: Who and why? *Educational Psychology Review, 13*(2), 93–114.

Sánchez, B., Colón, Y., & Esparza, P. (2005). The role of sense of school belonging and gender in the academic adjustment of Latino adolescents. *Journal of Youth and Adolescence, 34*(6), 619–628.

Sanders, M. G. (1997). Overcoming obstacles: Academic achievement as a response to racism and discrimination. *The Journal of Negro Education, 66*(1), 83–93.

Scott, M. S., Perou, R., Urbano, R., Hogan, A., & Gold, S. (1992) The identification of giftedness: A comparison of white, Hispanic and black families. *Gifted Child Quarterly, 36*, 131–139.

Skiba, R. J., Michael, R. S., Nardo, A. C., & Peterson, R. (2002). The color of discipline: Sources of racial and gender disproportionality in school punishment. *The Urban Review, 34*(4), 317–342.

Skiba, R. J., & Rausch, M. K. (2006). Zero tolerance, suspension, and expulsion: Questions of equity and effectiveness. In C. M. Everston & C. S. Weinstein (Eds.), *Handbook of classroom management: Research, practice, and contemporary issues* (pp. 1063–1092). Mahwah, NJ: Lawrence Erlbaum.

Skiba, R. J., & Rausch, M.K. (2008). School disciplinary systems: Alternatives to suspension and expulsion. In G. G. Bear & K. M. Minke (Eds.), *Children's needs III: Development, prevention, and intervention* (pp. 87–102). Bethesda, MD: National Association of School Psychologists.

Smalls, C., White, R., Chavous, T., & Sellers, R. (2007). Racial ideological beliefs and racial discrimination as predictors of academic engagement among African American adolescents. *Journal of Black Psychology, 33*(3), 299–330.

Spencer, M. B., Noll, E., Stoltzfus, J., & Harpalani, V. (2001). Identity and school adjustment: Revisiting the "acting White" assumption. *Educational Psychologist, 36*(1), 21–30.

Steele, C. M. (1997). A threat in the air: How stereotypes shape intellectual identity and performance. *American Psychologist, 52*(6), 613–629.

Sullivan, A. L., & A'Vant, E. (2009). On the need for cultural responsiveness. *Communiqué, 38*(3). Retrieved from http://www.nasponline.org/publications/cq/mocq383culturalresponsive.aspx

Tajfel, H., & Turner, J. (1986). The social identity theory of intergroup behavior. In S. Worchel & W. G. Austin (Eds.), *Psychology of intergroup relations* (pp. 7–24). Chicago, IL: Nelson.

Tenenbaum, H. R., & Ruck, M. D. (2007). Are teachers' expectations different for racial minority than for European American students? A meta-analysis. *Journal of Educational Psychology, 99*(2), 253–273.

Tsoi-A-Fratt, R. (2010). *We dream a world: The 2025 vision for black men and boys.* Washington, DC: Center for Law and Social Policy.

Tyson, K. (2006). The making of a "burden": Tracing the development of a "burden of acting white" in schools. In E.M. Horvat & C. O'Connor (Eds.), *Beyond acting white: Reframing the debate on black student achievement* (pp. 57–88). Lanham, MD: Rowman & Littlefield.

Tyson, K., Darity, W., Jr., & Castellino, D. R. (2005). It's not "a Black thing": Understanding the burden of acting White and other dilemmas of high achievement. *American Sociological Review, 70*(4), 582–605.

Weinstein, C., Curran, M., & Tomlinson-Clarke, S. (2003). Culturally responsive classroom management: Awareness into action. *Theory Into Practice, 42*(4), 269–276.

Wiggan, G. (2008). From opposition to engagement: Lessons from high achieving African American students. *The Urban Review, 40*(4), 317–349.

PART THREE

CULTURALLY RELEVANT PEDAGOGY IN URBAN CLASSROOMS

CHAPTER EIGHT

Developing Culturally Relevant Classrooms FOR Urban African American Students

H. RICHARD MILNER IV

In this chapter, I outline some of what we—those of us in education—have come to know about how to develop culturally relevant classrooms for urban[1] African American students. It is important to note that, although the target group of this chapter is Black students, many of the practices and ideas outlined are transferable to other school contexts and other groups of students. I also discuss why it is critical to develop culturally relevant spaces for urban African American students, especially during a time when urban educators struggle to meet the complex and multifaceted needs of these students in urban educational settings. At the heart of this discussion is the question of what culturally relevant pedagogy is and how urban educators develop learning environments that are grounded in and from the cultural experiences of urban African American students. More than a set of principles, ideas, or practices, what I hope to demonstrate and advocate in this chapter is that culturally relevant pedagogy is more of a state of being or mindset than a specific or prescribed set of principles or practices.

In an important chapter called "Yes, but How Do We Do It? Practicing Culturally Relevant Pedagogy," Gloria Ladson-Billings (2006) shares an interaction that she had with a prospective teacher. This teacher expressed the following to her: "Everybody keeps telling us about multicultural education, but nobody is telling us how to do it!" (p. 30). Perplexing to many of those in her audience,

Ladson-Billings laments "Even if we could tell you how to do it, I would not want us to tell you how to do it" (p. 39). There are at least two important points involved in Ladson-Billings' response to the prospective teacher who questioned how to "do" multicultural education and culturally relevant teaching. For one, teachers, including urban, provide educational experiences to a range of students who bring an enormous range of diversity into the learning environment. There are no one-size-fits-all approaches to the work of teaching. It is critical that urban teachers are mindful of the students they are teaching and the range of needs they bring into the classrooms. Moreover, the social context that shapes urban students' experiences is vast and integral in a complex way to what decisions are made; to how the decisions are made; and to why urban students' needs vary from year to year, classroom to classroom, and school to school. A second point that can be taken from Ladson-Billings's response is that no one tells us how to "do democracy" (p. 39); we just do it.

In a similar light, urban teachers who practice culturally relevant pedagogy do so because it is consistent with what they believe and who they are. Their belief system guides their practices. In short, teachers practice culturally relevant pedagogy because they believe in it and think that it is the right practice to foster, support, create, and enable students' learning opportunities. Teachers practice democracy for similar reasons. People are not told how to do democracy; rather, they practice democracy because they believe in its fundamental principles and ideals (Ladson-Billings, 2006).

Before expounding upon how (and why) urban teachers develop culturally relevant classrooms for urban African American students, I highlight some prevailing assumptions and realities about these students, particularly in urban school settings. Addressing the needs of African American students in urban schools is multilayered, and there are numerous factors and dimensions to addressing their needs. I am certainly not suggesting that creating culturally relevant classrooms automatically results in some magical academic outcomes for urban African American students. It is important that urban educators do not think of these approaches as the panacea to students and teachers' problems. Thinking about urban African American students and their experiences, worldviews, behaviors, and outcomes is an important task that should be continuously studied and addressed—from policies to practices—in order to meet these students' needs. After a discussion of needs of urban African American students, I shift to another discussion that elucidates culturally relevant pedagogy. I then showcase the practices of a teacher who develops a culturally relevant classroom in an urban school setting. I conclude this chapter with implications and conclusions that have a strong emphasis on educational equity and social action.

AFRICAN AMERICAN STUDENTS' EXPERIENCES IN URBAN SCHOOLS

There is no single African American[2] culture.[3] The term African American denotes an ethnic group of people—not a singular static cultural group; there is a wide range of diversity among and between African Americans, although there are some consistencies inherent to the experiences of African Americans (Banks, 2006; Milner, 2008). For instance, African Americans share a history of slavery, Jim Crow, and other forms of systemic discrimination and racism that binds them. African Americans also possess a shared history of spiritual grounding, tenacity, and resilience that they have maintained through some of the most horrific situations that human beings have had to endure (Anderson, 1988). However, although there are shared experiences, there are also many differences among African Americans. Take, for instance, the variance between former Secretary of State Condoleezza Rice and current National Football League (NFL) player Michael Vick (currently playing for the Philadelphia Eagles). The differences between these two African Americans are significantly greater than those of gender. Although Rice and Vick are both African American and share some similarities between them, there are countless differences as well. Thus, it is critical that readers of this chapter do not essentialize or generalize the points discussed about African Americans herein, and it is critical that they do not consider the ideas discussed about African Americans to be static and pejorative.

What seems to be clear about the education of urban African American students is that they have been consistently underserved and undereducated in urban PK–12 schools across U.S. society (Irvine, 1990; Tillman, 2004; Woodson, 1933). Where urban African American students are concerned, Ladson-Billings (2000) wrote: "As a group, African Americans have been told systematically and consistently that they are inferior, that they are incapable of high academic achievement. Their performance in school has replicated this low expectation for success" (p. 208). In essence, urban teachers often have low expectations for their urban African American students, and they teach down to them, often watering down the curriculum and not planning adequately to meet their needs (Milner, 2009). Urban teachers sometimes fail to see the brilliance in these students, because they are not equipped to recognize their talents, creativity, and intellectual prowess (Milner, 2008). They often see difference and being different (that is, in terms of students' conceptions, beliefs, convictions, values, and behaviors that are inconsistent with their own) as wrong. Moreover, urban teachers may equate the different ways in which African American students express themselves (through discourse, for instance), dress, or approach and address an issue (Milner, 2009) as involving a deficit or deficiency (Ford, 1996). The common idea is that different means deficient or substandard, and urban teachers are not prepared to recognize that excellence emerges in various contexts and among various groups of students including African American students in urban schools (Milner, 2008; Morris, 2004).

African American students are grossly underrepresented in gifted education and overrepresented in special education (Artiles, Klingner, & Tate, 2006; Ford, 2006; Moore, Ford, & Milner, 2005). Where trends in gifted education are concerned, Ford (2006) found: "Sadly, I have seen little progress relative to demographic changes—Black and Hispanic students continue to be as underrepresented in gifted programs today as they were 20 years ago" (p. 2). Although the educational experiences of urban African American students in general are often dismal at best, the experiences of African American males are often even more troubling. In a report from the Schott Foundation for Public Education entitled *Public Education and Black Male Students: A State Report Card,* Holzman (2004) explained:

> In many school districts, up to 70 percent of black boys who enter 9th grade do not graduate four years later with their peers. In most districts, black boys are disproportionately assigned to special education and nearly absent from advanced placement classes. (p. 2)

In short, Holzman reveals that "In 2001/2002 59% of African-American males did not receive diplomas with their cohort[s]" (p. 4). When focused on urban cities and graduation patterns, the author illustrates that "New York City and Chicago, for example, enrolling nearly 10% of the nation's Black male students between them, fail to graduate 70% of those with their peers" (p. 4).

More recent data substantiate these earlier findings. According to the National Center for Education Statistics (2007), African American students graduate at a significantly lower rate than their White student counterparts: In 2005, a graduation rate of 60.3% for African American students compared to 80.4% for White students. Further, in 2005, the percentage of high school dropouts was disproportionately higher for African American students than for White students: 10.4% compared to 6%, respectively. These trends seem to persist, although some data suggest that African American students are improving in these areas.

In addition to these troubling realities regarding retention and attrition for urban African Americans in school, these students are expelled from classes at an alarming rate. Skiba, Michael, Nardo, and Peterson (2002) analyzed the disciplinary records of 11,001 students in 19 middle schools in a large urban Midwestern public school district during the 1994–1995 academic year and report a "differential pattern of treatment, originating at the classroom level, wherein African American students are referred to the office for infractions that are more subjective in interpretation" (p. 317). Different behaviors are often equated with insubordination: Teachers may see urban African American students as defiant and disrespectful.

The Skiba et al. (2002) study illustrates that students of color overwhelmingly receive harsher punishments for misbehavior than do their White counterparts. As an example, the authors describe a fistfight at a high school football game in Decatur, Illinois. This event resulted in the school superintendent recommending that all seven of the African American students involved be expelled from school for two years. In a very similar situation involving all White students, a less severe punishment was granted. The real question is: Why are some groups of students— particularly African American students—punished more severely and more frequently than are others? The reality is that when African American students are not in the classroom due to office referrals and consequently in and out of school as a result of suspension and expulsion, they are missing out on important instructional time (Davis & Jordan, 1994). Their performance on academic measures is thusly affected. Based on what I have come to know about successful practices of urban teachers, I am doubtful that practices like culturally relevant pedagogy are prevalent in spaces in which African American students' experiences are so disturbing. I turn now to elucidate the construct of culturally relevant pedagogy.

CULTURALLY RELEVANT PEDAGOGY

The term *culturally relevant pedagogy* is often used to discuss or describe the theory of culturally relevant teaching, whereas the term *culturally relevant teaching* is used to describe the practice of the theory (Ladson-Billings, 1994, 2006). In this section and subsequent sections of the chapter, I use both *pedagogy* and *teaching* interchangeably. Over the years, researchers have made a compelling case for the importance of developing culturally relevant curricula and instruction for students, even African American students, in the urban PK–12 classroom (cf. Foster, 1997; Howard, 2001; Ladson-Billings, 1994). Ladson-Billings (1992), the scholar responsible for coining and conceptualizing culturally relevant pedagogy, maintains that it is an approach that:

> serves to empower students to the point where they will be able to examine critically educational content and process and ask what its role is in creating a truly democratic and multicultural society. It uses the students' culture to help them create meaning and understand the world. Thus, not only academic success, but also social and cultural success is emphasized. (p. 110)

Central to this approach is the notion that teachers develop skills to understand the complexities of students' cultural ways of experiencing the world. Moreover, the construct suggests that students develop a critical consciousness and that they move beyond spaces where they simply or solely consume knowledge without critically examining it. So, the idea is that teachers create learning environments in which students can develop voice and perspective and are allowed to participate (more fully) in the multiple discourses available in a learning context (Milner, 2008). For example, Ladson-Billings (1994) explains,

> Culturally relevant pedagogy uses student culture in order to maintain it and to transcend the negative effects of the dominant culture. The negative effects are brought about, for example, by not seeing one's history, culture, or background represented in the textbook or curriculum . . . culturally relevant teaching is a pedagogy that empowers students intellectually, socially, emotionally, and politically by using cultural referents to impart knowledge, skills, and attitudes. (pp. 17–18)

Urban educators who develop culturally relevant spaces see students' culture as an asset, not a detriment to their success (Banks, 2006). In other words, they actually use students' culture in their curriculum planning and implementation, and they also allow students to develop the skills to question how power structures are created and maintained in U.S. society. In this sense, the teacher is not the only, nor the main, arbiter of knowledge (McCutcheon, 2002).

In culturally relevant spaces, students are expected and empowered to develop intellectually and socially to build skills to make meaningful and transformative contributions to society. In addition, culturally relevant pedagogy is an approach that helps students "see the contradictions and inequities that existed in their local community and the larger world" (Ladson-Billings, 1992, p. 382). Through culturally relevant teaching, urban teachers prepare students with the skills to question inequity and fight against the many isms and phobias that they encounter, while enabling students to transfer what they have learned through classroom instructional/learning opportunities to other experiences both inside and outside of school (Milner, 2008).

TENETS OF CULTURALLY RELEVANT PEDAGOGY

Three interrelated tenets shape Ladson-Billings' conception of culturally relevant pedagogy: (a) academic achievement, (b) cultural competence, and (c) sociopolitical consciousness. The theory behind this type of pedagogy—similar to theoretical orientations in other disciplines—has taken on multiple and varied meanings depending on the researcher building from it and for what purpose it is being used. Ladson-Billings (2006) expresses her regret for using the term academic achievement in her first iteration of the theory, partly because people immediately equated academic achievement with student test scores. What Ladson-Billings actually envisions, however, is that culturally relevant pedagogy allows for and facilitates student learning. In other words, she is interested in ascertaining "what it is that students actually know and are able to do as a result of pedagogical interactions with skilled teachers" (p. 34). Thus, the type of academic achievement she envisions has to do with teachers being able to help students understand why they are learning what they are learning in spaces where students can develop the knowledge and skills necessary for success.

Cultural competence, the second tenet of culturally relevant pedagogy, is not necessarily about helping teachers develop a set of static information about differing cultural groups in order to develop some sensitivity toward the "other culture." Rather, cultural competence is first about students' cultural acquisition, not that of the teachers. Such a position on cultural competence runs counter to the ways in which other disciplines, such as medicine, clergy, and social work, might think about the concept (Ladson-Billings, 2006). What Ladson-Billings means by cultural competence is "helping students to recognize and honor their own cultural beliefs and practices while acquiring access to the wider culture, where they are likely to have a chance of improving socioeconomic status and making informed decisions about the lives they wish to lead" (p. 36).

Cultural competence also concerns the ability of teachers to help foster student learning about themselves, others, and how the world works to function effectively in it. The idea is that, in order to have a seat at the table of those in power, students must deeply understand who those in power are. This allows them to participate in and contribute to the conversation and ultimately to challenge, change, and transform power structures such as sexism. Thus, cultural competence is about developing a deepened knowledge about the self and the self in relation to others (Milner, 2008).

The third tenet of culturally relevant pedagogy, sociopolitical consciousness, is about focusing on the micro- and macrolevel matters that have a bearing on urban teachers' and students' lived experiences (Ladson-Billings, 2006). The idea that occurrences, such as the unemployment rate, that play a meaningful role in national debates as well as in local realities for teachers and students should be incorporated into curricula and instructional opportunities to enable both teachers and students' consciousness. Ladson-Billings (2006) stresses that sociopolitical consciousness is not about teachers pushing their own political and social agendas in the classroom; rather, it is about helping "students use the various skills they learn to better understand and critique their social position and context" (p. 37). Although Ladson-Billings has outlined the three main features of the theory (e.g., academic achievement, cultural competence, and sociopolitical consciousness), the theory has grown, developed, and evolved in some important ways.

OUTCOMES OF CULTURALLY RELEVANT CLASSROOMS

One important question regarding culturally relevant urban classrooms has to do with the relationship between culturally relevant pedagogy and student outcomes; that is, what are student outcomes when their classroom contexts are shaped by and grounded in culturally relevant pedagogy? The answer to this question is not one that, I believe, can be answered by looking exclusively at students' test score performance. Rather, the outcomes of culturally relevant urban classroom contexts seem to extend far beyond what might be measured on a standardized exam. Grounded in Ladson-Billings's ideology, as well as in my own research and the studies of others (Howard, 2001; Milner, 2008), student outcomes can be captured in at least three broad categories, especially if readers are willing to think of African American student outcomes as being prevalent and possible beyond traditional test measures.

One outcome of urban African American students who experience culturally relevant classrooms seems to be empowerment (Ladson-Billings, 2006). Students are empowered to examine what they are learning more intently, to create and construct their own meanings, to succeed academically and socially, and to gauge contradictions and inequities both in- and outside of school. In addition, culturally relevant classrooms allow urban African American students to see their culture in the curriculum and instruction, and students are encouraged to maintain this focus. And third, in culturally relevant classrooms, urban African American students are challenged through learning opportunities that are innovative and through learning opportunities that allow them to meaningfully understand the sociopolitical nature of society (Ladson-Billings, 2006). In Figure 1, I attempt to capture and summarize some of the outcomes of culturally relevant urban classrooms.

Culturally Relevant Pedagogy
EMPOWERS students to • examine educational content and processes • create and construct their own meanings • succeed academically and socially • see contradictions and inequities in local and larger communities **INCORPORATES** student culture in • curriculum and teaching • maintaining a focus on students' culture • transcending the negative effects of the dominant culture **CREATES** classroom contexts that • are challenging and innovative • focus on student learning (and consequently academic achievement) • build cultural competence • link curriculum and instruction to sociopolitical realities

Fig. 1. An Outcomes Summary

A LOOK AT A CULTURALLY RELEVANT TEACHER

In this section, I showcase a teacher from a study I conducted during the 2005–2006 academic year at Bridge Middle School who developed a culturally relevant classroom setting.[4] Although I describe the successful practices of an African American teacher, it is important to note that urban teachers from any racial or ethnic background can be (and are!) classified as culturally relevant teachers (cf., Cooper, 2003; Ladson-Billings, 1994). In addition, although I am focusing on the practices of a teacher rather than a classroom, readers should keep in mind that it is teachers who develop the kinds of classroom contexts that can be described as culturally relevant. This is true for urban classrooms, as well as suburban and rural settings. Thus, there is an inseparable connection between who teachers are, what they believe, what they do, and the classroom milieu that is constructed and sustained over a period of time (Milner, 2008).

Mr. Jackson is a male African American mathematics and science teacher who, at the time of the study, had been teaching for 7 years as a certified teacher but had been in the district for 10 years working as an assistant or substitute teacher the remaining three years. Mr. Jackson always wore a shirt, tie, and most of the time a suit jacket. He wore glasses and could be found standing in front of his classroom door between classes. He often reminded students (i.e., students whom he had taught as well as others) to "be mindful of the time," as he warned them not to be late for class. He had a deep love and appreciation for music, and this love and appreciation filtered into his curriculum development and teaching. In particular, Mr. Jackson enjoyed jazz, pop, R & B, classical, and hip-hop music; music was almost always playing softly during his mathematics and science classes. In the following section, I focus on four recurrent themes that capture Mr. Jackson's culturally relevant classroom: (a) the value of learning, (b) targeting power and image among students, (c) immersion in students' world(s), and (d) the intersection of music and learning.

The Value of Learning

Mr. Jackson stresses that his pedagogy and classroom are shaped by the idea of helping his students find the value and relevance of school for their lives. In other words, because students often "care most" about impressing their friends and because they are often more interested in what is happening in other aspects of their lives (e.g., dating, sports, and other hobbies) than in school, Mr. Jackson realizes that it is critical for him to help them see school as a "hip" and "cool" place to be. With this in mind, he wants his students to see the value of school and the value of learning. Further, Mr. Jackson shares,

> The biggest struggle in most urban schools is getting over the 'It's not cool to learn fac-
> tor.' Once you break those barriers and you get your classroom management in check
> everything rolls pretty smooth. But that [the idea that school is not cool] is a microcosm
> of our society.

Mr. Jackson feels that, "The biggest struggle is getting . . . the children to understand how important education is and that it is ok to act cool and be smart and intelligent" at the same time. In class, Mr. Jackson targets and "hooks" the students whom other students in the school view as "cool" or hip.

As in all schools, there is a power structure among the students at Bridge Middle School. In some schools, the student athletes are at the top of the hierarchy. In other schools, the valedictorian is considered to be the cool, popular, and powerful student. At Bridge Middle School, according to Mr. Jackson and based on my observations, the athletes and cheerleaders are often held in the highest esteem among their peers. At school, Mr. Jackson works to get the students who are considered popular and cool on his "side" in the classroom and to engage them in the learning of the classroom. In this way, Mr. Jackson develops a classroom setting that promotes and stresses the importance of learning and doing well in school. Mr. Jackson believes that once students witness the cool students being actively involved in learning opportunities that the majority of other students will get connected. In essence, Mr. Jackson is attempting to foster a value of learning by targeting the "most powerful" students in his class to serve as implicit role models for their classmates.

Targeting Power and Image Among Students

Mr. Jackson believes that targeting powerful students is critical from the very beginning of the school year and that it is necessary to use such power as an anchor for the engagement and learning of all students. In essence, he wants to get the popular students to embrace his vision for the class, so that other students will follow their lead. As an example of this, Mr. Jackson shares:

> I try to target the coolest. I try to target the toughest. I try to target the most popular stu-
> dents, and I get them to understand and follow my vision. And once I get them, the rest of
> the class usually follows.

It is important to note that Mr. Jackson is not suggesting that he does not want his students to develop the critical consciousness that is such a powerful feature of culturally relevant teaching. What he is suggesting is that, fundamentally, he needs to create a classroom context in which students are committed to learning and engaging in classroom learning opportunities. So, when he mentions that he wants students to follow his vision, what he is suggesting is that he wants students to follow a vision of a value for learning and perceiving school and education as cool and hip.

Mr. Jackson could not stress enough the power and influence that students have on each other. In many respects, students' peers are more important to them than their teachers or even their parents. The most popular students at the school have a great deal of power and influence, and he understands that he must get those students on his side for the sake of learning and relevance in the classroom. He states:

> You have to get the people who have the most influence—the peer influence is very big in their world, very big. So if you get the toughest kids, the strongest kids, the most powerful kids, you get them to buy in, then you have got it [for the entire class].

In class, it is obvious that Mr. Jackson has the buy-in from the entire group of students—even those students who are considered the most popular and/or the toughest.

Still, Mr. Jackson stresses that consistency in the way students are treated is very important in the context. In fact, he considers it as an important feature in developing a successful classroom at the urban school. As an example of this thinking, he says:

> I don't care what your [power] status is—you are going to get consequences. I don't care if you are the big linebacker bully in the school, or if you are the quiet little girl who is eighty pounds and never does anything. I want you serious about your work [engaging in the learning]. So, you have to be careful not to let some people off because kids are watching you do that.

In a sense, Mr. Jackson is pointing to issues of image and perceptions among students. Further, he believes that students are watching what happens in the classroom, how he handles situations, whether he is being "fair, firm, and consistent." Mr. Jackson is mindful of this and works to make sure his students have a positive image of him and what is going on in the classroom.

Moreover, although he stresses the importance of targeting "powerful" students to create a strong classroom context, he also emphasizes the importance of perceived fairness, equity, and consistency among his students. It is quite likely that image and perception play a role in his wearing of shirt and tie each day. His life story—his experiences with other more advanced teachers in other schools—leads him to believe that his dress is an important part of his own "image" and power as a teacher. In Mr. Jackson's words, "Teachers should dress for where they are going not necessarily where they are currently." It is this statement that really connects to one of his teaching principles: He wants his students to envision life beyond their current situations. He also aspires to become a principal at some point in the future, and he is dressing for where he is going, not necessarily where he is presently.

As Mr. Jackson explains, students talk to each other about what is happening in the classroom. Both image and perception are central to the decisions he makes in the classroom. Further, targeting the most popular students—in terms of the images students possess of themselves and others—is another important feature of the classroom context he co-develop with his students. In addition, based on my observations, it is clear in his classes that Mr. Jackson immerses himself in his students' worlds.

Immersion in Students' Worlds

It is arguable that the most admirable aspect of Mr. Jackson's pedagogical approach and his ability to develop a culturally relevant classroom is his deep level of interest in, knowledge about, and connections to the life experiences of his students. He is conscious of what is going on in the students' lives both *inside* and *outside* of the classroom, and he works very hard to ensure that he remains current in what is happening in the students' worlds. In his words, students

> implement things from their world into their academic setting. So, if I am doing math problems, I am going to have problems with stuff that comes out of the rap world or the video game world. . . . Just recently, our basketball team was doing really well, and I used the players in the math assignments, and that gets them engaged.

Mr. Jackson is not talking about incorporating students' world experiences from time to time. Rather, he is referring to teachers' actually keeping their worlds in the curriculum and teaching—consistently. From my observations, the students look forward to word problems or examples with "real-world" relevance. They often correct minor errors teachers or students make about the number of points a player scored for example. Their corrections may seem to be insignificant or trivial to others but are a big deal to the students because it is their reality—an actuality that is important to them. They want and expect the examples to tell the truth about their life worlds from a phenomenological perspective.

I often wonder how Mr. Jackson is able to stay so current with what is happening with the middle school urban students with whom he works. For example, he is able to quote the lyrics of hip-hop music, memorize the names of the most popular professional athletes, and has a strong knowledge base of the latest movies that are out. He is, in a sense, immersed in pop culture. In my interview with him, Mr. Jackson explains why he believes he is so connected to the world of his students:

> The reason I know what is happening in their world is that I live in their world. I have a 14 year old; I have an 11 year old; I have an 8 year old. I know the world they came from with my 8 year old, and I know where they are with my 11 year old . . . I know where they are going with my 14 year old. Because I teach in middle school, I am right around 11- and 12-year-old range [students] . . . And I am a DJ—I like the rap music myself. I play rap music. I feel like a kid at heart sometimes, so I kind of stay in touch with them in that way too.

It is important to note that Mr. Jackson does not believe that it is impossible for other teachers to immerse themselves in students' worlds—even if they do not have children around the same age as the students at Bridge Middle School. To the contrary, he believes that teachers should learn about their students' worlds and use what they learn to enhance the learning that takes place in and out of the classroom:

> You have to immerse yourself in their world in some form or fashion. I am just lucky to come from the world that I teach in. I came from that world. I truly live in that world, so I am immersed already in my natural life. So if I were in a system where the students came from a different world, I would just have to immerse myself in their world.

In other words, he does not believe that teachers should make excuses for why they cannot learn about and engross themselves in the worlds of their students. As an example, he explains: "You have to understand their desires, wants, and needs and dislikes . . . You have to implement that in your academics because if they are not interested, then they are not going to learn." It is clear that there is a direct connection between the immersion of a teacher in the world of students and the learning opportunities that are available in a classroom.

As previously mentioned, Mr. Jackson has a genuine interest in and affection for music, which is a major part of his teaching repertoire. He believes that teachers should use the personal experiences they have as assets, just as he believes teachers should allow students to use the experiences they have in the classroom as assets. One asset that Mr. Jackson brings into the classroom is knowledge of and an interest in (hip-hop) music.

Intersection of Music and Learning

Another important feature of Mr. Jackson's culturally relevant classroom at Bridge Middle School is his implementation of music in the classroom. To recap, music is almost always playing in his classroom, and students from other classes frequently visit the room—just to see what is being played on any particular day. When asked about the relevance and reasoning behind his implementation of music in the classroom, Mr. Jackson states,

> Well, it's nothing new. It was actually used in ancient Egypt where they used drums and instruments in the classroom. I do it for a couple reasons. Number one reason is kind of selfish—I like it . . . its like people like to go take smoke breaks or eat chocolate—I like to listen to music. And, it soothes me. It's usually jazz, sometimes some soft rock, [or] some soft R & B, but it's usually jazz, occasionally classical. The research states that when you play soft music, it calms students down and if you continue to play it, it kind of works as association—when students take tests, and you play the same songs [as what was played when covering the material] they can remember something about the assignment [or content] through the sound of the song—through association.

The students enjoy the class perhaps because the teacher offers something different than what typically occurs in classrooms, in which students come in, sit down, listen to a lecture, do work sheets, and are dismissed (Haberman, 1991). Stated in a different way, I heard students in the hallway or cafeteria report that they were ready to "get to Jackson's class." They were eager to find out the lesson plan of the day and/or week.

One learning opportunity, in the form of a game, that the students seemed to really enjoy was what Mr. Jackson called "science feud." During these feuds, he does not play soft music; he plays music that students can dance to—music that is relevant and responsive to student interests. And, the students love it! The basic structure of the game is not too innovative. Similar to the popular game show *Family Feud*, the students answer questions that he poses to them about some aspect of science. These questions are usually aligned with content standards covered in the class. In essence, the game serves as a form of review for upcoming examinations. The hook is not necessarily that the teacher plays music during the game, as this happened on the game show too, which plays a violin version of square dance music. The hook is the *particular type* of music being played. It is the kind of music that the students want to hear, consistent with what they listen to during their free time at school and also what they listen to outside of school. It is this kind of music that makes students want to be in the teacher's class. As the students approach the front of the room to answer questions during "science feud," Mr. Jackson typically plays music that the students appreciate (e.g., R & B or hip-hop). In his words,

> I'll stop the music, and I'll ask a question and they [the students] have to hit the table. The first one to hit the table and get the answer correct [sic], gets a point. And the team that wins, I'll let them leave class early or get to leave first or whatever. The sixth graders I had who are now in seventh or eight grade—they'll still come by when I have it going on and they say "I wanna play, I wanna play." They like it.

Because the students want to listen to the music, they study the material and try to answer the questions correctly. This case vignette is an example of culturally relevant pedagogy. It also represents an example of a teacher meeting students where they are.

IMPLICATIONS AND CONCLUSIONS

The practices I share of this teacher, Mr. Jackson, and what I classify as his ability to develop a culturally relevant classroom are important to consider. His mindset and decision making are grounded in social justice, and the practices that I describe move beyond the three main tenets of culturally relevant pedagogy that Ladson-Billings (2006) describes (e.g., academic achievement, cultural competence, and sociopolitical consciousness) to anchor and shape the theory. In Mr. Jackson's showcase, he develops a culturally relevant classroom through a focus on: (a) the value of learning, (b) targeting power and image among students, (c) immersion in students' world(s), and (d) the intersection of music and learning. As evident in the previous section, the social contexts of Bridge Middle School serve as a precursor to the creation of a powerful learning environment for the teacher and his students. In Mr. Jackson's teaching style, he is practicing social justice. Nieto (2010) declares that social justice is what education "needs to be about" (p. 228).

A point to remember is that developing culturally relevant classrooms requires teachers to use their heads and their hearts (Banks, 2003) to make meaningful decisions for student learning. There are no magic formulas, tricks, or predetermined theories or related practices that automatically guarantee that students will be successful in a social context of learning. The teaching and learning relationship is much too complex for such predeterminations. Developing culturally relevant classrooms, as Ladson-Billings explains, is more a state of mind than a set of specific practices that teachers employ. When teachers care about social justice and are committed to ensuring that all students equitably experience learning opportunities, students benefit (Milner, 2008). Thus, although I am hopeful that readers of this chapter will learn from the theoretical framings and practical implications outlined, I am more hopeful that they will develop a frame of mind to "do" culturally relevant pedagogy and to practice social justice based on what they know to be true about themselves and their students.

Much of what I outline here is transferable to other learning contexts, and teachers, including urban ones, have the ability to develop learning environments that can work to redress many of the negative experiences that African American students encounter through the educational system. As evident in the case of Mr. Jackson, teachers can be successful in all types of schools and with students from all racial, ethnic, and cultural backgrounds. Although structural and systemic issues (e.g., lack of resources or racism) may seem insurmountable, teachers cannot afford to use them as excuses for not developing classroom contexts that provide optimal learning opportunities for students and ones that are grounded in social justice. All students, especially urban African American students, possess a level of brilliance that needs to be tapped. In urgent times such as these, teachers must work to develop classroom contexts that validate who students are—classrooms that allow students to build the knowledge, skills, and attitudes necessary for academic success, social success, cultural competence, and sociopolitical consciousness.

NOTES

1. There is not a static definition or meaning of the term *urban*. Scholars define urban students, urban environments, and urban education in various ways. For instance, in general, urban education can be equated with inner-city schools or large metropolitan regions. When Weiner (2003) reviews the literature about urban education, she notes that it paints negative portraits of the urban context. She explains that the lack of success in urban schools is often described as a result of the "problems in students, their families, their culture, or their communities" (p. 305). To suggest that all, or even most, urban schools, neighborhoods, people, and other related contexts are substandard would be unfairly inaccurate. There is some powerfully rich knowledge, culture, and opportunity inherent in urban spaces, yet these resources are too often ignored and/or underexplored.

2. The terms "Black" and African American will be used interchangeably throughout this chapter.

3. *Culture* can be defined as a group of people who possess and share deep-rooted connections, such as values, beliefs, languages, customs, norms, and history. It is dynamic and encompasses a range of concepts that relate to its central meaning, such as identity (e.g., race and ethnicity), class, economic status, gender, sexual orientation, ability, and religion (among other categories).

4. Pseudonyms are used to mask the identity of the school and teacher. Constructed in 1954, Bridge Middle School is an urban school in a relatively large city in the southeastern region of the United States. According to a Bridge County real estate agent, houses in the community sell for between $120,000 and $175,000. There also is a considerable number of rental houses zoned to the school. Many of the neighborhood students from higher socioeconomic backgrounds who are zoned to Bridge attend private and independent schools in the city rather than attend the school. The practice of students attending private and independent schools rather than their zoned school is very common in the district. A large number of students from lower socioeconomic backgrounds attend the school. Bridge Middle School is considered a Title I school, which means that the school receives additional federal funds to assist students with instructional and related resources. During the 2006–2007 academic year, Bridge Middle School accommodated approximately 354 students. The most recent data available regarding student demographics (2005–2006) indicates that 59.8% of the students at Bridge were African American, 5.6% were Latin American, 31.6% were White, 0.3% were Native American, and

2.8% were Asian American, a truly diverse learning environment at least in terms of racial and ethnic diversity. The free and reduced lunch rate increased between the 2002 and 2006 academic years: from 64% to 79%. In 2006, there were 27 teachers at the school, with 45% of the faculty being African American and 55% being White. Seven of the teachers were male and twenty were female. For a more detailed account of Bridge Middle School, its teachers and students, and this research, read Milner's (2008) article *Disrupting Deficit Notions of Difference: Counter-Narratives of Teachers and Community in Urban Education.*

REFERENCES

Anderson, J. D. (1988). *The education of Blacks in the South, 1860–1935.* Chapel Hill: The University of North Carolina Press.

Artiles, A. J., Klingner, J. K., & Tate, W. F. (2006). Representation of minority students in special education: Complicating traditional explanations. *Educational Researcher, 35*(6), 3–5.

Banks, J. A. (2003). Teaching literacy for social justice and global citizenship. *Language Arts, 81*(1), 18–19.

Banks, J. A. (2006). *Cultural diversity and education: Foundations, curriculum, and teaching.* Boston, MA: Pearson.

Cooper, P. M. (2003). Effective white teachers of Black children: Teaching within a community. *Journal of Teacher Education, 54*(5), 413–427.

Davis, J. E., & Jordan, W. J. (1994). The effects of school context, structure, and experiences on African American males in middle and high school. *Journal of Negro Education, 63*(4), 570–587.

Ford, D. Y. (1996). *Reversing underachievement among gifted black students: Promising practices and programs.* New York, NY: Teachers College Press.

Ford, D. Y. (2006). Identification of young culturally diverse students for gifted education programs. *Gifted Education Press Quarterly, 20*(1), 2–4.

Foster, M. (1997). *Black teachers on teaching.* New York, NY: New Press.

Haberman, M. (1991). The pedagogy of poverty versus good teaching. *Phi Delta Kappan, 73*(4), 290–294.

Holzman, M. (2004). *Public education and black male students: A state report card.* The Schott Educational Inequity Index. Cambridge, MA: The Schott Foundation for Public Education.

Howard, T. C. (2001). Telling their side of the story: African American students' perceptions of culturally relevant teaching. *The Urban Review, 33*(2), 131–149.

Irvine, J. J. (1990). *Black students and school failure: Policies, practices and prescriptions.* New York, NY: Greenwood Press.

Ladson-Billings, G. (1992). Liberatory consequences of literacy: A case of culturally relevant instruction for African American students. *Journal of Negro Education, 61*(3), 378–391.

Ladson-Billings, G. (1994). *The dreamkeepers: Successful teachers of African American children.* San Francisco, CA: Jossey-Bass.

Ladson-Billings, G. (2000). Fighting for our lives: Preparing teachers to teach African American students. *Journal of Teacher Education, 51*(3), 206–214.

Ladson-Billings, G. (2006). "Yes, but how do we do it?": Practicing culturally relevant pedagogy. In J. Landsman & C. W. Lewis, *White teachers/diverse classrooms: A guide to building inclusive schools, promoting high expectations and eliminating racism* (pp. 29–42). Sterling, VA: Stylus.

McCutcheon, G. (2002). *Developing the curriculum: Solo and group deliberation.* Troy, NY: Educators' Press International.

Milner, H. R., IV. (2008). Disrupting deficit notions of difference: Counter-narratives of teachers and community in urban education. *Teaching and Teacher Education, 24*(6), 1573–1598.

Milner, H. R., IV. (2009). Preparing teachers of African American students in urban schools. In L. C. Tillman (Ed.), *The handbook of African American education* (pp. 123–140). Thousand Oaks, CA: Sage.

Moore, J. L., III, Ford, D. Y., & Milner, H. R., IV. (2005). Recruitment is not enough: Retaining African-American students in gifted education. *Gifted Child Quarterly, 49*(1), 51–67.

Morris, J. E. (2004). Can anything good come from Nazareth? Race, class, and African American schooling and community in the urban south and Midwest. *American Educational Research Journal, 41*(1), 69–112.

National Center for Education Statistics. (2007). Table 23-1: Status dropout rates of 16- through 24-year-olds, by race/ethnicity: October 1972–2005. In *The condition of education 2007* (NCES 2007-064). Retrieved from http://nces.ed.gov/pubs2007/2007064_App1.pdf

Nieto, S. (2010). Afterword. In H. R. Milner (Ed.), *Culture, curriculum, and identity in education* (pp. 223–230). New York, NY: Palgrave Macmillan.

Skiba, R. J., Michael, R. S., Nardo, A. C., & Peterson, R. L. (2002). The color of discipline: Source of racial and gender disproportionality in school punishment. *Urban Review, 34*(4), 317–342.

Tillman, L. C. (2004). (Un)intended Consequences? The Impact of the *Brown v. Board of Education* decision on the employment status of black educators. *Education and Urban Society, 36*(3), 280–303.

Weiner, L. (2003). Why is classroom management so vexing for urban teachers? *Theory into Practice, 42*(4), 305–312.

Woodson, C. G. (1933). *The mis-education of the Negro.* Washington, DC: Associated.

CHAPTER NINE

Using Culturally Relevant Pedagogy AND Social Justice TO Understand Mathematics Instructional Quality IN AN Urban Context

ROBERT Q. BERRY III AND TEMPLE A. WALKOWIAK

The quality of instruction plays a significant role in student outcomes (Sanders & Rivers, 1996) and educational experiences in mathematics. The National Mathematics Advisory Panel (NMAP; 2008) notes that differences in mathematics achievement among students can be attributed to differences in instructional quality and that these differences can "account for 12% to 14% of total variability in students' mathematics achievement gains during an elementary school year" (NMAP, 2008, p. 35). These variances in instructional quality are compounded "if students receive a series of effective or ineffective teachers" (NMAP, 2008, p. 35). Sutton and Krueger (2002) argue that mathematics instructional practices have changed very little over time and that improving mathematics instructional quality can lead to improvement in student outcomes. In addition, the education researchers assert that "many mathematics students spend much of their time on basic computational skills rather than engaging in mathematically rich problem-solving experiences" (Sutton & Krueger, 2002 p. 26). Palacios (2005) suggests that teachers who do not use high-quality mathematics instructional practices "are less likely to attempt to reach all students' learning needs or alter their teaching practices" (p. 23).

For those African American students in urban educational settings, Crocco and Costigan (2007) argue that there is a strong relationship between mathematics instructional quality and a mathematics curriculum that concentrates on the practice of basic skills and algorithms and does not integrate the contexts or the backgrounds of students. That is, they suggest that the quality of mathematics instruction students receive is lessened when the focus is on acquiring mathematics skills rather than on using mathematics to examine and understand problems or to develop critical mathematical literacy. It is unfortunate that the focus on basic skills in mathematics tends to dominate mathematics instruction in urban districts (Crocco & Costigan, 2007).

McKinney, Chappell, Berry, and Hickman (2009) examine the mathematics instructional practices in an urban school district and report that the urban teachers in this school setting used lectures; drill and practice; teacher-directed approaches; and memorization of algorithms, rules, and procedures as their primary instructional practices. High-quality mathematics instruction is not the norm for all students; in fact, many students of color in urban schools, particularly African American ones, are less likely to receive high-quality mathematics instruction.

MATHEMATICS EDUCATION EXPERIENCES OF AFRICAN AMERICAN STUDENTS

Course enrollment patterns are significant because there appears to be a correlation between mathematics instructional quality and the level of courses that students are enrolled in (Boston, 2008). Students enrolled in high-level mathematics courses receive more exposure to mathematics content and higher-quality mathematics instruction and experience mathematics in a way that allows them to make connections between mathematics and the real world (Tate, 2005). These students are able to see the relevance of mathematics in their lives; thus, they are able to develop a trajectory that includes mathematics in their future. The course enrollment patterns show that the percentage of African American students enrolled in high-level mathematics courses have not significantly changed over time (Lubienski, 2002; Davis & Martin, 2008; Tate, 2005). African American students report taking fewer college-preparatory courses than their peers (Lubienski, 2002; Strutchens & Silver, 2000; Tate, 2005). Moreover, African American students are more likely to report enrollment in lower-level courses (Tate, 2005). Because of course enrollment patterns, many African American students do not have the mathematics background to participate in the science, technology, engineering, and mathematics (STEM)-based job markets nor enroll in STEM-based majors in college. In consequence, there have been no significant increases in the number of African American students choosing STEM-based majors in college or entering into the STEM-based labor market (Martin, 2008; Tate, 2005).

In their analysis of the literature focusing on the mathematics experiences of African American students, Davis and Martin (2008) conclude that the literature reveals two important insights: First, a significant number of African American students often experience low-quality mathematics instruction that is designed to help them pass standardized tests in mathematics rather than develop the mathematical skills to become critical thinkers, problem solvers, and agents for change (Davis, 2008; Lattimore, 2003, 2005). Davis and Martin find support of this insight through a number of reports that reveal that African American students are inundated with mathematics instructional strategies that emphasize repetition, right-answer thinking that focuses on memorization and rote learning, and mathematics computational strategies. To support these instructional strategies, teachers primarily use worksheets, timed computational tests, and in-class practice tests that mirror standardized tests (Berry, 2005; Corey & Bower, 2005; Davis, 2008; Lattimore, 2003, 2005). For African American students, the use of low-quality mathematics instructional strategies coupled with the previously mentioned instructional materials situate mathematics as dis-engaging and present a view of "mathematics as irrelevant and decontextualized from their everyday experiences" (Davis & Martin, 2008, p. 20).

Davis and Martin's (2008) second insight focuses on mathematics as a gatekeeper for access to higher-level mathematics courses, gifted and honors programs, and future aspirations (Berry, 2005; Davis, 2008; Lattimore, 2005; Sheppard, 2006). Urban African American students are often denied access to higher level mathematics courses and advanced programs; in consequence, many of them are relegated to lower-level mathematics courses. Being denied access to higher-level courses denies African American students access to what Tate (2005) describes as the opportunity-to-learn (OTL) mathematics. OTL mathematics consists of three variables: (a) content exposure and coverage, (b) content emphasis, and (c) quality of instructional delivery (Tate, 2005). The content exposure and coverage variable focuses on the amount of time spent on mathematics topics and the depth of coverage of mathematics. The content emphasis variable focuses on the selection of topics within the mathematics curriculum and the selection of students for basic skills instruction or for higher-order skills instruction. The quality of the instructional delivery variable focuses on pedagogical strategies. Several studies suggest that African American students' content exposure and content emphasis in elementary and middle grades have primarily consisted of numbers and operations and computational skills, with little depth in other mathematics strands, such as algebra, geometry, data analysis and statistics, and measurement (Davis & Martin, 2008; Lattimore, 2005; Lubienski, 2002). It is plausible to conclude that exposure to a narrow band of mathematics content coupled with low quality of instruction denies many African American students the opportunity to learn mathematics. Thus, these students are often denied access into higher-level mathematics courses.

AFRICAN AMERICAN STUDENTS' MATHEMATICS ACHIEVEMENT IN 11 URBAN SETTINGS

The National Assessment of Educational Progress (NAEP) mathematics assessment gauges student mathematics achievement in grades 4, 8, and 12. The NAEP mathematics assessment is the only ongoing national assessment of mathematics achievement in the United States (Lutkus, Grigg, & Dion, 2007). It provides information about what students know and can do in mathematics. The Trial Urban District Assessment (TUDA), a special project of the NAEP, assessed the mathematics performance of 11 large urban districts (i.e., Charlotte, Austin, Houston, San Diego, New York, Boston, Atlanta, Los Angeles, Cleveland, Chicago, and Washington, DC) in 2003, 2005, and 2007. The NAEP data has been used to illustrate that factors, such as socioeconomic status, school policies, allocation of human and material resources, and classroom instructional practices,[1] can account for performance and quality disparities (Oakes, 1990; Secada, 1992; Strutchens & Silver, 2000; Tate, 1997).

Before discussing students' mathematics performance on the NAEP, it is important that urban education practitioners, policy makers, and researchers have a clear understanding of the contexts of the 11 TUDA school districts represented in this project. The school districts in this project represent large student populations that have generally higher concentrations of students of color, lower income families, and English Language Learners (ELLs) than other school districts nationally (Lutkus et al., 2007). In 2007, African American and Hispanic[2] students made up about 38% of fourth graders in the nation, but, in the 11 TUDA districts, the percentages were between 56% and 92%, respectively. The 11 TUDA districts had larger percentages of lower-income students, as measured by their eligibility for the National School Lunch Program; nationally 45% of students were eligible for the National School Lunch Program, but, for the TUDA districts, the eligibility ranged from 48% in Charlotte to 100% in Cleveland. The 11 TUDA districts also differed from the nation in the percentages of students who are ELLs and students with disabilities. In 2007, the national percentage of fourth-grade students who were ELLs was 11%, but in the 11 TUDA districts, it ranged from 3% in Atlanta to 48% in Los Angeles. That year, the national percentage of students with disabilities was 14%, whereas in TUDA districts it ranged between 10% in Atlanta to 21% in Boston.

Students' achievement on the NAEP mathematics assessment is described as "below basic," "basic," "proficient," and "advanced." Fourth graders performing at the basic level were expected to be able to estimate and use basic facts to perform simple computations with whole numbers and to show some understanding of fractions and decimals (Lutkus et al., 2007). The many African American fourth graders performing at the basic level in 2007 and 2005 focused primarily on whole-number computations with some experiences with fractions and decimals but were not able to solve real-world problems (National Center for Education Statistics [NCES], 2009). In terms of fourth graders performing at the proficient level, these students were expected to have a conceptual understanding of fractions and decimals and be able to solve real-world problems (Lutkus et al., 2007). Fourth graders performing at the advanced level were expected to be able to solve complex and nonroutine real-world mathematical problems and be able to justify their solutions to mathematics problems by explaining how they were achieved (Lutkus et al., 2007). The average scale national score on the NAEP in 2007 and 2005 indicates that African American fourth-grade students were not performing at proficient or advanced levels (NCES, 2009).

Eighth-grade students performing at the basic level were expected to have an understanding of arithmetic operations, including estimation, using whole numbers, decimals, fractions, and percents (NCES, 2009). For 2007 and 2005, the average scale score (a type of score calculated by a committee by a process of scaling the raw scores of thousands of students) for African American eighth grade students nationally indicates that they were not performing at the basic level; their score is below the basic level cutoff score. Rather, these students were performing at the below basic level (NCES, 2009), which indicates that their mathematical experiences had not moved beyond computations of numbers and that they had limited exposure to the areas that allow mastery of other content strands, such as algebra, geometry, and data analysis. Eighth-graders performing at the proficient level were expected to be proficient with algebra and functions, to compare and contrast mathematical ideas, to make inferences from data and graphs, to apply properties of informal geometry, and to accurately use the tools of technology (Lutkus et al., 2007; NCES, 2009). Eighth graders performing at the advanced level were expected to use number sense and geometric awareness to consider the reasonableness of an answer, to use abstract thinking to create unique problem-solving techniques, and to explain the reasoning processes underlying their conclusions (Lutkus et al., 2007; NCES, 2009).

Table 1. Average National Scale Scores in Mathematics for Fourth-Grade Students in General and for Black Students in Specific for 2007 and 2005

	Mathematics Achievement Levels			
	2007		2005	
TUDA Districts	Average Scale Scores	NAEP Assessment Levels	Average Scale Scores	NAEP Assessment Levels
Nation (All)	239	Basic	239	Basic
Nation (Black)	222	Basic	220	Basic
Atlanta	217	Basic	215	Basic
Austin	226	Basic	228	Basic
Boston	226	Basic	223	Basic
Charlotte	230	Basic	230	Basic
Chicago	213	Below Basic	208	Below Basic
Cleveland	210	Below Basic	215	Basic
Washington, DC	209	Below Basic	207	Below Basic
Houston	225	Basic	224	Basic
Los Angeles	216	Basic	209	Basic
New York	227	Basic	222	Basic
San Diego	222	Basic	221	Basic

Note. 214 is at the lower end of the score range for the basic level and 249 is at the lower end for the proficient level on the NAEP Mathematics Assessment.

Table 1 shows the average national scale scores for fourth-grade students in general and for African American fourth graders in specific for 2007 and 2005 (NCES, 2009). The average national scale score for all fourth graders is 239 for both 2007 and 2005. African American students' scale score, nationally and among the 11 TUDA districts, is below the wider national scale score for both years, at 222 in 2007 and 220 in 2005. The national scale scores for all fourth-grade students indicates that they were performing at the basic level, and African American students' national scale score also indicates that they were performing at the basic level. In 2007, African American fourth graders in eight TUDA districts performed at the basic level and three performed at the below-basic level. In 2005, African American fourth graders in nine TUDA districts performed at the basic level and two performed at the below-basic level. Table 2 shows the average national scale scores for eighth-grade students in general and for African American eighth graders in specific (NCES, 2009) in 2007 and 2005. The average scale score nationally for all eighth graders is 280 for 2007 and 278 for 2005. Black students' scale score, nationally and among the 11 TUDA districts, is below the national scale score for both years, at 259 in 2007 and 254 in 2005. For 2007

Table 2. Average National Scale Scores in Mathematics for Eighth-Grade Students in General and for Black Students in Specific for 2007 and 2005

	Mathematics Achievement Levels			
	2007		2005	
TUDA Districts	Average Scale Scores	NAEP Assessment Levels	Average Scale Scores	NAEP Assessment Levels
Nation (All)	280	Basic	278	Basic
Nation (Black)	259	Below Basic	254	Below Basic
Atlanta	253	Below Basic	242	Below Basic
Austin	265	Basic	262	Basic
Boston	263	Basic	256	Below Basic
Charlotte	267	Basic	264	Basic
Chicago	248	Below Basic	245	Below Basic
Cleveland	253	Below Basic	244	Below Basic
Washington, DC	245	Below Basic	241	Below Basic
Houston	265	Basic	257	Below Basic
Los Angeles	245	Below Basic	239	Below Basic
New York	258	Below Basic	257	Below Basic
San Diego	258	Below Basic	253	Below Basic

Note. 262 is at the lower end of the score range for the basic level and 299 is at the lower end for the proficient level on the NAEP Mathematics Assessment.

and 2005, the national scale scores for all eighth-grade students indicate that they were performing at the basic level, whereas Black students' national scale scores for these years indicate that they were performing at the below-basic level. In 2007, Black eighth graders in seven TUDA districts performed at the below-basic level, whereas in four districts they performed at the basic level. In 2005, African American eighth graders in nine TUDA districts performed at the below-basic level, whereas in two districts they performed at the basic level.

The TUDA findings indicate that in 2005 and 2007 Black fourth- and eighth-grade students in the 11 urban school districts had not developed a conceptual understanding of fractions and decimals and could not proficiently solve real-world problems (Lutkus, et al., 2007). In addition, these students were not able to solve complex and nonroutine real-world problems. As stated earlier, students performing at the proficient or advanced levels on NAEP were expected to be able to develop a conceptual understanding, make conjectures, reason mathematically, problem solve, and develop mathematical arguments (Lutkus, et al., 2007). Their scale scores suggest that African American fourth and eighth graders, in urban school districts, were experiencing low-quality mathematics instruction and were not experiencing mathematics instruction that leads to problem-solving proficiency and mathematical reasoning.

The achievement levels, as measured by the NAEP mathematics tests, may be indicative of the quality of instruction that these students receive. Wenglinsky (2002) examines how more than 7,000 students' mathematics achievement levels on the 1996 NAEP mathematics assessment were related to measures of teaching quality. In this study, he finds five variables of teacher quality that are related to student achievement, taking class size and socioeconomic status (SES) into account. The five variables concerning the teacher are: (a) whether his academic major was mathematics, (b) his professional development in higher-order thinking skills, (c) his professional development focusing on diversity, (d) hands-on learning, and (e) the level of his higher-order thinking skills. The findings suggest that teachers with a professional background in mathematics content, higher-order thinking skills, and professional development focusing on diversity build experiences to meet the academic, social, and cultural needs of students. With this in mind, Wenglinsky states: "Regardless of the level of preparation students bring into the classroom, decisions that teachers make about classroom practices can either greatly facilitate student learning or serve as an obstacle to it" (p. 7). Thus, teachers' pedagogical decisions and activities make a difference in the quality of mathematics instruction that students experience.

WHAT IS MATHEMATICS INSTRUCTIONAL QUALITY?

The publications *Mathematics Teaching Today: Improving Practice, Improving Student Learning* (National Council of Teachers of Mathematics [NCTM], 2007) and *Principles and Standards for School Mathematics* (NCTM, 2000) provide a vision for high-quality mathematics instruction. *Mathematics Teaching Today* defines standards for the teaching and learning of mathematics, and *Principles and Standards* outlines a vision for a mathematics classroom through a description of six principles (i.e., equity, curriculum, teaching, learning, assessment, and technology); five content standards (i.e., number and operations, algebra, geometry, measurement, and data analysis and probability); and five process standards (i.e., problem solving, reasoning and proof, communication, connections, and representation). However, critics of these publications argue that these documents are too visionary and lack specific kinds of constructive pedagogical methods that represent high-quality mathematics teaching (Ball & Rowan, 2004; Clements, 2007; Leonard, 2008; Martin, 2007).

Although a vision is necessary, many teachers also need a framework for understanding high-quality mathematics teaching as it plays out in the mathematics classroom. Several mathematics education researchers have worked to provide pedagogical constructs for high-quality mathematics instruction (Borko, Stecher, & Kuffner, 2006; Walkowiak, Berry, McCracken, Rimm-Kaufman, & Meyer, 2009). However, these constructs are meaningless if educators lack a clear understanding of the contexts in which students make connections in mathematical meaning. High-quality mathematics instruction must consider the contexts in which students come to know and understand mathematics. With this in mind, Walkowiak et al. (2009) identify seven constructs that represent the indicators of high-quality mathematics instruction for elementary mathematics: (a) the structure of a lesson, (b) students' use of mathematical tools, (c) the cognitive depth of the lessons, (d) a mathematical discourse community, (e) explanation and justification, (f) problem solving, and (g) connections and applications. Following is a detailed description of the seven constructs proposed by Walkowiak et al.:

1. *The structure of a mathematics lesson* refers to the sequence and coherence of a lesson. Mathematics lessons should be logical and coherent, leading students to a deeper understanding of mathematical concepts. When planning lessons, it is critical that teachers organize instruction so that key mathematical concepts are integrated (NCTM, 2000).

2. *Students' use of mathematical tools* refers to students creating and translating multiple representations of mathematical concepts through the use of symbols, graphs, pictures, words, charts, diagrams, and physical manipulatives. It is important that students use tools to build meaning and to represent and make sense of abstract mathematical ideas (NCTM, 2000, 2007).

3. *Cognitive depth of the lessons* relates to the types of mathematical tasks teachers provide that allow students to wrestle and explore central mathematical ideas (NCTM, 2007). The nature of the mathematical tasks is connected to cognition. For example, demanding tasks have a higher level of cognitive depth that involves connecting procedures to underlying mathematical concepts or completing complex nonalgorithmic tasks for which there are no prescribed approaches. Low-demanding tasks involve a lower amount of cognitive depth required for students and often involve performing exercises that students have memorized or procedural steps with no connections to underlying mathematical ideas (Stein, Smith, Henningsen, & Silver, 2000). Both high- and low-demanding tasks are appropriate in mathematics classrooms; however, appropriateness and frequency of use is a concern among researchers.

4. *A mathematical discourse community* involves representing, talking, writing, reading, listening, agreeing, and disagreeing about mathematical ideas (NCTM, 2007). When students are encouraged to participate in discourse

about mathematical ideas, they learn to communicate mathematically. Discourse provides multiple points of engagement and is a central part of what students learn and how they understand mathematics. In classrooms rich in discourse, teachers typically address mathematical thinking to encourage students to share their thinking about mathematics, rather than just a solution to a problem. Further, the teacher solicits students' ideas, questions, and input explicitly and frequently.

5. *Explanation and justification* is a part of the broader construct of discourse; the authors highlight it as a construct for high-quality teaching. A classroom community that fosters discourse among students may focus on checks for understanding without inviting reasoning and proof. Explanation and justification as a construct requires that teachers engage students in not only explaining how they obtain solutions but also in justifying why their chosen strategies are appropriate for arriving at such solutions.

6. *Problem solving* refers to grappling with a task for which the solution method is not already known (NCTM, 2000). Whereas the cognitive demand construct is focused on the teacher, problem solving is a student-focused construct. For example, it helps students learn mathematics by giving them the opportunity to clarify and extend their knowledge (NCTM, 2000).

7. *Connections and applications* within mathematics lessons are central to students' understanding of and appreciation for mathematics. Making connections within and among mathematical ideas provides students with an understanding of mathematics as a network of ideas rather than isolated facts and procedures. In addition, connections refer to relating mathematics to students' ways of knowing, to real-world contexts, and to other disciplines. Applications of mathematics to the real world provide context and relevance for students as to why mathematics is important. When connections and applications are made, students' understandings will likely be deeper and longer lasting (NCTM, 2000).

Research findings involving the seven constructs of mathematics instructional quality appear to indicate that students in urban contexts are not experiencing high-quality mathematics instruction. For example, Weiss, Pasley, Smith, Banilower, and Heck (2003) conducted an observational study of 31 primarily urban schools in the United States. These researchers find that in these schools: the *structure of a mathematics lesson* was lacking and students were not allowed opportunities for sense making and were not provided the coherence to develop deep mathematical understanding. They also find that *students' use of mathematical tools* impacts how they understand and use mathematical ideas. McKinney, Chappell, Berry, and Hickman (2009) studied teachers in an urban school district and report that the use of mathematics manipulatives and tools to connect abstract concepts to concrete tools were absent in these classroom settings. Research on *cognitive depth* suggests that there is an overrepresentation of low-level cognitively demanding tasks in mathematics lessons in urban classrooms (Stein, Smith, Henningsen, & Silver, 2000). Using *mathematical discourse* helps students integrate mathematical knowledge with their cultural ways of knowing. Lipka et al. (2005) conducted a study of culturally relevant instruction focusing on *mathematical discourse* and find that use of culturally relevant contexts enabled changes to teachers' relationships with the students. The teachers created what was called a "third-space" in which students could develop a mathematical identity within a cultural context that valued cultural mathematics knowledge alongside traditional mathematics knowledge.

Explanation and justification are critical components of students' mathematical experiences in classrooms. In a study involving Latino students in an urban school district, Gutstein (2003) concludes that teaching mathematics for social justice requires students to make conjectures, develop mathematical arguments, investigate ideas, justify answers, and validate their own thinking. Hiebert et al. (2005) analyze videos of mathematics instruction in American classrooms and find that 66% of students spent their time in mathematics practicing familiar procedures, rather than engaged in *problem solving*. It is plausible that this percentage may be higher in urban classrooms. Leonard, Davis, and Sidler (2005) investigate the use of culturally relevant problem-solving tasks with Black students in an urban school district and find the tasks to be engaging for the students and to improve their problem-solving strategies.

Connections and applications of mathematics topics and concepts is compatible with urban African American students' cultural ways of knowing and doing and can positively impact these students' mathematics identity and increase their opportunities to learn mathematics. This compatibility engages African American students to make mathematical *connections* with technology (e.g., Conant, Rosebery, Warren, & Hudicourt-Barnes, 2001; Leonard et al., 2005), sports (Nasir, 2002; Nasir, Hand, & Taylor, 2008), games (Nasir, 2005), or music (Albert, 2000). Through making these connections, Black students see applications to their lived realities and find *applications* for mathematics when they explore uses of mathematics (Davis, 2008).

The seven aforementioned constructs represent indicators of high-quality mathematics instruction. These constructs considerably overlap with culturally relevant pedagogy and teaching mathematics for social justice. In the remainder of this chapter, we suggest that that, if teachers have an understanding of African

American students' learning preferences, they can implement high-quality mathematics instruction through the use of culturally relevant pedagogy and teaching mathematics for social justice. Culturally relevant pedagogy and teaching mathematics for social justice compel teachers to implement high-quality mathematics instruction in which teachers connect mathematics to students lived experiences, students become problem solvers and doers of mathematics and use multiple mathematics content strands to engage with problem solving, and the pedagogy is engaging and relevant for both the teachers and students. We contend that the seven constructs of high-quality mathematics instruction are embedded in culturally relevant pedagogy and teaching mathematics for social justice.

LEARNING PREFERENCES

Because many African American students attend schools in urban settings, it is plausible to consider that culture is a significant socializing force and that it is essential to investigate the nature of teaching and learning preferences associated with the cultures of these students. Learning preferences can be described as ways individuals prefer to absorb, organize, and make sense of information. Learning preferences do not tell us about an individual's abilities or intelligence; rather, they provide an understanding as to why some tasks seem easier than others. There has been research on learning preferences that has examined ways to align teaching and learning styles that would result in greater outcomes for academically diverse students (Malloy, 2009; Pitts, 2009). Urban educators who understand learning preferences facilitate, structure, and validate successful learning for all students (Guild & Garger, 1998). Researchers have learned a great deal about learning preferences and how identifying teaching methods and teaching through learning preferences leads to improved academic engagement and academic achievement (Dunn et al., 2009; Pitts, 2009). Dunn et al. (2009) demonstrate that, when educators develop an understanding of learning preferences, the following occur: (a) positive changes in instructional quality, (b) an increased sensitivity toward meeting the needs of learners, (c) a stronger promotion of social justice and equity among teachers and students, (d) increased academic achievement, and (e) better discipline among students even when learning in their nonpreferred styles.

There appears to be no clear consensus concerning the terminology used to describe learning preferences or the factors identified as contributing to learning preferences. In fact, Pitts (2009) reports that researchers have identified approximately 127 factors contributing to learning preferences. In addition, researchers use different terms to describe similar learning preferences. For example, Shade (1997) uses the terms *relational* and *analytical* to describe divergent learning preferences, whereas Dunn and Dunn (1992) use *global* and *analytical* to describe similar preferences. Some urban learners have a relational preference approach to learning (Shade, 1997). Relational learning preference is characterized as the preference for freedom of movement, variation, creativity, divergent thinking, inductive reasoning, and focus on people. Dunn and Dunn describe global learners as similar to relational learners in preferring to master the big ideas or concepts before concentrating on the details. These individuals work well in dynamic environments and prefer to work with their peers and structure tasks in their own ways.

Urban learners, including African Americans, who have an analytical learning preference object to relations in a logical, diagnostic fashion with the ability to discern objects as discrete from their context (Shade, 1997). Analytical learners have a tendency toward impersonal learning preferences in social encounters. Dunn and Dunn (1992) describe analytical learners in a similar way to Shade (1997): as preferring information to be presented in a step-by-step sequential manner that builds toward the big ideas or conceptual understanding. These individuals prefer to learn in a quiet, formal setting; often have a strong emotional need to complete tasks; like to learn alone or one on one with a teacher; and prefer highly structured assignments.

People are not exclusively a product of their cultural and social contexts. Those individuals with seemingly similar backgrounds may experience the effects of cultural and social contexts in different ways (Irvine & York, 1995). Both culture and social contexts are neither static nor deterministic, and people are not the product of their culture or social contexts solely (Irvine & York, 1995). Although the literature on learning preferences is broader than the preferences presented here, this chapter uses the relational and analytical preferences, because these descriptors are far reaching. African American learners considerably overlap with the relational learning preference, with aggregates of holistic and field-dependent learning preferences (Malloy, 2009; Shade, 1997). The holistic learner seeks to synthesize divergent experiences to obtain the essence of these experiences. For example, the learner thrives on content tied into a larger whole and perceives cause and effect as separate entities. The kinesthetic mode is the primary method of information induction for holistic learners; thus, hands-on and active learning help tie concrete experiences to abstract concepts (Malloy, 2009; Shade, 1997). The field-dependent learner requires cues from the environment, prefers external structure, is people-oriented, is an intuitive thinker, and remembers material in a social context (Malloy, 2009; Shade, 1997). These learners, including urban, draw on their daily experiences to facilitate learning and prefer to gain an understanding of the interconnectedness and interdependence among ideas, items, and experiences for optimal learning to exist. Relational learners classify ideas, items, and experiences based on how things relate to each other and prefer experimentation, improvisation, and interaction with others and the environment (Malloy, 2009; Shade, 1997).

UNDERSTANDING CULTURALLY RELEVANT PEDAGOGY
AND TEACHING FOR SOCIAL JUSTICE

The literature makes it clear that teachers' pedagogical decisions, activities, beliefs, stereotypes, and expectations directly influence students' mathematical experiences and outcomes (Cousins-Cooper, 2000; Gay, 2000; NCTM, 2000,; Strutchens & Silver, 2000). Mathematics teaching as relational and multidimensional situates mathematics instruction as connected to students' social and cultural backgrounds (Franke, Kazemi, & Battey, 2007). Mathematics teaching as relational means knowing students' identities, histories, experiences, and social/cultural contexts (Gutstein, 2003). Mathematics teaching, as multidimensional, means interacting and forming relationships among multiple dimensions. These dimensions include teachers' pedagogical content knowledge, teachers' beliefs about mathematics teaching and learning, teachers' understandings about students' social and cultural contexts, and teachers creating an environment for mathematics learning (Lampert, 2004; Moschkovich, 2002).

Gutstein (2006) describes two broad frameworks of mathematical pedagogy that aim to prepare students for their future: (a) functional literacy and (b) critical literacy. Functional literacy is grounded in the notion that mathematics teaching should prepare students for the workforce. The kind of mathematics instruction students receive in the functional literacy context is dependent upon their conceptions and beliefs about their relative place in society. Teaching in terms of functional literacy prepares students to work in the service industry, as instruction within this framework is often computationally based with very little problem-solving or demanding tasks that are highly cognitive. Critical literacy is a pedagogy grounded in the notion that mathematics should be used to evaluate and critique systems and institutions as well as develop individual and social agency (Gutstein, 2006). This form of literacy prepares students to be critical thinkers, problem solvers, and agents for change. Culturally relevant pedagogy and teaching mathematics for social justice are examples of critical literacy that is grounded in the framework that suggests that teachers must use high-mathematics instructional quality to be effective.

Culturally relevant pedagogy requires urban mathematics teachers to attend to students' academic, social, and cultural understandings by using forms of communal, social, and political contexts as forms of official knowledge (Ladson-Billings, 1995). Culturally relevant pedagogy supports the following three goals for students: (a) experiencing academic success, (b) developing and/or maintaining cultural competence, and (c) developing critical consciousness (Ladson-Billings, 1994, 1995). In mathematics, academic success involves more than the acquisition of functional literacy; it includes acquiring the tools necessary to becoming a lifelong learner. Cultural competence involves "the ability to function effectively in one's culture of origin" (Ladson-Billings, 2000, p. 219). Critical consciousness consists of critical literacy in that it is about understanding the political nature of situations, critiquing the status quo, and proactively trying to change it (Ladson-Billings, 1995).

Teaching mathematics for social justice is not uniformly defined within the research literature. The definitions range from equal access, to advanced mathematics courses, to social reconfiguration spurred by the use of mathematics as a tool to understand social life and the inequities that exist within it (Gonzalez, 2009). Gonzalez (2009) defines teaching mathematics for social justice using four constructs: (a) access to high-quality mathematics instruction for all students; (b) curriculum focused on the experiences of marginalized students; (c) the use of mathematics as a critical tool to understand social life, one's position in society, and issues of power; agency; and oppression; and (d) the use of mathematics to transform society into a more just system. The seven constructs of high-mathematics instruction discussed previously address Gonzalez's first construct, access to high-quality instruction, in that they provide a framework for educators developing their lessons when teaching or observing mathematics instruction. Gonzalez's last three constructs overlap with culturally relevant pedagogy and critical literacy. Teaching for social justice should not simply be undertaken to increase participation in advanced mathematics courses, access to higher education, and entry into the workforce; in addition to doing all of those things, it should liberate urban students who are often seen as marginalized (Gonzalez, 2009; Martin, 2009). Gutstein (2006) refers to teaching mathematics for social justice as helping students to learn how to "read and write the world" with mathematics (p. 4).

Culturally relevant pedagogy and teaching for social justice is not a panacea. Rather, these pedagogies can provide frameworks that offer ways of integrating high mathematics instructional quality with culture and contexts. The assumption that these pedagogies are beneficial to students of color is tied to how teachers theoretically perceive culture and social justice (Leonard, 2008). Care should be taken not to trivialize or routinize culture or social contexts in the mathematics classroom to the extent that they become counterproductive or just another form of hegemonic practice (Ladson-Billings, 1995; Martin, 2007). A classic way in which mathematics teachers trivialize culture is by taking a contributions approach (Banks, 1993), in which they insert ethnic-sounding names into mathematics problems or use ethnic heroes and holidays to explore the mathematics contributions of cultures. These incorporations do not lead to high-quality mathematics instruction, a curriculum focusing on the experiences of students, mathematical empowerment, or the development of critical thinking.

EXAMPLES OF CULTURALLY RELEVANT PEDAGOGY
AND TEACHING FOR SOCIAL JUSTICE

There is a dearth of examples of culturally relevant pedagogy and teaching mathematics for social justice in the literature. Teaching mathematics for cultural relevance and for social justice requires that the development of mathematical tasks use a context that is relevant to urban African American students' lives. For example, many families are concerned about current and future economic circumstances. The following question addresses monetary and social issues: "What hourly wage would a single parent of two children have to earn in order to live above the poverty line in your state?" (Wiest, Higgins, & Frost, 2007) A multitude of factors should be considered when exploring this question, such as housing, food, transportation, child care, health insurance, clothing, and other essentials. In order to solve this problem, students should collect data on the factors listed above and determine the poverty level for their area. The mathematics in this problem requires students to engage in data collection and analysis, reasoning and problem-solving skills, and numerical computations, while considering real-world finances and other relevant variables (Wiest et al., 2007). This problem allows urban African American students to work collaboratively and encourages them to share ideas. It also allows for flexibility in how students approach the problem and compile different types of evidence to support their decisions. The process of working on this problem can guide urban African American learners toward understanding real-world contexts, exploring issues of social justice, and offering critiques of the world using mathematics.

Renner (2005) and a group of students used the Pythagorean Theorem to design a wheelchair ramp to make the front of their school handicap accessible (e.g., the school had been handicap accessible in the basement at the rear). The students were required to figure out the best place to put a wheelchair ramp, develop a scale drawing, and contact local contractors to find out building costs based on their measurements and calculations. They presented their designs and contractor bids for the wheelchair ramp to the school administration. The administration thanked the students for their work but did not use their suggestions for building a ramp. These experiences gave Renner and the students the opportunity to engage in discussions about issues of public and private facilities, the Americans with Disabilities Act, and budgetary priorities. A group of students offered to build the ramp themselves but school administration rejected their plans.

The Algebra Project (Moses & Cobb, 2001) is an example of a curriculum that is culturally relevant and incorporates social justice. In *Radical Equations: Math Literacy and Civil Rights,* Moses and Cobb (2001) describe access to algebra as a civil rights issue. The Algebra Project rests on three principles: (a) the centrality of involving families and community members, (b) understanding and becoming immersed in the communities, and (c) empowering young people to fight for their own liberation. The units in the Algebra Project are designed to engage students' creativity and mathematical reasoning. For example, an African drum unit is designed to pair a drummer and a teacher in lessons that teach fourth and fifth graders about ratios, proportions, fractions, and rates (Levine, 2005). Another example is a unit for sixth graders focusing on integers, in which African American students in Cambridge, Massachusetts, begin with a ride on a subway. The teacher asks questions that focus on their shifting environment, and the students draw pictures, construct models, and write descriptions (Levine, 2005).

The three examples of culturally relevant pedagogy and teaching mathematics for social justice presented here suggest that the use of relevant context close to the social, political, and cultural lives of students can provide opportunities for students, particularly urban African American ones, to develop deep mathematical understandings. When considering the constructs of mathematics of high instructional quality, one can argue that the examples presented here provide opportunities for teachers to design lessons that meet the standards of previously mentioned constructs. The examples show that teachers, including urban, can use contexts and cultural relevance to structure mathematics lessons that are coherent and focused on central mathematical ideas.

The wheelchair ramp example suggests that the use of the Pythagorean Theorem to structure a unit that explores the slope of a triangle to build a ramp offers a social and political application of an important mathematical concept. The Algebra Project examples suggest that using mathematical tools provides a connection for multiple representations of mathematical ideas. The hourly wage example shows that cognitive depth can be achieved through the use of an open-ended task, which requires students to use data to support their mathematical arguments. All of the examples situate mathematical discourse and explanation and justification as essential constructs for culturally relevant pedagogy, by allowing students to develop understandings of the social, political, and cultural underpinnings of the lessons. Problem solving is a broad construct to use for culturally relevant pedagogy and teaching for social justice, in that students grapple with mathematical problems as well as social and political problems. Thus, students use mathematics to tackle social and political issues. The aforementioned examples highlight that connections and applications are inherent in the tasks.

Although the examples presented of culturally relevant pedagogy and teaching mathematics for social justice provide a lens for incorporating these pedagogies and an understanding of students' engagement, it should not be interpreted that only these pedagogies can be used for mathematics teaching. Rather, students should learn mathematics in ways that capitalize on their strengths and help them compensate for their weaknesses. Urban African American students should be exposed to multiple instructional methods that would allow them to learn mathematics using their preferred ways of knowing. In addition, these students should learn new ways of thinking that are not necessarily based on their preferred ways of knowing (Malloy, 2009).

Traditional mathematics instruction has emphasized a pedagogy that advantages learners who prefer whole-class lecture format with teachers modeling strategies for solving a problem and students passively listening to the explanation (Tate, 2005). Generally speaking, the lecture is followed by students working alone on a large set of problems that reflect the lecture topic (Tate, 2005). The purpose of the lecture and problem set is to prepare students to produce correct responses to narrowly defined problems rather than using their experiential backgrounds to explore and understand mathematics in a contextual and conceptual manner (Tate, 2005). This instructional strategy is often coupled with curricular or ability grouping, with many urban African American students tracked into mathematics programs that focus on the mastery of low-level computational skills (Tate, 2005). Traditional mathematics pedagogy is less challenging pedagogically than teaching for cultural relevance or social justice, in that it does not require teachers to have an understanding of urban African American students' social, political, and cultural contexts. Contextualizing mathematics instruction requires that teachers understand the resources students bring to the learning environment and that teachers accommodate their instruction to meet the needs of academically and culturally diverse students.

CONCLUSIONS AND RECOMMENDATIONS

Teaching and learning mathematics by using culturally relevant pedagogy and infusing social justice principles can motivate urban African American students to use mathematics as a tool in ways that lead to social, political, and economic empowerment. It is critical that urban teachers understand the social, political, and economic contexts that impact these students' lives and mathematize these contexts, so that urban African American students can recognize social inequities and use mathematics to advocate for social, political, or economic change (Leonard, 2008). Culturally relevant teaching and teaching mathematics for social justice empower urban students, including African American ones, to use mathematics as a critical tool for understanding the world.

In order for students to experience mathematics in the ways described above, an overhaul of education must occur, including the preparation of teachers in their understanding of mathematical ideas and their real-world applications. Curriculum content and teacher knowledge should adapt over time to fit evolving contexts. Urban teachers should also be able to understand the underlying mathematics within given contexts and that the curriculum is not static. Further, they should be careful to avoid the assumption that culturally relevant teaching and teaching mathematics for social justice is a panacea. Although there are a common set of sociohistorical experiences that connect urban African American students of particular backgrounds together, neither the students nor their needs remain the same over time. When urban teachers integrate cultural relevance and social justice principles into their mathematics teaching, there is promise for improvement in mathematics instructional quality.

Equally as important, urban teachers should have confidence in their students' ability to succeed (Berry, 2008; Martin, 2009; Powell, 2004). Learning rigorous content and developing a strong mathematics identity are critical to achieving mathematics success. Culturally relevant teaching and teaching mathematics for social justice can potentially lead to the development of a strong mathematics academic identity that may encourage urban African American students to believe they have the ability to learn mathematics, understand the significance of mathematical knowledge, recognize the opportunities and the barriers presented by understanding mathematical knowledge, and develop the motivation and persistence to obtain mathematical knowledge (Martin, 2009).

Although it appears to be clear from the research that urban African American students are receiving low-quality mathematics instruction, there is a dearth of research that suggests focusing on ways to improve the instructional quality that African American students experience. Therefore, we suggest that more research is needed in the following areas: (a) teachers' understanding of mathematics instructional quality and their pedagogical decisions, (b) the instructional quality of mathematics and its impact on African American students' achievement in mathematics, and (c) effective ways to implement culturally relevant pedagogy and teaching mathematics for social justice, in a milieu that has focused on standardized testing.

NOTES

1. Classroom instructional practices are analogous with mathematics instructional quality.
2. To be consistent with the NAEP data, we use the terms *Black*, *White*, and *Hispanic*, although we acknowledge that differences of opinions exist as to the appropriateness of those terms. In addition, for the sake of simplifying the text, we use the term *race* very loosely to mean race or ethnicity, particularly in relation to the NAEP categories of Black, White, and Hispanic students.

REFERENCES

Albert, L. R. (2000). Lessons learned from the "five Men Crew." In M. E. Strutchen, M. L. Johnson, & W. F. Tate (Eds.), *Changing the faces of mathematics: Perspectives on African Americans* (pp. 81–88). Reston, VA: National Council of Teachers of Mathematics.

Ball, D. L., & Rowan, B. (2004). Introduction: Measuring instruction. *The Elementary School Journal, 105*(1), 3–10.

Banks, J. A. (1993). Multicultural education: Historical development, dimensions, and practice. *Review of Research in Education, 19*(1), 3–49.

Berry, R. Q., III. (2005). Voices of success: Descriptive portraits of two successful African American male middle school mathematics students. *Journal of African American Studies, 8*(4), 46–62.

Berry, R. Q., III. (2008). Access to upper-level mathematics: The stories of successful African American middle school boys. *Journal for Research in Mathematics Education, 39*(5), 464–488.

Borko, H., Stecher, B., & Kuffner, K. L., & Standards National Center for Research on Evaluation. (2006). *Using artifacts to characterize reform-oriented instruction: The scoop notebook and rating guide* (CSE Technical Report 707). Los Angeles, CA: National Center for Research on Evaluation.

Boston, M. D. (2008). *Using classroom artifacts as evidence of quality instruction in mathematics.* Paper presented at the annual meeting of the American Association of Colleges for Teacher Education, New Orleans, LA.

Clements, D. H. (2007). Curriculum Research: Toward a Framework for "Research-based Curricula." *Journal for Research in Mathematics Education, 38*(1), 35–70.

Corey, D. L., & Bower, B. L. (2005). The experience of an African American male learning mathematics in the traditional and the online classroom: A case study. *The Journal of Negro Education, 74*(4), 321–331.

Conant, F. R., Rosebery, A., Warren, B., & Hudicourt-Barnes, J. (2001). The sound of drums. In E. McIntyre, A. Rosebery, & N. Gonzalez (Eds.), *Classroom diversity: Connecting curriculum to students' lives* (pp. 51–59). Portsmouth, NH: Heinemann.

Cousins-Cooper, K. M. (2000). Teacher expectations and their effects on African American students' success in mathematics. In W. G. Secada, M. E. Strutchens, M. L. Johnson, & W. F. Tate (Eds.), *Changing the faces of mathematics: Perspectives on African Americans* (pp. 15–20). Reston, VA: National Council of Teachers of Mathematics.

Crocco, M., & Costigan, A. (2007). The narrowing of curriculum and pedagogy in the age of accountability: Urban educators speak out. *Urban Education, 42*(6), 512–535.

Davis, J. (2008). *The lived realities and mathematics education of Black middle school students' living in a poor racially segregated community.* Paper presented at the American Educational Research Association, New York, NY.

Davis, J., & Martin, D. B. (2008). Racism, assessment, and instructional practices: Implications for mathematics teachers of African American students. *Journal of Urban Mathematics Education, 123*(1), 10–34.

Dunn, R. S., Honigsfeld, A., Doolan, L. S., Bostrom, L., Russo, K., Schiering, M. S., Suh, B., & Tenedero, H. (2009). Impact of learning-style instructional strategies on students' achievement and attitudes: Perceptions of educators in diverse institutions. *The Clearinghouse, 82*(3), 135–140.

Dunn, R. S., & Dunn, K. I. (1992). *Teaching elementary students through their individual learning styles.* Boston, MA: Allyn & Bacon.

Franke, M. L., Kazemi, E., & Battey, D. (2007) Mathematics teaching and classroom practices. In Frank K. Lester (Ed.), *Second handbook of research on mathematics teaching and learning* (pp. 225–256). Charlotte, NC: Information Age.

Gay, G. (2000). *Culturally responsive teaching: Theory, practice, and research.* New York, NY: Teachers College Press.

Guild, P. B., & Garger, S. (1998). *Marching to different drummers.* Alexandria, VA: Association for Supervision and Curriculum Development.

Gonzalez, L. (2009). Teaching mathematics for social justice: Reflections on a community of practice for urban high school mathematics teachers. *Journal of Urban Mathematics Education, 2*(1), 22–51.

Gutstein, E. (2003). Teaching and learning mathematics for social justice in an urban, Latino school. *Journal for Research in Mathematics Education, 34*(1), 37–73.

Gutstein, E. (2006). *Reading and writing the world with mathematics: Toward pedagogy for social justice.* New York, NY: Routledge.

Hiebert, J., & Stigler, J. (2000). A proposal for improving classroom teaching: Lessons from the TIMSS Video Study. *Elementary School Journal, 101*(1), 3–20.

Hiebert, J., Sigler, J. W., Jacobs, J. K., Givin, K. B., Garnier, H., Smith, M., & Gallimore, R. (2005). Mathematics teaching in the United States today (and tomorrow): Results from the TIMSS 1999 Video Study. *Educational Evaluation and Policy Analysis, 27*(2), 11–132.

Irvine, J. J., & York, D. E. (1995). Learning styles and culturally diverse students: A literature review. In J. A. Banks & C. A. M. Banks (Eds.), *Handbook of research on multicultural education* (pp. 484–497). New York, NY: Macmillan.

Ladson-Billings, G. (1994). *The dreamkeepers: Successful teachers of African American children.* San Francisco, CA: Jossey-Bass.

Ladson-Billings, G. (1995). Toward a theory of culturally relevant pedagogy. *American Educational Research Journal, 32*(3), 465–491.

Ladson-Billings, G. (2000). Fighting for out lives: Preparing teachers to teach African American Students. *Journal of Teacher Education, 51*(3), 206–214.

Lampert, M. (2004). When the problem is not the question and the solution is not the answer: Mathematical knowing and teaching. In T. P. Carpenter, J. A. Dossey, & J. L. Koehler (Eds.), *Classics in mathematics education research* (pp. 152–171). Reston, VA: National Council of Teachers of Mathematics.

Lattimore, R. (2003). African-American students struggle on Ohio's high stakes test. *The Western Journal of Black Studies, 27*(2), 118–126.

Lattimore, R. (2005). Harnessing and channeling African American children's energy in the mathematics classroom. *Journal of Black Studies, 35*(3), 267–283.

Leonard, J. (2008). *Culturally specific pedagogy in the mathematics classroom: Strategies for teachers and students.* New York, NY: Routledge/Taylor & Francis.

Leonard, J., Davis, J. E., & Sidler, J. L. (2005). Cultural relevance and computer-assisted instruction. *Journal of Research on Technology in Education, 37*(3), 263–284.

Levine, D. (2005). Radical equations. In E. Gutstein & B. Peterson (Eds.), *Rethinking mathematics: Teaching social justice by the numbers* (pp. 90–96). Milwaukee, WI: Rethinking Schools.

Lipka, J., Hogan, M., Parker, J., & Yanez, E. (2005). Math in a cultural context: Two case studies of a successful culturally bases math project. *Anthropology and Education Quarterly, 36*(4), 376–395.

Lubienski, S. T. (2002). A closer look at black-white mathematics gaps: Intersections of race and SES in NAEP achievement and instructional practices data. *Journal of Negro Education, 71*(4), 269–287.

Lutkus, A., Grigg, W., & Dion, G. (2007). *The nation's report card: 2007 trial urban district assessment in mathematics* (NCES Publication No. 2008–452). Washington, DC: National Center for Education Statistics. Retrieved from http://nces.ed.gov/pubsearch/pubsinfo. asp?pubid=2008452

Malloy, C. E. (2009). Instructional strategies and dispositions of teachers who help African American students gain conceptual understanding. In D. B. Martin (Ed.), *Mathematics teaching, learning, and liberation in the lives of Black children* (pp. 123–144). Mahwah, NJ: Lawrence Erlbaum.

Martin, D. B. (2007). Beyond missionaries or cannibals: Who should teach mathematics to African American children? *The High School Journal, 91*(1), 6–28.

Martin, D. B. (2009). Liberating the production of knowledge about African American children and mathematics. In D. B. Martin (Ed.), *Mathematics teaching, learning, and liberation in the lives of black children* (pp. 3–36). New York, NY: Routledge.

McKinney, S. E., Chappell, S., Berry, R. Q., III, & Hickman, B. T. (2009). An examination of the instructional practices of mathematics teachers in urban schools. *Preventing School Failure, 53*(4), 278–284.

Moschkovich, J. (2002). A situated and sociocultural perspective on bilingual language learners. *Mathematical Thinking and Learning, 4*(2/3), 189–212.

Moses, R. P., & Cobb, C. E., Jr. (2001). *Radical equations: Math literacy and civil rights.* Boston, MA: Beacon Press.

Nasir, N. S. (2002). Identity, goals and learning: Mathematics in cultural practice. *Mathematical Thinking and Learning, 4*(2/3), 211–245.

Nasir, N. S. (2005). Individual cognitive structuring and the sociocultural context: Strategy shifts in the game of dominoes. *The Journal of Learning Sciences, 14*(1), 5–34.

Nasir, N. S., Hand, V., & Taylor, E. V. (2008). Culture and mathematics in school: Boundaries between "cultural" and "domain" knowledge in the mathematics classroom and beyond. *Review of Research in Education, 32*(1), 187–240.

National Center for Education Statistics. (2009). *The nation's report card: Mathematics 2009 trial urban district assessment* (NCES Publication No. 2010–452). Washington, DC: U.S. Department of Education. Retrieved from http://nces.ed.gov/nationsreportcard/pdf/dst2009/2010452rev.pdf

National Council of Teachers of Mathematics. (2000). *Principles and standards of school mathematics.* Reston, VA: Author.

National Council of Teachers of Mathematics. (2007). *Mathematics teaching today: Improving practice, improving student learning.* Reston, VA: Author.

National Mathematics Advisory Panel. (2008). *Foundations for success: The final report of the National Mathematics Advisory Panel.* Washington, DC: U.S. Department of Education.

Oakes, J. (1990). Opportunities, achievement and choice: Women and minority students in science and mathematics. *Review of Research in Education, 16*(1), 153–222.

Palacios, L. (2005). *Critical issue: Mathematics education in the era of NCLB—principles and* standards. Retrieved from http://www.ncrel.org/sdrs/areas/issues/content/cntareas/math/ma500.pdf

Pitts, J. (2009). Identifying and using a teacher-friendly learning-styles instrument. *Clearing House: A Journal of Educational Strategies, Issues and Ideas, 82*(5), 225–231.

Powell, A. (2004, July). *The diversity backlash and the mathematical agency of students of color.* Paper presented at the International Group for the Psychology of Mathematics Education, Bergen, Norway. Retrieved from http://www.eric.ed.gov/PDFS/ED489450.pdf

Renner, A. (2005). Designing a wheelchair ramp. In E. Gutstein & B. Peterson (Eds.), *Rethinking mathematics: Teaching social justice by the numbers* (pp. 88–89). Milwaukee, WI: Rethinking Schools.

Sanders, W. L., & Rivers, J. (1996). *Cumulative and residual effects of teachers on future student academic achievement.* Knoxville, TN: The University of Tennessee Value-Added Research and Assessment Center.

Secada, W. (1992). Race, ethnicity, social class, language and achievement in mathematics. In D. Grouws (Ed.), *Handbook of research on mathematics teaching and learning* (pp. 146–164). New York, NY: Macmillian.

Shade, B. J. (1997). African-American cognitive patterns: A review of the research. In B. J. Shade (Ed.), *Culture, style and the educative process: Making schools work for racially diverse students* (pp. 70–91). Springfield, IL: Charles C. Thomas.

Sheppard, P. A., IV. (2006). Successful African-American mathematics students in academically unacceptable high schools. *Education, 126*(4), 609–625.

Stein, M. K., Smith, M. S., Henningsen, M., & Silver, E. A. (2000). *Implementing standards-based mathematics instruction: A casebook for professional development.* New York, NY: Teachers College Press.

Stein, M. K., Smith, M. S., & Silver, E.A. (1999). The development of professional developers: Learning to assist teachers in new settings in new ways. *Harvard Educational Review, 69*(3), 237–269.

Strutchens, M., & Silver, E. (2000). NAEP findings regarding race/ethnicity: Students' performance, school experiences, and attitudes and beliefs. In E. A. Silver & P. A. Kenney (Eds.), *Results from the seventh mathematics assessment of the National Assessment of Educational Progress* (pp. 45–72). Reston, VA: National Council of Teachers of Mathematics.

Sutton, J., & Krueger, A. (2002). *EDThoughts: What we know about mathematics teaching and learning.* Aurora, CO: Mid-Continent Research for Education and Learning.

Tate, W. F. (1997). Race ethnicity, SES, gender and language proficiency trends in mathematics achievement: An update. *Journal for Research in Mathematics Education, 28*(6), 652–679.

Tate, W. F. (2005). *Access and opportunities to learn are not accidents: Engineering mathematical progress in your school.* Greensboro, NC: Serve.

Walkowiak, T. A., Berry, R. Q., III, McCracken, E. R., Rimm-Kaufman, S. E., & Meyer, J. P. (2009). *The Validation of an Observational Measure of Mathematics Instruction.* Paper presented at the 31st Annual Meeting of the North American Chapter of the International Group for the Psychology of Mathematics Education, Atlanta, GA.

Weiss, I. R., Pasley, J. D., Smith, P. Sean, Banilower, E. R., & Heck, D. J. (2003). *Looking inside the classroom: A study of K–12 mathematics and science education in the United States.* Chapel Hill, NC: Horizon Research.

Wenglinsky, H. (2002). *How teaching matters: Bringing the classroom back into discussions of teacher quality.* Princeton, NJ: Milken Family Foundation.

Wiest, L. R., Higgins, H. J., & Frost, J. H. (2007). Quantitative literacy for social justice. *Equity & Excellence in Education, 40*(1), 47–55.

CHAPTER TEN

Bridging THE Culture OF Urban Students TO THE Culture OF Science: The Roles of Culturally Relevant Pedagogy, Discursive Identity, AND Conceptual Continuities in the Promotion OF Scientific Literacy

BRYAN A. BROWN, MATTHEW KLOSER,
AND J. BRYAN HENDERSON

"We build too many walls, and not enough bridges."

—SIR ISAAC NEWTON

Science holds an important position in the United States. It is unfortunate that it has often been considered accessible to only our most intellectually talented students. As the Sputnik Era energized science education reform, an educational pipeline was created for many of these talented students to enter scientific careers (Deboer, 1991). In consequence, many Americans that did not fit the mold of traditional science students did not consistently or systematically engage with science during their primary and secondary educations. More recently, the National Research Council (NRC; 1996) and the American Association for the Advancement of Science (AAAS; 1993) shifted their focus from developing a pipeline of scientists and engineers to developing a scientifically literate citizenry. In theory, this new approach heeds Newton's words, as walls once built to stratify the scientific elite from the general population have been replaced with bridges connecting a diverse range of people to science.

However, there is an irony in Newton's call for bridges that is difficult to ignore. Newton's contributions in physics and mathematics helped establish norms in the scientific community that have determined the appropriate nature of subsequent scientific questions, evidence, discourse, and even scientific journal article formats (Bazerman, 1988). Newton, among others, pursued questions and established methods and forms of communication consistent with his own culture—questions and methods that philosophers of science from similar backgrounds eventually codified as "true science" in gatherings, such as the Vienna Circle. Rather than create a bridge, Newton's body of work has actually helped create a scientific paradigm whose walls have alienated many people. Those wanting to engage in scientific discourse must communicate using specific vocabulary and grammar that diverges from common vernacular and diverse communicative styles. Thus, if the science curriculum and instruction is to be made truly salient to all, it should find ways to build academic bridges that facilitate a scientifically literate citizenry among today's diverse learners. As many urban students, particularly African Americans, initially engage the work of Newton, Darwin, and the like, we contend that too few bridges connect the established scientific content and culture in what students already experience and understand in their everyday lives.

Given that science education plays a central role in the creation of new knowledge structures, it is up to science educators to dictate whether these structures can ultimately function as walls or bridges. Building bridges stands at the forefront of science education's challenges, and, if science is to become a viable option for urban African American students, educators should be equipped with the proper pedagogical tools to build bridges between student culture and the culture of science. This chapter explores notions of cultural relevance, language, identity, and conceptual development that should be considered if such bridge building is to be efficacious for urban African American students.

SCIENTIFIC LITERACY

The notion of "scientific literacy" has provided a conceptual goal based on which science educators can build curricula, instruct students, and assess their understanding. Given the contemporary push for such scientific literacy to reach beyond merely those who seek to practice science professionally, one influential group, AAAS, has established the goal that, by the time Halley's Comet next shoots through the night sky in 2061, all Americans will have achieved scientific literacy. Indeed for nearly 30 years, the science education community has pushed for more widespread scientific literacy in the hope that the United States can remain a dominant social, scientific, and economic player on the world stage (Arons, 1983; AAAS, 1989).

As an idea, scientific literacy offers a unique contrast to other ways of conceptualizing and assessing what people know about science. Brokering the term "literacy" with those concerned with reading/language arts offers science educators a unique way of framing learners and citizens as either "literate" or "illiterate" citizens. Such a construction enables the community to set a goal to achieve a nation of individuals who are, in fact, scientifically competent. By contrast, many European assessments of how people understand scientific ideas describe the process as the "public understanding of science." Although the differences in the phrases that the different cultures use are subtle, "scientific literacy" provides a nonrelative, seemingly objective framework that can be used to gauge how people reason, analyze, and understand the world.

Although significant obstacles on reaching widespread scientific literacy remain, none is more striking than the lack of consensus surrounding this concept's definition. Even though it has a nonrelative framework, the concept of scientific literacy has remained abstract for American educators since Hurd coined the term in 1958 (Rutherford & Ahlgren, 1990). In the absence of a strong definition, many educators, including urban, have created a science literacy myth in which acceptable definitions include "the simplistic view that any exposure to science contributes [to] scientific literacy, to . . . the naïve view that scientific literacy means being able to think like a scientist" (Shamos, 1995, p. 47). Whether myth or reality, the notion of scientific literacy has opened a veritable Pandora's Box in defining America's science education goals. DeBoer (pp. 591–593, 2000) summarizes the diversity of scientific literacy literature into nine categories: (a) teaching and learning about science as a cultural force in the modern world, (b) preparation for the world of work, (c) teaching and learning about science that has direct application to everyday living, (d) teaching students to be informed citizens, (e) learning about science as a particular way of examining the natural world, (f) understanding reports and discussions of science that appear in the popular media, (g) learning about science for its aesthetic appeal, (h) preparing citizens who are sympathetic to science, and (i) understanding the nature and importance of technology and the relationship between technology and science.

As DeBoer's list indicates, whereas some advocate for scientific literacy that includes aesthetics and implementation, technology, and philosophy, others have argued that a scientifically literate citizenry is a more than a knowledgeable citizenry, it is a participatory citizenry (Brossard & Shanahan, 2006; DeBoer, 2000;

Roth & Lee, 2002). Proponents of this latter perspective advocate that literacy emerges when communities interact and participate in decisions and actions related to scientific phenomena (Roth & Lee, 2002). They thus suggest that scientific literacy not only includes scientific knowledge and practices but also involves the context in which interactions occur, decisions are made, and opinions are swayed (Roth & Lee, 2002). Stated in a different way, they see scientific literacy as no more than science praxis (Roth & Lee 2002; Roth, 2007).

Participation in the scientific community, however, requires particular discourses and language—facets that may create walls for many students who have little exposure or connection to conventional scientific discourse. Some science educators have focused on this literal interpretation of literacy (Halliday & Martin, 1993; Norris & Phillips, 2003). Latour and Woolgar's (1986) anthropological account of the science laboratory generalized the scientific experience not as one of experimentation but rather of literary inscription. They observe machines providing volumes of recorded measures, logs filled with annotations, and reference journals spread throughout the workspace. The desk, not the lab bench, provides the most engagement and excitement (Latour & Woolgar, 1986). Indeed, science uses language as a tool that incorporates technical terms and innovative grammatical structures to convey specific meaning effectively and efficiently (Halliday & Martin, 1994). In this sense, Halliday and Martin (1994) and Norris and Phillips (2003) underscore the essential nature of language in science education in claiming that "the language of science has become the language of literacy" (Halliday & Martin, 1993, p. 11). As a result, many students and members of the public who fail to connect with this discourse have felt alienated from scientific participation (Halliday & Martin, 1993).

In sum, building bridges between students and the scientific enterprise remains difficult not because K–12 urban education lacks an ultimate goal but because the goal cannot be defined clearly. This abstraction creates significant difficulties for teachers as they try to build bridges from student prior knowledge to an ill-defined goal that differs among scholars and educators. In his synthesis, DeBoer (2000) argues that science teachers can and should choose their own working definition of scientific literacy that addresses the needs of their students and community. To extend our metaphor, under these conditions, urban teachers attempt to build bridges to the scientific community, but the bridges may lead to different locations based on the students involved. Thus, the objective, nonrelative framework is lost and students initially isolated from practices within the world of science will have to continue to climb walls, if not try and avoid them altogether.

Given the potential pitfalls of working with a loose conception of scientific literacy, we choose to focus this chapter on a more specific facet of science comprehension. That is, our subsequent references to scientific literacy are effectively references to the degree to which urban African American students understand the major explanatory stories about science and ideas about how that knowledge is shaped and accepted (Osborne, 1998). Within this working definition, urban African American students are theoretically able to use knowledge and language shaped in science classrooms to participate as voting citizens, analyze science in the media, sympathize with the work of practicing scientists, and engage in scientific practices themselves (DeBoer, 2000). We argue that, if such a conception of scientific literacy is indeed among the primary goals of urban science educators, science curriculum and instruction cannot be cut out of the picture. Indeed, variations of urban African American students with respect to prior knowledge, cultural capital, and life experiences dictate that teachers may need to use a multitude of pedagogical strategies to reach ends concerned with the fulfillment of more specific scientific standards. This is especially true for reaching and connecting with urban African American students. Hence, we advocate the need to erect urban educational bridges spanning the existing chasm between one's culture and the more nonrelative culture surrounding science. We also point to pedagogy that has such bridge building in mind and provide evidence of how it can be put into practice without necessarily compromising standards. Having established the need for bridges to span what is effectively a cultural divide between student and science culture. In the remainder of this chapter, we suggest that bridge building behooves us to pay careful attention to urban African American students' language practices, developing scientific identities that are intimately tied to language use and creating conceptual continuities between prima facie student interpretations of science and the ultimate understandings science educators wish to enfranchise.

A CULTURAL DIVIDE

Building educational bridges implies that a gap exists between the tools students bring to the classroom and those necessary to participate in the scientific enterprise. But what exactly is the gap that must be spanned? Simply put, this issue is linked to culture. Science has been described as maintaining a unique epistemological framework (Sandoval, 2003), detailed representational practices (diSessa, 1983, 2002) and complex linguistic patterns (Halliday & Martin, 1993; Lemke, 1990), such that learning science is learning to participate in a new culture (Lee, 2001; Valeras & Kane, 2009). In order for students to achieve Osborne's (1998) goals of understanding the explanatory stories and ideas of science, bridges should span the diverse cultures of individual students and the established culture of science. This goal ultimately requires focusing on language practices, establishing conceptual continuities, and defining urban African American students' scientific identity.

Teaching and learning science consists of far more than the transmission and reception of knowledge. Rather, it involves the transmission and reception of a specific culture in terms of its unique epistemology, language practices, and methods. Because science has worked to generate a culture of objective scientific practice, science teaching has been seen as immune from critiques of cultural bias and hegemony (Brickhouse, 1994). For example, literature courses are often condemned as culturally unresponsive when diverse groups of students read books that perpetuate hegemonic perspectives. On the contrary, science classes have been conceived as being culturally neutral and immune from being taught from a culturally relevant perspective (Brown, 2004). The paradigm that guides this thinking operates on the assumption that if all students have to learn the language, epistemology, and knowledge of science, then why does science teaching bear the responsibility of culturally relevant instruction? Such a perspective often builds walls between science and urban African American students, as they find their language practices, identity, and cultural epistemology devalued in science classrooms (Brown, 2004; Gilbert & Yerrick, 2001).

Unlike other disciplines, such as history or English, that have multiple paradigms from which one analyzes texts, events, and perspectives, science suggests that its involvement occurs through one means—the universal scientific paradigm. Science, therefore, homogenizes cultures into one paradigm and ignores diverse cultural and linguistic practices. The National Science Standards and Benchmarks for Scientific Literacy, do, however, emphasize the importance of relating science to one's daily life—an important pedagogical bridge. Many urban classrooms fail to make these connections. Although the standards do not narrowly suggest only one scientific method, many textbooks and classrooms convey a sense of uniformity. It results in the perpetuation of a Kuhn-ian paradigm, in which members of the community operate within the current constraints and perspectives unless a revolution replaces it with another unitary position (Kuhn, 1962). The philosophy of science negates, a priori, the possibility of tapping into diverse perspectives as an authentic means of engaging science.

This acute conception of what does and does not constitute a scientific perspective creates somewhat of a catch-22. Classrooms that incorporate all aspects of the science standards, including content, investigation, and sociohistorical perspectives, do so within an established scientific paradigm defined not by a single race or gender but definitively by a single scientific culture that has historically favored White males. On the other hand, urban classes that fail to meet these standards present an equally uniform, dogmatic perspective reliant on memorization and recall. In either case, with the nature of science calling for ardent objectivity, culturally relevant frameworks for science teaching are difficult to identify.

Indeed, most students, especially urban African American ones, bring experiences, conceptions, and misconceptions to the science classroom that do not align with the supposedly culturally neutral scientific paradigm but nevertheless are scientific in nature. Moll, Amanti, Neff, and Gonzalez's (1992) *funds of knowledge* notion captures these important components for minority students and students of low socioeconomic background. For example, a student assembling electronics in the living room learns explicitly about foundational elements of electronics, implicitly about properties of electricity and circuits, and may learn about scientific ideas such as controlling variables when performing a test. Urban African American students also bring language-related funds of knowledge to the science classroom, but they are often ignored more than prior experiences. If science education wishes to build bridges instead of walls, urban educators should connect African American students' existing language practices with those acceptable in the science community and connect these students' prior experiences and knowledge to existing theories, laws, and concepts. In short, urban educators should shape and use diverse tools and resources that students bring to the classroom in order to create a common scientific paradigm in which all students can engage.

BUILDING BRIDGES: CULTURAL RELEVANCE WITHOUT COMPROMISE

Culturally Relevant Pedagogy

In attempts to build a research base of best practices for teaching urban students, scholars have engaged in years of research on culturally grounded teaching (Banks, 1993; Gay, 2000; Hollins, 1996; Irvine, 1990; Ladson-Billings, 1999; Nieto, 1999; Villegas-Lucas & Lucas, 2003). Banks's (1993) work on multicultural education has highlighted the need to recognize the subtle differences and complexities associated with teaching urban African American students. This research and similar studies highlight how the growing need for pedagogical content knowledge (PCK) is insufficient if it is not thoroughly embedded in a rich understanding of PCK for African American students (Gay, 2000; King, 2003; Shulman, 1987).

Early forms of research on culturally relevant instruction highlight the need to recognize the values and resources embedded in urban African American students' cultural ways of being (Banks, 1993; King, 2003). Scholars built on Pierre Bordieu's notion of cultural capital to argue that a transition needed to occur to help urban teachers see the value of African American students' culture, so they could teach these students to participate in classroom culture. To this end, King (1994) argues that urban teachers require a deep knowledge about both academic and African American cultures to accomplish this task. As urban teachers develop a clear sense of *who* their students are, they play the role of cultural broker and help them adapt to the academic culture in their own cultural way. For example, cultural wars have been fought for decades in relation to the concept of evolution. Urban teachers, who know the scientific evidence and theories as well as African American students' cultural leanings on the issue, tend to have more success in teaching the content than those who completely ignore the perspective of the urban student culture.

The subtle difference between asking students to adapt academic culture to their own cultural identity versus asking them to assimilate into mainstream academic culture is key to the success of culturally relevant instruction. Ladson-Billings (1992) explains this principle in describing how urban African American parents are able to recognize the difference between teachers who operate on an assimilation versus an accommodation model:

> The parents defined success as the kind of teaching that encouraged their children to choose academic excellence, while at the same time it allowed them to maintain a positive identification with their own heritage and background. These parents were aware of the possible (and perhaps, likely) alienating effects of education on African American children. (p. 382)

In this chapter, we adopt Ladson-Billings's perspective on the relationship between academic identification and school performance. More specifically, we assume that the need to maintain cultural objectivity in science causes much of the conflict between urban African American students' culture and the culture of science. In light of this dilemma, we are concerned that if science teaching does not recognize the dilemma that exists between urban African American students' identity and classroom learning, many of these students are likely to be alienated from science. The first step, it seems, is for urban teachers, parents, and students to acknowledge the cultural difference and then establish instructional practices that help bridge these gaps.

If modern conceptions of scientific literacy are to go beyond what is understood by urban education experts and become relevant to the personal needs of science students—the majority of whom will not practice science professionally—science instruction demands consideration of the cultural nuances that an ever-diversifying student body brings to the table. The benefit of such cultural relevance includes the possibility of enfranchising wider appeal and student motivation to learn scientific concepts that could otherwise be easily chalked up as abstract, book-ish, and only relevant to the confines of urban classrooms in which they are taught. Effective urban educators recognize students' existing knowledge as a starting point not an obstacle for instruction. When classroom instruction is tied to the specific activities in urban African American students' everyday lives, the curriculum becomes more culturally relevant and, in theory, more interesting to them.

Project-Based Learning

How can urban African American students' existing knowledge be woven into contemporary science curriculum? Marx, Blumenfeld, Krajcik, and Soloway's (1997) project-based science (PBS) is one viable example. PBS crafts curricular units based on a driving question that requires a summative product. In essence, urban teachers design projects with an underlying question, such as "Will breathing the air in my city make me sick?" or "How do I stay on my skateboard?" (p. 345). Students first identify the necessary lines of study pertinent to the aforementioned questions, and then peer groups are formed to investigate selected issues over the course of several weeks. In compiling such research, urban African American students have the opportunity to bring their respective funds of knowledge into the curriculum. It then becomes the responsibility of the instructor to help tie students' funds of knowledge into scientific concepts that can aid them in making sense of the investigations they have selected. Another feature of PBS is that urban African American students are given latitude in how they wish to pursue their chosen line of study. This stands in contrast to more conventional scripted activities. Such projects may indeed be "hands-on," but they are not necessarily "minds on." Students can become easily preoccupied with merely following directions in prescribed projects (Tobin, Tippins, & Gallard, 1994).

Incorporating pedagogies like PBS, science educators have the opportunity to situate scientific learning within the context of the culturally relevant issues that African American students bring into the classroom. As Lave (1988) has argued, knowledge retention can be powerfully linked to the environment or context in which the acquisition of information takes place, and such projects allow urban African American students to explore their everyday concerns inside the classroom. For instance, the creation and maintenance of community gardens in New York City has shown positive effects for urban science learners (Calabrese-Barton, 2007) and increases the possibility of internalizing scientific thinking and concepts.

However, in a historically common critique of attempts to broaden the notion of scientific literacy, can the latitude of pedagogies like PBS give urban African American students standards for science proficiency? Although community gardens may help African American students learn some material, does the time commitment and narrow focus prevent students from becoming scientifically literate? Does PBS threaten to compromise standards that have been set to allow the United States to competently tackle the technological problems of the future? Does allowing science instruction to be individualized and culturally relevant result in a situation in which fundamentals simply do not get taught (Kromhout & Good, 1983). Results from PBS instruction in the Detroit Public Schools suggest otherwise. Marx et al. (2004) tested the efficacy of a three-year PBS curriculum, involving nearly 8,000 students in grades 6 through 8. At the time of the study, Detroit Public Schools had a student population in which 91% of the students were African American, and approximately half of the total student population lived in families that were at or below the poverty line. Marx et al. find that on written assessments measuring science content knowledge and science processes, student achievement from pre- to posttest increased for each of the study's three years. They claim that with proper professional development, urban teachers can incorporate culturally relevant pedagogy like PBS, so that "students who are low achievers in science can succeed in standards-based, inquiry science" (p. 1063). Achievement gains have been reported not only on the researcher-developed multiple-choice and free-response assessments but also on some standardized tests (Rivet & Krajcik, 2004; Songer, Lee, & McDonald, 2003).

Project-based learning taps into urban African American students' funds of knowledge and provides the freedom to explore questions and develop solutions within their own contexts. A major component of PBS and PBS-like instruction is discourse and language practices accessible to students that engage them in meaningful conversations. Discussions in the science classroom can evoke more active student engagement with the material, promote the skills necessary to work in a collaborative environment, and allow urban teachers to interact with many more African American students than do traditional didactic methods (DeBoer, 1991). In most cases, science discourses create obstacles to student learning in that they conflict with students' identities and discursive practices. This suggests that more careful attention needs to be paid to student discursive practice in science reform that champions discussion as part of the bridge-building effort.

Discursive Identity

Urban educators are now beginning to recognize how acquiring science literacy can be viewed as the development of a scientific identity. In essence, the very construct of scientific literacy assumes some fundamental things about who the literate individual is as a person, including an expectation of his individual's intellectual skills, knowledge resources, epistemology, and language use. Informed by a sociolinguistic framework, it can be assumed that, in every linguistic exchange (e.g., written, read, spoken, and enacted), speakers and listeners coconstruct meaning through interactions that serve to position them as particular types of people (Agar, 1994; Fishman, 1989; Gee, 1999, 2002). In a dialogue, the language of a disciplinary knowledge like science requires individuals to symbolically cue their identity by making use of the language and symbols of science. Engaging in these discourse practices is not neutral with respect to students' identity. As a result, the very use of science discourse practices is rich with implications of culture and identity and must be explored through a lens that makes these interactions visible.

Although perspectives of the interactional parameters of classroom discourse have been central to analyses of science learning (Kelly, 2005; Lemke, 1990), explorations of identity have made little progress in explaining what an identity dilemma seemingly is. This refers to an undesirable quid pro quo in the urban science classroom in which African American students must eschew their established identity for the sake of functioning appropriately within the scientific paradigm (Gilbert & Yerrick, 2001). In such cases, a perspective on identity has the potential to illuminate how identity shapes the interactive modes of classroom discourse and, in turn, scientific literacy in general.

Many sociocultural perspectives on identity offer a nonstatic framework (Gee, 2002; Wenger, 1998; Wortham, 2003). For instance, Gee (2002) explains how identity "can change from moment to moment in the interaction, can change from context to context, and of course, can be ambiguous or unstable" (p. 99). Although identity is understood as a framework for characterizing "who" an individual is understood to be, it is subject to a number of dynamic interpretations. As urban students, including African American ones, interact, they use their histories and interpret cues of moment-to-moment interaction to make an assessment of "who" they understand the other participants to be (Nasir & Saxe, 2003). On the other hand, urban African American students can use their knowledge of these relationships to send messages about their identity to others. As an example, consider those urban students perceived to "sound Black." Such individuals often engage, actively or passively, in discursive activities that allow others to interpret their diction and/or behaviors as "Black." Based on this example, identity signals a broad set of domains that may be evoked and socially constructed in the moment. The shared assumptions that individuals carry about what an African American person sounds or acts like can frame how the cues embedded in talk or behavior shape how the listener, observer, or speaker interprets the identities they associate with the discourse (Brown, 2004; Nunberg, 2004)

We, in turn, advocate that urban science educators adopt a teaching disposition sensitive to the notion that discursive messages may contribute to how urban African American students' scientific identity is constructed (Fishman, 1989; Gumperz, 1982). As such, language can be used as a powerful tool to shape how African Americans affiliate and share membership in the science classroom (Fishman, 1989). Applying this lens to an assessment of science literacy development suggests that the language and symbols of science can be used as a source for identity construction (Gee, 1999, 2002; Gumperz, 1982; Wortham, 2003).

Since the late 1990s, several studies have recognized how scientific discourses intersect with students' identity (Anderson, Holland, & Palinscar, 1997; Gilbert &

Yerrick, 2001) and how language mediates interaction and knowledge acquisition (Halliday & Martin, 1993; Lemke, 1990). For example, Gilbert and Yerrick's (2001) award-winning publication explains how students' views of science are uniquely connected to their language identity dilemma. To this end, they argue that those who choose to participate in the culture of science and its language practice are seen to be acting "White," whereas those who reject the culture and language of science are seen as maintaining a "Black" identity. Further, this body of work illustrates how language serves as a mediator of identity relationships and how African American students' awareness of these interactions has the potential to influence their mode of class engagement.

Gilbert and Yerrick (2001) underscore research findings that indicate how cultural and linguistic components of science classrooms generate emotive feelings of conflict and marginalization (Brickhouse, 1994; Brown, 2004). When taking the relationship between language, identity, and classroom interaction into account, research exploring the language-identity dilemma can provide insights into how African American students gain access to science. If science teaching and learning are explored from a perspective that assesses the social significance of science language use, research may begin to gain a greater understanding of how interpersonal and intrapersonal contexts can shape learning outcomes.

As urban African American students traverse their cultural borders, they are often forced to learn to appropriate their identities associated with membership in multiple cultural groups. This is a bridge that urban science teachers should help these students build to repeatedly cross between their normal identity and that of their science-based selves. To understand how these identities are enacted and impact learning, we argue for the need to recognize how the construction of discursive identity takes place (Brown, 2004; Brown, Reveles, & Kelly, 2005). The act of communicating identity through language practices provides the basis for what constitutes a discursive identity. The idea is that individuals select genres of language with the knowledge (e.g., tacit or implicit) that others will interpret their discourse as a signal of their cultural membership (Brown, 2004).

Science education research has been slow to explore how the discursive coconstruction of student identities shapes science learning. If urban educators adopt the linguistic assumption that all language practices are associated with some cultural membership and identity, they should not assume that acquiring science literacy is a culturally neutral process. In fact, it is believed that the acquisition of science literacy is firmly rooted in urban students' acquiring a mastery of science discourse.

Given the assumption that acquiring a mastery of science discourse is essential for any African American student, including urban, to learn science, two tenets of language learning are particularly problematic: First, all language is associated with the culture of those who use the language (Agar, 1994; Nunberg, 2004). This suggests that learning and using the language of science can be problematic if instruction does not incorporate a culturally affirming approach to science teaching. In this way, culturally relevant pedagogy (CRP) should include a framework that addresses how to decrease the impact of potential issues of language and identity. A second language-learning problem is associated with students' cognition. If urban African American students are taught science in a language that they are familiar with, then their conception of the phenomenon is inhibited by the mode of instruction being offered. On the other hand, if these students are taught both language and concepts simultaneously, one could argue that African American students are being confronted with two unique walls to climb: The first is the wall of cultural affiliation that they face in choosing to participate in the language of science. During this process, urban African American students may be accused of acting White (Gilbert & Yerrick, 2001; Fordham, 1996). The second wall involves students lacking a clear conception of the content because of unfamiliar language used to introduce the concepts. Together, these language-learning challenges call for a greater understanding of how to construct bridges that urban African American students can realistically cross.

Conceptual Continuities

Culturally relevant science pedagogy should bridge not only urban African American students' native language practices and those deemed acceptable by the scientific community but also their native conceptions and those established by science. As urban science educators think about ways to improve access for their African American students, they may benefit from an improved ability to recognize the continuities that exist between students' native ways of understanding the world and those valued in education. Building on existing research that has explored how urban students' everyday literacy practices can be used for classroom learning (Hull & Shultz, 2001; Mahiri, 2004; Morrel, 2005), it is believed that science education could benefit from building similar bridges between everyday practice and canonical science, including language usage (Rosebery, Warren, & Conant, 1992).

Studies of everyday language practices have shown that appropriating everyday language practices can assist students, including urban African American ones, in their cognition process (Rosebery et al., 1992). Over the years, research on language in science has explored the grammar, rhetorical structure, and technical terminology of science discourse, but little science education research has compared the functionality of alternative genres of talk to their impact on science cognition and achievement.

Linguists have suggested that as humans experience the world, we conceptualize our experiences with the available language resources (Sapir, 1949). Therefore, a culturally relevant framework recognizes how students' own medium of expression relates to those valued in science (Sapir, 1949). Framing native discourses as assets, as opposed to deficits, can address major challenges associated with language use and science learning. If urban educators begin instruction in a language that African American students already know, they are better equipped to gain a clear conception of the idea being taught (Brown & Ryoo, 2009). Using a "double speak" approach—articulating the scientific word or phrase immediately followed by the concept in common vernacular—provides a bridge not only in terms of discursive identity but also for creating conceptual continuities between these seemingly disparate worlds. As Hammer (2000) explains, "Much of naïve instructional practice is characterized by inappropriate presumptions regarding the resources students have available" (p. 53). In large part, this inappropriate analysis is associated with naïve urban teachers not understanding the role of discourse. When urban science teachers operate with a singular perspective on science language, a "right or wrong" dichotomy pervades, and they fail to acknowledge partial understandings. Understandings expressed in alternative genres are also made invisible. By placing a high premium on academic language—without recognizing the value of African American students' discursive resources—urban science teachers' burn bridges before they are even constructed. Therefore, a CRP should identify the conceptual continuities embedded in urban African American students' native language as a way to work within their initial resources and still achieve the original goal intended for all students.

Research on intuitive science understanding led to the development of learning theories, describing how people come to understand the world. Posner, Strike, Hewson, and Gertzog (1982) introduced and later revised a "conceptual ecology" as an overarching rationale for understanding how urban African American students come to understand phenomena. This framework, commonly known as conceptual change, explains how urban African American students advance from intuitive understandings to reconstructed scientific understandings. Although conceptual change has been widely accepted as a theory for understanding student learning, it is not without its critics.

One of the primary critiques of this body of work put forth claims about the limits of its effectiveness. Over the years, education scholars have argued that conceptual change is limited in that it only describes learning that occurs when students hold a clear understanding of a phenomenon. These same scholars have thus argued for a more gradual alteration of students' perspectives. In 2002, Vosniadou claimed that students change perspectives gradually rather than drastically. Other scholars have argued that students' misconceptions are merely erroneous categorizations of concepts, which would make conceptual change a simple reassignment of concepts.

The idea that students' science concepts exist in stark discrepant contrasts was challenged by a number of education scholars who argue for the recognition of students' native conceptual understandings. DiSessa (2002) identifies how conceptual change perspectives serve as foundational transformations between native understandings of the world and their scientific counterparts. It is the challenge of reconciling the relationship between native conceptions and those valued by science that both serves as the foundation of this study and is often tightly linked with issues of language and identity. If urban students develop complex understandings of the world in settings outside of science, the conceptual change perspective helps urban education scholars understand how scientific understandings are developed through alternative discourses. Further, using students' native ways of understanding the world as a means to help bridge their conceptual understanding has the potential to be fruitful to students' learning.

A precedent exists for student learning through conceptual continuities. In 1984, DiSessa described how individuals transition from the direct experience to scientific understanding, by writing about the role of continuities between intuitive and scientific understanding:

> What we wish to take from Goethe is the sense that direct experience in only mildly altered form can play a significant role in the understanding of 'abstract' matters and his sense of continuity from naïve to scientific apprehension of the world. (p. 16)

Linguists have long argued that an individual's ability to conceptualize is directly connected to the culture of discourse made available to her (Whorf, 1956). As urban African American students come to understand the world, they develop discursive practices that enable them to organize it. Without a perspective that accounts for the roles of alternative discursive repertoires in understanding learning, much of our understanding about their conceptualization is limited to those instances where they are applying linguistic repertoires commensurate with science. Urban student populations, however, possess conceptions of the natural world whether they engage in scientific discourse or common vernacular. This does not ensure that the concepts are correct, but by using existing language and understanding, urban science teachers can activate prior knowledge and use the correct elements of discourse to build deeper understanding.

IMPLICATIONS AND CONCLUSIONS

America's science education goals as articulated by the NRC and AAAS illustrate the shift from science as reserved for elite intellectuals to science as a discipline accessible and indeed necessary for all individuals. Removing this social wall, however, has not successfully equipped all Americans with the requisite knowledge and skills to be deemed scientifically literate by any definition (and as we have seen, there are many). This is especially true for students of color, English Language Learners, and students of low socioeconomic status. And walls remain firmly ensconced for many students who struggle to identify themselves with the scientific paradigm—a way of thinking, speaking, and justifying. If all Americans are to be scientifically literate by 2061, urban science educators need to begin to recognize where bridges can be built starting now.

CRP appears to be a good starting point. In specific, urban science teachers should focus on helping urban African American students create an identity that helps them navigate the science classroom within the context of their home life and culture. The options are two-fold: Urban teachers can help students create a single identity to flexibly adapt to multiple environments or help students develop the skills necessary to assume the proper and distinct identities valued in each specific science arena. Both options ensure that CRP is not equated with lower standards but rather with meeting national standards in unique ways that embrace one's background. Indeed, we have seen how PBS is one such way to incorporate the principles of CRP into praxis and do so without necessarily compromising standards.

As the very essence of bridge building concerns linking student culture with the historically nonrelative culture of science, language becomes a central issue in reconciling unique personal identities with the identity of a scientifically literate citizen. Therefore, in order to enfranchise scientifically literate identities, at least with respect to our explanation-driven conception of literacy borrowed from Osborne (1998), we argue that urban teachers need to focus more acutely on the role that discourse plays in science learning. Last, we maintain that because native student interpretations and language practices involve elements of understanding that can indeed be parlayed into a more coherent and literate take on science, urban science teachers should use linguistic tools available in the classroom to form a conceptual continuity that bridges urban African American students' prior experience and science discourse and use it effectively to construct correct science meaning.

As a body of research, much remains to firmly connect scientific literacy with CRP, discursive identity, and conceptual continuities. If urban science teachers are able to accomplish this task, then perhaps the walls that Newton helped create will be replaced with the bridges he called for—linkages that will allow future generations of urban science learners to participate in an advanced scientific society.

REFERENCES

Agar, M. (1994). *Language shock: Understanding the culture of conversation.* New York, NY: William Morrow.

American Association for the Advancement of Science. (1993). *Benchmarks for science Literacy.* New York, NY: Oxford University Press.

Anderson, C., Holland, J., & Palincsar, A. (1997). Canonical and sociocultural approaches to reform in science education: The story of Juan and his group. *Elementary School Journal, 97*(4), 359–383.

Arons, A. B. (1983). Achieving wider scientific literacy. *Daedalus, 112*(2), 91–122.

Banks, J. A. (1993). Multicultural education: Historical development, dimensions, and practice. *Review of Research in Education, 19*, 3–49.

Bazerman, C. (1988). *Shaping written knowledge.* Madison: University of Wisconsin Press.

Brickhouse, N. (1994). Bringing in the outsiders: Reshaping the sciences of the future. *Journal of Curriculum Studies, 26*(4), 401–416.

Brossard, D., & Shanahan, J. (2006). Do they know what they read? Building a scientific literacy measurement instrument based on science media coverage. *Science Communication, 28*(1), 47–63.

Brown, B. A. (2004). Discursive identity: Assimilation into the culture of science and its implications for minority students. *Journal of Research in Science Teaching. 41*(8), 810–834.

Brown, B. A., Reveles, J. M., & Kelly, G. J. (2005). Scientific literacy and discursive identity: A theoretical framework for understanding science education. *Science Education, 89*(5), 779–802.

Brown, B. A., & Ryoo, K. (2008) Teaching science as a language: A "content-first" approach to science teaching. *Journal of Research in Science Teaching, 45*(5), 525–664.

Calabrese-Barton, A. (2007). Science learning in urban settings. In S. Abell & N. G. Lederman (Eds.), *Handbook of Research on Science Education* (pp. 319–344). Mahwah, NJ: Lawrence Erlbaum.

DeBoer, G. E. (1991). *A history of ideas in science education.* New York, NY: Teachers College Press.

DeBoer, G. E. (2000). Scientific literacy: Another look at its historical and contemporary meanings and its relationship to science education reform. *Journal of Research in Science Teaching, 37*(6), 582–601.

DiSessa, A. (1983). Phenomenology and the evolution of intuition. In D. Gentner & A. Stevens (Eds.), *Mental models* (pp. 15–32), Hillsdale, NJ: Lawrence Erlbaum.

DiSessa, A. (2002). Why conceptual ecology is a good idea. In M. Limon & L. Mason (Eds.), *Reconsidering conceptual change: Issues in theory and practice* (pp. 29–60). Dordrecht, Holland: Kluwer Press.

Fishman, J. A. (1989). Language, ethnicity, and racism. In *Language & ethnicity in minority sociolinguistic perspective.* Philadelphia, PA: Multilingual Matters.

Fordham, S. (1996). *Blacked out: Dilemmas of race, identity, and success at Capital high.* Chicago, IL: The University of Chicago Press.

Gay, G. (2000). *Culturally responsive teaching.* New York, NY: Teachers College Press.

Gee, J. (1999). What is literacy? In C. Mitchell & K. Weiler (Eds.), *Reviewing literacy: Culture and the discourse of the other.* Westport, CT: Bergin & Garvey Press.

Gee, J. P. (2002). Identity as an analytic lens for research in education. *Review of Research in Education, 25*, 99–125.

Gilbert, J., & Yerrick, R. (2001). Same school, separate worlds: A sociocultural study of identity, resistance, and negotiation in rural, lower track science. *Journal of Research in Science Teaching, 38*(5), 574–598.

Gumperz, J. (1982). *Language and social identity.* Cambridge, UK: Cambridge University Press.

Halliday, M. A. K., & Martin, J. R. (1993). *Writing science: Literacy and discursive power.* Pittsburgh, PA: University of Pittsburgh Press.

Hammer, D. (2000). Student resources for learning introductory physics. *American Journal of Physics Teachers, 68*, S52–S59.

Hollins, E. (1996). *Transforming curriculum for a culturally diverse society.* Mahwah, NJ: Lawrence Erlbaum.

Hull, G., & Schultz, K. (2001). Literacy and learning out of school: A review of theory and research. *Review of Educational Research, 71*(4), 575–611.

Irvine, J. (1990). *Black students and school failure.* New York, NY: Greenwood Press.

Kelly, G. (2005). Discourse, description, and science education. In R. Yerrick & W.-M. Roth (Eds.), *Establishing scientific classroom discourse communities: Multiple voices of research on teaching and learning* (pp. 79–108). Mahwah, NJ: Lawrence Erlbaum.

King, J. E. (2003). Culture-centered knowledge: Black studies, curriculum transformation and social action. In J. A. Banks & C. A. McGee-Banks (Eds.), *The handbook of research on multicultural education* (2nd ed.; pp. 349–380). Jossey-Bass.

Kromhout, R., & Good, R. (1983). Beware of societal issues as organizers for science education. *School Science and Mathematics, 83*(8), 647–650.

Kuhn, T. (1962) *The structure of scientific revolutions.* Chicago, IL: University of Chicago Press.

Ladson-Billings, G. (1999). Just what is critical race theory and what's it doing in a nice field like education. In L. Parker, D. Deyhele, & S. Villenas (Eds.), *Race is . . . race isn't: Critical race theory and qualitative studies in education* (pp. 7–30). Boulder, CO: Westview Press.

Latour, B., & Woolgar, S. (1986). An anthropologist visits the laboratory. In B. Latour & S. Woolgar (Eds.), *Laboratory life: The construction of scientific facts* (pp. 43–90). Princeton, NJ: Princeton University Press.

Lave, J. (1988). *Cognition in practice: Mind, mathematics, and culture in everyday life.* Cambridge, UK: Cambridge University Press.

Lee, O. (2001). Culture and language in science education: What do we know and what do we need to know? *Journal of Research in Science Teaching, 38*, 499–501.

Lemke, J. (1990). *Talking science: Language, learning and values.* Norwood, NJ: Ablex.

Mahiri, J. (2004). *What they don't learn in school: Literacy in the lives of urban youth.* New York, NY: Peter Lang.

Marx, R. W., Blumenfeld, P. C., Krajcik, J. S., & Soloway, E. (1997). Enacting project-based science. *Elementary School Journal, 97*(4), 341–358.

Marx, R. W., Blumenfeld, P. C., Krajcik, J. S., Fishman B., Soloway, E., Geier, R., & Tal, R. T. (2004). Inquiry-based science in the middle grades: Assessment of learning in urban systemic reform. *Journal of Research in Science Teaching, 41*(10), 1063–1080.

Moll, L. C., Amanti, C., Neff, D., & Gonzalez, N. (1992). Funds of knowledge for teaching: Using a qualitative approach to connect homes and classrooms. *Theory into Practice, 31*(1), 132–141.

Morrell, E. (2005). Toward a critical English education: Reflections on and projections for the discipline. *English Education, 37*(4), 312–322.

Nasir, N. S., & Saxe, G. B. (2003). Ethnic and academic identities: A cultural practice perspective on emerging tensions and their management in the lives of minority students. *Educational Researcher, 32*(5), 14–18.

National Research Council. (1996). *National Science Education Standards.* Washington, DC: National Academies Press.

Nieto, S. (1999). Culturally relevant cases: A personal reflection and implications for teacher education. In M. A. Lundeberg, B. B. Levin, & H. L. Harrington (Eds.), *Who learns what from cases and how? The research base for teaching with cases* (pp. 179–196). Mahwah, NJ, and London, UK: Falmer Press.

Norris, S. P., & Phillips, L. M., (2003). How literacy in its fundamental sense is central to scientific literacy. *Science Education, 87*(2), 224–240.

Nunberg, G. (2004). *Going nucular: Language, politics, and culture in confrontational times.* New York, NY: Public Affairs.

Osborne, J. (1998). Science education for the twenty-first century. *Eurasia Journal of Mathematics, Science & Technology Education, 3*(3), 173–184.

Posner, G. J., Strike, K. A., Hewson, P. W., & Gertzog, W. A. (1982). Accommodation of a scientific conception: Towards a theory of conceptual change. *Science Education, 66*(2), 211–227.

Rivet, A. E., & Krajcik, J. S. (2004). Achieving standards in urban systemic reform: An example of a sixth-grade project-based science curriculum. *Journal of Research in Science Teaching, 41*(7), 669–692.

Rosebery, A., Warren, B., & Conant F. (1992). Appropriating scientific discourse: Findings from language minority classrooms. *The Journal of Learning Sciences, 2*(1), 61–94.

Roth, W., & Lee, S. (2002). Scientific literacy as collective praxis. *Public Understanding of Science, 11*(1), 1–14.

Roth, W. M. (2007). Communication as situated, embodied practice. In T. Ziemke, J. Zlatev, & R. Frank (Eds.), *Embodiment: Vol 1. Body, language, and mind.* Berlin, Germany: Mouton de Gruyter Press.

Rutherford, J., & Ahlgren, A. (1990). *Science for all Americans.* New York, NY: Oxford University Press.

Sandoval, W. A. (2003). Conceptual and epistemic aspects of students' explanations. *Journal of the Learning Sciences, 12*(1), 5–51.

Sapir, E. (1949). *Selected writings in language, culture, and personality.* Berkeley: University of California Press.

Shamos, M. H. (1995). The myth of scientific literacy. *Liberal Education, 82*(3), 44–50.

Shulman, L. (1987). Knowledge and teaching: Foundations of the new reform. *Harvard Educational Review, 57*(1), 1–22.

Songer, N. B., Lee, H. S., & McDonald, S. (2003). Research towards an expanded understanding of inquiry science beyond one idealized standard. *Science Education, 87*(4), 490–516.

Tobin, K., Tippins, D. J., & Gallard, A. J. (1994). Research on instructional strategies for teaching science. In D. L. Gabel (Ed.), *Handbook of research on science teaching and learning* (pp. 45–93). New York, NY: Macmillan.

Valeras, M., & Kane, J. (2009). Language undertheorized: Conceptual metaphors and conceptual change. *Human Development, 29,* 3–5.

Villegas-Lucas, A., & Lucas, T. (2003). Preparing culturally responsive teachers. *Journal of Teacher Education, 53*(1), 20–32.

Vosniadou, S. (2002). On the nature of naive physics. In M. Limon & L. Mason (Eds.), *Reconsidering conceptual change: Issues in theory and practice* (pp. 61–76). Dordrecht, Holland: Kluwer Press.

Wenger, E. (1998). *Communities of practice: Learning, meaning, and identity.* Cambridge, UK: Cambridge University Press.

Whorf, B. (1956). *Language, thought, and reality: Selected writings of Benjamin Lee Whorf.* Cambridge, MA: The MIT Press.

Wortham, S. (2003). Accomplishing identity in participant-denoting discourse. *Journal of Linguistic Anthropology, 13*(2), 1–22.

PART FOUR

URBAN SCHOOL LEADERSHIP AND OUTREACH

Urban School Administrators: A Grassroots Approach TO No Child Left Behind Mandates

CHRISTOPHER DUNBAR JR. AND LAURA MCNEAL

Across the United States, many states struggle to address pervasive challenges associated with efforts to increase achievement in urban schools. No Child Left Behind (NCLB) mandates, the federal government's response to failing schools, have proven to be ineffective in improving school outcomes for many African American students who attend urban school systems. The central tenets of NCLB's approach to reform in response to failing schools require districts to implement a series of mandates designed to raise student achievement outcomes. Urban schools failing to achieve Adequate Yearly Progress (AYP), a measurement of progress implemented by NCLB, are subject to a range of sanctions of varying degrees, starting with a warning and requirement to create a reform action plan to avoid more severe sanctions (e.g., school reconstitution or closures). Despite persistently low student achievement among urban African American students, many of these failing schools have successfully improved their academic performance by opting to forgo the NCLB corrective mandates and implement their own proscribed remedy (Mead, 2007). For example, instead of replacing the entire staff (one of the mandates of NCLB), the principals in these schools opt to hire retired teachers as coaches for struggling teachers and use data gathered weekly to assess students' academic strengths and weaknesses in an effort to focus on and address the problems.

In lieu of closing these urban schools, as required by NCLB, many state departments and urban school districts choose to allow failing schools to remain open. In such cases, principals are often empowered to develop corrective measures to improve student achievement. Popular and scientific literature suggests that principals have a major role in schools. This is especially true for failing schools in urban communities. This chapter presents the findings of urban principals who turned around failing schools.

Although several research studies have been conducted on the impact of NCLB mandates on achievement outcomes, few studies, if any, have focused on failing schools in the reconstitution stage that successfully achieved AYP without following NCLB reconstitution mandates (Plank & Dunbar, 2007). Therefore, in this chapter, we present findings that can help policy makers and district-level administrators better understand how urban school principals in the reconstitution stage of NCLB managed not to comply with NCLB reconstitution mandates yet still make AYP.

REVIEW OF THE LITERATURE

For decades, urban educators, researchers, and policy makers have attempted to provide an analysis that offers factors that explain the gross disparities in achievement between African American and Whites students (Ferguson, 2003). The realization that a large achievement gap has persisted, despite over a half century of efforts to improve educational opportunities, brought issues of student access, equity, and achievement to the awareness of the broader public. As a result, stakeholders in urban education have begun to re-evaluate the current U.S. education system in an effort to develop more effective educational reform measures (McNeal, 2008; Talbert-Johnson, 2004). For example, NCLB, which amended the Elementary and Secondary Education Act of 1965, was signed into law on January 8, 2002. The primary objective of this legislation is to address public concern regarding the increasingly high number of failing public schools, particularly in urban contexts.

The founding principle of NCLB is the notion that educators should be held accountable for the academic performance of all students (McNeal, 2008). Under this act, schools, districts, and states are required to demonstrate that 100% of students have achieved grade-level proficiency in reading and mathematics by the year 2013 (Bell, 2003; Greene, 2004; Wenglinsky, 2004). To ensure that schools fulfill this mandate, NCLB requires that they establish a benchmark for proficiency standards to determine whether they along with their school districts are making AYP toward 100% student proficiency (Christie, 2002; Rebell & Wolff, 2008). In specific, public schools, including urban ones, are required to demonstrate an increase in the percentage of students that meet or exceed the state-wide annual achievement objectives for achieving AYP. In an effort to close the achievement gap, the act also requires schools and districts to distinguish annual achievement gains for specific subgroups of students, such as African Americans, Caucasians, Asian/Pacific Islanders, Latin Americans, Native Americans/Native Alaskans, economically disadvantaged students, students with disabilities, and students with limited English proficiency. If any subgroup of students fails to demonstrate an increase in annual achievement outcomes, the entire school is classified as not achieving AYP. NCLB's requirement that all students demonstrate progress is intended to reduce the current achievement gap in America's schools (Christie, 2002; Manning & Kovach, 2003; Petersen & Young, 2004).

NCLB not only requires that schools and districts measure whether students are achieving AYP, but it also requires them to issue annual report cards detailing a comparison of student performance on state-wide academic assessments within the state (Darling-Hammond, 2006; Smith, 2005; Wenglinsky, 2004). The school's progress information located within *The Nation's Report Card*, issued by the U.S. Department of Education, is required to be dis-aggregated by students' race, gender, poverty, English proficiency, and disability. The legislative intent behind this requirement is to make parents aware of achievement outcomes in their child's school and to increase school accountability for student success (Darling-Hammond, 2006; Hass, Wilson, Cobb, & Rallis, 2005).

In accordance with NCLB, schools failing to meet annual achievement objectives are required to follow mandatory school improvement efforts, which are categorized into three escalating intervention stages: During the first stage, schools failing to demonstrate AYP are issued a warning and required to develop a school plan in consultation with school staff, parents, district-level leadership, and external experts to address the poor academic performance of students (Buchanan, 2004). In this stage, schools are also required to provide students with options for transferring to nonfailing schools.

Schools that fail to make AYP for two consecutive years move into stage two, the *corrective stage*, at which point they are categorized as being in need of improvement. Schools in this stage are required to develop a building-level improvement plan, continue to provide students with the option of transferring to a nonfailing school, and supply students with free supplemental education services; they are entitled to receive technical assistance from the district.

Schools designated as being in the corrective stage are also required to take at least one of the following actions: (a) replace school staff deemed relevant to the school's failure to make AYP, (b) significantly increase management authority at the school level, (c) appoint an outside expert to advise the school on its progress toward making AYP, (d) extend the school year or school day, (e) restructure the internal organizational structure of the school, or (f) implement a new scientifically based curriculum that includes providing professional development for all relevant staff. Several of these actions constitute a partial reconstitution of the school and occur during the first and second stages of accountability as mandated by NCLB.

The third stage of accountability under NCLB is termed *reconstitution*. Reconstitution occurs, when after two full school years of corrective action, the school continues to fail to make AYP. This stage requires schools to adopt alternative governance arrangements consistent with state law. Acceptable arrangements include: (a) reopening the school as a public charter; (b) replacing all or most of the staff, which may include the principal and others viewed as relevant to the school's failure to make AYP; (c) entering into a contract with an entity, such as a private management company, in order for the school to operate as a public school; (d) turning over the operation of the school to the state, if permitted by state laws and agreed to by the state; or (e) any other major restructuring of a school's governance arrangement consistent with the act's requirements.

A cursory examination of *The Nation's Report Card* suggests that student achievement is on the rise in America's schools (National Center of Educational Progress [NAEP], 2007). However, a more vigilant examination reveals that a substantial number of schools are currently in the final reconstitution stage (i.e., restructuring) for failing to meet AYP. According to Mead (2007), approximately 1,750 schools in 42 states were in NCLB's restructuring stage in the 2005–2006 school years. To this end, the number of schools in the final stages of NCLB sanctions is expected to grow dramatically in the next few years, especially for schools in urban settings.

PURPOSE OF STUDY

The purpose of our study is to understand how urban school principals implement the required mandates of the reconstitution stage under NCLB. This stage requires schools that have not made AYP for two years, during the corrective stage, to reconstitute or reconfigure the school. This means possibly closing the school, displacing teachers, becoming a charter school, or coming under the control of a management organization.

The urban principals we interviewed all led schools that were in the reconstitution stage. Yet, instead of following the set of mandates designated by NCLB mandates, they opted to use other forms to address the academic needs of their urban students. We posed a series of questions to garner an understanding of what principals knew about NCLB, including their knowledge of supplemental services provided under the mandate and what, if any, impact the Act had on their ability to lead and move their school off the list of schools not making AYP. In this study, we uncovered multiple methods of academic improvement utilized by school leaders and their explanations for implementing alternative routes to improve student scores in order to remove their schools from the list of schools not meeting AYP.

CONCEPTUAL FRAMEWORK

Coombs (1980) provides an analysis of noncompliance with education policy that forms the conceptual lens for this study. The author asserts that, in order for a policy to have a substantive impact, change in the behavior of target individuals must occur. By focusing on the prescription (i.e., set of guidelines) that is embedded in a policy and determining the extent of a school's compliance, researchers can assess the success of its implementation. Based on Coombs's work, the following factors can be used to explain why target schools may not comply with policy mandates: (a) lapses or ambiguities in communication, (b) insufficient resources, (c) an objection to the policy itself (i.e., to its goals or assumptions), (d) distaste for the action required, or (e) doubts about the authority upon which the policy is based or that authority's agents. Again, for the purpose of this study, we used Coombs's framework to better understand the actions of urban principals to improve educational outcomes for their students.

METHODS

In this study, we use a qualitative approach that allows us to look beyond everyday ways of seeing social life in an effort to understand it in novel ways. Qualitative research involves complex issues of interpretation. It consists of moving back and forth between theory and evidence. Further, this research approach involves the art of interpretation. It also requires the researcher to develop a "sociological imagination" in an effort to understand the world (Mills, 1959); that is, to develop the capacity to see individual issues within a larger social context. Developing a sociological imagination involves theorizing. In this study, we see theory as creating a story about some event or piece of the social world. The mission of modern sociology is the analysis and understanding of the patterned conduct and social pressures of society on the basis of the values and attitudes on which individual and collective participation in social life exists/rest (Glesne, 2006).

Participants

We purposely selected five principals because they were leaders in urban schools that were in (at least) the second year of the corrective stage, requiring them to reconstitute their schools. The principals represent two urban school districts and one urban public charter school in Michigan that serves grades K–12. The principals we interviewed range in age, from 28 to 50 (the average age is 39), with 5% being female and 95% male. The racial/ethnic distribution is 75% African American, 23% White, and 2% Latin American. Pseudonyms are utilized for the urban schools and principals.

DATA COLLECTION AND ANALYSIS

Utilizing an interviewing protocol, we asked the urban principals a series of open-ended questions that focus on their perceptions and experiences of working in a reconstituted school and about the impact and effectiveness of NCLB's reconstitution mandates for addressing poor student achievement within their schools. We also asked the principals to pinpoint specific intervention strategies that enable their schools to achieve AYP. In essence, we used an interviewing format designed to promote an environment conducive to collecting viable qualitative data (Glesne, 2006; Creswell, 2008).

We tape recorded the interviews, which lasted between 60 and 90 minutes, and transcribed them with the intent of discovering emerging themes. Participants had an opportunity to review the transcriptions to assure accuracy throughout the study (Glesne, 2006; Creswell, 2008). As themes emerged, we organized the data into individual categories, highlighting similarities and differences in respect to approaches utilized to improve academic outcomes for students.

FINDINGS

School leaders in this study elected not to comply with mandated reconstitution procedures outlined in NCLB but instead used other means to address the needs of their particular schools. Coaches were hired to reteach teachers in areas of reading and mathematics, one school requiring staff to meet on weekends to develop a plan in an effort to better prepare students for Michigan Education Assessment Program (MEAP) exams and another collecting student academic data and convening weekly to devise a set of guidelines to support the academic improvement of their students.

Dr. James Culver

The Polk Intermediate School District was undergoing a rapid shift in student population at the time of our study. Enrollments and revenues had fallen steadily in recent years as families moved to the suburbs and students moved to charter schools and neighboring school districts. As a result, the district had closed 10 buildings in the years prior and expected to close another 10 in the coming decade. As school administrators struggled to address the declining student enrollment, they also undertook the daunting task of addressing schools failing to meet NCLB standards due to low student achievement outcomes.

Members of our research team conducted an interview with Dr. James Culver, the Curriculum Director of Elementary and Middle Schools in the Polk School District, to understand what steps were taken by the district and school leaders to address the needs of their schools that we currently in NCLB's reconstitution stage. Our research team collected additional data directly from two schools identified as currently in NCLB's reconstitution stage, Westlake and Jackson middle schools.

Westlake Middle School

Westlake is a public magnet school that serves approximately 552 seventh and eighth graders. It made AYP in the 2004–2005 school years. However, it did not make AYP in previous years; therefore, it has been identified by the State Department of Education as in need of improvement for the 2005–2006 school year. Because Westlake is a Title 1 school, NCLB mandates all parents of its students to transfer their children to schools that have made AYP. In addition, parents are entitled to free supplemental educational services, another provision supported by NCLB. The researchers discovered that the school principal, Mr. Hilliard, implemented the following measures in an effort to increase student achievement outcomes and transform Westlake into a high-performing school: (a) professional development training, (b) school improvement team, and (c) school-wide reform initiatives. It is ironic that although these school improvement measures were approved through NCLB, they were steps that should have been implemented prior to reaching the third stage of required reconstitution.

Professional Development Training

Principal Hilliard implemented a two-tier professional development training program that utilized external and internal resources. Teachers were provided with an academic support coach funded through a Title 1 Grant, and administrators were granted a professional development program for failing schools that are in NCLB's final phases. The academic support coach was trained by the State Department of Education and began working in October of 2005. The primary responsibility of the coach was to help staff work collaboratively with teachers to implement the objectives outlined for administrators. According to Principal Hilliard, professional development training was created to help change behaviors that inhibited the high achievement of students and to help school staff become vested in school improvement efforts.

School Improvement Team

Principal Hilliard created a school improvement team to assist him in carrying out the successful implementation of his school improvement strategies. The central goal of the team was to overcome challenges to successful school improvement, such as failure to complete assigned tasks and resistance to change. At first, the school improvement team was scheduled to meet once a month. However, Principal Hilliard indicates that, as the school year progressed, the school improvement team met more frequently in preparation for upcoming state assessment testing. Although Principal Hilliard's decision to implement a school improvement plan may have assisted in the school's efforts to achieve AYP, this action is a corrective measure that is mandated for stage two of NCLB mandates, whereas this school is actually in stage three, which requires the more drastic sanction of reconstitution.

In this school district, principals leading low-performing schools are required to attend periodic reviews with their supervisor, a representative of the Polk School District, and another principal. During these reviews, principals present their school improvement plan for feedback. The panel of reviewers evaluates what the principal has developed in the plan and provides him with a score based on a standard evaluation rubric created by the district. This information is shared with the school staff, and the process is repeated to assess the plan's strengths and weaknesses.

The panel of reviewers suggested that Principal Hilliard's school improvement team expand its focus from two content areas (the previous year's focus) to four content areas. The primary factor to which it attributed the school's improved scores is the annual math and language arts assessment test mandated by the state, which assisted the improvement team in evaluating whether the school's strategies were improving student learning outcomes.

Although Principal Hilliard revealed that the school improvement team exceeded his expectations for improving student achievement outcomes, he also shared some challenges encountered due to external factors. For example, according to Principal Hilliard, Westlake Middle School did not receive the previous year's student test results until late March, when they should have arrived by early January. The failure to distribute the student test scores in a timely manner represents a lapse in external communication (highlighted in Coombs's conceptual framework) and a reason for target individuals' noncompliance with policy prescriptives, such as NCLB. In other words, if schools are held to educational outcome assessments, then they need to receive test results in a timely manner, which would allow them to address the problems and subsequently place administrators in a stronger position to address students' academic needs.

As a result of this two-month delay in receiving student test scores, the school improvement team got off to a late start in reviewing testing scores to develop curriculum strategies to address student weaknesses. According to Principal Hilliard, receiving the testing results two months late created additional challenges, thus exacerbating an already-dire situation. Once the state test scores were evaluated, the school improvement team initiated several curricular changes to enhance student achievement outcomes. For example, the team integrated a literacy and writing framework throughout the various content areas. The team also designed a template providing strategies to assist teachers in enhancing existing learning improvement mandates. For example, teachers were asked to develop a more challenging curriculum integrating the higher levels of the learning objectives contained in Bloom's taxonomy, which would improve students' analytical skills and go beyond having students fill in the blanks. As a result, the teachers asked students to summarize and critically evaluate class material rather that to simply write a short answer.

School-Wide Reform Initiatives

Principal Hilliard implemented several school-wide reform initiatives, including an Accelerated Reader program, a peer evaluation process, and changes in curriculum instruction. These reform initiatives were created based on observations made by the school improvement team and the principal. More specifically, the reform efforts were designed to enhance student achievement outcomes, with the goals of increasing student literacy, improving the quality of classroom instruction, and enhancing the overall quality of the school's education services through personnel staff development. According to Principal Hilliard, the school hired an additional academic support coach to assist him in conducting classroom observations to evaluate the effectiveness of school-wide reform initiatives and identify any additional areas in need of improvement. In the classroom observations, the support coach revealed the following:

> We may stay 20 to 30 minutes, come out and discuss what we see and how things are going. We also study student work to see how it has changed over the past year. As a result, our discussions have changed, what we look for has changed. Additionally, our overall approach

to learning has changed. When we began assessing classroom learning environments, we observed teachers doing a whole lot of work and students not doing much. Teachers were lecturing the majority of class time and giving students the answers, as opposed to a student-centered learning approach which allows the students to utilize their critical thinking skills and application of knowledge to find the answers. We also noticed that a lot of students were struggling to read the class material which made it difficult for them to fully participate in class activities.

After the observations, the principal and academic support coach had several conversations about what they found and developed strategies to address the school's areas of weakness. One strategy, an Accelerated Reader program, was developed to reduce classroom size and target students with poor reading skills. Another strategy provided teachers with the opportunity to travel to high-achieving schools in other cities to observe effective teaching techniques that could be integrated into their existing curriculums. The opportunity to travel to other schools and view "best practices" helped teachers understand how to both identify and address adaptive and technical challenges within their classroom settings.

The data collected from Westlake Middle School illuminates the school's non-compliance with NCLB mandates by opting to implement Stage 2 (the corrective stage) interventions when the school's failure to achieve AYP for three consecutive years actually places them in the third stage, reconstitution. However, Principal Hilliard's efforts successfully increased the quality of professional development, improved staff relations, and implemented a more rigorous curriculum. Thus, despite the principal's decision not to comply with the third stage of NCLB, the context-specific strategies he implemented improved student outcomes. According to Coombs (1980), the principal's actions represent "belief based non-compliance," which occurs when target individuals doubt the effectiveness of the policy's proscribed behavior and impact (i.e., reconstitution).

RESISTANCE TO CHANGE

Principal Hilliard highlighted many of his successful school improvement efforts, and he also shared some of the challenges. He noted that there had been resistance to change on the part of some teachers, suggesting that despite his classroom improvement efforts, many teachers continued to teach the way they had always taught, because they failed to see the added value in using a new unfamiliar approach. For example, four teachers were selected to attend a training session, which introduced a different writing process that involves using prompts to encourage students to both draw and write. When these teachers brought back the information to share with their colleagues, they encountered great resistance, with their fellow teachers suggesting that the changes failed to align with their existing teaching philosophy. Thus, instead of using the new writing method that focused more on examining student progress and less on a particular skill set, teachers continued their traditional approach to teaching, which focused on perfection as opposed to student growth. According to Principal Hilliard, "This approach usually meant the student would do the first writing and the teacher would redo it for the student."

The new process entailed a more constructivist learning approach, which required students to sound out the mis-spelled words and critically assess what they should do differently to produce better writing. Principal Hilliard responded to the teacher resistance by creating an environment that made all teachers feel valued, using teacher appreciation lunches and various other morale-building activities. Principal Hilliard also conducted staff retreats once a month, designed to help teachers embrace the recommended changes. By the end of the semester, all of the teachers adopted the new writing process and testing results indicated immense improvement in student writing and reading.

ACTION AND BY WHOSE AUTHORITY?

This section reflects two factors embedded within Coombs's policy framework: (a) distaste for the action required and (b) doubts about the authority upon which the policy is based, or the agents of that authority. Principal Hilliard, a change agent for the district, described how teachers demonstrated distaste for the implementation of his policy directives because they conflicted with their current teaching philosophy. The teachers' collective decision not to comply with his classroom improvement efforts, in essence, thwarted his attempt to introduce new policy directives (i.e., writing processes). The teachers' actions also demonstrated their distaste for the principal's programmatic directives, as well as their confidence in his leadership.

Jackson Middle School

Jackson Middle School, which educates approximately 544 seventh and eighth graders, has consistently failed to raise student achievement outcomes. This is evident by the classification of this school as in need of improvement for the 2005–2006, Year 5, academic school year by the state's Department of Education. Seventh-grade students attending the school scored below half the state average in listening and math and just above half of the state average in reading and writing. At the time of the study, the current principal, Cheryl Evans, had been a school administrator for nine years, with the last three years spent at Jackson Middle School. In an interview with Principal Evans, the research team asked how long the school had been under corrective action. She responded: "Let's see. At least, we're number five and holding, because we made AYP last year, so we started at zero, and now we are at level five, so it has to be for the last five years."

In our discussions with Principal Evans, she revealed that she initiated the following school improvement efforts to raise student achievement outcomes: (a) professional development, (b) school-wide programs, (c) improved special education services, and (d) supplemental education services.

Professional Development: Working With the Hand We've Been Dealt

We asked Principal Evans to tell us about the professional development programs she initiated for teachers. Before answering this question, the principal began to inform us about the skill deficits of students enrolled in her school and how that shaped and influenced her professional development training. Principal Evans stated,

> Many of our kids came to us from elementary school with third grade or lower reading levels. And, it's very difficult to have a third grade reading level with seventh grade reading material. One of the first things we took on was helping teachers to help kids to read. The majority of our students struggle in reading comprehension.

According to Principal Evans, testing results reveal that 85% of students could not read the required material or comprehend what they were reading.

The principal described that after assessing the academic challenges of students, she focused her school reform efforts on improving reading instruction in her school. She highlighted how the composition of the school's staff created challenges in her efforts to improve reading instruction. She even discussed how teacher placement within the district contributed to poor student learning outcomes due to the mis-match between students' needs and teacher skill level. She shared that her middle school staff consisted of a combination of K–8 certified teachers and 9–12 secondary certified teachers. She suggested that most of the 9–12 teachers "hadn't a clue about how to teach children to read." To remedy this gross disparity in teacher skill levels, Principal Evans identified teachers who excelled in literacy instruction and commissioned those teachers to train other teachers. The principal's use of internal resources to conduct professional development for the staff significantly raised students' literacy levels at Jackson Middle School and helped build camaraderie among the teaching staff.

In this section, Principal Evans's discussion of barriers to substantive reform aligns with one of the five tenets described in Coombs's noncompliance framework:

inadequate resources. At Jackson Middle School, this applies to the lack of highly qualified teachers to teach literacy; in addition, the incongruence regarding teachers' skill level and student needs. According to Coombs (1980), target individuals often understand the policy mandates issued to them but simply do not have the "wherewithal to comply" (p. 888). However, despite the lack of resources, Principal Evans successfully addressed her teaching staff's skill deficit by developing her own context-specific policy prescriptive.

School-Wide Programs Developed

Principal Evans created several school-wide programs in addition to teacher professional development training programs to improve student reading and writing skills. For example, Jackson Middle School held ALL Write Days, which required students to write all day in their content areas. The primary objectives of All Write Days were to emphasize the importance of writing to students and improve their writing scores. English Language Acquisition (ELA) teachers scored the student writing to assess their progress. Steps were also taken to ensure that students transitioning from feeder elementary schools into Jackson Middle School were equipped with the necessary skills and knowledge to perform at grade level.

Staff members from Jackson Middle School met with staff from the feeder elementary schools to communicate exactly what the students needed to know to successfully transition into middle school. Principal Evans indicated that their meetings revealed that many of the staff from the feeder elementary schools did not know what the content expectations were for the sixth grade. In response, colleagues assisted one another in a collective effort to meet students where they were academically. They also took additional steps to ensure that future students were better prepared by communicating to feeder schools what students need to know to succeed at the next level.

With the support of a new superintendent, Jackson Middle School is moving to institute gender-specific classrooms and, by next year, gender specific schools. The principal noted that this strategy "has helped tremendously." In class, the girls and boys feel more confident in responding to queries aloud because the threat of appearing "not smart" to the other gender has been removed. Other strategies include using Black Board Configuration, an organizational tool for teachers; Reading Apprenticeship, an instructional approach; Step Up to Writing, a writing program; and Block Scheduling, a type of scheduling that enables students to devote 84 minutes every day exclusively for writing.

Supplemental educational services (SES) providers offered another opportunity for students to get extra academic support. However, Principal Hilliard revealed several problems with the SES providers. To begin, providers were hired by the teachers but were not compensated. In addition, the materials necessary to teach the children were not provided to them. Also, Principal Evans vehemently opposed the notion that children who do poorly in school during the day will perform better in an after-school program that resembles the day-school program, often featuring the same teachers. The principal added, "The Supplemental After School Programs (SES) directed by Bush and NCLB are really not doing anything to help us with our kids." The principal, however, believed some of the aforementioned strategies are steps in the right direction for improving AYP scores.

Evans's school-wide improvement programs, such as All Write Day, demonstrate a grassroots effort; that is, one in which changes happen within and by members of the organization. The lapse and ambiguities in communication between the feeder elementary schools and middle schools correlates with Combs's noncompliance framework. As a result, sixth-grade students entering Jackson Middle School arrive several grades behind their peers in other districts. Furthermore, according to Principal Evans, the district's SES has not provided the support prescribed by NCLB mandates. For example, the principal indicated a lapse or ambiguity in communication in which teachers were not compensated for their services. Second, teachers were not provided with adequate resources to implement their curriculum. In specific, Principal Evans found that the practice of allowing the same teachers who teach in a failing school to provide supplemental education services fails to serve our students' academic needs. For these reasons, the principal clearly articulated her strong opposition to NCLB policy.

Improved Education for Special Education Students

Principal Evans noted that her school had approximately 125 special education students, only 20% of whom were exempt from taking the high-stakes exam (i.e., JEP). She also pointed out that there were a number of students who fit into an area she described as "gray." Although these students were struggling in regular education classes, they were not eligible for special education services. In an effort to address their needs, the principal convened a meeting of regular and special education teachers to enable them to devise strategies that would improve these students' AYP scores. One of the strategies implemented to increase special education student outcomes was "looping", which is a practice in which students stay with the same teacher for two consecutive years.

The looping framework is designed to help teachers better serve special-needs students by being familiar with the student's individual needs and learning styles due to the extended instructional period. According to Principal Evans, the looping practice at Jackson Middle School significantly raised the test scores of students who did not qualify for special education services but required additional assistance. This is yet another example of this principal leading and not simply managing a failing school.

CARVER FALLS PUBLIC SCHOOLS

Carver Falls is one of the largest cities in a Midwest state, with a population of approximately 198,000. The city is bordered by several smaller cities, creating an urbanized community of approximately 700,000. The district, as a whole, achieved AYP status for the 2004–2005 school years.

In our meeting with District Superintendent Thomas, he stressed the need to "do the right thing" for children regardless of the NCLB mandates. In other words, his actions are not necessarily dictated by NCLB mandates but rather by addressing the academic deficiencies of students who attend the Carver Falls Public School (CFPS) District. Superintendent Thomas revealed that the use of data is an ongoing process that drives instruction in his district. In addition, the district utilized a data review process to systematically review data, plan intervention strategies, adjust instruction, and assess the effectiveness of those adjustments to ensure that all students achieve the district's goals. All schools in the districts participated in this process. At each site, the data review involved grade-level teams, an instructional leadership team, and an external data review team. He indicated that many of his students need academic support particularly in the area of reading. As a result, reading intervention became the primary focus under his leadership. Superintendent Thomas commented that, although the JEP testing data is important, it is not the data that the district uses to evaluate student learning. The following sections contain interviews with principals from three elementary schools, who discuss methods used to identify and address student academic needs. All three schools achieved AYP during the 2004–2005 academic year, yet because they did not achieve AYP in the previous years, the state Department of Education identified these schools as in need of improvement, either Year 4 or 5, for the 2005–2006 school years.

Hewitt Elementary

Hewitt Elementary School is a PK–5 public magnet school. It serves approximately 376 students. In 2006, student scores on the JEP tests fell below the state average in every category. In reading, on which the district placed its emphasis, 59% of the third graders met or exceeded state standards, whereas the state average was 87%. Fifty-three percent of the fourth graders met or exceeded the state standards in reading, whereas the state average was 83%. Fifty-four percent of the fifth graders met or exceeded state standards, whereas the state average was 83%. In our discussions with the school principal, he indicated that he improved student achievement by addressing grade-level content deficiencies and implementing data-driven interventions.

Grade-Level Content Deficiencies

The principal revealed that Hewitt had focused on reading and reading intervention for the past four years, as prescribed/mandated by the district's superintendent. In our interview with the superintendent, he stated that his decision to infuse reading programs into the schools and to regularly test and review the data was his approach to understanding students' academic deficiencies in his district, regardless of NCLB mandates. "We're here to help all children not just students in low-performing schools."

The superintendent placed the emphasis on identifying students with similar skill deficits and then putting them into groups to address their particular academic needs. School staff conducted progress monitoring testing every three to four weeks and performed benchmark testing four times a year. In addition, the school uses a test called Dynamic Indicators for Basic Early Literacy Skills (DIBELS), which consists of reading comprehension testing, mathematics testing using multiple assessments, and a test that measures all grade-level content deficiencies (GLCD). This test is taken monthly.

Data-Driven Interventions

Teachers also used monthly writing prompts. The Instructional Leadership Team and the Intervention Learning Team worked together to synthesize the data to discover any weaknesses. Good practices were discovered and passed onto other teachers. Time was then devoted to sharing ideas, setting goals, implementation, and forming an intervention plan for the next round of data collection. This cycle was repeated every four to five weeks. In each round, students were given DIBELS to help teachers identify their abilities and weaknesses and subsequently group them into homogeneous units in which concerted efforts would be placed on improving areas of weakness. It appears that this school's efforts to improve academic deficiencies were aligned with the superintendent's focus outline. The fact that there was not as great of an alignment with the tenets prescribed by NCLB comes as no surprise, being that the superintendent made it clear that complete adherence to NCLB was not his primary focus, which is another example of Coombs's (1980) policy-based noncompliance (i.e., refusal to comply with policy because of having misgivings about the policy itself). As stated earlier, the district's goal was to uncover student academic weaknesses and work toward their improvement. The principal ended the interview by stating,

> It's like steering a boat. It's a slow process that can be frustrating. So to maintain the positive focus and energy and to do what's best for kids, even if it doesn't align with NCLB, and realize that you can't make changes over night and you can't do everything that's hard. I don't know any teachers who don't want their kids to be successful.

Daley Elementary School

Daley Elementary is a public magnet school that serves approximately 391 K–5 students. In 2006, its student scores on the JEP tests also fell below the state averages in every category. For example, in the area of reading, 67% of the third graders meet or exceed the state standard for that year; the state average is 87%. In writing, 47% of third graders at Daley meet or exceed the state standard; the state average is 52%. In math, 79% of the third graders meet or exceed the state standard; the state average is 87%. The scenario was similar for fourth and fifth graders in their respective areas of testing. Fourth graders are behind the state averages in both reading and math, and fifth graders are behind state averages in reading, science, writing (which is 1% short of meeting the state average) and math. Daley achieved AYP in the 2004–2005 school year; however, because it did not achieve AYP in previous years, the state Department of Education identified this school as "in need of improvement, Year 5" for 2005–2006.

During our discussions, the principal at Daley explained that this school was very data driven. For example, he stated:

> We have an intervention team and we progress. We do interventions Monday through Thursdays. Thursday afternoon we meet to look at the (ability) groups then change the (composition) groups based on the data. Fridays we look at progress, monitor and move kids around constantly to where they need to be. This has helped out a lot!

Data are compiled according to the percentages of students who have been identified as "at risk," "some risk," or "low risk." By the middle of the year, more students are moved into the low-risk category because of their achievement gains, which is the central goal of the intervention. Reports are compiled that indicate how children are doing in the three primary content areas of math, reading, and writing. The intervention team then does the monitoring and reports the findings to the teachers. The teachers then adjust their lesson plans and meet again to see where and if additional adjustments are necessary. Two days prior to the external data meeting, grade-level meetings are held to review data, detailing what progress, if any, students have made since the last data collection. Lesson plans are constantly adjusted and kids are moved to appropriate ability groups. The principal stated,

"We use the data to guide us." According to the principal, these intervention efforts have successfully increased student achievement outcomes at Daley.

Princeton Park Elementary School

Princeton Park Elementary is a PK–5 public magnet school that serves approximately 204 children. In 2006, student scores on JEP tests fell below the state average in all categories. In reading, 70% of Princeton Park third graders met or exceeded state standards in reading for that year. In writing and math, third graders scored 44% and 61%, respectively, whereas the state averages are 52% and 87%. Fourth graders scored 76%, 43%, and 48% in reading, writing and math, respectively, whereas the state averages are 83%, 55%, and 82%. Fifth graders scored 50%, 27%, 15%, and 32% in reading, science, writing, and math, respectively, whereas the state averages are 80%, 77%, 63%, and 32%. The school achieved AYP in 2004–2005; however, because it did not achieve AYP in previous years, the state Department of Education identified this school as in need of improvement in 2005–2006.

In our discussions with the principal at Princeton Park Elementary, we discovered that he also implemented data-driven interventions that involved changing classroom structure based on student achievement levels. More specifically, the Princeton Park principal spoke about the amount of monitoring, testing, and assessments that go on in their effort to understand where students are academically and then place them in ability groups based on their skills or deficits. The principal explained,

> It helps us to reach our goals because we have people to examine data more closely. We have a trained person to help us with the data. If you know exactly what kids need to focus on, you can move them in a direction that will address their specific needs. In the past, when there was no trained individual to help us analyze data, *we were sometimes spinning our wheels and not assisting the kids who really needed help.*

The superintendent's stated position is to help all children in a district in which poor reading skills play a critical role in schools failing to make AYP. So, despite mandates to reconstitute, he elected to employ district-level strategies to improve the academic outcomes of students. In this respect, his noncompliance may be due, in part, to what Coombs describes as a distaste for the action required (reconstitution) and an objection to the policy itself.

Marshall Academy Public Charter School

Marshall Academy is a K–6 public charter school that serves approximately 228 students. In 2006, students' scores on JEP tests fell below the state average in all categories except fourth-grade writing, in which 60% met or exceeded the state standard, exceeding the state average of 55%, which represents students who meet or exceed the state standard. In reading, writing, and math, 59%, 22%, and 56% of third graders, respectively, met or exceeded the state standard for that year. Fourth graders met or exceeded the state standard in reading, writing, and math 70%, 60%, and 47%, respectively; however, these percentages fell below the state averages. Fifth graders met or exceeded state standards in reading, science, writing, and math 50%, 50%, 41%, and 27%, respectively. The school achieved AYP progress in 2004–2005, but because it had not achieved AYP in previous years, the state Department of Education identified this school as "in need of improvement Year 4" for 2004–2005.

An interview with the school's Chief School Administrator, Dr. Davis, reveals that the school had undergone many struggles before his arrival in 2000. The school had failed to achieve AYP for several years, enrollment had dropped, and the superintendent was replaced. In addition, the building was "filthy" and not in compliance with safety codes. As a result, the school was closed on the first day of classes under Dr. Davis's leadership. After evaluating the existing school environment, Dr. Davis developed an action plan that involved the following: (a) addressing core problem areas, (b) creating a learning environment in which all members are vested in student success, and (c) taking an unconventional approach to school improvement rather than adopting the sanctions recommended by NCLB.

Addressing Core Problem Areas

Dr. Davis immediately recognized the need for additional funding to address the school's structural issues. He began to write proposals for grants to purchase computers, rewire the building, and make the necessary structural changes to bring the building up to safety codes. The school received grant funding to remedy the school's structural defects and for the purchase of computers and staff technology training. After achieving this first milestone, Davis identified the core changes that needed to occur to further his school improvement efforts. He instructed the school improvement team to develop a better framework for addressing student discipline concerns. The team responded by developing a uniform set of guidelines detailing what steps school staff should take to address discipline issues. The guidelines also detailed appropriate sanctions and due process procedures for students involved in disciplinary matters. After addressing the school's disciplinary procedures, Dr. Davis assigned the school improvement team with the task of improving student achievement outcomes.

Dr. Davis explained that the school increased the allotted time for reading to address student deficiencies in reading comprehension. In addition, every staff member who did not have training from the State Language Proficiency Program (SLPP) was sent to an external consulting firm to receive training. Teachers used the training they received at SLPP every day to teach students how to use grammar correctly. A language arts consultant was also brought in for two days to train teachers on what the JEP test entailed. Last, the school secured a $100,000 grant from the Department of Education to help underperforming schools through a program called Project Connect. This program also trains teachers in the areas of language arts and curriculum development. The most important aspect of this program for the teachers was access to a wealth of information. The school utilized this program for two years. The school was also given an additional consultant who trained teachers on all aspects of MEAP. Dr. Davis's school improvement initiatives created a substantive impact by increasing student achievement in reading and writing. He increased achievement outcomes by overcoming one of the barriers to noncompliance, insufficient resources, illustrated in Coombs's noncompliance framework. He did this by securing external funding to help fund professional development training for teachers. This is another example of school leaders in NCLB's final reconstitution stage successfully improving achievement outcomes without adhering to NCLB school improvement mandates.

Vested Interest in Student Success

The principal inspired school staff, families, and the surrounding community to take a vested interest in student success by building community–family partnerships and providing teachers with competitive salaries. For example, the school instituted a formal program that increased family participation in school improvement efforts. One of the key aspects of the program involved increasing parent-teacher interactions by keeping the school open from noon until 7:00 p.m. Through the program, entire families participated in a structured program designed to enhance family and school partnerships. The principal also increased teacher salaries, making them competitive with those of surrounding school districts by utilizing grant funding. In addition, the school received consecutive Title 1 improvement grants of $45,000 to hire coaches who assisted teachers in school improvement efforts during staff retreats. Defining the most challenging barriers to student achievement was the focus of the first-year retreat, whereas the second-year retreat focused on leadership. The coaches encouraged teachers to take responsibility for success and failures in the school. It is interesting that the school principal indicated that the coaches were not as helpful as he had hoped. Rather, he described two stellar teachers on the staff as being the most helpful in the school's effort to achieve AYP. In his words, "They [the teachers] showed everybody how it could be done." They modeled appropriate teaching and focused on the needs of children. In addition, all teachers (according to their contract) were obligated to volunteer several times during the year to tutor students for the JEP test. The principal attributed the success of the students to this level of commitment and investment in student success by his staff.

Unconventional Approach

Dr. Davis attributed the success of his school reform efforts to his decision to create context-specific school reform strategies, as opposed to adopting NCLB's "one-size-fits-all" reconstitution options. In addition, Dr. Davis stressed the importance of the school board's hands-off approach in the beginning stages of the school reform efforts, at which point progress toward increasing student achievement appeared stagnant. In the first three years after his arrival (2001–2004), the school did not achieve AYP; however, the school achieved AYP in the 2004–2005 school year once his intervention strategies had time to solidify. We asked Dr. Davis about the student use of SES and NCLB's school choice mandates. He replied that, despite informing parents of their SES and school choice options, only 20 students had participated in SES and even fewer exercised school choice options over the past couple of years. When we asked Dr. Davis if conforming to NCLB sanctions was the primary impetus for his school's success in being removed from the failing schools list, he responded, "No . . . [his staff was] simply determined and committed to help their children succeed."

Further, Dr. Davis believed that NCLB sanctions had minimal effect on his decisions and approach in improving academic outcomes for his students. His belief is that NCLB is a one-size-fits-all prescription to fix all low-performing schools and does not go far enough in considering the context of specific schools. As stated earlier, his school had many structural problems with the school facility itself that NCLB did not address. According to Coombs's framework for analysis, Dr. Davis objected to the policy itself and doubted the authority on which the policy was based, as well as having a distaste for the required action. Dr. Davis also stated that he had to take matters into his own hands by writing grants, selling his ideas to teachers, and involving parents in the education of their children.

CONCLUSION

After conducting this study, we learned of several actions implemented in schools to increase student academic outcomes without having to reconstitute schools. Despite not following NCLB mandates that called for overhauling schools, schools in this study were able to achieve AYP the following year. We learned that multiple problems existed for school leaders, which were not specifically addressed by NCLB mandates. In other words, NCLB mandated sanctions without critically understanding the context for which they were prescribed. Principals asserted that the policy did not provide substantive resources to fully implement SES or school choice options. In other words, the mandate simply consisted of symbolic words without the significant support to make options "real" for "real" families.

In addition, there was significant resistance to adhering to prescribed mandates, because individuals charged with their implementation objected to the policy itself and the authority upon which the policy was based. Principals and staff were able to make a difference in student academic outcome through leading and not simply managing. Principals, through their leadership, created opportunities for teachers to improve their teaching strategies. According to interviewees, teachers collectively shelved their autonomy in the interest of school-wide improvement. They began to teach with their "doors open," so to speak. What we mean here is that teaching and learning became an open-door collective effort to change the school culture and climate from one in which teachers "closed the doors to their rooms" and continued teaching the way they always had to one in which there was a school-wide effort to improve academic outcomes for all students.

After achieving AYP for two consecutive years, the schools in this study made a fresh start on their AYP clock. It remains to be seen whether their respective improvements will be enough to sustain their efforts to remain off the list of schools not achieving AYP. Despite NCLB sanctions recommended for schools at this stage, none of these schools elected to undertake these options. To the contrary, the schools participating in this study successfully turned their schools around through innovative, context-specific intervention strategies. It appears that the threat of having to reconstitute may have been the catalyst needed to make necessary changes to improve student achievement. However, the threat seemingly was not enough to force these schools or their districts to carry out the NCLB mandates.

REFERENCES

Bell, L. I. (2003). Strategies that close the gap. *Educational Leadership, 60*(4), 32–34.

Buchanan, B. (2004). Defining Adequate Yearly Progress. *American School Board Journal, 191*(2), 10–13.

Christie, K. (2002). States address achievement gaps. *Phi Delta Kappan, 84*(2), 102–103.

Coombs, F. S. (1980). The bases of noncompliance with a policy. *Policy Studies Journal, 8*(6), 885–892.

Creswell, J. W. (2008) *Educational research: Planning, conducting, and evaluating quantitative and qualitative research* (3rd ed.). Upper Saddle River, NJ: Pearson.

Darling-Hammond, L. (2006). No Child Left Behind and high school reform. *Harvard Educational Review, 76*, 642–669.

Ferguson, R. (2003). Teachers' perceptions and expectations and the black-white test score gap. *Urban Education, 38*(4), 460–507.

Glesne, C. (2006). Becoming qualitative researchers. Boston, MA: Pearson Education/Allyn & Bacon.

Greene, L. E. (2004). No child left behind: Meeting the challenges. *Principal, 83*(5), 12–38.

Hass, E., Wilson, G., Cobb, C., & Rallis, S. (2005). One hundred percent proficiency: A mission impossible. *Equity and Excellence, 38*(3), 180–189.

Manning, J. B., & Kovach, J. A. (2003). The continuing challenges of excellence and equity. In B. Williams (Ed.), *Closing the achievement gap: A vision for changing beliefs and practices* (120–131). Alexandria, VA: ASCD.

McNeal, L. (2008). NCLB: Adequate yearly progress. In C. Russo (Ed.), *Encyclopedia of School Law.* Thousand Oaks, CA: Sage.

Mead, S. (2007). Easy way out: "Restructured" usually means little has changed. *Education Next, 7*(1), 52–56.

Mills, C. W. (1959). *The sociological imagination.* London, UK: Oxford University Press.

No Child Left Behind Act of 2001, PL 107-110 (January 8, 2002).

Petersen, G. J., & Young, M. D. (2004). The no child left behind act and its influence on current and future district leaders. *Journal of Law & Education, 33*(4), 343–363.

Plank, D., & Dunbar, C. (2007). Michigan: Over the first hurdle. In F. M. Hess & C. E. Finn (Eds.), *No remedy left behind* (pp. 202–222). Washington, DC: AEI.

Rebell, M., & Wolff, J. R. (2008). Meaningful educational opportunity: A vital and viable mission for NCLB. *Educational Horizons, 86*(4), 203–205.

Smith, E. (2005). Raising standards in American schools: The case of no child left behind. *Journal of Education Policy, 20*(4), 515–525.

Talbert-Johnson, C. (2004). Structural inequities and the achievement gap in urban schools. *Education and Urban Society, 37*(1), 22–36.

Wenglinsky, H. (2004). Closing the racial achievement gap: The role of reforming instructional practices. *Education Policy Analysis, 12*(64), 1–22.

CHAPTER TWELVE

The Fast AND THE Serious: Exploring THE Notion OF Culturally Relevant Leadership

FLOYD D. BEACHUM AND CARLOS R. MCCRAY

Modern American schools operate in a social, political, and economic context of considerable uncertainty. Rapidly changing international political realities, the continuing explosion of development and use of technology in all aspects of modern life, and rhetoric about the importance of education far stronger than the fiscal priorities actually given to American schools serve to create conditions in which it is increasingly difficult to bring about the promised "effectiveness" for any group of students.

—BUNYAN BRYANT AND ALAN H. JONES, 1993, P. 5

The aforementioned context for American schooling is an outgrowth of the technological advancement and progress of the 21st-century society. "The more complex society gets, the more sophisticated leadership must become" (Fullan, 2001, p. ix). To this end, leaders surely impact the culture of an organization.

Organizational culture can be defined as the "underlying values, beliefs and principles that serve as a foundation for the organization's management system, as well as the set of management practices and behaviors that both exemplify and reinforce those principles" (Denison, 1990, p. 2). On the other hand, organizational culture can also be observed according to the perspective of the individuals within the organization regarding their shared cultural experiences (e.g., students within a school). Damen (1987) states, "Culture is learned and shared human patterns or models for living" (p. 367). More specifically, Wilson (2009) defines cultural traits as "shared outlooks, modes of behavior, traditions, belief systems, worldviews, values, skills, preferences, styles of self-presentation, etiquette, and linguistic patterns" (p. 15). Our major premise in this chapter is to establish a rationale and present a leadership framework that focuses on context and culture as a model for urban school administrators to lead, manage, and flourish. Our secondary purpose is to present this framework as a way to create positive urban school cultures for students in the interest of social justice.

The language of social justice is slowly being infused into K–12 education. In school leadership, the theory of social justice tends to outpace the practice (Beachum & McCray, 2010a). What is needed is an approach to social justice that carefully blends the best of theoretical concepts with the realities encountered in everyday urban school practice (Theoharis, 2009). We assert that social justice in urban school leadership should be relationship driven, holistic, and morally grounded (Dantley, Beachum, & McCray, 2008). This chapter seeks to address the issues of relationships in K–12 schools, offer a broader vision of urban school leadership, and encourage ethical action on the behalf of students in the interest of social justice.

In the early part of the 20th century, Mary McLeod Bethune encouraged educators to invest in the potential and promise of students. She argues, "We have a powerful potential in our youth, and we must have the courage to change old ideas and practices so that we may direct their power toward good ends" (Lynch, 2006, p. 37). In far too many instances, urban students are characterized as lazy, unmotivated, violent, and/or hopeless (Beachum & McCray, 2008; Dyson, 1997; Ginwright, 2004). Unless educators' perceptions about urban students are changed, they will fail to meet Bethune's challenge.

In this rapidly changing and increasingly diverse society, new urban school leadership is needed. Because both organizational culture and the cultures of individuals within schools are important to overall organizational effectiveness (Cox, 1994), administrators need leadership that recognizes culture as an organizing principle. We are suggesting that urban school administrators could benefit from what we are calling culturally relevant leadership. After explaining this framework, we discuss further implications for theory and practice.

CONTEXT AND CULTURE: RATIONALE FOR CULTURALLY RELEVANT LEADERSHIP

In the 21st century, the United States continues along a path of increasing racial/ethnic, language, and religious diversity (Irvine, 2003). Demographic changes across the American educational landscape present many challenges for urban school administrators (Obiakor, 2001; Madsen & Mabokela, 2005). On a daily basis, educational professionals often find themselves in situations marked by complexity and opportunity. Thus, it is critical that they develop effective ways of addressing specific areas of demographic change, the homogeneity of the teaching force, and the creation of a diversity-affirming organizational culture.

As previously noted, there is a continual trend toward greater racial/ethnic diversity in the United States. This trend is often related to population increases of people of color and the increasing net immigration rates for nonwhite groups in upcoming years (Madsen & Mabokela, 2005; U.S. Department of Commerce, 1996; Villegas & Lucas, 2002). It is quite likely that the population increase will have a direct impact on who is educated in American K–12 urban schools, as well as the quality of education they receive. According to National Center for Education Statistics (1998), students of color account for the majority of the K–12 enrollment in California, Hawaii, Mississippi, New Mexico, Texas, and the District of Columbia. Demographic trends such as these are juxtaposed with the fact that the core of teachers is overwhelmingly homogenous. In fact, the teaching force in the United States is largely White and female (Kunjufu, 2002; Mizialko, 2005). Across the country, white female teachers comprise the majority of the teaching positions in elementary and middle schools, as well as the teaching positions in preschool and kindergarten settings (Hancock, 2006). This, in and of itself, is not a bad thing; how these teachers interact with and educate diverse students is the area of most concern. Hancock (2006) asserts:

> The reality that White women are on the front lines of urban education is clearly evident. While we continue to recruit and retain minority teachers, it is critical that we also focus our attention on helping to educate White women teachers about the realities of teaching students who may hold a different sociopolitical, sociocultural, and socioeconomic perspective. (p. 97)

In addition, Kunjufu (2002) posits that African American teachers, too, sometimes have negative attitudes and low expectations of African American students, including urban. Put simply, issues surrounding teacher expectations, students of color, and appreciation for diversity have relevance to all educators in the organization (Banks, 2001; McCray, Alston, & Beachum, 2006). The responsibility for greater organization (e.g., climate and culture) falls upon the leadership.

Urban schools are becoming increasingly diverse and complex. As a result, urban school leaders are forced to find ways to maximize the potential of school staff, as well as address the many challenges in today's urban schools (Cox, 1994; Fullan, 2001). Organizational effectiveness in urban schools is impacted by the organizations' culture and leadership. Cox (2001) notes that most organizations have cultures that are somewhere between "toxic and deadly" (p. 12), where issues of diversity are concerned. In reference to schools, Banks (2001) indicates that school culture is the responsibility of all members of the organization and school staff must be actively engaged in creating an environment that is empowering and nurturing for all students, especially those from racially and ethnically diverse groups. In addition, Madsen and Mabokela (2005) state:

> A school's organizational culture establishes how its participants will approach issues of diversity. Thus, school norms and their cultural nuances establish the work climate that will accommodate and lead to greater flexibility on diversity-related issues. Schools need to understand how gender, race, national origin, and work specialization create microculture groups. (p. 3)

Therefore, it is reasonable to believe that effective urban leadership is an educational imperative. This kind of leadership recognizes that all children and youth have the ability to excel academically and succeed in life. These urban leaders purposefully seek to learn from their students, staff, and community in their effort to achieve the goals of the school (Lindsey, Roberts, & Campbell-Jones, 2005). They also acknowledge the fact that, historically, many U.S. schools have not served all students well (Beachum & McCray, 2010b, 2011; Perry, 2003; Morris, 2009).

Urban leadership requires vision (Beachum & Obiakor, 2005; Kouzes & Posner, 1995), and school leaders who embrace notions of social justice are vested in the idea that the school should serve the needs of all students, regardless of race/ethnicity, gender, social class, sexual orientation, ability status, or religious beliefs (Bogotch, Beachum, Blount, Brooks, & English, 2008; Frattura & Topinka, 2006; Marshall, 2004). According to the context and future outlook of urban schools, what is needed is a leadership perspective that is culturally relevant. The extant scholarly literature includes descriptions of culturally relevant teaching. There is also research connecting notions of leadership and diversity. In this chapter, we seek to illuminate this research and present a new theoretical framework for urban educational leaders.

REVIEW OF RELEVANT LITERATURE

Culturally Relevant Pedagogy

Urban education scholars have long argued that teaching styles should be culturally appropriate to the student populations being taught (Beachum & McCray, 2008, 2011; Gay, 2000; Ladson-Billings, 1994; Lee, 1995; Milner, 2006; Shade, Kelly, & Oberg, 1997). Though there is agreement on this basic notion, there are still differences in terms of how teaching styles should be implemented; leading to the divergence in the ways they are referred to: for instance, as "culturally congruent" (Au & Jordan, 1981; Au & Kawakami, 1994), "culturally responsive" (Erickson, 1987, Gay, 2000), and "culturally relevant" (Ladson-Billings, 1994). These approaches are clearly necessary because the past practice of simply trying to infuse some ethnic content into the curriculum was ineffective in meeting the needs of culturally diverse students (Cuban, 1972). In the long run, however, these approaches only began to define, describe, and detail effective teaching practices when working with students from ethnically and racially diverse backgrounds.

In a 1981 case study, Au and Jordan investigate the ways in which Hawaiian students learn to read in a program known as the Kamehameha Early Education Program (KEEP). They discover that the key to the program's success is its focus on sound–symbol relationships instead of comprehension. This emphasis is very similar to the Hawaiian linguistic pattern of "talk story." The researchers conclude that Hawaiian students view reading as a storytelling or socially interactive experience. KEEP's emphasis on cultural similarity led Au and Jordan to coin the term "culturally congruent" as a teaching style.

Gloria Ladson-Billings (1994) builds upon the established designation of culturally congruent when she coins the term "culturally relevant pedagogy" in her study of highly effective teachers of African American students. Ladson-Billings asked teachers and parents to nominate teachers they believed were successful. Those who were nominated twice were included in her study. The teachers participated in interviews, and they allowed Ladson-Billings to observe their classrooms. In this study, the researcher finds incredible similarities among the teachers deemed successful. They encourage equitable relationships with their students, desire students to take responsibility for their learning, and exhibit a passion for their profession. In addition, these teachers are culturally competent and encourage critical consciousness in their students.

Ladson-Billings (1995, p. 160) asserts that good teaching starts with teachers who use a culturally relevant pedagogy. In order for it to be effective, students should: (a) experience academic success, (b) develop and/or maintain cultural competence, and (c) develop a critical consciousness through which they challenge the status quo of the current social order. Thus, culturally relevant pedagogy should be incorporated into the curriculum as a means of "empowering students intellectually, socially, emotionally, and politically" (Ladson-Billings, 1994, p. 18).

Academic achievement is another important aspect of culturally relevant pedagogy; it is usually fostered by "the cultural knowledge, prior experiences, frames of reference, and performance styles of ethnically diverse students" (Gay, 2000, p. 29). In order for culturally diverse students to succeed and successfully navigate through formal education, teachers and leaders must incorporate methods of communication and learning into a framework that maintains the integrity of students' cultural backgrounds. Such a framework encourages respect and recognition of students' backgrounds, care and concern about their educational experiences, and encouragement and support as students develop a critical consciousness.

Leadership for Diversity in K–12 Schools

Leadership as a notion remains intriguing, allusive, and important. According to Short and Greer (2002), leadership is obscure and puzzling, and strangely fascinating and alluring. Until recently, educational administration, including urban, has been greatly shaped by notions like scientific rationalism and paradigms such as logical positivism. Scientific rationalism focuses on the efficiency of the organization, division of labor, and standardization, with an emphasis on impersonality and objectivity (Cunningham & Cordeiro, 2006; Hoy & Miskel, 1991). Notions of leadership are evolving from their origins of control, management, and close oversight into democratic decision making, relationship building, and empowerment (Cunningham & Cordeiro, 2003; Beachum & Obiakor, 2005; Short & Greer, 2002). This new leadership perspective is essential as organizations deal with daily flux and increased organizational agility. "Leadership, then, is not mobilizing others to solve problems we already know how to solve, but to help them confront problems that have never yet been successfully addressed" (Heifetz, 1994, p. 15). This purposeful paradigmatic shift is an educational imperative for dealing with the increasing diversity of urban K–12 schools.

The 21st century will continue to be characterized by increased racial and ethnic diversity (Cox, 1994). As such, urban schools will have to deal with many diversity-related challenges and changes (Beachum & McCray, 2004, 2011; Crosby, 1999; Kunjufu, 2002; Obiakor, 2001; McCray, Wright, & Beachum, 2007). Leadership is crucial in dealing with this diversity (Cox, 2001). The current racial context offers unique opportunities to expand leadership frontiers beyond traditionalist perspectives and antiquated ideologies that have ignored diversity and marginalized urban African American students (Dantley, 2002). Expounding on the dominant notions in educational leadership, Dantley (2002) asserts:

> [Educational leadership] has borrowed idioms and syntax from economics and the business world all in an effort to legitimate itself as a valid field. Inherent in such a theoretical heritage are also the concomitant ideological persuasions and embedded predispositions that inform the discourses from which educational leadership has borrowed. The penchant for rationality, order, and empiricism that inspires these positivist abstractions is hardly crafted in a frictionless social or ideological environment, although their maxims would lead one to believe that they have been birthed from an ahistorical and apolitical context. (p. 336)

Dantley has clearly enunciated that the overreliance on outdated positions (and scientific-rational approaches) is problematic. He implies that to overemphasize rationality is to ignore the irrational ways of people, to try to regulate disorder is to negate the natural chaos in organizations (especially urban schools) and to disregard the sociohistorical and political context is disheartening and disingenuous. When urban leadership fails to take diversity seriously, African American students in urban schools are often disfranchised by a conspiracy of mediocrity (Beachum & Obiakor, 2005; Sergiovanni, 1992).

When urban leadership creates a school culture that is student centered, it lessens the chance of prejudice among students, faculty, and staff (Banks, 2001; McCray et al., 2006). Researchers have discovered that students and teachers tend to bring socially and culturally biased feelings to school (Kailin, 2002; Tatum, 1997). In essence, urban leaders should foster serious and sincere conversations around issues of race/ethnicity, gender roles, class, and oppression (Dantley, 2005; Gause, 2005).

THEORETICAL FOUNDATIONS FOR CULTURALLY RELEVANT LEADERSHIP

The preceding review of literature sets the groundwork for the further exploration of culturally relevant leadership. With this notion being in its infancy, it is necessary to build and borrow from other similar and relevant frameworks. Villegas and Lucas (2002) developed a framework for preservice teachers. The model consists of educational continua that locates preservice teachers along a spectrum. It is made up of three dichotomous frames that the researchers did not make rigid, so that preservice teachers would not be easily lumped into one of the categories within the three frames. The frames are as follows: (a) social dyconsciousness: the social consciousness, deficit perspective; (b) the affirming perspective; and (c) the educator as technician: the educator as change agent perspective. In the following section, we propose three alternative frames for leadership, which are informed by the work of Villegas and Lucas (2002) and the other relevant literature. These frames include: liberatory consciousness, pluralistic insight, and reflexive practice.

Liberatory Consciousness

Liberatory consciousness is informed by critical consciousness and seeks to raise awareness levels and increase knowledge. Many urban school leaders have an educational view that does not connect the problems of urban African American students to larger structural inequalities (Beachum & Obiakor, 2005; Gorski,

2006; Villegas & Lucas, 2002). School leaders should work actively toward raising consciousness levels to balance the scales of excellence and equity in education (Obiakor & Beachum, 2005). Along these lines, Duncan-Andrade (2008) advocates for a liberatory pedagogy that seeks to end oppression and free students from the reigns of injustice. Liberatory consciousness includes the recognition of ideas such as the systemic nature of social inequality (i.e., denying the fallacy of us all being equal) and the affirmation of identity (i.e., suggesting that we all deserve to be treated with respect and supported in the teaching/learning process, as opposed to being dehumanized, disrespected, or devalued; McCray, 2008; Schmidt, 2005; Tatum, 1997, 2007; Villegas & Lucas, 2002).

Liberatory consciousness has great potential for educational leadership. Many educators and scholars support the idea of raising consciousness levels (Freire, 1973; Kailin, 2002; Ryan, 2006; Villegas & Lucas, 2002; West, 2004). The liberation aspect of this concept was well pronounced by Milner (2006) in writing, "Completeness for the oppressed begins with liberation. Until liberation is achieved, individuals are fragmented in search of clarity, understanding, and emancipation. This liberation is not outside of us or created or accomplished through some external force. Rather, it begins with a change in thinking" (p. 85). The essence of a liberatory consciousness is a change in thinking for educators, making them realize their own power with students and colleagues and their potential in society. Further, it involves raising levels of awareness and consciousness for students, educators, and administrators; understanding the systemic nature of oppression; and recognizing the link between the greater injustices in society and contemporary schooling.

Pluralistic Insight

Pluralistic insight deals with educators' attitudes toward students. It shuns a deficit perspective, wherein one "believes the dominant culture is inherently superior to the cultures of marginalized groups in society" (Villegas & Lucas, 2002, p. 35). Educators' attitudes and expectations can significantly impact students' school experiences (Beachum & McCray, 2008; Irvine, 1990; Kunjufu, 2007; Obiakor, 2001). The concept of pluralistic insight leans toward an affirming and positive notion of students that acknowledges the uniqueness of their experiences and their rich diversity. In discussing the history of notions of intelligence in education, Tatum (2007) explains the heart of the problem:

> ...the long tradition of stereotypical representations of Black and Latino people in popular culture as either stupid, lazy, dangerous, hypersexual, or all of those things combined ... [gives us] a situation in which it is very likely that Black and Latino children will enter school situations in which they are disadvantaged from the beginning by a teacher's lowered expec-

> tations as compared to those he or she may have for the White students in the class. This is a crucial point. I am not saying that most or many teachers are actively, consciously racist in their belief system (though of course some are). But we are all products of our culture and its history. Regardless of our own racial or ethnic backgrounds, we have all been exposed to racial stereotypes and flawed educational psychology, and unless we are consciously working to counter their influence on our behavior, it is likely that they will shape (subtly perhaps) our interactions with those who have been so stereotyped. (p. 52)

Pluralistic insight recognizes that we all have biases and perceptions, but we also have a greater responsibility to challenge these notions. According to Obiakor, Obiakor, Garza-Nelson, and Randall (2005), "We must begin to understand that traditional educational programs are loaded with discriminatory practices, unrealistic expectations, disproportionate representations, and illusory conclusions. It is important that we shift our paradigms and powers as we look for innovative ways to solve urban problems" (p. 29). In order to have pluralistic insight, we must encourage educational leaders to promote cultures of high expectations (Kunjufu, 2002; Tatum, 2007). Pluralistic insight is comprised of an understanding of the impact of attitudes on learning, a challenge to the stereotypical characterizations of others, and the adoption of an attitude of high expectations for all students and for all teachers.

Reflexive Practice

A crucial component of the concept of reflexive practice is educators viewing their practice as evolutionary. Reflexive practice views educators (i.e., teachers and administrators) as change agents who utilize culturally relevant pedagogy and practices for increased student success. In essence, this frame asserts that educational leaders engage in ongoing praxis (i.e., reflection and action). McCray et al. (2004) suggest that the work of educators is not viewed as linearly objective but rather is connected to the surrounding community of the school and the external society. In reference to educators, Villegas and Lucas (2002) state:

> While education has the potential to challenge and transform the inequities in society, without intervention, schools tend to reproduce those inequities by giving greater status to the ways of thinking, talking, and behaving of the dominant cultural group. Those with this perspective recognize that teaching is a complex activity that is inherently political and ethical. They are aware that institutional structures and practices do not exist in a vacuum, but that people build and sustain them, whether consciously or unconsciously. (p. 55)

McCray et al. also find in their research that some school leaders are more beholden to dominant cultural groups and political status quo than others. Thus, reflexive practice actively opposes the denigration, alienation, and stigmatization of students and communities that could result from the aforementioned complex educational context in favor of action. Reflexive practice activities include:

1. *Showing students genuine respect.* All students value, want, and deserve respect. It is up to educational leaders to model respect and it will generally be reciprocated. Expounding on the notion of respect, Garrison-Wade and Lewis (2006) opine, "Even adults seek the same in their personal interactions. Unfortunately, too often teachers forget that respect is important. They sometimes unintentionally belittle students. Once respect is lost, it is nearly impossible to regain" (p. 154).

2. *Taking the time to build relationships with faculty and students.* Relationships are an important component of modern organizations; at the same time, they tend to be at the heart of many problems in organizations (Covey, 1989). Therefore, educational leaders should build collegiality among their staff (e.g., special recognition awards, off-site retreats, collaborative planning times, etc.). These leaders should also make the time to build relationships with students, even as busy administrators. Educators can get through to students more easily when they have taken the time to build a significant relationship with them (Beachum & Obiakor, 2005; Kunjufu, 2002).

3. *Reflect, amend, and change (RAC).* In the long run, educational leaders are responsible for the school organization and the people within its walls. This responsibility requires them to make difficult decisions, so it is important for educational leaders to take the time to engage in RAC. Although the hectic schedule and constant pace of the school day may be daunting, urban leaders should take the time to reflect. An effective way to reflect is through journaling, which provides an opportunity to think back over situations from the day and remember what has happened. After reflection, urban leaders can then amend or rethink some of the decisions that had to be made quickly, (e.g., a disciplinary infraction by a student, a comment to the local newspaper, a student-sponsored social event on campus, etc.). After reflection and amendment, urban leaders can go back and change her decisions or behaviors as necessary. In a similar vein, Jacobson (2008) writes,

> Although it is challenging and uncomfortable, it is our responsibility as educators to overcome our discomfort through reflective practice where, as professionals, we come to understand why we do what we do, or how we feel the way we do. (p. 97)

Reflexive practice goes beyond the commonplace notion of being a reflective practitioner and views the educational leader as an agent for change and advocate/ alliance builder for the school, and encouraging a bias toward action.

CULTURALLY RELEVANT LEADERSHIP FOR STUDENT SUCCESS

On the whole, culturally relevant leadership is a mechanism for fostering greater student success and social justice. African American success in urban school contexts can be defined as making good grades, performing well on standardized tests, staying in school, feeling respected and appreciated in school, and realizing their true potential in the world as well as recognizing their own self-worth. Social justice leaders operate with an acute understanding of how "race, class, gender, disability, sexual orientation, and other historically marginalizing factors in the United States" (Theoharis, 2009, p. 11) have influenced and impacted K–12 urban schools. In the culturally relevant leadership framework, the school leader starts with the "self," by freeing his mind through liberatory consciousness. Then, the leader is forced to confront negative images and stereotypes, which ideally results in a change in attitude toward pluralistic insight. In the end, reflexive practice hopefully changes the way the school leader operates on a daily basis. In addition to the ideas previously mentioned, we suggest that school leaders encourage greater student success by taking the following steps:

1. *Encourage and support diverse teaching methods.* Teachers should be allowed to explore multiple ways of teaching and learning. This would require school leaders to allow room for experimentation and possible *implementation dips.* An implementation dip is a temporary drop in performance when a new innovation is used (Fullan, 2001). School leaders would play more of a supportive role in instructional leadership, not just an evaluative one. In this kind of environment, teachers would be allowed to investigate, inspire, experiment, reflect, revise, relearn, and change with the approval of administration. At the same time, they would be held accountable because their goal is student success.

2. *Create thoughtful learning communities that focus on student learning.* The notion of teachers sharing teaching strategies, having collaborative planning time, and collectively looking at student data is a relatively new phenomenon. For many years, teachers operated in silos within their own classrooms, fostering a closed culture marked by isolation and autonomy (Wagner, 2001). The duty to educate all students, according to empirical evidence, means that the old ways of operating should be revisited. Urban leaders should work to create the time and space for teachers to collaborate as well as organize professional development activities around student learning (Hord & Sommers, 2008). A practice-based activity for teachers is a concept called *lesson study* (see http://www.tc.edu/lessonstudy/index.html), where teachers work together in planning a lesson.

3. *Share leadership opportunities and value multiple voices.* The culturally relevant leader should look for opportunities to build leadership capacity among teachers. More specifically, this means identifying responsibilities and encouraging teachers to take on more of them, speak to broader audiences, and think beyond their immediate classrooms. In a similar sense, it is important that school leaders value the voices of all in the organization. "The administration and faculty together set the standards that the teachers work to achieve. Through their collaboration, they experience the freedom, ownership, and accountability they need to accomplish the job" (Singleton & Linton, 2006, p. 227). This requires the leader to make space even for dissent (not disrespect). Fullan (2001) reminds us that skeptics can be valuable in the organization, because they remind us of things we may have overlooked. Skeptics are different from cynics who tend to be negative and undermine the organization's mission.

4. *Connect the school with the community.* Schools are often intricately connected to the communities in which they reside. Thus, educational leaders must support efforts to involve the community at large in the life of the school. "Schools can never divorce themselves from the communities where they exist" (Swaminathan, 2005, p. 195). Urban leaders should create opportunities for dialogue, invite speakers, host events, and build coalitions with the external community. According to Singleton and Linton (2006), "The administration leads the effort to reach out to all parents and members of the community." They go on to elaborate, stating that when such outreach is effective, "parents and other community members do not feel disfranchised nor do they feel intimidated due to their own personal educational attainment, English language skills, racial description, economic status, dress, or perceptions of school derived from their own personal experiences. Families know that their voice matters in school affairs" (p. 227).

Together these suggestions help create an educational context were student success can increase.

CONCLUSION

This chapter is focused on "the fast and the serious." This statement is meant to be symbolic for educational leaders. Fast refers to education leaders who tend to be quick to acknowledge diversity and provide superficial activities like overemphasizing cultural dress, food, and art. Such urban educators also fall prey to believing in a reframing of multicultural education (and culturally relevant approaches) that places comfort before change (McCray et al., 2006). Gorski (2006) warns those who advocate for and believe in multicultural (or culturally relevant) approaches that they "must not turn multicultural education into human relations, relativistic concept that values every perspective. Multicultural education [and culturally relevant leadership] is not about validating every perspective but about eliminating racist, sexist, homophobic, classist, and other oppressive perspectives and policies from schools and society" (p. 76). The serious urban leaders are those who make sincere efforts to embrace culturally relevant leadership as a viable strategy for leading schools toward equity, excellence, and social justice. Culturally relevant leadership is informed by the following frames: (a) liberatory consciousness, (b) pluralistic insight, and (c) reflexive practice. It builds upon a long tradition of multicultural and diversity-related research yet traverses new pedagogical landscapes that inform the work of teacher-leaders and administrators who address the school organization. Culturally relevant leadership may very well be a way to bring about much-needed change in our schools. In an exposition on systemic change, Tatum (2007) insightfully articulates the heart of culturally relevant leadership when she states:

> Singing in concert with others leads to a more powerful result than singing alone, and of course, change happens more quickly at the institutional level when the focus shifts from the individual to the systemic—to the policies and practices that cut across classrooms... In order for system-wide change to take place, there must be leadership at the highest levels to support the examination of continuing educational inequities. (p. 79)

REFERENCES

Au, K., & Jordan, C. (1981). Teaching reading to Hawaiian children: Finding culturally appropriate solutions. In H. Trueba, G. Guthrie, & K. Au (Eds.), *Culture and the bilingual classroom: Studies in classroom ethnography* (pp. 139–152). Rowley, MA: Newbury.

Au, K., & Kawakami, A. (1994). Cultural congruence in instruction. In E. Hollins, J. King, & W. Hayman (Eds.), *Teaching diverse populations: Formulating knowledge base* (pp. 5–23). Albany: State University of New York Press.

Banks, J. A. (2001). Multicultural education: Characteristics and goals. In J. A. Banks & C. H. McGee-Banks (Eds.), *Multicultural education: Issues and perspectives* (4th ed., pp. 3–30). New York, NY: Wiley.

Beachum, F. D., & McCray, C. R. (2004). Cultural collision in urban schools. *Current Issues in Education, 7*(5). Retrieved from http://cie.asu.edu/volume7/number5/

Beachum, F. D., & McCray, C. R. (2008). Dealing with cultural collision: What Pre-Service educators should know. In G. Goodman (Ed.), *Educational psychology: An application of critical constructivism* (pp. 53–70). New York, NY: Peter Lang.

Beachum, F. D., & McCray, C. M. (2010a). Cracking the code: Illuminating the promises and pitfalls of social justice in educational leadership. *International Journal of Urban Educational Leadership, 4*(1), 206–221.

Beachum, F., & McCray, C. (2010b). Through the fire: How pretext impacts the context of African American educational experiences. In G. Goodman (Ed.), *Educational psychology reader: The art and science of how people learn* (pp. 230–250). New York, NY: Peter Lang.

Beachum, F. D., & McCray, C. R. (2011). *Cultural collision and collusion: Reflections on hip-hop culture, values, and schools.* New York, NY: Peter Lang.

Beachum, F. D., & Obiakor, F. E. (2005). Educational leadership in urban schools. In F. E. Obiakor & F. D. Beachum (Eds.), *Urban education for the 21st century: Research, issues, and perspectives* (pp. 83–99). Springfield, IL: Charles C. Thomas.

Bogotch, I., Beachum, F. D., Blount, J., Brooks, J., & English, F. (2008). *Radicalizing educational leadership: Dimensions of social justice.* Rotterdam, Netherlands: Sense.

Bryant, B., & Jones, A. H. (1993). *Seeking effective schools for African American children: Strategies for teachers and school managers.* San Francisco, CA: Caddo Gap Press.

Covey, S. R. (1989). *The 7 habits of highly effective people: Powerful lessons in personal change.* New York, NY: Free Press.

Cox, T., Jr. (1994). *Cultural diversity in organizations: Theory, research, and practice.* San Francisco, CA: Berrett-Koehler.

Cox, T., Jr. (2001). *Creating the multicultural organization: A strategy for capturing the power of diversity.* San Francisco, CA: Jossey-Bass.

Crosby, E. A. (1999). Urban schools: Forced to fail. *Phi Delta Kappan, 81*(4), 298–303.

Cuban, L. (1972). Ethnic content and "white" instruction. *Phi Delta Kappan, 53*(5), 270–273.

Cunningham, W. G., & Cordeiro, P. A. (2003). *Educational leadership: A problem-based approach* (2nd ed.). Boston, MA: Allyn & Bacon.

Cunningham, W. G., & Cordeiro, P. A. (2006). *Educational leadership: A problem-based approach* (3rd ed.). Boston, MA: Allyn & Bacon.

Damen, L. (1987). *Culture learning: The fifth dimension on the language classroom.* Reading, MA: Addison-Wesley.

Dantley, M. (2002). Uprooting and replacing positivism, the melting pot, multiculturalism, and other impotent notions in educational leadership through an African American perspective. *Education and Urban Society, 34*(3), 334–352.

Dantley, M. (2005). African American spirituality and Cornel West's notions of prophetic pragmatism: Restructuring educational leadership in American urban schools. *Educational Administration Quarterly, 41*(4), 651–674.

Dantley, M., Beachum, F. D., & McCray, C. (2008). Exploring the intersectionality of multiple centers within notions of social justice. *Journal of School Leadership, 18*(2), 124–133.

Denison, D. (1990). *Corporate culture and organizational effectiveness.* New York, NY: Wiley.

Duncan-Andrade, J. (2008). Developing social justice educators: How can the subject tell the truth about itself? In G. Goodman (Ed.), *Educational psychology: An application of critical constructivism* (pp. 1–11). New York, NY: Peter Lang.

Dyson, M. E. (1997). *Race rules: Navigating the color line.* New York, NY: Vintage.

Erickson, F. (1987). Transformation and school success: The politics and culture of educational achievement. *Anthropology & Educational Quarterly, 18*(4), 355–356.

Frattura, E. M., & Topinka, C. (2006). Theoretical underpinnings of separate educational programs: "The social justice challenge continues." *Education & Urban Society, 38*(3), 327–344.

Freire, P. (1973). *Pedagogy of the oppressed.* New York, NY: Seabury Press.

Fullan, M. (2001). *Leading in a culture of change.* San Francisco, CA: Jossey-Bass.

Garrison-Wade, D., & Lewis, C. W. (2006). Tips for school principals and teachers: Helping black students achieve. In J. L. Landsman & C. W. Lewis (Eds.), *White teachers/diverse classrooms: A guide to building inclusive schools, promoting high expectations, and eliminating racism* (pp. 150–161). Sterling, VA: Stylus.

Gause, C. P. (2005). Navigating stormy seas: Critical perspectives on the intersection of popular culture and educational leader-"ship." *Journal of School Leadership, 15*(3), 333–345.

Gay, G. (2000). *Culturally responsive teaching: Theory, research, and practice.* New York, NY: Teachers College Press.

Ginwright, S. A. (2004). *Black in school: Afrocentric reform, urban youth, and the promise of hip-hop culture.* New York, NY: Teachers College Press.

Gorski, P. (2006). The unintentional undermining of multicultural education: Educators at the crossroads. In J. L. Landsman & C. W. Lewis (Eds.), *White teachers/diverse classrooms: A guide to building inclusive schools, promoting high expectations, and eliminating racism* (pp. 61–78). Sterling, VA: Stylus.

Hancock, S. D. (2006). White women's work: On the front lines of urban education. In J. Landsman & C. W. Lewis (Eds.), *White teachers/diverse classrooms: A guide to building inclusive schools, promoting high expectations, and eliminating racism* (pp. 93–109). Sterling, VA: Stylus.

Heifetz, R. (1994). *Leadership without easy answers.* Cambridge, MA: Harvard University Press.

Hord, S. M., & Sommers, W. A. (2008). *Leading professional learning communities: Voices from research and practice.* Thousand Oaks, CA: Corwin Press.

Hoy, W. K., & Miskel, C. G. (1991). *Education administration: Theory and practice.* Boston, MA: McGraw-Hill.

Irvine, J. J. (1990). *Black students and school failure.* New York, NY: Greenwood Press.

Irvine, J. J. (2003). *Educating teachers for diversity: Seeing with a cultural eye.* New York, NY: Teachers College Press.

Jacobson, T. (2008). Teacher and family relationships. In G. Goodman (Ed.), *Educational psychology: An application of critical constructivism* (pp. 95–112). New York, NY: Peter Lang.

Kailin, J. (2002). *Antiracist education: From theory to practice.* Lanham, MD: Rowman & Littlefield.

Kouzes, J. M., & Posner, B. Z. (1995). *The leadership challenge.* San Francisco, CA: Jossey-Bass.

Kunjufu, J. (2002). *Black students—Middle class teachers.* Chicago, IL: African American Images.

Kunjufu, J. (2007). *An African centered response to Ruby Payne's poverty theory.* Chicago, IL: African American Images.

Ladson-Billings, G. (1994). *The dreamkeepers: Successful teachers of African-American students.* San Francisco, CA: Jossey-Bass.

Ladson-Billings, G. (1995). But that's just good teaching! The case for culturally relevant pedagogy. *Theory into Practice, 34*(3), 159–165.

Landsman, J., & C. W. Lewis (Eds.), *White teachers/diverse classrooms: A guide to building inclusive schools, promoting high expectations, and eliminating racism* (pp. 93–109). Sterling, VA: Stylus.

Lee, C. D. (1995). Signifying as a scaffold for literary interpretation. *Journal of Black Psychology, 21*(4), 357–381.

Lindsey, R. B., Roberts, L. M., & Campbell-Jones, F. (2005). *The culturally proficient school: An implementation guide for school leaders.* Thousand Oaks, CA: Corwin Press.

Lynch, M. (2006). *Closing the racial academic achievement gap.* Chicago, IL: African American Images.

Madsen, J. A., & Mabokela, R. O. (2005). *Culturally relevant schools: Creating positive workplace relationships and preventing intergroup differences.* New York, NY: Routledge.

Marshall, C. (2004). Social justice challenges to educational administration: Introduction to a special issue. *Educational Administration Quarterly, 40*(1), 5–15.

McCray, C. R. (2008). Constructing a positive intrasection of race and class for the 21st century. *Journal of School Leadership, 18*(2), 249–267.

McCray, C. R., Alston, J. A., & Beachum, F. D. (2006). Principals' perceptions of multicultural education and school climate. *Multicultural Learning and Teaching, 1*(1), 12–22.

McCray, C. R., Wright, J. V., & Beachum, F. D. (2004). An analysis of secondary school principals' perceptions of multicultural education. *Education, 125*(1), 111–120.

McCray, C. R., Wright, J. V., & Beachum, F. D. (2007). Beyond *Brown*: Examining the perplexing plight of African American principals. *Journal of Instructional Psychology, 34*(4), 247–255.

Milner, H. R. (2006). But good intentions are not enough: Theoretical and philosophical relevance in teaching students of color. In J. Landsman & C. W. Lewis (Eds.), *White teachers/diverse classrooms: A guide to building inclusive schools, promoting high expectations, and eliminating racism* (pp. 79–90). Sterling, VA: Stylus.

Mizialko, A. (2005). Reducing the power of "whiteness" in urban schools. In F. E. Obiakor & F. D. Beachum (Eds.), *Urban education for the 21st century: Research, issues, and perspectives* (pp. 176–186). Springfield, IL: Charles C. Thomas.

Morris, J. E. (2009). *Troubling the waters: Fulfilling the promise of quality public schooling for Black children.* New York, NY: Teachers College Press.

National Center for Education Statistics. (1998). *Data file: 1996–97 common fore of data public elementary and secondary school universe.* Washington, DC: U.S. Government Printing Office.

Obiakor, F. E. (2001). *It even happens in "good" schools: Responding to cultural diversity in today's classrooms.* Thousand Oaks, CA: Corwin Press.

Obiakor, F. E., & Beachum, F. D. (2005). Urban education: The quest for democracy, equity, and excellence. In F. E. Obiakor & F. D. Beachum (Eds.), *Urban education for the 21st century: Research, issues, and perspectives* (pp. 3–19). Springfield, IL: Charles C. Thomas.

Obiakor, F. E., Obiakor, P. H., Garza-Nelson, C., & Randall, P. (2005). Educating urban learners with and without special needs: Life after the Brown case. In F. E. Obiakor & F. D. Beachum (Eds.), *Urban education for the 21st century: Research, issues, and perspectives* (pp. 20–33). Springfield, IL: Charles C. Thomas.

Perry, T. (2003). Up from the parched earth: Toward a theory of African-American achievement. In T. Perry, C. Steel, & A. G. Hilliard (Eds.), *Young gifted and Black: Promoting high achievement among African-American students* (pp. 1–108). Boston, MA: Beacon.

Ryan, J. (2006). *Inclusive leadership.* San Francisco, CA: Jossey-Bass.

Schmidt, S. L. (2005). More than men in white sheets: Seven concepts to the teaching of racism as systemic inequality. *Equity & Excellence in Education, 38*, 110–122.

Sergiovanni, T. J. (1992). *Moral leadership: Getting to the heart of school improvement.* San Francisco, CA: Jossey-Bass.

Shade, B. J., Kelly, C., & Oberg, M. (1997). *Creating culturally responsive classrooms.* Washington, DC: American Psychological Association.

Short, P. M., & Greer, J. T. (2002). *Leadership in empowered schools: Themes from innovative efforts.* Upper Saddle River, NJ: Prentice Hall.

Singleton, G. E., & Linton, C. (2006). *Courageous conversations about race: A field guide or achieving equity in schools.* Thousand Oaks, CA: Corwin Press.

Swaminathan, R. (2005). Building community in urban schools: Promises and challenges. *Urban education for the 21st century: Research, issues, and perspectives* (pp. 187–198). Springfield, IL: Charles C. Thomas.

Tatum, B. D. (1997). *Why are all the Black kids sitting together in the cafeteria? And other conversations about race.* New York, NY: Basic Books.

Tatum, B. D. (2007). *Can we talk about race? And other conversations in an era of school resegregation.* Boston, MA: Beacon Press.

Theoharis, G. (2009). *The school leaders our children deserve: Seven keys to equity, social justice, and school reform.* New York, NY: Teachers College Press.

U.S. Department of Commerce. (1996). *Current population reports: Population projections of the United States by age, sex, race, and Hispanic origin: 1995 to 2050.* Washington, DC: Author.

Villegas, A. M., & Lucas, T. (2002). *Educating culturally responsive teachers: A coherent approach.* Albany: State University of New York Press.

Wagner, T. (2001). Leadership for learning: An action theory of school change. *Phi Delta Kappan, 82*(5), 378–383.

West, C. (2004). *Democracy matters: Winning the fight against imperialism.* New York, NY: Penguin Press.

Wilson, W. J. (2009). *More than just race: Being Black and poor in the inner city.* New York, NY: Norton.

CHAPTER THIRTEEN

Reaching Out: Partnering With THE Families AND Communities OF African American Urban Youth

MAVIS G. SANDERS, GILDA MARTINEZ-ALBA,
AND MICHELLE D. WHITE

In urban communities throughout the United States, African American youth overcome significant obstacles each day to accomplish high levels of academic success and educational attainment. Brian, Jessica, Dorothy, and Jim, recipients of full college scholarships through the Ron Brown Scholars Program, are a few of these young people.[1] The stories of their lives, which follow, are at once inspiring and instructive.

Brian: *Learning in multiple contexts*

Brian grew up in an urban African American and Latino neighborhood in the western part of United States. While growing up, he balanced his time between going to school and working in a local barbershop. He enjoyed and felt comfortable in both environments. The local barbershop was a focal point growing up because of the importance of having the "right hairstyle" and the sense of belonging that it provided. He said the climate was one in which sports, politics, and cars, as well as many other topics, were discussed in "verbal contests" between and among clients who spanned several generations.

Thanks to his "strong support network," which included his family and a school counselor who encouraged him to apply for the Ron Brown Scholarship, he was able to graduate from high school and attend Princeton University. He graduated with a bachelor's degree in education policy and decided to pursue a doctorate in education at the University of California, Berkeley.

His ultimate goals include being "a good healthy person and happy in life." When asked if his education had helped him to realize these goals, he responded, "I am definitely happy. My education is different than just my schooling. . . . I see it as my experiences in different places where I get information and find different ways to take advantage of it." He also said that a big impact on his success has been his "ongoing participation in events and activities" that helped him to stay focused and encouraged him to continue to challenge himself.

Community institutions, including the barbershop, remain important to him. He still goes there every two weeks to get a cut or "lined up." When he does, he believes he is not only attending to his hair but also to himself. Barbershop visits leave him feeling "renewed inside and out." These visits often include up to two hours of waiting, but he welcomes this as a time to listen to everyone around him and their opinions.

Jessica: *Building bridges across continents*

Jessica grew up in an urban area in the mid-Atlantic region of the United States. In seventh grade, she had the opportunity to visit Nigeria, her parents' birthplace. She was very excited to meet everyone from her family's village, especially those from a photo she had looked at many times over the years. In the photo, there were many children whom she hoped to meet and to see now that they were much older. What she did not realize was that many of the children in the photo had died. When she found out, she was "horrified."

She had never had a friend in the United States die; therefore, she did not expect this outcome. The children died from diarrhea, measles, and other causes. While in Nigeria, Jessica and her mother (a nurse) went to visit hospitals filled with sick children. The hospitals were not in walking distance from her family's village, and because many people in the village did not own cars or had to work, they had not gotten vaccinated.

This trip proved to be a life-altering experience. Jessica went on to study the history of science and medicine at Yale University and decided to pursue a career in medicine. After completing her medical education, she plans to return to Nigeria to organize and create more hospitals to lower childhood mortality rates.

When she was asked, "What would you recommend to help students succeed?" she quickly responded, "Family support and having a lot of communication with teachers and guidance counselors." Jessica added that public libraries provided "a safe, quiet space to study after school."

Dorothy: *Celebrating self and others*

After her father died in a car crash when she was only five years old, Dorothy was adopted by her aunt and uncle who lived in an urban area in the Midwest. Her adoptive parents gave her new opportunities. As a result of their support and her hard work, she achieved the academic success required to attend various community organized summer programs. These programs took her to places throughout the United States and the world. She said, "By visiting other states and countries, I was able to enjoy other cultures, yet celebrate my own." At the end of high school, she was accepted to Harvard University, where she decided to study government.

She stated that "a support system, follow through, positive reinforcement, and high expectations" were keys to her academic success. Her adoptive parents were "consistently aware of where she was at all times," which helped to structure her journey through adolescence and the education pipeline. She believed that, as a result of her education, she now has "more opportunities" and "more control over what happens" in her life. She feels like she "can do anything."

Jim: *Advocating for education*

Jim grew up with his mother in a housing project in the northeastern part of the United States. Drug dealers were a regular part of the community that he walked through every day to get to his apartment, but he did not let that discourage him. His mother's support helped him to maintain a positive attitude and outlook on life.

After school, he helped tutor students. Because of the horrible conditions in his community, Jim felt that "some of these students were destined for an unfortunate future." In other words, without some intervention, Jim saw many of these students' futures as the same as those of the people who sold drugs in his community.

After graduating from high school, Jim attended Cornell University, where he studied economics. When asked what support students need to help them succeed, he stated, "The value of education needs to be re-emphasized in our households." He also explained that parental involvement, mentoring programs, and believing that "school is cool" were some of the most important factors that helped him to succeed. He further added, "Church members, teachers who took a genuine interest in me, and being fortunate enough to be surrounded with likeminded peers made all the difference."

Prominent in the success stories of these youth and hundreds of others like them is the support of caring adults in their schools, families, and communities. Both education theory and research indicate that, when there is cooperation and collaboration among adults, students benefit (Henderson & Mapp, 2002; Sanders & Sheldon, 2009). To ensure that such collaboration is the norm and not the exception, it is critical that teachers, administrators, and school staff develop comprehensive school-based partnership programs involving the school, family, and community. Such programs acknowledge and facilitate various types of family and community involvement and are implemented to achieve important goals for students' learning and success (Epstein & Associates, 2009). Effective partnerships require educators to adopt a philosophy and practice of education that recognizes the separate and overlapping influences of students' schools, families, and communities in their learning and development (Comer, 2004; Epstein, 2001). This approach to education helps to ensure that urban youth like Brian, Jessica, Dorothy, and Jim receive the collaborative support that is critical for their academic success and well-being (Sanders, 1998; Sanders & Herting, 2000).

In this chapter, we discuss different types of family and community involvement in the education of urban African American youth. We also present current research describing the importance of this involvement for students' school success. In the concluding section, we offer practical recommendations for urban educators who seek to build stronger connections with their students' families and communities. By following these recommendations, educators can begin to build more socially just schools for the urban children and youth they serve.

Defining Family and Community Involvement

Family involvement is commonly defined as the participation of parents in all aspects of their children's education and growth (National Parent Teacher Association, 2000). By this definition, the term *parent* should include guardians, grandparents, siblings, or extended family members acting in the parental role (Weiss, Kreider, Lopez, & Chatman, 2005). Although the basic definition of family involvement appears simple, it is a complex construct that covers a broad range of parental attitudes and behaviors (McDermott, 2008; Patrikakou, Weissberg, Redding, & Walberg, 2005). It is a dynamic construct influenced by a variety of factors, and, at its best, an adaptive construct that responds to students' changing needs over time (Hill & Chao, 2009; Patrikakou, et al., 2005).

There are two broad categories that are often used to distinguish different types of parent involvement: (a) home-based involvement and (b) school-based involvement. Home-based involvement refers to activities, such as monitoring, homework, or rewarding school success, that occur in the home. School-based involvement refers to activities, such as participation in school decision-making committees or classroom volunteering, that occur in the school. Home–school communication, including parent–teacher conferences, interim progress reports, and newsletters, is a third category that is viewed as separate and distinct from the two others but is central to their effective implementation (Patrikakou et. al, 2005).

Although these broad categories begin to show the breadth and variety of parent involvement behaviors, an increasingly common framework that captures greater nuance was developed by Epstein (1995). The researcher categorizes family involvement into six types: (a) *parenting:* establishing home environments that support children as healthy individuals; (b) *communicating:* engaging in effective two-way communication about school programs and children's progress; (c) *volunteering:* providing help and support for school programs and student activities; (d) *learning at home:* helping children at home with homework and curricular-related decisions and activities; (e) *decision making:* participating in educational decision making, improvement, and reform efforts; and (e) *collaborating with the community:* identifying and utilizing resources and services from the community to strengthen and support schools, students, and their families.

A brief overview of these six types of involvement and how schools can support them follows:

1. *Parenting.* According to Bronfenbrenner (1985), family relationships and interactions have a profound impact on the development of the child and her interactions and success in the larger society. He asserts:

> The family determines our capacity to function effectively and to profit from experience in the other settings of life—school, peer group, higher education, business, community, and the nation as a whole. In all these settings, what we learn, as well as what we can contribute, depends on the families we come from and the families in which we now live. This is true from early childhood until the day we die. (p. 6)

McDermott (2008) characterizes good parenting as a challenging and complex process. In order for parents to raise healthy children who become ethical and productive members of society, it is critical that they are able to respond to children's emotional, physical, and intellectual needs over time. Further, to do so, most parents need support from families, friends, colleagues, social service providers, educators, or all of the above (Bronfenbrenner, 1985; McDermott, 2008). This support is especially important for low-income urban parents who have more limited economic, political, and social capital than middle- and upper-income families (Horvat, Weininger, & Lareau, 2003). Low-income urban parents are more likely to be employed in service occupations characterized by low earnings, inflexible work schedules, fewer opportunities for full-time employment, and limited benefits, such as health insurance, paid vacations, or holidays (U.S. Department of Labor, 2005). Unstable housing and greater residential mobility are also more prevalent in low-income urban communities (Koball, Douglas-Hall, & Chau, 2005).

When urban schools provide families with access to information, social support, and resources to help meet the challenges of effective parenting, positive outcomes for students are achieved. For example, longitudinal research conducted about the Chicago Child-Parent Center Program finds that families that received such support had fewer incidents of child abuse and neglect (Reynolds & Clements, 2005). Moreover, these families' children experienced reductions in special education placements, grade retention, delinquency, and high school dropout (Reynolds & Clements, 2005).

However, in order for the efforts of schools to be most effective, educators must engage in meaningful dialogue with families in order to better understand their needs and concerns (Epstein & Associates, 2009). The term *dialogue* is intentionally chosen here to mean that parties "talk *with* each other, not *at* each other," as individuals in a community working on behalf of children and youth (Brock, 2010, p. 129).

2. *Communicating.* Communication between families and schools is essential for collaborative support of children's learning and development (Eccles & Harold, 1996; Davis-Kean & Eccles, 2005). When urban educators effectively communicate with families through strategies such as face-to-face meetings, disseminating materials regarding ways to support children's learning at home, and making telephone calls both as a matter of routine and when children experience problems or challenges, low-performing students make significant achievement gains in both reading and mathematics (Westat & Policy Studies Associates, 2001). Moreover, parents have greater access to information and materials to support their children's learning and a greater appreciation of their role in their children's education (Davies, 1993).

However, home–school communication can also be a source of conflict and tension, especially in schools serving low-income, ethnically diverse populations (Lawrence-Lightfoot, 1978, 2003). DeCastro-Ambrosetti and Cho (2005) find that teachers often blame the home and parents for the low academic performance of culturally and linguistically diverse students. The researchers conclude, "As long as this rift between home and school exists, communication between parents and teachers will continue to be strained and hindered" (p. 45). This means that to foster the academic success of diverse students, teachers not only have to adapt curriculum and pedagogy (Nieto, 2000) but also their interactions with students' families.

In her seminal work, *Developing Home-School Partnerships: From Concepts to Practice*, Swap (1993) asserts that effective communication between parents and educators is based on a relationship in which each respects the other's contribution and expertise, boundaries are clear, conflicts are dealt with openly and respectfully, and interactions are rewarding (in that they support children's socioemotional growth, intellectual development, and school success). In today's increasingly diverse urban schools, effective communication by urban teachers also means that one form or style of communication cannot be privileged over others. When urban teachers rely too heavily on print communication and middle-class forms of interaction and discourse, low-income African American communities are often marginalized (Jaime & Russell, 2010; Lareau, 1987). Urban schools can facilitate this type of involvement by creating formal and informal and traditional and nontraditional opportunities for home–school communication—opportunities that are coconstructed with parents and students.

3. *Volunteering.* Volunteering typically occurs at the school (e.g., tutoring students and participating in field trips) or through the school at family members' homes or offices (e.g., preparing materials for learning activities and telephoning other parents about educational events; Epstein & Associates, 2009). Volunteering has been found to benefit students, educators, and the volunteers themselves. For example, volunteer aids in urban classrooms have been found to enhance teacher effectiveness and increase student achievement in the areas of reading and grammar regardless of students' grade levels, sex, aptitude, and ethnicity (Holzmiller, 1982). Other education researchers contend that volunteering is one way in which diverse families can share their "funds of knowledge" or the knowledge and skills that households have accumulated over time to function effectively (Moll, Amanti, Neff, & Gonzalez, 1992). By incorporating families' funds of knowledge in educational activities throughout the academic year, urban schools make teaching and learning more personal, relevant, and culturally responsive experiences for the students they serve (Swap, 1993). Urban schools can increase this type of involvement by offering volunteers meaningful opportunities and training (Henderson, Mapp, Johnson, & Davies, 2007; Sanders & Sheldon, 2009). Many urban schools create parent rooms or centers to provide family and community volunteers a welcoming place to meet, plan activities, and carry out tasks. By providing space for volunteers, urban schools communicate to families the importance of their contribution to the school and students (Johnson, 1994). In some urban schools, these parent centers are also sites for community meetings and extended services for families, including GED, ESL, and computer classes (Sanders & Lewis, 2004).

4. *Learning at home.* Summarizing two decades of research on families' involvement at home on their children's school success, Henderson and Mapp (2002) report:

- When parents are involved in their children's education at home, the children do better in school.
- A home environment that encourages learning is more important to student achievement than income, education level, or cultural background.
- When children and parents talk regularly about school, children perform better academically.

According to Scott-Jones (1995), the benefits of families' involvement at home can occur through a variety of interactions, which she categorizes into three levels: (a) valuing, (b) monitoring, and (c) helping. *Valuing* refers to parents communicating to their children the value of education and their expectations and aspirations for their children's success in school. *Monitoring* refers to parents' oversight of their children's activities and behaviors directly and indirectly related to school. Parents can also support learning at home by *helping* their children practice and master academic tasks as "experts" or "colearners." This type of involvement, although not witnessed by the school, can be supported by specific school actions.

Ongoing research by Hoover-Dempsey, Walker, and Sandler (2005) explains factors that influence if and how families will be involved in their children's learning. These factors include: (a) parents' sense of efficacy at helping their children succeed in school, (b) demands on parents' time and energy, and (c) general and specific invitations and demands for involvement from children and schools. To encourage this type of involvement, Hoover-Dempsey and colleagues recommend that schools implement an interactive homework program like Teachers Involve Parents in Schoolwork (TIPS), which is discussed later in this chapter, and create additional assignments and opportunities that encourage parents to talk with students about general or specific aspects of school. By offering specific, time-limited, developmentally appropriate suggestions for home-based involvement, urban schools can help families increase engagement in their children's learning at home and build parents' sense of efficacy at involvement in the process.

5. *Decision making.* Family involvement in decision making may include being a school board member, a participant on a parent advisory or other school-based committee, or an active member of a parent-teacher organization. Areas in which parents may be involved in school decision making include goal setting, development, implementation and evaluation of program activities, personnel decisions, and funding allocations. Cotton and Wikelund (2001) report that parent involvement in decision making is one of the most controversial types of involvement

because educators are reluctant to encourage parents to become partners in governance. The researchers found that, although education administrators agree that parents should be involved with schools in a variety of ways, they disapprove of parent involvement in administrative areas, such as teacher selection and evaluation, the selection of texts and other teaching materials, or setting budget priorities.

Yet, others believe that parent involvement in decision making is critical to school improvement and excellence, especially in urban communities. Comer (2005), for example, observed different degrees and patterns of school involvement among families and created a three-level model to account for this variation. According to Comer, Level 1 involvement includes parenting, communicating, and learning at-home activities as described previously. Level 2 involvement consists of volunteering activities. Level 3 involvement features decision making through providing service on planning and management teams or curriculum and other school committees. Comer further asserts that this third level of parent involvement can transform and empower urban families to become agents of positive change within their schools and communities.

However, unless urban educators commit to making their schools more democratic institutions, parents may never penetrate beyond the margins of urban education decision making. Writing from a social justice perspective, Fine (1993) argues:

> Without a commitment to democratically restructuring schools and communities, parental involvement projects will end up helping families (or not) rather than transforming public life. Without an image of parents and educators working across lines of power, class, race, gender, status, and politics, toward democracies of difference, each group is likely to feel they have gotten no hearing, and will default to their respective corners shrouded in private interests and opposition. (p. 6)

Urban schools intent on increasing this type of involvement should actively recruit parents from a variety of backgrounds, provide these parents with the tools needed to act as family representatives and advocates, and assist school personnel to work collaboratively across differences of ethnicity, class, and gender (Sanders & Epstein, 2000).

6. *Collaborating with the community.* A final way in which families can be involved in their children's education is through linking up with community organizations that support children's cognitive, social, and emotional development. Urban adolescents who reported support from adults in their families, schools, and community-based organizations, such as the church, reported more positive school behavior and academic self-concepts, as well as higher school grades, than

students who did not have this broad-based support (Sanders, 1998; Sanders & Herting, 2000). Community organizations that provide academic support and enrichment during nonschool hours are especially important for urban African American students' academic success (Sanders & Campbell, 2007).

Community-based organizations can also help urban families to achieve the goals of parenting previously discussed. When urban parents have access to community organizations that provide assistance with health care, food, housing and heating, or information on how to better support their children's learning, they can be helped to create home environments that provide the structure and stability associated with students' school success (Bronfenbrenner, 1985). Urban schools can support this process by acting as resource brokers. Small (2006) defines resource brokers as "organizations possessing ties to businesses, non-profits and government agencies rich in resources" (p. 274). According to Small, through formal and informal interactions, institutional resource brokers can increase neighborhood residents' access to a variety of information and services. Because of their relative stability and resilience to political and economic shifts, schools, including urban ones, are uniquely positioned to act in this capacity. Empirical studies further highlight the importance of family and community involvement for the educational success of African American urban youth. These studies are described in the following section.

Research on Family and Community Involvement and African American Urban Youth

The research on African American family involvement mirrors major findings on the influence of parent involvement on school outcomes for the general population. For example, a recent meta-analysis, including 52 studies on parent involvement and educational outcomes, finds that parent involvement has a positive overall effect on a variety of academic variables, regardless of ethnicity (Jeynes, 2007). Although the general effects of family involvement are consistent across ethnic and racial groups, some differences have been identified. In a separate meta-analysis of 21 studies on family involvement and educational outcomes for children of color, Jeynes (2003) finds that parental involvement overall has a positive impact on the achievement of all students of color but that it "benefited African American and Latinos more than Asian Americans" (p. 214).

In a longitudinal study of over 2,000 African American families, Wu and Qi (2006) find that parental encouragement shows the most significant and consistent effects on child academic achievement, both concurrently and longitudinally. For example, children of parents who emphasized the importance of knowing the alphabet and numbers in kindergarten achieved higher levels in reading and math in kindergarten and first grade, as well as reading in third grade, than students whose parents did not. Moreover, when parents believed that their children were equal to or better in certain general developmental areas (e.g., attention or articulation) than other children of the same age, the positive effects of such beliefs persisted into subsequent years of schooling. In addition, parents' perceptions of how their children were doing academically in the first and third grades showed positive concurrent and longitudinal effects on children's reading, math, and general knowledge or science test scores (Wu & Qi, 2006).

Research further suggests that urban teachers' classroom and family engagement practices together with family and community involvement has a stronger impact on student achievement than factors such as income and family structure. For example, Ferguson, Clark, and Stewart (2002) examine the impact of school and family process factors and noninstructional factors on urban student achievement. They define school and family process factors as teachers' estimates of students' time spent on classroom learning, teacher perception of student capabilities, teacher–parent communication patterns, parental standards for student academic pursuits, and students' patterns of out-of-school time use. Noninstructional factors consist of family income and background. The study reveals that the process factors have profoundly higher effects on student achievement than the noninstructional factors. Specifically, 51% of the variation in student test scores was accounted for by the school and family process factors. Together, these factors nearly eliminated the effects of student ethnicity and the socioeconomic status (SES) of the families on student achievement (Ferguson, Clark, & Stewart, 2002).

Underscoring the importance of "community" in school, family, and community partnerships, Ferguson et al. (2002) conducted a series of studies that show the positive effects of out-of-school high-yield learning activities (e.g., leisure reading, writing, studying, being tutored) on urban students' academic achievement. In a study conducted in Bakersfield, California, Ferguson and colleagues found that high-achieving urban youth spent more time in out-of-school high-yield learning activities than low achievers. In the elementary grades, high achievers spent 7 hours and 56 minutes per week involved in out-of-school learning activities compared to 7 hours for low-achieving students. Although the 56-minute difference is not statistically significant at the elementary level, high school students show a statistically significant difference of 6 hours and 25 minutes per week. High-achieving high school students engaged in 15 hours 14 minutes per week of structured out-of-school learning activities, compared to only 8 hours and 49 minutes per week for low-achieving students (see Fig. 1). High-achieving students were also found to spend more time engaged in learning activities in the classroom than low-achieving students. The researchers conclude that the cumulative effect of the differences in the combined in- and out-of-school weekly learning

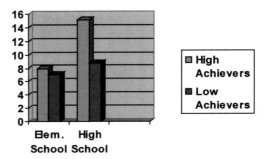

Fig. 1. *Hours per Week Involved in Out-of-School Learning Activities of High- and Low-Achieving Students*
Note. Adapted from *Closing the Achievement Gap in Suburban and Urban School Communities*, 2002, by R. F. Ferguson, R. Clark, and J. Stewart. Naperville, IL: North Central Regional Educational Lab.

time for low- and high-achieving students contributed to expanding gaps in their achievement (Ferguson et al., 2002).

Ferguson and colleagues (2002) find that, beyond participation in out-of-school learning activities, the quality of urban students' engagement in such activities influenced achievement outcomes. More specifically, the researchers examined the effects of students' involvement in two areas of out-of-school learning activities: (a) high-yield literacy activities (e.g., reading, writing, and studying) and (b) high-yield enrichment activities (e.g., hobbies and playing games). They also find that high achievers generally were involved at a higher quality level in high-yield activities than low achievers.

Other studies also highlight the importance of students' access to well-designed, out-of-school-time learning activities. In an evaluation of California's After School Learning and Safe Neighborhoods Partnerships Program, which serves over 963 schools and 97,000 students, Blank, Melaville, and Shah (2003) find "large improvements in achievement among the lowest-performing students in reading [4.2% of participants moved out of the lowest quartile on the SAT-9 compared to only 1.9% of all students state-wide] and in math [2.5% of participants moved out of the lowest quartile compared to only 1.9% state-wide]" (p. 23). There is a direct relationship between gains in math and levels of participation in the program. Students who participated in the program for 7.5 months or more improved their scores by 2.5 times compared to students who did not participate. The study also shows improvements in school attendance, particularly among highly truant students. There was also a marked reduction in school suspensions among middle school students, which is associated with improved social skills and behaviors and improved feelings of safety.

Thus, research shows the benefits of excellent classroom instruction and family and community engagement for students' school success. It underscores the importance of schools reaching out to the families and communities of African American urban youth to provide more equitable educational opportunities and generate more equitable educational outcomes. In the next section, we offer recommendations to help schools begin the process of building comprehensive partnerships with their students' families and communities.

RECOMMENDATIONS FOR IMPROVING SCHOOL, FAMILY, AND COMMUNITY PARTNERSHIPS

Recommendation #1: Create Opportunities for Home–School–Community Dialogue

Urban parents and teachers share a stake in and represent the strongest and most direct correlates to student achievement. It is, thus, imperative that teacher–parent communication move beyond quarterly conferences and field trip dates to authentic dialogue. Hoover-Dempsey et al. (2005) note that teachers and schools can strengthen parent engagement in students' education. According to the researchers, by clearly stating and demonstrating a belief that parents play a critical role in their children's learning, educators can influence the construction of the parental role toward active, rather than passive, involvement. By creating and maintaining an environment that actively values and respects parents' voices and presence, while empowering parents with specific strategies to increase student success, schools express their desire for family engagement (Hoover-Dempsey et al., 2005, p. 48).

Nevertheless, these efforts require coordination and ongoing dialogue between parents, teachers, community partners, and students. To facilitate this process, urban schools can create a committee of stakeholder representatives to evaluate, design, and organize home–school communication efforts (Sanders & Epstein, 2000). These schools might also create and maintain logs to track communication activities and to measure their effects on student test scores, grades, attendance, and behavior. When organizing these activities, urban schools should be flexible and willing to deviate from conventional practices to meet the needs of their urban families. Providing child care, translation into languages spoken by families, assistance with transportation, and extended and nontraditional times and settings for meetings are several strategies that schools can adopt to meet families' specific needs (Epstein & Associates, 2009; Nieto, 2000; Swap, 1993). For example, community recreation centers and local churches can be ideal locations for parent meetings. In addition, schools can partner with these and other community organizations to offer tutoring, mentoring, counseling, and other services as needed for families and students.

Improved home–school communication also requires ongoing professional development for teachers. Administrators, therefore, have a significant role to play in developing school-wide programs for family and community engagement (Sanders & Sheldon, 2009). They should take responsibility for organizing professional development opportunities to ensure that teachers use research-based strategies to support parents and students. Administrators should also take responsibility for overseeing the collection and analyses of data to measure the effectiveness of the family outreach strategies used in the school. Principal leadership, then, is needed to facilitate the types of family–teacher interaction that can make a positive difference in the education and lives of African American urban youth.

Recommendation #2: Implement Interactive Homework to Enhance Home-Based Involvement and Home–School Interaction and Communication Around Curricular Issues

Whereas some parents are comfortable helping their children with schoolwork, others require greater assistance. One strategy to encourage greater parent engagement in children's learning at home is the TIPS process (see http://www.partner-shipschools.org for more information). This research-based interactive homework approach was designed, developed, and tested by Epstein and Associates (2009). TIPS encourages students in elementary and secondary schools to conduct conversations and other interactions with family members in order to improve their parents' understanding of what they are learning in school and facilitate home discussions about schoolwork. TIPS assignments are designed to require no more than 15–20 min of families' active engagement. Further, TIPS prototypes can be revised and supplemented to match any curriculum. When well-designed and regularly assigned (e.g., two to four times per month), TIPS has been shown to have a positive influence on students' academic achievement.

For example, a study of TIPS Language Arts included 683 students in grades 6 and 8 in two urban middle schools, in which over 70% of the students qualified for free or reduced-price lunch (Epstein, Simon, & Salinas, 1997). The urban middle school students shared writing prompts, ideas, and drafts of stories or essays and conducted "family surveys" to discover their family members' experiences. Analyses statistically controlled for parent education, student grade level, attendance, fall report card grades, and fall writing sample scores to identify the effects of TIPS interactive homework assignments on students' writing skills in the winter and spring. The researchers also found that students who completed more TIPS assignments with their parents improved their writing scores from fall to winter and from winter to spring, regardless of their initial abilities.

In a similar study, Van Voorhis (2007) used a quasi-experimental design to compare the math achievement of students in classrooms in which teachers assigned interactive math homework (treatment) to the achievement of students in classrooms in which teachers did not incorporate this type of homework (control). Her study found significant differences in achievement between students and families in the treatment and control groups. Urban students—who were assigned interactive math homework—reported greater family involvement in math, as well as higher levels of achievement, compared to students in the control condition. In a separate study on TIPS science assignments, Van Voorhis (2003) found that families whose children received weekly interactive homework in science tended to be more involved in the homework, and students in these families tended to get higher grades in science, compared to students whose teachers did not assign the interactive science homework. Because TIPS assignments request parent feedback, they also help to increase parent–teacher communication around critical issues of curriculum and instruction.

When implementing TIPS in diverse urban classrooms, teachers should take steps to ensure that as many families as possible have the opportunity to fully participate. First, urban teachers should find out the best days to assign interactive homework. Because African American families often have different work and leisure schedules, they should be given two to three days to complete each TIPS assignment. Second, TIPS assignments should begin and end with home–school communications that are translated into the languages spoken by students' families. Third, urban teachers should ensure that they fully explain TIPS to both students and families to ensure that students understand their role as "doers" of the homework and parents understand their role as homework partners. Last, urban teachers should adopt a broad definition of "parents" and assist students to identify one or several family members, including older siblings, extended family members, mentors, and tutors, as their homework partners prior to assigning TIPS (Epstein, 2001).

Recommendation #3: Partner With Community Organizations Like the Public Library to Increase Students' Out-of-School Learning Time

It is increasingly clear that high-achieving African American students spend more time in school and out of school engaged in learning activities guided by competent caring adults. Parents often spend a great deal of time, effort, and money trying to find constructive after-school and summer learning activities for their children. Urban schools can support this process by partnering with community institutions to offer such programs at the school or a community site, or by providing information to parents about local community institutions and activities that can support students' achievement and success. One such community institution is the library (Martinez, 2007, 2008).

Libraries are natural places to find free selections of readings, in print or online, that are of interest to all students. Moreover, urban African American students who are given regular opportunities to visit libraries read more often, with more ease, and are more interested in returning to libraries than students who are not provided with such opportunities (Ramos & Krashen, 1998). Having a library card can also keep students interested in reading, by giving them the opportunity to check out their own books (Robinson, 2006). Librarians are always available to assist students in finding books of interest. They not only want to provide support for reading motivation and academic success but also aspire to create lifelong readers (Crowley, 2008). According to Dengel (1994), "If, as the saying goes, it takes a whole village to raise a child, then the library should be the hub of that village" (p. 39). Urban schools can partner with public libraries to ensure that urban African American families have library cards; know about summer reading programs, story times, and other library activities; and know their children's reading levels as well as strategies with which to interact around written text.

In addition, teachers in urban schools can build their classroom libraries and enhance materials offered in their school media centers by borrowing books from their local libraries. Libraries provide extensions for teachers to check out books for longer periods of time than are afforded to regular patrons. Urban teachers can also check out more books than regular patrons by simply stating that they are teachers. If the community library does not have sufficient materials that reflect urban students' and families' interests and experiences, teachers should advocate for them by speaking to the librarians. Through this engagement, educators in urban schools can help to ensure that their students have equal opportunities to access print, which is part of the American Library Association's mission (American Library Association, 2009).

Both education research and practice show that urban educators best serve their African American students when they work with families and stakeholders in their communities (Marsh & Turner-Vorbeck, 2010). Thus, it is important that urban teachers move beyond the school walls to explore what their African American students' communities have to offer. Community libraries are important and relevant places to begin this exploration.

CONCLUSION

Although teacher competency remains the strongest correlate to student achievement, parent and community involvement also significantly influences student success and can directly impact teachers' perceptions and expectations of urban

African American students. In a synthesis of nearly a decade of research, the Coalition for Community Schools reports that teachers tend to have higher expectations for students whose parents are significantly involved in school. In addition, these students go on to have higher test scores and grades than students whose parents are not highly involved (Blank et al., 2003).

Such research underscores the need for school administrators, faculty, and staff to facilitate school, family, and community partnerships that embrace a broad definition of family involvement. In this chapter, we recommend strategies that promote more effective home–school communication, greater home–school interaction around curricular issues, and more extensive outreach to community institutions. Through such efforts, within a comprehensive framework of school, family, and community partnerships (see Epstein & Associates, 2009), urban educators can ensure that their urban African American youth have the types of learning opportunities and supports experienced by Brian, Jessica, Dorothy, and Jim. In so doing, these urban educators contribute to more socially just urban schools.

NOTE

1. Students' names have been changed to ensure anonymity and confidentiality. Student vignettes were crafted from interview data and student essays. Featured students are recipients of Ron Brown scholarships. The Ron Brown Scholars Program was established in 1996 to provide academic scholarships, service opportunities, and leadership experiences for young African Americans who show outstanding promise (see www.ronbrown.org). To read more about these students and other Ron Brown Scholars, see *I Have Risen: Essays by African-American Youth* (Fix, 2006).

REFERENCES

American Library Association. (2009). "Sample programming ideas: Showcase the vastness of your library's resources." Retrieved from http://www.ala.org/ala/issuesadvocacy/advleg/publicaware-ness/campaign@yourlibrary/prtools/sampleprogramming.cfm

Blank, M., Melaville, A., & Shah, B. (2003). *Making the difference: Research and practice in community schools.* Washington, DC: Coalition for Community Schools, Institute for Educational Leadership.

Brock, R. (2010). Debunking the myths about the urban family: A constructed conversation. In M. Marsh & T. Turner-Vorbeck (Eds.), *(Mis)understanding families: Learning from real families in our schools* (pp.126–144). New York, NY: Teachers College Press.

Bronfenbrenner, U. (1985). The three worlds of childhood. *Principal, 64*(5), 6–11.

Comer, J. (2004). *Leave no child behind: Preparing today's youth for tomorrow's world.* New Haven, CT: Yale University Press.

Comer, J. (2005). The rewards of parent participation. *Educational Leadership, 62*(6), 38–42.

Cotton, K., & Wikelund, K. (2001). *Parent involvement in education.* Retrieved from http://education-northwest.org/webfm_send/567

Crowley, B. (2008). Lifecycle librarianship. *Library Journal, 133*(6), 46.

Davies, D. (1993). Benefits and barriers to parent involvement from Portugal to Boston to Liverpool. In N. F. Chavkin (Ed.), *Families and schools in a pluralistic society* (pp. 205–216). Albany: State University of New York.

Davis-Kean, P., & Eccles, J. (2005). Influences and challenges to better parent-school collaborations. In E. Patrikakou, R. Weissberg, S. Redding, & H. Walberg (Eds.), *School-family partnerships for children's success* (pp. 57–76). New York, NY: Teachers College Press.

DeCastro-Ambrosetti, D., & Cho, G. (2005). Do parents value education? Teachers' perceptions of minority parents. *Multicultural Education, 13*(2), 44–46.

Dengel, D. J. (1994). Raising the quality quotient: Library outreach to child care providers. *School Library Journal, 40*(7), 36–39.

Eccles, J. S., & Harold, R. D. (1996). Family involvement in children's and adolescents' schooling. In A. Bloom & J. F. Dunn (Eds.), *Family-school links: How do they affect educational outcomes?* (pp. 3–34). Mahwah, NJ: Lawrence Erlbaum.

Epstein, J. (1995). School/family/community partnerships: Caring for the children we share. *Phi Delta Kappan, 76*(9), 701–712.

Epstein, J. (2001). *School, family and community partnerships.* Boulder, CO: Westview Press.

Epstein, J. L., & Associates (2009). *School, family and community partnerships: Your handbook for action* (3rd edition). Thousand Oaks, CA: Corwin Press.

Epstein, J. L., Simon, B. S., & Salinas, K. C. (1997). Effects of teachers involve parents in schoolwork (TIPS) language arts interactive homework in the middle grades. *Research Bulletin, 18*, 1–4.

Fager, J., & Brewster, C. (1999, March). *By request: Parent partners: Using parents to enhance education.* Portland, OR: Northwest Regional Educational Laboratory.

Ferguson, R. F., Clark, R., & Stewart, J. (2002). *Closing the achievement gap in suburban and urban school communities* (Policy issue). Naperville, IL: North Central Regional Educational Lab.

Fine, M. (1993). (Ap)parent involvement: Reflections on parents, power, and urban public schools, *Teachers College Record, 94*(4), 682–729.

Fix, S. (2006). *I have risen: Essays by African-American youth.* Charlottesville, VA: CAP Charitable Foundation.

Halsey, P. (2005). Parent involvement in junior high schools: A failure to communicate. *American Secondary Education, 34*(1), 57–69.

Henderson, A., & Mapp, K. (2002). *A new wave of evidence: The impact of school, family, and community connections on student achievement.* Austin, TX: Southwest Educational Development Laboratory.

Henderson, A., Mapp, K., Johnson, V., & Davies, D. (2007). *Beyond the bake sale: The essential guide to family-school partnerships.* New York: The New Press.

Hill, N., & Chao, R. (2009). *Families, schools, and the adolescent: Connecting research, policy, and practice.* New York, NY: Teachers College Press.

Holzmiller, R. (1982, November). *Utilizing regression methodology to investigate the effects of volunteer aides on student achievement* (ED228333). Paper presented at the Annual Meeting of the California Educational Research Association, Sacramento, CA.

Hoover-Dempsey, K., Walker, T., & Sandler, H. (2005). Parents' motivations for involvement in their children's education. In E. N. Patrikakou, R. P Weissber, S. Redding, & H. J. Walber (Eds.), *School-family partnerships for children's success* (pp. 40–55). New York, NY: Teachers College Press.

Horvat, E., Weininger, E., & Lareau, A. (2003). From social ties to social capital: Class differences in the relations between schools and parent networks. *American Educational Research Journal, 40*(2), 319–351.

Jaime, A., & Russell, C. (2010). Reaching Native American families to increase school involvement. In M. Marsh & T. Turner-Vorbeck (Eds.), *(Mis)understanding families: learning from real families in our schools* (pp. 145–161). New York, NY: Teachers College Press.

Jeynes, W. (2003). A meta-analysis: The effects of parental involvement on minority children's academic achievement. *Education and Urban Society, 35*(2), 202–218.

Jeynes, W. (2007). The relationship between parental involvement and urban secondary school student academic achievement. *Urban Education, 42*(1), 82–110

Johnson, V. R. (1994). *Parent centers in urban schools: Four case studies.* Baltimore, MD: Center on Families, Communities, Schools & Children's Learning.

Koball, H., Douglas-Hall, A., & Chau, M. (2005). *Children in Urban Areas are Increasingly Low Income.* New York, NY: National Center for Children in Poverty.

Lareau, A. (1987). Social class differences in family-school relationships: The importance of cultural capital. *Sociology of Education, 60*(2), 73–85.

Lawrence-Lightfoot, S. (1978). *Worlds apart: Relationships between families and schools.* New York, NY: Basic Books.

Lawrence-Lightfoot, S. (2003). *The essential conversation: What parents and teachers can learn from each other.* New York, NY: Random House.

Marsh, M., & Turner-Vorbeck, T., Eds. (2010). *(Mis)understanding families: learning from real families in our schools.* New York, NY: Teachers College Press.

Martinez, G. (2007). Libraries, families, and schools: Partnership to achieve school reading readiness- a multiple case study of Maryland public librarians (UMI No. 3172648). *Dissertation Abstracts International, 66*(04), 1302A.

Martinez, G. (2008). Public libraries–community organizations making outreach efforts to help young children succeed in school. *The School Community Journal, 18*(1), 93–104.

McDermott, D. (2008). *Developing caring relationships among parents, children, school, and communities.* Los Angeles, CA: Sage.

Moll, L. C., Amanti, C., Neff, D., & Gonzalez, N. (1992). Funds of Knowledge for Teaching: Using a qualitative approach to connect home and classrooms. *Theory Into Practice, 31,* 131–141.

National Parent Teacher Association. (2000). Building successful partnerships: A guide for developing parent and family involvement programs. Bloomington, IN: National Educational service.

Nieto, S. (2000). *Affirming Diversity* (3rd ed.). New York, NY: Longman.

Patrikakou, E., Weissberg, R., Redding, S., & Walberg, H. (Eds.; 2005). *School-family partnerships for children's success.* New York, NY: Teachers College Press.

Ramos, F., & Krashen, S. (1998). The impact of one trip to the public library: Making books available may be the best incentive for reading. *Reading Teacher, 51*(7), 614–615.

Reynolds, A., & Clements, M. (2005). Parental involvement and children's school success. In E. Patrikakou, R. Weissberg, R. S. Redding, & H. Walberg (Eds.), *School-family* (pp. 109–130). New York, NY: Teachers College Press.

Robinson, L. (2006). *Adapting literacy activities for young children.* Retreieved from http://www.wiu.edu/thecenter/articles/adaptlit.html.

Sanders, M. (1998). The effects of school, family, and community support on the academic achievement of African American adolescents. *Urban Education, 33*(3), 385–409.

Sanders, M. G. (2005). *Building school-community partnerships: Collaboration for student success.* Thousand Oaks, CA: Corwin Press.

Sanders, M., & Campbell, T. (2007). Securing the ties that bind: Community involvement and the educational success of African-American children and adolescents. In J. F. L. Jackson (Ed.),

Strengthening the educational pipeline for African Americans: Informing policy and practice (pp. 141–164). Albany: State University of New York Press.

Sanders, M. G., & Epstein, J. L. (2000). The National Network of Partnership Schools: How research influences educational practice. *Journal of Education for Students Placed At Risk, 5*(1/2), 61–76.

Sanders, M., & Herting, J. (2000). Gender and the effects of school, family and church support on the academic achievement of African-American urban adolescents. In M. G. Sanders (Ed.), *Schooling students placed at risk: Research, policy, and practice in the education of poor and minority adolescents* (pp. 141–161). Mahwah, NJ: Lawrence Erlbaum.

Sanders, M.G., & Lewis, K. (2004). Partnerships at an urban high school: Meeting the parent involvement requirements of No Child Left Behind. *E-Journal of Teaching and Learning in Diverse Settings, 2*(1), 1–21.

Sanders, M., & Sheldon, S. (2009). *Principals Matter: A guide to comprehensive programs of school, family, and community partnerships.* Thousand Oaks, CA: Corwin Press.

Scott-Jones, D. (1995). Parent–child interactions and school achievement. In B. Ryan, G. Adams, T. Gullotta, R. Weissberg, & R. Hampton (Eds.), *The family school connection* (pp. 75–107). Thousand Oaks, CA: Sage.

Small, M. L. (2006). Neighborhood institutions as resource brokers: Childcare centers, interorganizational ties, and resource access among the poor. *Social Problems, 53*(2), 274–292.

Swap, S. (1993). *Developing home-school partnerships: From concepts to practice.* New York, NY: Teachers College Press.

U.S. Department of Labor (2005). *A Profile of the Working Poor, 2003*: Washington, DC: Author.

Van Voorhis, F. L. (2003). Interactive homework in middle school: Effects on family involvement and science achievement. *Journal of Educational Research, 96*(6), 323–338.

Van Voorhis, F. L. (2007, April). *Can math be more meaningful: Longitudinal effects of family involvement on student homework.* Paper presented at the annual meeting of the American Educational Research Association (AERA), Chicago, Illinois.

Weiss, H., Kreider, H., Lopez, M., & Chatman, C. (2005). *Preparing educators to involve families.* Thousand Oaks, CA: Sage.

Westat & Policy Studies Associates. (2001). *The longitudinal evaluation of school change and performance in Title I schools.* Washington, DC: US Department of Education.

Wu, F., & Qi, S. (2006). Longitudinal effects of parenting on children's academic achievement in African American families. *Journal of Negro Education, 75*(3), 415–430.

PART FIVE

PERSPECTIVES AND INSIGHTS IN POSTSECONDARY CONTEXTS

CHAPTER FOURTEEN

Inside Information
on High-Achieving
African American Male
College Students

FRED A. BONNER II AND JOHN W. MURRY JR.

Often characterized as a national crisis, the plight of African American males in PK–12 urban education contexts is at best heartrending and at worst tragic. According to data included in the Schott Foundation for Public Education's 2008 edition of *Given Half a Chance: The Schott 50 State Report on Public Education and Black Males* (Schott Foundation for Public Education, 2008), a disproportionate number of African American males did not obtain their high school diplomas in 2005/2006, and African American males are two times likely to not graduate with their class in New York, Florida, and Georgia public school settings.

The Schott Report further states that trends of this sort are evidence of a demographic group that is frequently marginalized and deprived a quality education. The schooling experiences for African American males in the PK–12 urban contexts reflect the perils this cohort endures in postsecondary settings. Equally grim are data, reported in publications like the *Minorities in Higher Education Twenty-Second Annual Status Report* (2006), revealing that African American students are not faring well in postsecondary either. National data from the elementary, secondary, and postsecondary levels provide reason for educators, researchers, and policy makers invested in the success of African American male populations to take pause. It is important to recognize that the "faces behind the numbers" do not represent the entire population of African American males throughout the educational pipeline (i.e., at elementary, secondary, and postsecondary levels). For many, the problems are where the story ends, when it comes to framing the educational experiences for African American males; however, the discourse falls short of providing a holistic view of the diversity of educational achievement represented within the group.

A counterpoint to the lack of achievement is a surplus of talent found to exist among this group, yet a focus on high-achieving or academically gifted African American males is an academic pursuit that has prompted very little attention. An even greater void is found to exist in studying these high achievers in higher education settings (Bonner, 2001; Fries-Britt, 1998; Harper & Quaye, 2009; Hébert, 2006). Thus, this chapter initiates a discourse highlighting the factors that most positively influence the academic outcomes for high-achieving African American male college students, particularly those who matriculated from urban PK–12 public school settings. Subjects including critical race theory (CRT), underidentification and underachievement, identity development, social and cultural capital, and generational (millennial) influences and impact are used to frame the issues, as well as link educational pipeline experiences. Each subject stresses implications for higher education in terms of both academic/career and student affairs structures.

CRITICAL RACE THEORY

Throughout American society, racism is a pervasive force. Its reach permeates all aspects of American life, including the arena of public education. Solorzano, Ceja, and Yosso (2000), in citing Lorde (1992), define racism as the "belief in the inherent superiority of one race over all others and thereby the right to dominance" (p. 61). It is believed that racism affects the achievement of ethnic minorities, particularly African American males. Most education experts agree that there is no single inclusive definition of CRT; however, as a theory or framework, it provides education researchers with a better means for understanding and examining how "racial subordination is among the critical factors responsible for the continued production of racialized disparities and opportunity gaps" for high-achieving African American males in urban school contexts (Harper, Patton, & Wooden, 2009, p. 392). CRT, an outgrowth of critical legal studies, was developed as a theory to better understand and study societal issues involving race. It is based on seven basic tenets:

1. Racism is ingrained or naturalized aspect of American society and is firmly embedded in our educational system.

2. The ideals of a color-blind society, in which educational achievement is based on meritocracy, objectivity, neutrality, and equal opportunity, are invalid.

3. The experiential knowledge of ethnic-minority students provides a far better way than the former premises of understanding barriers that exist in achieving real educational opportunity.

4. Interest convergence advances educational success for African American students only to the extent that the self-interests of the White majority are furthered through the educational system.

5. History is revised to paint a more accurate description of the real experiences of Black students in an urban setting.

6. Racism is a mechanism whereby White Americans are able to control the allocation of resources and power in public education for their own benefit.

7. Claims made by many White educators that meritocracy decides educational achievement and opportunity must be continually challenged to fight against White supremacy (Dixson & Rousseau, 2005; Harper et al., 2009; Ladson-Billings & Tate, 1995; Lynn, 2004; Mutua, 2006; Patton, McEwen, Rendon, & Howard-Hamilton, 2007; Stovall, 2006; Teranishi & Briscoe, 2008).

Several of the tenets of CRT are well demonstrated. Many White teachers, school counselors, and administrators in urban public schools, as well as in other school settings throughout the United States, believe that their educational institutions are meritocratic systems and provide equal opportunity to all students. These same education professionals are convinced that their educational institutions are color-blind, when it comes to race (Bergerson, 2003). Bergerson (2003) suggests that "because merit is so highly valued, it is difficult to convince whites that people of color are systematically excluded from opportunities to succeed, by individual racism as well as racist structures and institutions" (p. 53). Aligned with this notion, Dixson and Rousseau (2005) assert that there are "both individual-level 'microaggressions' in the form of lowered teacher expectations as well as more macro-level forms of institutional racism in which school-wide programs lack the courses and rigor necessary for students to succeed in higher education" (p. 12). On another note, Hussar and Bailey (2009) indicate that, in fall 2006, 77.3% of elementary and secondary school students in urbanized areas were persons of color. Thus, there is a racial imbalance between the students and teachers. Many of the urbanized schools have a majority of teachers who are not persons of color. These teacher and student trends are thought to perpetuate barriers to the benefits of education that students of color, including African American males, face in achieving true social justice.

Another important aspect of CRT is the reliance upon experiential knowledge gained by high-achieving African American males in urban school districts. Public school officials should accept the notion that "racism, like capitalism, is an accepted structural phenomenon centered on maintaining the status quo" in our public schools (Stovall, 2006, p. 250). And much could be learned by school officials about "teachers' interactions with students of color in urban settings and a more complex analysis [provided] of what happens" in the K–12 educational environment in an effort to challenge the status quo (Chapman, 2007, p. 156). DeCuir and Dixson (2004) explain that the experiential knowledge of African American students is transmitted in the form of telling a story that "aims to cast doubt on the validity of accepted premises or myths, especially ones held by the majority" (p. 27). To excel in urban academic settings, African American males usually must first overcome the perception that they are intellectually inferior to White students and are not suited for the rigors of higher education.

At the postsecondary level, Patton et al. (2007) suggest that student affairs administrators have used student development theory "to make sense of attitudes, behaviors, norms, and outcomes among college students since the late 1970s" (p. 39); however, the use of CRT has not gained a real foothold in research on college students. They suggest that the impact of racism on African American male students has not been fully explored and offer five specific recommendations for using CRT to better inform student affairs practice in higher education. Patton et al. assert that student affairs leaders should "challenge, question, and critique traditional theoretical perspectives" (p. 48) of student development theory and practice, while recognizing that racism is deeply rooted in colleges and universities and maintaining that the status quo is unacceptable. They also note that student affairs practitioners in graduate programs should "reflect on how often racial perspectives are incorporated into reading materials, class discussions, and assignments. Such individuals should be mindful of the roles that race, power, and privilege play in classroom dynamics, particularly in predominately White settings" (p. 49). Further, the authors suggest that student affairs officials should adopt a CRT perspective in their daily practice to better understand realities of racial experience for Black and other ethnic minority students. Further, they also recommend that student affairs professionals become "knowledgeable about and aware of their own racial identities, honestly evaluate themselves in terms of their understanding of race and racism, and recognize how their knowledge, awareness, and racial identity influences their decisions, policies, and interactions with students from diverse backgrounds" (p. 49).

It is unfortunate that most White educators do not believe they engage in racism. In fact, many posit that academic achievement in public education is based on merit. But, Bergerson (2003) concludes, "Whites do not want to consider race and racism as everyday realities, because doing so requires them to face their own racist behaviors as well as the privileges that come from being white" (p. 53).

UNDERIDENTIFICATION AND UNDERACHIEVEMENT

Underidentification and underachievement are both contributors to the lack of African American male inclusion in gifted and talented programming in the PK–12 environment (Bonner, Jennings, Marbley, & Brown, 2008). Several education scholars (Fashola, 2005; Ford, 2003; Ford, Moore, & Milner, 2005; Grantham, 2004; Hopkins, 1997; Hrabowski, Maton, & Greif, 1998; Kunjufu, 2005, Polite & Davis, 1999; Whiting, 2006) have illustrated this point. According to the U.S. Office for Civil Rights (2002), African American males, nationally, have been underrepresented by as much as 50% in gifted and talented programming. On another note, Schott Foundation of Public Education (2008) reports African American males comprise 9% of the public school enrollments but less than 4% of the students identified for gifted and talented programming.

What often happens is that these data become static and cyclical, ultimately leading to an ongoing struggle for African American male populations. Across school settings and particularly in urban school contexts, African American males are too often viewed as troublemakers and lacking clearly defined future goals (Milner, 2007, p. 240). The limbo status prescribed for this demographic group offers limited opportunities for educational growth and the realization of educational potential.

As a plausible example to illustrate the problems that are created for African American males in urban school contexts, data were extrapolated from *Public Education and Black Male Students: A State Report Card* (Holzman, 2004), a report produced by the Schott Foundation for Public Education. This report highlights graduation rates among school districts with African American male enrollments of 10,000 or more. Using Texas as an example, graduation rates for 2001/2002 are listed as 35%, 37%, and 40% for the cities of Houston, Dallas, and Ft. Worth, respectively. In addition, these numbers represent a 26%, 9%, and 15% gap between African American and White male populations in these urban centers (Holzman, 2004). High-achieving African American students are not pardoned from the conditions that plague their counterparts who are less academically successful. Milner (2007) offers information on ways to frame spaces that allow opportunity to flourish across achievement levels. His suggestions, in the form of five central principles, provide important information for those seeking to support high-achieving students, particularly African American male students. The following suggestions can serve as a clarion call to those who educate these students:

1. Envision life beyond the present.
2. Know yourself in relation to others.
3. Speak possibility and not destruction.
4. Care and demonstrate care.
5. Change your thinking to change your action.

Higher education institutions are on the receiving end of years of underidentification and underachievement processes that have exacted a profound impact on high-achieving African American male cohorts. In addition, the profound lack of research and literature conducted on high-achieving African American males in postsecondary education further compounds the lack of specific interventions that are set in place (Bonner, 2001; Fries-Britt, 1998; Harper & Quaye, 2009; Hébert, 2006). For example, Hébert (2006) states: "Giftedness does not end with a student's high school graduation. The challenge of designing the best educational experiences for gifted students in universities is one that the gifted education community has not adequately addressed" (p. 27). In both academic and student affairs divisions, it is worth noting that this student population, despite its academic prowess, has had to interface with schooling environments that supported deficit views of their potential. According to Harper and Quaye (2009), it is the model of deficit thinking that has led to disengagement and disenchantment among African American males who in the "eyes of the academy" have struggled to overcome negative views and perceptions related to their academic potential. Thus, finding ways to recognize the academic abilities of these high-achieving males in public forums can provide counternarratives that can dispel perceptions that they do not possess scholastic potential. Programmatic initiatives that combine academic and student affairs efforts to showcase these students' talents provide potentially novel approaches—examples of such initiatives are highlighted in the recommendations section of this chapter.

IDENTITY DEVELOPMENT

The ways in which identity is developed has been investigated over the years by a considerable number of researchers (Cross, 1971, 1978, 1991; Helms, 1990; Phinney, 1996). Over the last three decades or so, several scholars have specifically focused on the identity development processes that populations of color undergo (Cross, 1971, 1978, 1991; Helms, 1990). A concentrated focus on African American males and identity development is highlighted in a chapter included in

Michael Cuyjet's book, *African American Men in College*. One particular section in this chapter, by Bonner and Bailey (2006), connects identity and self-esteem development processes and shows how these two constructs are far from being mutually exclusive. Their choice of topics, such as academic dis-identification, lack of academic resilience, stereotype threat, and cool pose, from their estimation, contribute either directly or tangentially to notions of how African American males frame their identities. In consequence, these topics render many implications for PK–12 settings, as well as higher education institutions.

Perhaps one of the more salient forms of identity development among African American males, particularly those who occupy urban education settings, is the notion of racial identity development. According to Helms (1990), racial identity development is a perceived or shared sense of collective identity based on the views among individuals that they share a common racial heritage with a specified group. The theoretical models of two researchers, in particular, have occupied a place of prominence in the discussions of racial identity development: Molefi Asante's (1988) Afrocentric cultural identity development model and William Cross Jr.'s (1971) Negro-to-Black conversion model. According to Bonner, Lewis, Bowman-Perrott, Hill-Jackson, and James (2010), although both of these typologies offer tools for critical insight, it is Cross's (1971, 1991, 1995) model, with its subsequent revisions, that provides a more comprehensive framework with which to underscore identity development experiences among high-achieving African American males.

Cross's model identifies four stages—pre-encounter, encounter, immersion, and internalization—each of which describes "self-concept" issues involving race and concomitantly addresses attitudes that the individual holds regarding Black and White social groups. According to Bonner et al. (2010), each theme is emblematic of the evolving sense of self as a racial being, as well as a deepening understanding of how the individual develops a healthy racial identity development. Harper and Quaye (2007) contend that, for urban African American male students,

> urban schools are uniquely positioned to contribute to the development of racial identity. In many instances, they are the primary force in the socialization of Black adolescents. If this process culminates in the internalization of a positive racial self-concept, students are likely to internalize behaviors and attitudes that contribute to academic achievement. When this process is co-opted by ignorance and inflexibility, the end result is the adoption of a view of Black racial identity that impedes the process of teaching and learning. (p. 236)

Harper and Quaye's statement also holds true for the high-achieving African American. What is important to recognize about the PK–12 urban educational context is that these males are often struggling with multiple competing forms of identity (e.g. cultural, gender, and so forth). Whiting (2006) affirms that it is important to consider the relationships that exist among identity, race, and gender roles. Thus, although this section is grounded in a discussion of racial identity development, much is to be said about the struggles of being African American, high-achieving, and male. For some, embracing the label "high-achieving" means suppressing one's "African American identity." To this end, being academically successful is seen as antithetical to being Black.

PK–12 urban school experiences are critical in setting the stage for successful academic and social transitioning as well as matriculation in higher education. It is important for academe to recognize the experiences that urban African American males bring to the higher education setting and find valuable ways to promote a positive racial self-concept. According to Hébert (2002), for many high-achieving African American male college students, it is the synergy created from positive influences that prepare these young men to not only achieve in higher education but also "in a society that does not always respect and value them" (p. 60). By electing to enroll high-achieving African American males, colleges and universities are at best derelict and at worst hypocritical if they sidestep their educational role of ensuring that these students are living up to their academic potential.

SOCIAL AND CULTURAL CAPITAL

The education literature suggests that African American students from lower socioeconomic environments graduate from high school and matriculate into higher education at a much lower rate than do African American counterparts from middle-class and higher socioeconomic strata (Perna & Titus, 2005). This is also the plight of many high-achieving African American males in urban schools. In order to fully appreciate this phenomenon and understand the daunting academic challenges faced by high-achieving African American males that successfully navigate public education in an urban setting, the influences of cultural and social capital should be considered.

Cultural capital, a term conceived by French sociologist Pierre Bourdieu, suggests that in large part students' success in public education is due to the cultural skills, vocabulary, background, and manners he acquires from his parents and other adult acquaintances (Livingstone & Sawchuk, 2000; Perna & Titus, 2005). According to Bourdieu and Passeron (1977), students obtain what they term an "educational inheritance" from their parents. For students with well-educated parents, their inheritance is often viewed more favorably by teachers, school counselors, and administrators than is the inheritance of students from less-educated homes (Dika & Singh, 2002; Freeman, 1997). Those students with greater social capital receive increased attention and resources that improve their chances of success in the public school educational system. In other words, African American students who possess more social capital typically have parents with a larger family income than many African American students from poor and working-class homes. This socioeconomic conundrum can be amplified by attending urban public schools (Livingstone & Sawchuk, 2000).

Perna and Titus (2005) suggest that social capital is developed largely based on forming individual relationships and social networks and maintaining these social structures. In an extensive review of literature, Dika and Singh (2002) assert that social capital is based principally on two relational factors: The first factor involves the interaction between a student and her parents, and the second factor relates to relational interactions a student's parents have with other adults, particularly those adults associated with the public school that their child attends. This raises the following question: "Why is social capital important in the context of high-achieving African American students in urban settings?" The answer is that research suggests that students who possess more social capital achieve higher educational outcomes in terms of grades, test scores, high school graduation, and ultimately enrollment in higher education (Coleman, 1988; Dika & Singh, 2002; Freeman, 1997). Although meager research exists examining the connection between cultural capital and high-achieving African American males in urban public schools, there is some reason to believe that African American male students who possess higher cultural capital may be better able to take advantage of the educational opportunities offered by public schools. This advantage is due to these students having acquired or inherited the norms of the predominate social class through exposure to the arts gained by going to museums, attending the theater, reading literature at home, and participating in travel (Bennett & Savage, 2004; Livingstone & Sawchuk, 2000). As a result, inherited cultural capital allows African American male students to better interact with teachers and school counselors and to achieve greater academic success, based on being able to project middle-class values and culture. Further, Bennett and Savage (2004) conclude that possessing cultural capital may be the key to determining individuals' social position and status in American society.

In addition, access to social capital better positions students for receiving enhanced institutional resources from teachers and school counselors (Stanton-Salazar, 1997). There is a limited amount of research that indicates that African American male students acquire social capital principally through relationships and interactions with their parents, peer group members with similar academic orientations, and their parents' relationships and interactions with school officials and other like-minded parents (Dika & Singh, 2002; Ecclestone, 2004; Stanton-Salazar, 1997). More resources are needed to assist urban public schools develop effective programs focused on helping parents facilitate discussions with their children concerning the importance of education, career aspirations, and expectations; peer group selection; and extracurricular activities. Parents who are actively engaged with teachers, school counselors, and other school officials often see higher academic achievement from their children (Perna & Titus, 2005; Reay, 2004). Cultural development and parental involvement are two major keys to academic achievement in both public school and higher education settings.

At a time when most colleges and universities seek greater racial and ethnic diversity in their student bodies, scarce research is available on the impact of cultural and social capital on African American males in higher education. According to the literature that does exist, it is probable that colleges and universities receive larger numbers of admission applications from high-achieving African American male students from urban schools who bring cultural and social capital into their public school experience (Freeman, 1997). This is particularly true at exclusive four-year institutions (Anderson, 2005; Goyette & Mullen, 2006).

The question for student affairs officials is how to help students develop and acquire these forms of capital, According to Perna and Titus (2005), college advisors and other student affairs professionals should find ways to encourage parents to stay involved in their student's higher education experience, including helping them to build networks to acquire needed educational and social resources. What works to increase the college attendance rate for one ethnic minority group may not work for another. Therefore, college officials need to understand that a strategy to promote cultural capital and academic success in one ethnic minority group may not work for all ethnic minority groups. Differences exist between ethnic minority groups, which should be taken into account, when developing college preparation programs (Perna & Titus, 2005).

GENERATIONAL (MILLENNIAL) INFLUENCES AND IMPACT

Conversations centering on student culture should focus on generational cohort influences. Students who are currently enrolled in our nation's schools are often referred to by generational researchers, William Strauss and Neil Howe, as "millennials." In their book Millennials Rising, these authors identify this group as individuals who were born roughly between the years 1982 and 2000. Although myriad distinctions set this group apart from the generations that have preceded them, some of the more salient findings have been the sheer size as well as the amount of diversity that is represented within this population. This population is recognized as the largest and most diverse generation in U.S. history. In the article "The Progressive Politics of the Millennial Generation," Leyden, Teixeira, and Greenberg (2007) state:

> The size of the Millennial Generation is so great partly because many Millennials are children of the Boomers (the "echo boom"). The size of the generation is also boosted by the children of the unprecedented numbers of immigrants in the last several decades. The Millennials are the most diverse generation by far, with almost 40 percent belonging to minority groups, Hispanics in particular. (para. 12)

The framework that has been utilized to highlight some common attributes found to exist across and within this population is referenced in Strauss and Howe as centering on seven descriptive terms: "special," "sheltered," "confident," "team-oriented," "conventional," "pressured," and "achievers." Each one of these descriptors connects to create a unique generational cohort experience (Bonner et al., 2010). However, despite the utility of this framework, its heuristic abilities, when applied to populations of color, are somewhat incomplete. Limitations are inherent in its application of frameworks, models, and theories, which have been developed in monocultural contexts and subsequently applied in multicultural settings. Thus, these descriptive terms are primarily reflective of the experiences of majority (i.e., White) Millennials. They are potentially incongruent with the culture, mores, and traditions found to exist among diverse groups.

For African American males in urban school environments, these terms may constitute an even greater challenge to be applicable to their experiences. For example, the term "special," as explained by Howe and Strauss (2000), is emblematic of the treatment that has been meted out by parents to their children who are Millennials. In specific, this generation has always been told that they are special, and all of the accoutrements associated with their special status have been made available to them (e.g., supportive parents—sometimes overly supportive, hence the moniker "helicopter parent"—material wealth, trophies, and accolades). These students, in turn, grow to expect this treatment not only within their community and family units but also in organizational and institutional settings external to these enclaves.

According to Debard (2004), "It follows not only that these students are to be considered special by those who would provide for their student service needs because of the high expectations placed on them but also that they would perceive themselves as special and highly expectant" (p. 35). Yet, the application of the moniker "special" to the experiences of the urban African American male may be at best loosely coupled and at worst nonapplicable to their engagements with family, friends, the school setting, and society. In actuality, these males may experience social contexts as providing them with verbal and nonverbal messages that they are anything but special. Boyd (2007) asserts:

> A *black* man is more than six times as likely as a white man to be slain. The trend is most stark among *black* men fourteen to twenty-four years old: They were implicated in a quarter of the nation's homicides and accounted for 15 percent of the homicide victims in 2002, although they were just 1.2 percent of the population, according to the Bureau of Justice Statistics; *Black* men are nine times as likely as white men to die from AIDS, and life expectancy *for black* men is 62.9 years—more than six years shorter than that of white men. More than half of the nation's 5.6 million *black* boys live in fatherless households, 40 percent of which are impoverished; The suicide rate among young *black* men has doubled since 1980; One in four *black* men has not worked for at least a year, twice the proportion of male non-Hispanic whites or Latinos. And trends suggest a third of *black* males born today will spend time in prison; More *black* men earn their high school equivalency diplomas in prison each year than graduate from college. (p. 2; emphasis added by author)

Thus, "special" may not be a term that adequately describes what many of these males have experienced. And, for the high-achieving African American male, additional complexities are associated with their status. They range from the internecine battle against peers who view their academic acumen as being uncool to school environments that view their high-achieving trait as counterintuitive to their existence. Therefore, "special" is not often the label they choose to apply to themselves.

In positioning themselves to respond to the needs of the Millennial generation, higher education institutions, too, are often misinformed about the nuances of the moniker "special" in its application to populations of color and subsequently create misaligned programs and policy structures based on this misinformation. High-achieving urban African American males—who have managed to successfully negotiate the K–12 terrain—are often in need of postsecondary settings that are not aimed at the reproduction of the hegemonic and oppressive structures that framed their earlier school existence. To this end, Cuyjet (2006) posits: "It is critical to understand how African American men perceive the institution—and, perhaps more important, how they perceive that institutions sees them" (p. 240). It also important for higher education institutions to unpack the relevant identities that comprise these males, such as gender, intellectual status, and race.

RECOMMENDATIONS AND CONCLUSION

By providing inside information on such a complex and multifaceted population, this chapter has attempted to shed much-needed light on this population. The respective sections include critical discourse on what the previous literature has provided as well as that of both authors. Based on this information, it is clear that student affairs professionals and faculty members should consider incorporating the tenets of critical race theory into their professional practice. This process may very well require training in graduate-level programs and professional development subsequent to graduate school. It is critical that these professionals gain a better understanding of the pernicious effects of racism and how race plays a major part in the overall academic experience of high-achieving African American males in academe. It is also important that these professionals come to understand that the very institutions they serve often help perpetuate White dominance over populations of color. With this in mind, it is unlikely that professionals in U.S. colleges and universities will see the eradication of racism anytime in the near future. It is also important for administrators and faculty to come to terms with and accept the fact that their predominately White institutions of higher education are not color-blind and that student academic success is not based solely on merit but often hinges on other factors. Beneath the surface, subtle forms of racism, such as micro-aggressions, are encountered by students of color on a daily basis. Acknowledging these racial realities is an important first step in truly leveling the academic playing field for students of color. Last, both student affairs professionals and faculty should consider the recommendations about utilizing critical race theory espoused by Patton et al. (2007).

Recommendations for student affairs and academic affairs units regarding cultural and social capital specific to high-achieving Black males from urban schools should begin with a commitment to helping this student population develop the assets identified as critical to educational success. This commitment should first begin by recognizing that each minority subgroup is unique. Specific strategies should be carefully designed to ensure a successful postsecondary experience. Assisting high-achieving African American males in building supportive social networks with faculty, student affairs professionals, and other student populations is one strategy that can be achieved. On another note, it is important that African American male students, including high-achieving, are provided with adequate opportunities to develop mentor relationships with college officials. Such relationships can help these students obtain the necessary skills to navigate the confusing maze of selecting a major and courses, registration, and myriad other issues. Further, high-achieving African American males should be encouraged to examine fields of study typically eschewed by this cohort.

Academic and student affairs divisions should function from an asset model approach, as opposed to the deficit model approach that emphasizes underidentification and underachievement. Such an approach would allow for opportunities not only to recognize but also to celebrate success. Emphasizing asset approaches as opposed to deficit modeling is necessary in shifting the campus climate.

The paradigm shift begins by showcasing the abilities of those African American males who are capitalizing on their educational experiences. Academic convocations, award ceremonies, and recognition banquets for the expressed purpose of providing a forum for celebrating successes are warranted. In addition, student affairs divisions could connect to larger organizational entities such as the American College Personnel Association (ACPA) or the National Association of Student Personnel Administrators (NASPA) in an effort to recognize this population of students. NASPA, in particular, has developed a knowledge community (KC) or alliance dedicated to *Men and Masculinities*. Partnering with this entity to create meaningful programmatic and policy-oriented initiatives could prove to be quite fruitful. In addition, the expertise of student affairs organizations specifically targeted at providing insight for populations of color, such as the NASAP, could serve as yet another invaluable source of information.

Recommendations for academic and student affairs divisions related to identity development is captured by Bonner and Bailey (2006) in their statement, "The establishment of a positive identity for African American male collegians rests on their ability to establish some sense of agency. . . . one that not only recognizes the importance of the identity development process but also supports this process through altruistic dialogue" (p. 40). The altruistic dialogue mentioned here speaks to the importance of these individuals bringing their "whole" selves to the higher education setting. Thus, academic and student affairs divisions could provide opportunities for urban male students to engage in learning communities that support their identity development as high-achieving African American males. The core of a true undergraduate experience is cultivating the whole student, resisting the reductionist tendency to bifurcate the student's existence between academic and social polarities. Therefore, bringing both academic and student affairs best practices together through learning community contexts could allow urban high-achieving African American males to experience all facets of their identity in an affirming and safe space.

Last, recommendations for academic and student affairs divisions specific to the urban high-achieving male who occupies the millennial category should take into account differences among this population and majority (i.e., White) populations. Each label that has been used to categorize the Millennial population needs to be filtered through different lenses. Thus, the academic and student affairs divisions should look at mirroring what many women of color have done in the academy; to be specific, they have created *sister circles*, which serve as supportive enclaves. Perhaps, *brother triangles* (the triangle selected due to its representation as the strongest shape) could provide needed support for this population. The establishment of these groups often provides rich information and focused group reporting of the issues that are most important to their academic and social integration on campus. In addition, these groups reveal that the needs of African American millennial males who also happen to be high achieving is not only unlike their White millennial peers but is also unlike the needs articulated by other African American males who are not designated as high achieving.

Data that emerges from these triangles can be used to inform contemporary academic and student affairs practices. In essence, the overarching goal of this recommendation, as well as the others that preceded it, is that success for high-achieving African American males, particularly those from urban settings, should transition from being "insider" information to "outsider" practices if education professionals are to truly effect change.

REFERENCES

Anderson, G. M. (2005). In the name of diversity: Education and commoditization and consumption of race in the United States. *The Urban Review, 37*(5), 399–423.

Asante, M. K. (1988). *The Afrocentric idea.* Philadelphia, PA: Temple University Press.

Bennett, T., & Savage, M. (2004). Introduction: Cultural capital and cultural policy. *Cultural Trends, 13*(2), 7–14.

Bergerson, A. A. (2003). Critical race theory and white racism: Is there room for white scholars in fighting racism in education? *Qualitative Studies in Education, 16*(1), 51–63.

Bonner, F. A., II. (2001). *Academically gifted African American male college students: A phenomenological study.* Monograph of the National Research Center for the Gifted and Talented, in conjunction with Yale University, University of Connecticut, and University of Georgia, and the U.S. Department of Education.

Bonner, F. A., III, & Bailey, K. W. (2006). Enhancing the academic climate for African American college men. In M. J. Cuyjet (Ed.), *African American Men in College* (pp. 24–46). San Francisco, CA: Jossey-Bass.

Bonner, F. A., II, Jennings, M., Marbley, A. F., & Brown, L. (2008). Capitalizing on leadership capacity: Gifted African American males in high school. *Roeper Review, 30*(2), 93–103.

Bonner, F. A., II, Lewis, C. W., Bowman-Perrott, V., Hill-Jackson, L., & M. James. (2010). Definition, identification, identity and culture: A unique alchemy impacting the success of gifted African American males in school. *Journal for the Education of the Gifted, 33*(2), 176–202.

Bourdieu, P., & Passeron, J. C. (1977). *Reproduction in education, society and culture.* Beverly Hills, CA: Sage.

Boyd, H. (2007). It's hard out here for a black man! *Black Scholar, 37*(3), 2–9.

Chapman, T. K. (2007). Interrogating classroom relationships and events: Using portraiture and critical race theory in education research. *Educational Researcher, 36*(3), 156–162.

Coleman, J. S. (1988). Social capital in the creation of human capital. *The American Journal of Sociology, 94*, S95–S120.

Cook, J. B., & Córdova, D. (2006). *Minorities in higher education twenty-second annual status report.* Washington, DC: American Council on Education.

Cross, W. E., Jr. (1971). The Negro-to-Black conversion experience: Towards the psychology of Black liberation. *Black World, 20*(9), 13–27.

Cross, W. E., Jr. (1978). The Thomas and Cross models of psychological nigrescence: A literature review. *The Journal of Black Psychology, 5*(1), 13–31.

Cross, W. E., Jr. (1991). *Shades of black: Diversity in African American identity.* Philadelphia, PA: Temple University Press.

Cross, W. E. (1995). The psychology of nigrescence: Revising the Cross model. In J. Ponterotto, J. M. Casas, L. A. Suzuki, & C. M. Alexander (Eds.), *Handbook of multicultural counseling* (pp. 93–122). Thousand Oaks, CA: Sage.

Cuyjet, M. J. (2006). Helping African American men matriculate: Ideas and suggestions. In M. J. Cuyjet (Ed.), *African American men in college* (pp. 237–249). San Francisco, CA: Jossey-Bass.

DeBard, R. (2004). Millennials coming to college. In M. D. Coones & R. DeBard (Eds.), *Serving the millennial generation. New directions for student services, 106* (pp. 33–45). San Francisco, CA: Jossey-Bass.

DeCuir, J. T., & Dixson, A. D. (2004). "So when it comes out, they aren't surprised that it is them": Using critical race theory as a tool of analysis of race and racism in education. *Educational Researcher, 33*(5), 26–31.

Dika, S. L., & Singh, K. (2002). Applications of social capital in educational literature: A critical synthesis. *Review of Educational Research, 72*(1), 31–60.

Dixson, A. D., & Rousseau, C. K. (2005). And we are still not saved: Critical race theory in education ten years later. *Race Ethnicity and Education, 8*(1), 7–27.

Ecclestone, K. (2004). Learning in a comfort zone: Cultural and social capital inside an outcome-based assessment regime. *Assessment in Education, 11*(1), 29–47.

Fashola, O. (2005). *Educating African American males: Voices from the field.* Thousand Oaks, CA: Corwin Press.

Ford, D. Y. (2003). Two other wrongs don't make a right: Sacrificing the needs of diverse students does not solve gifted education's unresolved problems. *Journal for the Education of the Gifted, 26,* 283–291.

Ford, D. Y., Moore, J. L., III, & Milner, H. R., IV. (2005). Beyond cultureblindness: A model of culture with implications for gifted education. *Roeper Review, 27,* 97–103.

Freeman, K. (1997). Increasing African Americans' participation in higher education. *Journal of Higher Education, 68*(5), 523–550.

Fries-Britt, S. (1998). Moving beyond black achiever isolation: Experiences of gifted black collegians. *The Journal of Higher Education, 69*(5), 556–576.

Goyette, K. A., & Mullen, A. L. (2006). Who studies the arts and sciences? Social background and the choice and consequences of undergraduate study. *Journal of Higher Education, 77*(3), 497–538.

Grantham, T. (2004). Multicultural mentoring to increase black male representation in gifted programs. *Gifted Child Quarterly, 48*(3), 232–245.

Harper, S. R., Patton, L. D., & Wooden, O. S. (2009). Access and equity for African American students in higher education: A critical race historical analysis of policy efforts. *The Journal of Higher Education, 80*(4), 389–414.

Harper, S. R., & Quaye, S. J. (2007). Student organizations as venues for black identity expression and development among African American male student leaders. *Journal of College Student Development, 48*(2), 127–144.

Harper, S. R., & Quaye, S. J. (Eds.). (2009). *Student engagement in higher education: Theoretical perspectives and practical approaches for diverse populations.* New York, NY: Routledge.

Hébert, T. P. (2002). Gifted black males in a predominantly white university: Portraits of achievement. *Journal for the Education of the Gifted, 26*(1), 25–64.

Hébert, T. P. (2006). Gifted university males in a Greek fraternity: Creating a culture of achievement. *Gifted Child Quarterly, 50*(1), 26–41.

Helms, J. (Ed.). (1990). *Black and White racial identity theory, research, and practice.* Westport, CT: Praeger.

Holzman, M., (2004). *Public education and Black male students: A state report card.* Schott Educational Inequity Index, Cambridge, MA: The Schott Foundation for Public Education.

Hopkins, R. (1997). *Educating Black males: Critical lessons in schooling, community, and power.* Albany: State University of New York Press.

Hrabowski, F. A., III, Maton, K. I., & Greif, G. L. (1998). *Beating the odds: Raising academically successful African American males.* Oxford, UK: Oxford University Press.

Howe, N., & Strauss, W. (2000). *Millennials rising: The next great generation.* New York, NY: Vintage.

Hussar, W. J., & Bailey, T. M. (2009). *Projections of education statistics to 2018* (37th ed.). Washington, DC: National Center for Education Statistics.

Kunjufu, J. (2005). *Hip hop street curriculum.* Chicago, IL: African American Images.

Ladson-Billings, G., & Tate, W. (1995). Toward a critical race theory of education. *Teachers College Record, 97*(1), 47–68.

Leyden, P., Teixeira, R., & Greenberg, E. (2007). *The progressive politics of the millennial generation.* Retrieved from http://www.newpolitics.net/node/360?full_report=1

Livingstone, D. W., & Sawchuk, P. H. (2000). Beyond cultural capital theory: Hidden dimensions of working class learning. *Review of Education/Pedagogy/Cultural Studies, 22*(2), 121–146.

Lorde, A. (1992). Age, race, class, and sex: Women redefining difference. In M. Andersen & P. Hill Collins (Eds.), *Race, class, and gender: An anthology* (pp. 495-502). Belmont, CA: Wadsworth.

Lynn, M. (2004). Inserting the "race" into critical pedagogy: An analysis of "race-based epistemologies." *Educational Philosophy and Theory, 36*(2), 153–165.

Milner, H.R. (2007). African American males in urban schools: No excuses—teach and empower. *Theory into Practice 46*(3), 239–246.

Mutua, A. D. (2006). The rise, development and future directions of critical race theory and related scholarship. *Denver University Law Review, 84,* 329–394.

Patton, L. D., McEwen, M., Rendon, L., & Howard-Hamilton, M. F. (2007). Critical race perspectives on theory in student affairs. *New Directions for Student Affairs, 120,* 39–53.

Perna, L. W., & Titus, M. A. (2005). The relationship between parental involvement as social capital and college enrollment: An examination of racial/ethnic group differences. *Journal of Higher Education, 76,* 485–518.

Phinney, J. S. (1996). When we talk about American ethnic groups, what do we mean? *American Psychologist, 51*(9), 918–922.

Polite, V., & Davis, J. (1999). *African American males in school and society: Practices and policies for effective education.* New York, NY: Teachers College Press.

Reay, D. (2004). Education and cultural capital: The implications of changing trends in education policy. *Cultural Trends, 13*(2), 73–86.

Schott Foundation for Public Education. (2008). *Given half a chance: The Schott 50 state report on public education and Black males.* Cambridge, MA: Author.

Solorzano, D., Ceja, M., & Yosso, T. (2000). Critical race theory, racial microaggressions, and campus racial climate: The experiences of African American college students. *The Journal of Negro Education, 69*(1/2), 60–73.

Stanton-Salazar, R. D. (1997). A social capital framework for understanding the socialization of racial minority children and youth. *Harvard Educational Review, 67*(1), 1–40.

Stovall, D. (2006). Forging community in race and class: Critical race theory and the quest for social justice in education. *Race Ethnicity and Education, 9*(3), 243–259.

Teranishi, R. T., & Briscoe, K. (2008). Contextualizing race: African American college choice in an evolving affirmative action era. *The Journal of Negro Education, 77*(1), 15–26.

U.S. Office for Civil Rights. (2002). *2002 office for civil rights elementary and secondary school survey projections and documentation.* Washington, DC: U.S. Department of Education: Author.

Whiting, G. W. (2006). Promoting a scholar identity among African American males: Recommendations for gifted education. *Gifted Education Press Quarterly, 20*(3), 2–6.

CHAPTER FIFTEEN

In the Pursuit of Excellence: Examining the Effects of Racial Identity on African American College Students' Academic Orientations

LATRELLE D. JACKSON, W. MAX PARKER,
AND LAMONT A. FLOWERS

Academic development and social development at the undergraduate level occur through multifaceted processes that interconnect and are influenced by many variables including precollege experiences and institutional characteristics (Chickering & Reisser, 1993; Evans, Forney, & Guido-DiBrito, 1998; Pascarella & Terenzini, 1991, 2005). Given the developmental progression of college students' intellectual and affective traits, many students experience challenges as they attempt to adjust to a learning environment different from the one in high school (Flowers, 2004; Skowron, Wester, & Azen, 2004). Aside from the general student concerns about performing well in the classroom, selecting an appropriate college major, and establishing an identity (Chickering & Reisser, 1993), African American college students often grapple with questions, such as how to understand and develop their racial identity in the context of a college campus. Additionally, depending on the historical and contemporary context of the institution, African American college students may also feel marginalized and alienated.

To assist student affairs professionals with helping students develop appropriately in college, educational researchers have repeatedly examined the factors that impact academic achievement in college (Astin, 1993; Cohen & Wills,

1985; Cokley, 2002; Parker & Flowers, 2003; Pascarella & Terenzini, 1991, 2005; Steele, 1992). The research literature in this area has addressed key individual-level variables (Astin, 1993; Cokley, 2001; Moore, Lovell, McGann, & Wyrick, 1998; Pascarella & Terenzini, 1991, 2005; Van Laar, 2000) and institutional-level variables (Maton & Hrabowski, 2004; Pascarella, 1980; Osborne, 1997; Terenzini, Pascarella, & Blimling, 1999). The connection between these two major categories of variables determines whether the learning environment will support student development (Pascarella & Terenzini, 1991, 2005). However, some of this research is limited in scope and does not apply to African American students because it does not take into account cultural variables (e.g., racial identity) that often impact student learning. Because research indicates that racial identity questions and issues arise early in African American students' development and continue during their schooling and throughout their lifespan (Tucker & Herman, 2002), several researchers have noted a particular need for recommendations, pedagogical strategies, and methods for teaching character development and academic success skills for African American students at the K-12 curricular level (Gay, 2000; King, 2005; Murrell, 2002; Pierce, Lemke, & Smith, 1988; Piro & Lorio, 1991). To fully explore potential success strategies, researchers will need to continue to study African Americans at an early age because, as these youths mature, their behavioral responses to academic and community environments will not merely be defined by internal forces or external forces but also by their perceptions of the larger systemic elements (e.g., race, gender, ethnicity, class, nationality) and other personality constructs (Ginwright, Cammarota, & Noguera, 2005). Furthermore, it has been shown that students' worldviews, academic outlooks, and self-concepts influence their ability to navigate educational settings (Mitchell & Dell, 1992; Phinney, Dennis, & Osorio, 2006; Rowley, Sellers, Chavous, & Smith, 1998; Steele & Aronson, 1995; Sutton & Kimbrough, 2001; Taylor & Howard-Hamilton, 2001).

Given the previously discussed information, we recommend that to develop successful, strategic, and integrated academic success practices, it should be understood that learning occurs as new information is synthesized in light of previously mastered concepts (Dewey, 1938). The noted theorist Piaget (1952) describes this process as assimilation and accommodation. In light of this developmental process that occurs in college and throughout the lifespan (Chickering & Reisser, 1993; Erikson, 1968), researchers have established a direct connection between racial identity, academic achievement, and student engagement among African American students (Parker & Flowers, 2003; Taylor & Howard-Hamilton, 2001). For example, believing that one can achieve established goals is a necessary precursor to fully engaging in the purpose-driven process of obtaining a college education. This line of thinking has notable implications for students of color, particularly African Americans (Essandoh, 1995). With value-laden cultural references present in every key aspect of life, it is vital to identify the messages that African American students must discard or embrace to propel their academic pursuit of excellence (Gushue & Sicalides, 1997; Ward, 2004). Given the fact that many researchers have empirically supported the notion of racial and ethnic differences in achievement, it is critically important to delineate these central core influences for African American students in hopes of increasing their chances for college success (Demo & Parker, 1987).

ACADEMIC ORIENTATIONS OF STUDENTS FROM URBAN HIGH SCHOOLS

In light of reported differences in academic experiences, African American students from urban high schools may be at an even greater disadvantage given their previous educational experiences (Reid & Moore, 2008) and the resulting academic orientations and racial identity that may have been developed (Kenny et al., 2007). Moreover, it has been suggested that urban educators may be able to advance social justice in education by learning how to best prepare urban high school students to achieve academic excellence in a manner that is comparable to their peers in other high school settings (Kenny et al., 2007). Research regarding the preparation of African American college students who matriculated from urban high schools suggests that educators and school leaders may need to focus on this population prior to their enrollment in college, and even once they are on campus. This is important because some students may need special interventions to ensure that they are academically and socially successful with regard to making the right decisions and developing a healthy racial identity that promotes increased levels of self-respect, citizenship development, and a greater focus and awareness concerning how best to pursue academic and career goals in college (Reid & Moore, 2008). This recommendation may be an important goal for all students; however, research suggests that the structural and organizational elements of urban schools may further exacerbate this challenge for African American students who graduate from these types of high school environments. For example, Holland and Farmer-Hinton (2009) find that school size has an inverse relationship with college-preparatory experiences for high school students (e.g., participating in activities at school that encourage college attendance and promote success in college). Holland and Farmer-Hinton's data support the relevance of particular variables of interest to researchers who may be looking for a parsimonious model and operational definition of "college culture." In their study, Holland and Farmer-Hinton note, "College culture reflects environments that are accessible to all students and saturated with ever-present information and resources and ongoing formal and informal conversations that help students to understand the various facets of preparing for, enrolling in, and graduating from postsecondary academic institutions as those experiences specifically pertain to the students' current and future lives" (p. 26). This definition is relevant to our discussion of the relationship between academic orientations and racial identity in college, because if urban high school students are not receiving adequate college preparation skills, this may negatively impact their ability to perform well in college (Reid & Moore, 2008).

It should be noted that it is not our intention to suggest that all students who attend urban high schools will be negatively impacted and need special interventions in college, because it is well known that many of these students are resilient and do well academically (Reis, Colbert, & Hébert, 2005); however, the empirical findings in the studies by Holland and Farmer-Hinton and Reid and Moore suggest that school size is negatively associated with the development of the skills and dispositions that students need to be prepared for college-level academic tasks. Thus, although more research is needed to expand our knowledge regarding urban high school students and college readiness issues, these findings indicate that urban educators and researchers need to explore the correlation between school size and student preparation as well as provide practical recommendations to support urban high school students.

In urban high school environments, some African American students may not be engaged in the school culture or feel a sense of belonging because of the lack of mentors and opportunities for growth (Hemmings, 2007; Holt, Bry, & Johnson, 2008). Even urban African American students who do well academically in these types of environments may not be prepared for the rigors of postsecondary education (Reid & Moore, 2008). For example, some urban African American students may question their academic abilities once they find themselves in courses that they are underprepared for, in comparison to their peers with different precollege experiences. These students may need what might be considered remedial college readiness training and related experiences to learn how to adjust to the many transitional and developmental tasks and issues they will face in college. Chickering and Reisser (1993) indicate that the first major issues college students face are academic in nature, as they seek to overcome the differences in the levels of work from secondary to postsecondary education. Thus, an essential element of student development services may be to provide students from urban environments appropriate academic counseling to gain an understanding of these students' racial identities and assess their academic orientations. As additional justification for this recommendation, in Kenny et al.'s (2007) qualitative study of 16 urban high school students, the researchers note, "students did not reveal a critical consciousness of how oppression and racism might affect their achievement" (p. 342). Kenny et al.'s finding supports the notion that, although some students from urban high school schools may perceive and realize barriers to their academic success, they may be at the initial stages of their racial identity development process, which may further cause difficulties in college, where they are often confronted with even more psychosocial and intellectual struggles and challenges.

RACIAL IDENTITY DEVELOPMENT

Some of the major contributors to racial identity development theory are African American scholars, such as Hall, Cross, and Freedle (1972). Their work was influenced greatly by the societal conditions Black people encountered in the civil rights movement of the 1960s (Cross, 1991). Although identity development has been researched from numerous perspectives over the years, African American racial identity development models began to surface in the counseling psychology and psychotherapy literature in the 1970s in response to the civil rights movement. Helms (1990) summarizes this time as an era when theorists wanted to present models that were salient to the psychotherapy process. Two key themes emerged during this period: the client as a problem (CAP) and Nigrescence or racial identity development (NRID) models. Each one has significant implications for conceptualizing race from a meaning-making perspective and understanding the impact racial views have on successful life choices.

The CAP approach was groundbreaking in nature due to the time of its initiation, the 1960s, and the fact that at that time, African American leadership was crossing the boundaries of mainstream culture (Williams, 1987). However, many Whites viewed the social phenomenon of African Americans being assertive in their struggle for equal respect and treatment as aggressive and unpredictable (Caplan, 1970; Cheek, 1976; Helms, 1985, 1990). The undercurrent of concern was based on the lack of psychological models addressing the process by which people develop healthy identities in spite of racial discrimination and oppression (Acosta, Yamamoto, & Evans, 1982). This void in the scholarly literature initiated the development of models that incorporated a strengths-based perspective.

One of the best aspects of the CAP approach is the link it made to societal influences in shaping identity; however, the portrayal of an unpredictable, aggressive hostility was of limited benefit in understanding the complexities of African American identity development. NRID allowed for a more flexible understanding of identity influences—both internal and external sources. From the description of Nigrescence "as the developmental process by which a person 'becomes Black' where Black is defined in terms of one's manner of thinking about and evaluating oneself and one's reference groups rather than in terms of skin color per se" (Helms, 1990, p. 17), it followed that a person–environment interplay is involved in shaping identity. A focus on how much one identifies with the majority White culture (Akbar, 1979), as well as frameworks for healthy Black identity development, also surfaced during this time (Cross, 1971; Dizard, 1970; Jackson, 1975; Vontress, 1971a, 1971b). NRID blossomed through the foundational works of Cross (1971, 1978, 1980) and other researchers who sought to refine the model (Vandiver, Cross, Worrell, & Fhagen-Smith, 2002).

As the knowledge and understanding of racial identity advanced, scholars began to approach this area of research from a developmental perspective. Based on this concept, Janet Helms, a leading scholar on racial identity development, asserts that racial identity refers to a sense of group or collective identity based on the idea that one shares a common racial heritage with a particular group. In general, she defines racial identity development as the manner in which one identifies with his racial group. An expansion of the definition of racial identity development that occurred after her work includes the following qualities: (a) a reflection of how close to or how far from one's racial group a person feels, (b) a subjective judgment about the degree to which one accepts or rejects her racial group, (c) an estimation of how important race is to an individual, (d) part of the self-concept related to membership within a racial group, and (e) a dynamic and ever-changing force that is influenced by many factors, such as individual experiences, personally meaningful events in one's environment, societal and family messages, and observations of how group members are treated in society (Helms, 1995). Helms also defines "Black" racial identity as the extent to which Blacks identify with other Blacks and accept or reject identities resulting from racial victimization. Later, Helms and Cook (1999) advance the notion that an important developmental life goal is to understand and properly negotiate the challenges of perceived and realized negative racial attitudes about oneself and others. Racial identity has also been viewed as a measure of the importance that members of an ethnic group place on their cultural heritage (Parham & Helms, 1981; Thompson, Anderson, & Bakeman, 2000).

In a landmark article, "The Negro-to-Black Conversion Experience: Toward a Psychology of Black Liberation," Cross (1971) discusses initial applications of racial identity theory to counseling and student affairs. Cross developed the article into the Nigrescence model. Nigrescence is a process of attitudinal, behavioral, and perceptual changes based on how the individual sees himself, how he sees their racial group, and how he views the White majority. His original Nigrescense model consists of the following four stages: (a) pre-encounter, (b) encounter, (c) immersion-emersion, and (d) internalization. Cross (1991), then, added a fifth stage called "internalization-commitment." Told in a different way, following an extensive study of African Americans, Cross described Black racial identity development as a progressive continuum along five stages.

Pre-Encounter

At the pre-encounter stage, the African American individual may view the world through the eyes of White dominant culture and, in general, may view Whites as socially and intellectually superior (Cross, 1991, 1995; Helms, 1990). African Americans, at this stage are not necessarily anti-African American but rather are usually mis-educated about the African American experience. Thus, race is not essential to their well-being. For example, at the pre-encounter stage, African American individuals may be more likely to operate from a European perspective and on a predominantly White college campus would associate mostly with White Americans. The pre-encounter stage may also be manifested by a lack of racial focus in defining oneself. Those in this stage do not identify race as an important descriptor when conceptualizing their identity. In contrast, other variables are seen as more salient (e.g., gender, socioeconomic status, etc.). Some individuals, at this stage, may even affiliate with the majority culture and deny their African American heritage in order to be more in line with the majority culture (Abrams & Trusty, 2004; Cross, 1995; Helms, 1995). They also may tend to engage the world from a Eurocentric framework by idealizing things in White culture and negating the value of things associated with African American culture.

Encounter

When significant experiences occur for individuals at the pre-encounter stage (e.g., discrimination, cultural affirmations), a shift emerges to the encounter stage (Cross, 1991, 1995; Helms, 1990). Thus, the encounter stage is prompted by key events that engender feelings and perceptions that may cause African Americans to begin to reinterpret their worldviews with respect to race and identity. As a result, individuals may begin to question discrepant treatment of people and make connections to racial identity variables. During this stage, focus may be directed to the salience of race and notions regarding racial inferiority. This struggle may be profound in that it agitates the foundation of previously held notions and opens the door for new schemas of racial identity. In this transitional stage, African American individuals have experiences that may cause them to rethink their positions and ideologies concerning African Americans and Whites. Given the major changes in perspectives associated with the encounter stage, the African American individual is in a state of flux characterized by uncertainty and confusion. There are two necessary parts of the encounter stage according to Cross (1991): First, the African American individual must have an encounter, and, second, she must internalize the encounter (i.e., recognize the significance of the encounter experience and consider how it impacts her previously held views about African Americans and Whites). The internalization process is necessary for individuals to progress through the encounter stage.

Immersion/Emersion

As individuals transition to the next stage, immersion/emersion, they may be torn between conflicting messages and the emotions associated with those messages (Cross, 1991, 1995; Helms, 1990). The result may be behavioral and thought patterns that are different from those of the majority culture. During the immersion portion of the phase, individuals may immerse themselves in African American culture and refrain from excessive contact with White Americans. In addition, they may idealize African American people, while distancing themselves from White Americans. In the immersion-emersion stage, African American people initially focus totally on African Americans to the exclusion of Whites. They may attempt to connect with the African American community, seeing it as their main source of support. Unity among African American people is an important goal of this stage. At this stage, certain African American individuals believe that African American people should learn how to live totally independent of White people. Some individuals at this level also experience anger or hostility as they work to redefine their identity schema. These emotions may serve as productive energy by helping one to channel interest into educating oneself about African American culture and engage with other supportive African Americans, which constitutes the emersion portion of the phase. By doing this, they become less reactive, and their anger and hostility may even diminish. It should also be noted that the emersion aspect of this phase describes a developmental process that eventually may result in having a new understanding of oneself as well as beginning to embrace people from other cultures in meaningful ways.

Internalization

Once individuals reach the internalization stage, they often have achieved a sense of racial peace (Cross, 1991, 1995; Helms, 1990). After a great deal of self-examination, individuals may become less defensive about issues of race. Many of their racial identity development conflicts are resolved, during this phase, which may lead to the development of a deeper sense of security in themselves as African American individuals. By this stage, the strife associated with self-definition has decreased, paving the way for a comfortable connection with one's racial group. Those in the internalization stage may experience a greater degree of personal freedom to value themselves, along the range of identifiers (e.g., race, socioeconomic status, sexual orientation, etc.) and may value others who are culturally different. Although individuals still consider African Americans as their primary reference group, they approach the world from a more pluralistic perspective. Thus, friendships with White people may be renegotiated and anti-White feelings may be minimized (Thompson et al., 2000).

Internalization-Commitment

The last stage is internalization-commitment (Cross, 1991, 1995). During this stage, the process of identity integration continues, along with a greater appreciation of others. One's sense of self is grounded in one's racial identity development and serves as the framework by which one makes meaningful connections with others. This stage is often noted by increased political activism and continued commitment to Blacks. African American people in this stage attempt to eliminate racism of all oppressed people. The goal is to seek personal and interpersonal harmony regarding race and culture. Their ideas and feelings about African Americans are more mature and realistic than in the previous stages.

Summary of Racial Identity Development

Cross' (1971, 1991, 1995) work presents a healthy model of African American identity development that is inclusive of environmental influences (e.g., majority culture) and validates the internal process of identity integration. Helms (1990, 1995) advances this work, by drawing attention to the psychological movement within the stages, conceptualizing the need for emotional processing. Helms suggests that individuals must reconcile data gathered from racially inspired experiences as they shift through the stages of racial identity development. In her reformulation of racial identity development, Helms (1995) uses "statuses" as opposed to "stages" in her theory, describing a sequential progression and suggesting that thoughts and actions are categorically defined by one's status at a given time (Abrams & Trusty, 2004). She proposed this change because the notion of a stage did not seem to account for the dynamic processes involved in one's racial identity development; individuals may simultaneously exemplify characteristics of more than one stage. Thus, Helms offered the term statuses as a means to explain the schemas that are associated with the various arenas for racial identity development and noted that they are what identity measures tap into (Thompson et al., 2000). Stated in a different way, Helms (1995) views racial attitudes and behaviors as dynamic and evolving rather than static, which is why she refers to the various qualities of racial identity as statuses rather than stages (Helms, 1995; Ponterotto, Casas, Suzuki, & Alexander, 1995). It should be noted that several researchers have currently redeveloped these ideas and theories (Cross & Vandiver, 2001; Vandiver, 2001; Vandiver, Fhagen-Smith, Cokley, Cross, & Worrell, 2001; Worrell, Cross, & Vandiver, 2001). However, in the present study, we decided to focus on the earlier theories because of the weight of the research evidence that supports the propositions describing the interpersonal and psychosocial transitions of African Americans.

Purpose of the Study

Viewed collectively, the racial identity development model and related research literature illustrate the importance of worldview and an individual's environment. Thus, it is likely that how well an African American student navigates a college career depends largely on the educational setting as well as her racial identity development pattern or status. It is also likely that an African American student's racial identity development may be utilized to help filter the information he receives from peer, familial, and institutional exchanges and serve as stimuli for growth. Focusing on the goal of African American student excellence and success in college, this study examines the effects of racial identity development on African American students' academic orientations.

METHOD

The conceptual framework for the study is based on many research investigations on the effects of college attendance on student persistence and academic achievement. One line of this research suggests that student background factors and precollege characteristics impact college students' postsecondary outcomes (Chickering & Reisser, 1993; Pascarella, 1985; Pascarella & Terenzini, 1991, 2005; Robbins et al., 2004; Tinto, 1993). As such, the conceptual framework in this study is influenced by the viewpoint that an African American student's background and precollege characteristics (e.g., age, gender, etc.) affect her academic orientations (Dennis, Phinney, & Chuateco, 2005; Schunk, 1989, 1991). It has also been shown that institutional characteristics influence student outcomes. In accordance, a categorical variable measuring college racial composition was added to the analytical model. Also, student development research suggests that students' academic experiences in college are needed to help explain students' educational outcomes (Astin, 1993; Pascarella & Terenzini, 1991, 2005; Terenzini et al., 1999; Terenzini, Springer, Pascarella, & Nora, 1995; Terenzini & Wright, 1987). Thus, we use variables assessing students' academic experiences in the analytical model of the present study (i.e., year in school, grade point average).

Participants

The sample for this study consists of 435 African American students from five historically Black college and universities (HBCUs) and two predominately White institutions (PWIs), located in the Southeast. They were recruited by several collaborators among the participating institutions. The total sample is made up of approximately 59% females and 41% males. It contains the following distribution of students: freshmen (32%), sophomores (18%), juniors (20%), and seniors (30%). The average age range of the sample is 19–21. At the time of the study, 54% of the total sample attended HBCUs and 46% attended PWIs. In the HBCU sample, there are approximately 51% females and 49% males. In the PWI sample, there are approximately 69% females and 31% males.

Variables

The dependent variables for this study consist of scales from the Survey of Academic Orientations (SAO) (Beck & Davidson, 2001; Davidson, Beck, & Silver, 1999). The SAO is a 36-item, Likert-type scale (1 = *strongly disagree* to 5 = *strongly agree*). For each item, students were asked to rate the extent to which each statement describes their attitudes, perceptions, or behaviors. Higher scores on the SAO scales are interpreted as higher levels of the particular perceptions and behaviors, as assessed by the scale. The SAO consists of the following six scales: (a) reading for pleasure, (b) academic apathy, (c) academic efficacy, (d) mistrust of instructors, (e) creative expression, and (f) structure dependence. The reading for pleasure scale measures the extent to which a student likes to read books that interest him. The academic apathy scale measures the degree to which students are willing to expend energy to achieve academically. The academic efficacy scale measures a student's perceptions of her academic ability. The mistrust of instructors scale measures a student's perceptions of whether they believe their instructors intentionally impede their academic progress. The creative expression scale measures the extent to which students pursue opportunities to be creative. The structure dependence scale measures the extent to which students prefer focused learning environments in college. Detailed information about the dependent, independent, and control variables are shown in Table 1.

Because the purpose of this study is to determine the impact of racial identity attitudes on academic orientations, the primary independent variables that are of interest to us are African American students' racial identity attitudes as measured by the Racial Identity Attitude Scale (RIAS-B) (Helms, 1990; Parham & Helms, 1981). Using the RIAS-B, we measured the following four of the five stages of racial identity attitudes from Cross's (1971, 1991, 1995) racial identity theory, referring to them as statuses rather than stages, following Helms: (a) pre-encounter: viewing the world from a White frame of reference; (b) encounter: transitioning from idealizing Whites to viewing African Americans more positively; (c) immersion-emersion: embracing African Americans and partially rejecting some aspects of White culture; and (d) internalization: having a positive attitude toward one's own racial group and being more tolerant of the White majority. The RIAS-B (short form) consists of a 30-item, Likert-type scale (1 = *strongly disagree* to 5 = *strongly agree*). For each item, we asked students to rate the extent to which each statement described their attitudes and perceptions. Higher scores on the RIAS-B are associated with higher statuses of racial identity. The RIAS-B has demonstrated evidence of construct validity (Ponterotto & Wise, 1987). The RIAS-B has also been tested to examine the statistical properties of the items and has shown a high degree of internal consistency. Cronbach's alpha values of .69, .50, .67, and .79 are the established values for the pre-encounter, encounter, immersion-emersion, and internalization statuses, respectively (Helms, 1990). As shown in Table 2, in the present study, we obtained Cronbach's alpha values of .69, .31, .61, and .73 from the sample participants. The encounter status is comprised of only three items (Helms, 1990). It is quite possible that the small number of items for this scale contributed to the low reliability coefficient obtained from data in the present study. The three other alpha reliabilities are moderate to low but fairly consistent with previous research (Helms, 1990); thus the statuses were considered appropriate for the present study. However, we acknowledge that this particular measurement issue may have introduced a limitation in the present study.

Procedures

As shown in Table 2 and Table 3, we computed means and standard deviations (Hays, 1994) for each variable and a correlation coefficient between each scale of the SAO and the RIAS-B. Utilizing ordinary least squares regression (Berry &

Table 1. Operational Definitions of Variables

DEPENDENT VARIABLES

Academic Orientations

Reading for Pleasure: This six-item scale measures a student's tendency to read material that has not been assigned for class (Cronbach's alpha = .79).

Academic Apathy: This six-item scale measures a student's perspectives regarding her likelihood to exert effort in pursuing academic pursuits (Cronbach's alpha = .59).

Academic Efficacy: This six-item scale measures a student's perceptions and ideas concerning his ability to achieve academically (Cronbach's alpha = .59).

Mistrust of Instructors: This six-item scale measures the extent to which students believe that course instructors support them in the classroom (Cronbach's alpha = .66).

Creative Expression: This six-item scale measures a student's tendency to pursue creative activities (Cronbach's alpha = .75).

Structure Dependence: This six-item scale measures the extent to which a student requires a clear and focused instructional environment (Cronbach's alpha = .59).

INDEPENDENT VARIABLES

Pre-Encounter: This six-item scale measures the degree of agreement with a student's worldview from the majority perspective (Cronbach's alpha = .69).

Encounter: This three-item scale measures a student's perception of their initial racial identity transition (Cronbach's alpha = .31).

Immersion-Emersion: This six-item scale measures the process of pursuing knowledge and experiences pertaining to African American culture (Cronbach's alpha = .61).

Internalization: This nine-item scale measures an individual's perspectives regarding one's racial group as well as other racial groups (Cronbach's alpha = .73).

CONTROL VARIABLES

Age: A categorical variable based on a self-reported measure of the respondent's age (1 = 18 or younger; 2 = 19- to 21-years-old; 3 = 22- to 25-years-old; 4 = 26- to 35-years-old; 5 = 36-years-old or older).

Gender: A categorical variable (1 = female, 0 = male).

Racial Composition of the Institution: A categorical variable (1 = Attended a historically Black institution; 0 = Attended a predominantly White institution).

Year in School: A categorical variable (1 = Freshman; 2 = Sophomore; 3 = Junior; 4 = Senior).

Grade Point Average: A categorical variable based on a respondent's self-reported grade point average (1 = A; 2 = A–, B+; 3 = B; 4 = B–, C+; 5 = C, C–, or lower).

Table 2. Means and Standard Deviations of the Variables and Cronbach's Alpha for the Survey of Academic Orientations and Racial Identity Attitude Scale

Variable	Mean	Standard Deviation	Cronbach's Alpha
Age	2.08	.90	
Gender	.59	.49	
Racial Composition of the Institution	.54	.50	
Year in School	2.49	1.22	
Grade Point Average	2.84	1.15	
Academic Orientations			
Reading for Pleasure	19.95	5.05	.79
Academic Apathy	16.25	4.16	.59
Academic Efficacy	19.82	4.10	.59
Mistrust of Instructors	18.09	3.93	.66
Creative Expression	22.66	4.05	.75
Structure Dependence	21.73	3.62	.59
Racial Identity Attitudes			
Pre-Encounter	11.10	3.92	.69
Encounter	7.65	2.12	.31
Immersion-Emersion	13.65	3.60	.61
Internalization	33.10	5.19	.73

Table 3. Correlation Matrix of the Survey of Academic Orientations and Racial Identity Attitude Scale

Scales	A	B	C	D	E	F	G	H	I	J
A. Reading for Pleasure		−.130	.191*	−.014	.503*	.104	−.134	.175*	.055	.335*
B. Academic Apathy			−.296*	.360*	−.124	.023	.323*	.183*	.151*	−.121
C. Academic Efficacy				−.350*	.216*	−.035	−.277*	−.194*	−.074	.164*
D. Mistrust of Instructors					.101	.361*	.104*	.204*	.199*	.179*
E. Creative Expression						.360*	−.250*	.056	.043	.508*
F. Structure Dependence							−.112	.102	−.010	.435*
G. Pre-Encounter								.247*	.366*	−.298*
H. Encounter									.359*	.311*
I. Immersion-Emersion										.179*
J. Internalization										

Note. *p < .01.

Feldman, 1985; Cohen & Cohen, 1975; Pedhazur, 1997), each scale from the SAO was regressed on the four racial identity statuses, as measured by the RIAS-B (short form) and the entire set of control variables to estimate the direct effects of African American students' racial identity on their academic orientations, while applying statistical controls for the effects of age, gender, racial composition of the institution, year in school, and grade point average. As shown in Table 4, all statistical results were reported significant at $p < .01$.

RESULTS

The data analysis yielded six major findings. First, we found significant differences between the internalization status and the reading for pleasure scale ($B = .286$, $p < .01$). African American students who reported greater internalization of racial identity attitudes were more likely to read for pleasure. Second, the effects of the pre-encounter status on academic apathy was statistically significant ($B = .286$, $p < .01$). This result indicates that African American students in the pre-encounter status were less likely to expend effort in their academic pursuits. Third, the direct effects of the internalization status on academic efficacy was significant and positive ($B = .117$, $p < .01$). Thus, African American students at the internalization status were more likely to report that they had greater confidence in their academic abilities. Fourth, the effects of the internalization status on the mistrust of instructors scale was statistically significant ($B = .158$, $p < .01$). African American students who reported high values for the internalization status variable were also more likely to report that they were critical of their instructors. Fifth, the effects of internalization on creative expression was statistically significant ($B = .401$, $p < .01$). Thus, African American students in the internalization status were more likely to report that they were more likely to pursue creative activities. Sixth, African American students in the internalization status were also more likely to prefer greater structure in terms of their learning environment. Stated in a different way, the effects of the internalization status on structure dependence was statistically significant ($B = .322$, $p < .01$).

LIMITATIONS OF THE STUDY

Although the present study adds to our understanding of the impact of racial identity development on academic orientations, additional research is needed to account for some of the limitations in this study. The first limitation is that the institutional characteristics represented in this study may not apply to all institutions and all institutional contexts. The second limitation is that, although

Table 4. Summary of Regression Analysis

	B	β
Part A: Reading for Pleasure		
Pre-Encounter	−.061	−.047
Encounter	.182	.076
Immersion-Emersion	−.028	−020
Internalization	.286*	.300
$R^2 = .148$		
Part B: Academic Apathy		
Pre-Encounter	.286*	.272
Encounter	.216	.110
Immersion-Emersion	.023	.020
Internalization	−.031	-.040
$R^2 = .215$		
Part C: Academic Efficacy		
Pre-Encounter	−.186*	−.179
Encounter	−.370*	−.192
Immersion-Emersion	.045	.040
Internalization	.117*	.151
$R^2 = .249$		
Part D: Mistrust of Instructors		
Pre-Encounter	.093	.093
Encounter	.117	.063
Immersion-Emersion	.105	.098
Internalization	.158*	.210
$R^2 = .133$		
Part E: Creative Expression		
Pre-Encounter	−.067	−.065
Encounter	−.099	−.051
Immersion-Emersion	−.024	−.022
Internalization	.401*	.516
$R^2 = .298$		
Part F: Structure Dependence		
Pre-Encounter	.036	.039
Encounter	−.007	−.004
Immersion-Emersion	−.111	−.111
Internalization	.322*	.458
$R^2 = .200$		

Note. B = unstandardized regression coefficient; β = standardized regression coefficient *$p < .01$

the student sample contains African American students and represent a diverse population of African American college students, the sample does not include a representation of all African American college students (or even a random sample of African American college students); therefore, the findings may not resonate with the experiences or developmental patterns of all African American college students. A third limitation is that all of the data used in this study are based on student self-reported information. However, although standardized measures of academic achievement may be considered preferable to self-reported data (Pike, 1996), at least in terms of their psychometric properties, self-reported data have been shown to yield valid and reliable indicators of student perceptions, involvement, and development (Anaya, 1999; Pike, 1995). Another limitation of the study is that it is based heavily on racial identity development theory.

Although racial identity development theory has the advantage of helping counselors and student affairs professionals to understand and work with African American students more effectively, it should be noted that researchers and other student development personnel must not assume that because an individual looks African American, he only identifies with African Americans. It is equally necessary to acknowledge that an individual's racial identity status is not necessarily representative of her personality traits but is rather a dynamic, ever-changing, and evolving process influenced by many factors and stimuli. Moreover, because racial identity development theory does not fit everyone, it runs the risk of stereotyping ethnic minority individuals. Another limitation of racial identity development models is that there is an implied expectation that individuals proceed through the statuses in a linear direction, which is improbable and unlikely.

DISCUSSION AND IMPLICATIONS

A major statistical finding is that students who express sentiments most closely associated with the internalization status (i.e., being comfortable and self-assured as well as being open to diversity) are more likely to have positive academic orientations. Thus, with the primary goal being to help African American college students develop to higher levels, along the racial identity development continuum, utilizing racial identity development theory may be one way to begin to understand African American people in general and African American students in particular in a way that advances their academic outlook and academic belief system. Through African American racial identity development, student affairs professionals can clearly see that differences exist among African American college students and that those differences should be recognized and appreciated. Because differences exist, counseling, teaching, and student development activities should be designed to fit the racial and cultural values of the wide range of African American students' perspectives. The more familiar counselors are with the qualities of the various racial identity development statuses, the better they are able to apply them to fit student needs and concerns. It is also hypothesized that, through such knowledge and understanding, counselors can assist, diagnose, and treat African American students more effectively.

How effectively counselors or student affairs professionals function with African American students depends on both their knowledge of African American racial identity development theory and their awareness of their own racial identity development status. In accordance, a comprehensive understanding of racial identity development theory should be required for all academic counselors and student affairs professionals. A counselor with such an understanding is better equipped to identify when an African American student is probably in the pre-encounter status and therefore may prefer a White counselor over a counselor of color. Moreover, the counselor is able to recognize that perhaps an African American student perceives the White counselor as less critical and less judgmental than the African American counselor, especially if the African American counselor is in the immersion-emersion status. On the other hand, if the African American counselor is in one of the advanced statuses and is secure in his African American heritage, the pre-encounter African American student may feel safe and secure from fear of rejection. Thus, when counselors and student affairs professionals are aware of their and others' racial identity statuses, they may be more equipped or competent to help African American students work through issues related to race and culture.

Professionals who work with African American students at predominantly White institutions should be aware of the powerful influence and psychological consequences of racial identity. Moreover, they should be aware that some African American students may be treated differently by faculty, administrators, as well as other students. It is unfortunate that some African American students may internalize stereotypes and experience a variety of psychological and emotional consequences. Some of these consequences may include loneliness, low self-esteem, self-defeating behaviors, distortion of attractiveness, inability to form friendships, free-floating anxiety and depression, self-destructive behaviors and thoughts, feelings of invisibility, distortion of academic ability, and hopelessness and helplessness. Believing that racial issues are a thing of the past, coupled with not having an avenue to express racial concerns and cultural dynamics, many African American students, especially those in the pre-encounter status, may suppress their feelings about race and suffer many of the conditions just mentioned. Therefore, counselors and student affairs professionals should develop programs (e.g., focus groups, academic interventions, and other scholarly activities to encourage self-expression). In addition, innovative intellectual development programs and services designed to help students reach their goals while acknowledging their racial heritage are strongly encouraged. Moreover, institutions that infuse cultural components in their curriculum and social events tend to better equip students for the culturally affirming experiences that await them. Students attending settings that offer these features will have their cultural identity validated as they pursue their education.

In essence, those professionals working with student affairs, academic advisement, or the college campus mental health services can benefit from obtaining key information on the psychosocial characteristics of African American students in order to assist them in getting the services they need most, while supporting their academic mission (Dennis, Calvillo, & Gonzalez, 2008). Given the likely intersections of racial identity development and academic achievement, as supported by this study's statistical results, in order to further support African American students on college campuses, student affairs professionals, staff, administrators, and faculty should take several steps. These steps include continuing to increase efforts to examine both the cultural specifics and human universals of African American students and their issues, understanding their own psychosocial and personality characteristics; making a special effort to understand African American students within their specific cultural contexts; exploring personal assumptions and worldviews about African American people, culture, and values; and becoming more involved in a lifelong process of growth and change moving toward becoming a culturally skilled and a culturally sensitive multicultural and multiracial specialist.

Practical Implications for College Students From Urban High Schools

The primary impetus for this book is to provide information to ensure that African American students from urban high school environments have an equal opportunity of obtaining a college education. In light of the research highlighted in many of the chapters in this book, as well as empirical data describing the experiences of African American students in urban school settings (Reid & Moore, 2008), it is well known that the pursuit of excellence for African American students who attend urban high schools and ultimately college may be challenged and even suppressed prior to their enrollment in secondary education. Due to the fact that limited research in the scholarly literature has focused on the effects of attending an urban high school on African American students' college success from the standpoint of how faculty and student affairs professionals should adequately support this population of students, this chapter concludes with a discussion regarding some of the educational issues that urban African American students may experience in college based on their precollege experiences. If this information can be transferred into practice, high schools and postsecondary institutions may be closer to pursuing the type of social justice needed to expand educational opportunities for all Americans (Ginwright, Cammarota, & Noguera, 2005). In this regard, the pursuit of social justice may be broadly conceived as attempting to utilize resources to address issues that are faced by some populations and not by others. For example, if we know that some African American students who attend large urban schools may not receive adequate and timely information regarding college attendance, a social justice stance may require us to employ resources that would help to equalize educational opportunities and access to requisite knowledge for urban African American students.

Rodríguez (2008) notes that, although reducing school size may be important to help urban high school students realize student success outcomes, what may be more important is to focus on the relationships that educational personnel (e.g., teachers, school counselors, and educational leaders) have with students that can positively reinforce desirable academic orientations. This information may be relevant for urban school districts as they seek ways to utilize limited resources to support graduation and achievement outcomes in high schools. Perhaps, as reinforced by Rodríguez's work, a focus on developing positive social interactions among students and the school culture may enhance students' achievement outcomes. This may engender trust among urban students and educators in a way that promotes academic orientations that lead to more enhanced student perspectives that result in achievement.

A study by Reid and Moore (2008) further demonstrates that students from urban high school environments, even students with high grade point averages, may feel underprepared for the rigors of pursuing academic success in college. Reid and Moore's findings suggest that negative academic orientations that some students have with regard to their academic self-efficacy may result in tangible outcomes, such as underperforming in college and feeling as if they are not ready to handle college-level coursework. Some of the students in their study note specific areas in high school that promote these negative feelings and behaviors in college, citing the following topics: (a) a lack of opportunities to study abroad and learn deeply about other cultures, (b) a lack of focused attention on developing time management skills, (c) a lack of opportunities to develop skills to read and write in a way that best prepares them for college-level academic tasks, and (d) a lack of educational resources and curriculum options that are more advanced and promote higher-order thinking. Together, these and other factors result in college students developing racial and academic identities that are based on negative academic orientations and perspectives with regard to their intellectual abilities and self-concepts. Knowing this information may be helpful not only for urban high schools seeking to address these issues with their students but also for the student affairs professional seeking to provide a college environment that is both academically and socially beneficial for all students.

REFERENCES

Abrams, L., & Trusty, J. (2004). African Americans' racial identity and socially desirable responding: An empirical model. *Journal of Counseling and Development, 82*(3), 365–374.

Acosta, F. X., Yamamoto, J., & Evans, L. A. (1982). *Effective psychotherapy for low income and minority patients.* New York, NY: Plenum Press.

Akbar, N. (1979). African roots of Black personality. In W. Smith, K. Burlew, M. Mosley, & W. Whitney (Eds.), *Reflections of black psychology* (pp. 79–87). Washington, DC: University Press of America.

Anaya, G. (1999). College impact on student learning: Comparing the use of self-reported gains, standardized test scores, and college grades. *Research in Higher Education, 40*(5), 499–526.

Astin, A.W. (1993). *What matters in college? Four critical years revisited.* San Francisco, CA: Jossey-Bass.

Beck, H. P., & Davidson, W. D. (2001). Establishing an early warning system: Predicting low grades in college students from Survey of Academic Orientations scores. *Research in Higher Education, 42*(6), 709–723.

Berry, W. D., & Feldman, S. (1985). *Multiple regression in practice.* Newbury Park, CA: Sage.

Caplan, N. (1970). The new ghetto man: A review of recent empirical studies. *Journal of Social Issues, 26*(1), 57–73.

Cheek, D. (1976). *Assertive Black . . . puzzled White.* San Luis Obispo, CA: Impact.

Chickering, A. W., & Reisser, L. (1993). *Education and identity* (2nd ed.). San Francisco, CA: Jossey-Bass.

Cohen, J., & Cohen, P. (1975). *Applied multiple regression/correlation analysis for the behavioral sciences.* Hillsdale, NJ: Lawrence Erlbaum.

Cohen, S., & Wills, T. A. (1985). Stress, social support, and the buffering hypothesis. *Psychological Bulletin, 98*(2), 310–357.

Cokley, K. (2001). Gender differences among African American students in racial identity and its implications for academic psychosocial development. *Journal of College Student Development, 42*(5), 480–486.

Cokley, K. (2002). Ethnicity, gender, and academic self-concept: A preliminary examination of academic disidentification and implications for psychologists. *Cultural Diversity and Ethnic Minority Psychology, 8*(4), 378–388.

Cross, W. E., Jr. (1971). The Negro-to-Black conversion experience: Toward a psychology of Black liberation. *Black World, 20*(9), 13–27.

Cross, W. E., Jr. (1978). The Thomas and Cross models of psychological Nigrescence: A review. *Journal of Black Psychology, 5*(1), 13–31.

Cross, W. E., Jr. (1980). Models of psychological Nigrescence: A literature review. In R. Jones (Ed.), *Black Psychology* (2nd ed., pp.81–98). New York, NY: Harper & Row.

Cross, W. E. (1991). *Shades of black: Diversity in African-American identity.* Philadelphia, PA: Temple University Press.

Cross, W. E., Jr. (1995). The psychology of Nigrescence: Revising the Cross model. In J.G. Ponterotto, J. M. Casas, L. A. Suzuki, & C. M. Alexander (Eds.), *Handbook of multicultural counseling* (pp. 93–122). Thousand Oaks, CA: Sage.

Cross, W. E., & Vandiver, B. J. (2001). Nigrescence theory and measurement: Introducing the Cross Racial Identity Scale (CRIS). In J. G. Ponterotto, J. M. Casas, L. M. Suzuki, & C. M. Alexander (Eds.), *Handbook of multicultural counseling* (2nd ed., pp. 371–393). Thousand Oaks, CA: Sage.

Davidson, W. B., Beck, H. P., & Silver, N. C. (1999). Development and validation of scores on a measure of six academic orientations in college students. *Educational and Psychological Measurement, 59*(4), 678–693

Demo, R. M., & Parker, K. D. (1987). Academic achievement and self-esteem among black and white college students. *Journal of Social Psychology, 127*(4), 345–355.

Dennis, J. M., Calvillo, E., & Gonzalez, A. (2008). The role of psychosocial variables in understanding the achievement and retention of transfer students at an ethnically diverse urban university. *Journal of College Student Development, 49*(6), 535–550.

Dennis, J. M., Phinney, J., & Chuateco, L. I. (2005). The role of motivation, parental support, and peer support in the academic success of ethnic minority first-generation college students. *Journal of College Student Development, 46*(3), 223–236. doi: 10.1353/csd.2005.0023

Dewey, J. (1938). *Experience and education.* New York, NY: Macmillan.

Dizard, J. E. (1970). Black identity, social class, and black power. *Psychiatry, 33*(2), 195–207.

Erikson, E. H. (1968). *Identity: Youth and crisis.* New York, NY: Norton.

Essandoh, P. K. (1995). Counseling issues with African American college students in U.S. colleges and universities. *The Counseling Psychologist, 23*(2), 348–360.

Evans, N. J., Forney, D. S., & Guido-DiBrito, F. (1998). *Student development in college: Theory, research, and practice.* San Francisco, CA: Jossey-Bass.

Flowers, L. A. (2004). Examining the effects of student involvement on African American college student development. *Journal of College Student Development, 45*(6), 633–654.

Gay, G. (2000). *Culturally responsive teaching: Theory, research, and practice.* New York, NY: Teachers College Press.

Ginwright, S., Cammarota, J., & Noguera, P. (2005). Youth, social justice, and communities: Toward a theory of urban youth policy. *Social Justice, 32*(3), 24–40.

Gushue, G. V., & Sicalides, E. I. (1997). Helm's racial identity theory and Bowen's family system model: A case study. In C. E. Thompson & R. T. Carter (Eds.), *Racial identity theory* (pp. 127–145). Mahwah, NJ: Lawrence Erlbaum.

Hall, W. S., Cross, W. E., Jr., & Freedle, R. (1972). Stages in the development of black awareness: An exploratory investigation. In R. L. Jones (Ed.), *Black psychology* (pp.156–165). New York, NY: Harper & Row.

Hays, W. L. (1994). *Statistics* (5th ed.). Fort Worth, TX: Harcourt Brace College.

Helms, J. E. (1985). Cultural identity in the treatment process. In P. B. Pedersen (Ed.). *Handbook of cross-cultural counseling and therapy.* Westport, CT: Greenwood Press.

Helms, J. E. (Ed.). (1990). *Black and white racial identity: Theory, research, and practice.* Westport, CT: Greenwood Press.

Helms, J. E. (1995). An update of Helms's white and people of color racial identity models. In J. G. Ponterotto, J. M. Casas, L. A. Suzuki, & C. M. Alexander (Eds.), *Handbook of multicultural counseling* (pp. 181–191). Thousand Oaks, CA: Sage.

Helms, J. E., & Cook, D. A. (1999). *Using race and culture in counseling and psychotherapy: Theory and process.* Boston, MA: Allyn & Bacon.

Hemmings, A. (2007). Seeing the light: Cultural and social capital productions in an inner-city high school. *The High School Journal, 90*(3), 9–17.

Holland, N. E., & Farmer-Hinton, R. L. (2009). Leave no schools behind: The importance of college culture in urban public high schools. *The High School Journal, 92*(3), 24–43.

Holt, L. J., Bry, B. H., & Johnson, V. L. (2008). Enhancing school engagement in at-risk, urban minority adolescents through a school-based, adult mentoring intervention. *Child & Family Behavior Therapy, 30*(4), 297–318.

Jackson, B. (1975). Black identity development. In L. Golubschick & B. Persky (Eds.), *Urban social and educational issues* (pp. 158–164). Dubuque, IA: Kendall-Hall.

Kenny, M. E., Gualdron, L., Scanlon, D., Sparks, E., Blustein, D. L., & Jernigan, M. (2007). Urban adolescents' constructions of supports and barriers to educational and career attainment. *Journal of Counseling Psychology, 54*(3), 336–343.

King, J. (2005). *Black education: A transformative research and action agenda for the new century.* Hillsdale, NJ: Lawrence Erlbaum.

Maton, K., & Hrabowski, F. A. (2004). Increasing the number of African American PhDs in the sciences and engineering: A strengths-based approach. *American Psychologist, 59*(6), 547–556.

Mitchell, S., & Dell, D. (1992). The relationship between black students' racial identity attitude and participation in campus organizations. *Journal of College Student Development, 33*(1), 39–43.

Moore, J., Lovell, C., McGann, T., & Wyrick, J. (1998). Why involvement matters: A review of research on student involvement in the collegiate setting. *College Student Affairs Journal, 17*(2), 4–17.

Murrell, P. (2002). *African-centered pedagogy.* Albany: State University of New York Press.

Osborne, J. (1997). Race and academic disidentification. *Journal of Educational Psychology, 89*(4), 728–735.

Parham, T. A., & Helms, J. E. (1981). The influences of black students' racial identity attitude on preferences for counselor's race. *Journal of Counseling Psychology, 28*(3), 250–257.

Parker, M., & Flowers, L. A. (2003). The effects of racial identity on academic achievement and perceptions of campus connectedness on African American students at predominantly white institutions. *College Student Affairs Journal, 22*(2), 180–194.

Pascarella, E. T. (1980). Student-faculty informal contact and college outcomes. *Review of Educational Research, 50*(4), 545–595.

Pascarella, E. T. (1985). College environmental influences on learning and cognitive development: A critical review and synthesis. In J. C. Smart (Ed.), *Higher education: Handbook of theory and research* (Vol. 1, pp. 1–61). New York, NY: Agathon Press.

Pascarella, E. T., & Terenzini, P. T. (1991). *How college affects students: Findings and insights from twenty years of research.* San Francisco, CA: Jossey-Bass.

Pascarella, E. T., & Terenzini, P. T. (2005). *How college affects students: A third decade of research* (2nd ed.). San Francisco, CA: Jossey-Bass.

Pedhazur, E. J. (1997). *Multiple regression in behavioral research: Explanation and prediction* (3rd ed.). Orlando, FL: Harcourt Brace College.

Phinney, J., Dennis, J., & Osorio, S. (2006). Reasons to attend college among ethnically diverse college students. *Cultural Diversity and Ethnic Minority Psychology, 12*(2), 347–376.

Piaget, J. (1952). *The origins of intelligence in children.* New York, NY: International Universities Press.

Pierce, W., Lemke, E., & Smith, R. (1988). Critical thinking and moral development in secondary students. *The High School Journal, 71*(3), 120–126.

Pike, G. R. (1995). The relationships between self-reports of college experiences and achievement test scores. *Research in Higher Education, 36*(1), 1–22.

Pike, G. R. (1996). Limitations of using students' self-reports of academic achievement measures. *Research in Higher Education, 37*(1), 89–114.

Piro, J., & Lorio, J. (1991). Rationale and responsibilities in the teaching of critical thinking to American schoolchildren. *Journal of Instructional Psychology, 17*(1), 3–12.

Ponterotto, J. G., Casas, J. M., Suzuki, L. A., & Alexander, C. M. (1995). *Handbook of multicultural counseling.* Thousand Oaks, CA: Sage.

Ponterotto, J. G., & Wise, S. L. (1987). Construct validity study of the racial identity attitudes scale. *Journal of Counseling Psychology, 34,* 218–223.

Reid, M. J., & Moore, J. L., III. (2008). College readiness and academic preparation for postsecondary education: Oral histories of first-generation urban college students. *Urban Education, 43*(2), 240–261.

Reis, S. M., Colbert, R. D., & Hébert, T. P. (2005). Understanding resilience in diverse, talented students in an urban high school. *Roeper Review, 27*(2), 110–120.

Robbins, S. B., Lauver, K., Le, H., Davis, D., Langley, R., & Carlstrom, A. (2004). Do psychosocial and study skill factors predict college outcomes? A meta-analysis. *Psychological Bulletin, 130*(2), 261–288.

Rodríguez, L. F. (2008). "Teachers know you can do more": Understanding how school cultures of success affect urban high school students. *Educational Policy, 22*(5), 758–780.

Rowley, S., Sellers, R., Chavous, T., & Smith, M. (1998). The relationship between racial identity and self-esteem in African American college students. *Journal of Personality and Social Psychology, 74*(3), 715–772.

Schunk, D. H. (1989). Self-efficacy and achievement behaviors. *Educational Psychology Review, 1,* 173–208.

Schunk, D. H. (1991). Self-efficacy and academic motivation. *Educational Psychologist, 26*(3), 207–231.

Skowron, E., Wester, S., & Azen, R. (2004). Differentiation of self mediates college stress and adjustment. *Journal of Counseling and Development, 82*(1), 69–78.

Steele, C. (1992). Race and the schooling of African Americans. *Atlantic Monthly, 269*(4), 68–78.

Steele, C., & Aronson, J. (1995). Stereotype threat and the intellectual performance of African Americans. *Journal of Personality and Social Psychology, 69*(5), 797–811.

Sutton, E. M., & Kimbrough, W. M. (2001). Trends in black student involvement. *NASPA Journal, 39*(1), 30–40.

Taylor, C. M., & Howard-Hamilton, M. F. (2001). Student involvement and racial identity attitudes among African American males. *Journal of College Student Development, 36*(4), 330–336.

Terenzini, P. T., Pascarella, E. T., & Blimling, G. S. (1999). Students' out-of-class experiences and their influence on learning and cognitive development: A literature review. *Journal of College Student Development, 37*(2), 149–162.

Terenzini, P. T., Springer, L., Pascarella, E. T., & Nora, A. (1995). Influences affecting the development of students' critical thinking skills. *Research in Higher Education, 36*(1), 23–39.

Terenzini, P. T., & Wright, T. (1987). Influences on students' academic growth during four years of college. *Research in Higher Education, 26*(2), 161–179.

Tinto, V. (1993). *Leaving college: Rethinking the causes and cures of student attrition* (2nd ed.). Chicago: University of Chicago Press.

Thompson, C. P., Anderson, L., & Bakeman, R. (2000). Effects of racial socialization and racial identity on acculturative stress in African American college students. *Cultural Diversity and Ethnic Minority Psychology, 6*(2), 196–210.

Tucker, C. M., & Herman, K. C. (2002). Using culturally sensitive theories and research to meet the academic needs of low income African American children. *American Psychologist, 57*(10), 762–773.

Vandiver, B. J. (2001). Psychological nigrescence revisited: Introduction and overview. *Journal of Multicultural Counseling and Development, 29*(3), 165–173.

Vandiver, B. J., Cross, W. E., Jr., Worrell, F., & Fhagen-Smith, P. E. (2002). Validating the Cross Racial Identity Scale. *Journal of Counseling Psychology, 49*(1), 71–85.

Vandiver, B. J., Fhagen-Smith, P. E., Cokley, K. O., Cross, W. E., & Worrell, F. C. (2001). Cross's nigrescence model: From theory to scale to theory. *Journal of Multicultural Counseling and Development,* *29*(3), 174–199.

Van Laar, C. (2000). The paradox of low academic achievement but high self-esteem in African American students: An attributional account. *Educational Psychology Review, 12*(1), 33–61.

Vontress, C. E. (1971a). *Counseling Negroes.* Boston, MA: Houghton Mifflin.

Vontress, C. E. (1971b). Racial differences: Impediments to rapport. *Journal of Counseling Psychology, 18*(1), 7–13.

Ward, M. L. (2004). Wading through stereotypes: Positive and negative associations between media use and Black adolescents' conceptions of self. *Developmental Psychology, 40*(2), 284–294.

Williams, J. (1987). *Eyes on the prize: America's civil rights years, 1954–1965.* New York, NY: Penguin.

Worrell, F. C., Cross, W. E., & Vandiver, B. J. (2001). Nigrescence theory: Current status and challenges for the future. *Journal of Multicultural Counseling and Development, 29*(3), 201–213.

About The Editors

James L. Moore III is an associate provost in the Office of Diversity and Inclusion at The Ohio State University, where he also serves as the inaugural director of the Todd Anthony Bell National Resource Center on the African American Male. In addition, Dr. Moore is a professor of counselor education in the College of Education and Human Ecology. He has held other higher education positions at both University of South Carolina and Virginia Polytechnic Institute and State University. From 2006 to 2007, he took a leave of absence from The Ohio State University to accept the first Secondary School Counseling Coordinator position in the District of Columbia Public Schools.

Dr. Moore has a nationally and internationally recognized research agenda that focuses on how educational professionals, such as school counselors, influence the educational/career aspirations and school experiences of students of color (particularly African American males); sociocultural, familial, school, and community factors that support, enhance, and impede academic outcomes for K–20 (i.e., elementary, secondary, and postsecondary) African American students; recruitment and retention issues for students of color, particularly African Americans, in K–12 gifted education and for those high-potential college students in science, technology, engineering, and mathematics (STEM) majors; and social, emotional, and psychological consequences of racial oppression for African American males and other people of color in various domains in society (e.g., education, counseling, workplace, athletics, etc.). In a short span of time, Dr. Moore has made significant contributions in *school counseling, gifted education, urban education, higher education, multicultural education/counseling,* and *STEM education.* He has published over 85 publications and given over 150 scholarly presentations around the world, in countries including the United States, Canada, India, China, France, England, and Spain. He has also obtained over $4.5 million in grants and contracts.

Dr. Moore has biographies listed in *Outstanding Young Men in America* (1998 edition), *Academic Keys Who's Who in Education* (2003 edition), *Manchester Who's Who Among Professionals in Counseling and Development* (2005/2006 edition), *Prestige International Who's Who Registries of Outstanding Professionals* (2007 edition), and *Who's Who in Black Columbus* (2008, 2009, 2010, and 2011 editions).

He is the recipient of Brothers of the Academy's National Junior Scholar Award (2003), The Ohio State University's College of Education Distinguished Scholar Award (2004), the North Central Association for Counselor Education and Supervision Research Award (2004), Ohio School Counselor Association's Research Award (2004), American Educational Research Association's Division E Early Career Award in Counseling (2005), Ohio School Counselors Association's George E. Hill Counselor Educator Award (2005), Counselors for Social Justice's Ohana Award (2006), Phi Delta Kappa's Emerging Leaders Award (2007–2008), American Educational Research Association's Distinguished Scholar Award in Counseling–Division E (2008), National Association for Gifted Children's Early Scholar Award (2009), Institute for School-Based Family Counseling's Outstanding Contributions to School-Based Family Counseling (2009), National Association for Multicultural Education's Carl A. Grant Multicultural Research Award (2009), National Alliance of Black School Educators' W. E. B. Du Bois Higher Education Award (2010), Ohio State Black Graduate and Professional Student Caucus' Lawrence Williamson Jr. Service Award (2011), and is an inducted member in numerous professional and honor societies, such as Alpha Kappa Mu, Phi Kappa Phi, Phi Delta Kappa, Kappa Delta Pi, and Chi Sigma Iota.

Throughout the United States, Dr. Moore is a highly sought-after speaker. He has appeared in numerous documentaries, television and radio programs, and print media publications (i.e., newspapers, magazines, etc.). He has also frequently served as an education consultant and evaluator for a variety of school systems, state education departments, universities, and nonprofit agencies around the country.

Chance W. Lewis is the Carol Grotnes Belk Distinguished Professor and Endowed Chair of Urban Education at The University of North Carolina at Charlotte. Dr. Lewis teaches urban education graduate courses in the College of Education and coordinates its urban education doctoral program division. He also serves as the executive director of The University of North Carolina at Charlotte Urban Research and Policy Collaborative.

Over the years, Dr. Lewis has held a number of positions in K–12 and higher education settings. From 2006 to 2011, he served as the Houston Endowed Chair and associate professor of Urban Education in the College of Education at Texas A&M University. During that time, Dr. Lewis also served as the Co-director of the Center for Urban School Partnerships. From 2001 to 2006, he was an assistant professor of teacher education at Colorado State University, and, from 1994 to 1998, he was a business education teacher in East Baton Rouge Parish Schools in Baton Rouge, Louisiana, where he earned teacher of the year honors in 1997.

Dr. Lewis has over 100 publications, including 50+ refereed journal articles in some of the leading academic journals in urban education and teacher education. He has received over $4 million in grants and contracts from government agencies and private corporations. To date, Dr. Lewis has authored/coauthored/coedited six books: *White Teachers/Diverse Classrooms: A Guide to Building Inclusive Schools, Promoting High Expectations, and Eliminating Racism*; *The Dilemmas of Being an African American Male in the New Millennium: Solutions for Life Transformation*; *An Educator's Guide to Working With African American Students: Strategies for Promoting Academic Success*; *Transforming Teacher Education: What Went Wrong With Teacher Training, and How We Can Fix It*; *White Teachers/Diverse Classrooms: Creating Inclusive Schools, Building on Students' Diversity and Providing True Educational Equity*; and *Yes We Can! Improving Urban Schools Through Innovative Educational Reform*.

Because of Dr. Lewis's scholastic achievements, over 100 school districts and universities across the United States and Canada have contracted his services to provide professional development and conduct program evaluations. His achievements have been recognized throughout the country in the form of numerous awards, citations, and recognitions for his work.

About The Authors

Caroline A. Baker is an assistant professor in the Counseling and School Psychology Department at the University of Wisconsin, River Falls. Previously an elementary school counselor, Dr. Baker constantly seeks new ways to grow personally and professionally in regard to cultural awareness, knowledge, and skills. She aims to impart this passion to her counseling graduate students. Having lived in South Africa during apartheid, Dr. Baker witnessed racial and ethnic disparities of privilege. This experience, among others, contributes to her research agenda focusing on marginalized groups and best practices in multicultural education.

Floyd D. Beachum is the Bennett Professor of Urban School Leadership at Lehigh University. He is also an associate professor and program director for the Educational Leadership program in the College of Education. He received his doctorate in leadership studies from Bowling Green State University, with an emphasis in educational administration. His research interests include: leadership in urban education, moral and ethical leadership, and social justice issues in K–12 schools. He has authored several peer-reviewed articles on these topics in journals, such as the *Journal of School Leadership, Multicultural Learning and Teaching, Urban Education*, and *Journal of Cases in Educational Leadership*. In addition, he is co-editor of *Urban Education for the 21st Century: Research, Issues, and Perspectives* and co-author of two books, *Radicalizing Educational Leadership: Dimensions of Social Justice* and *Cultural Collision and Collusion: Reflections on Hip-Hop Culture, Values, and Schools*.

Robert Q. Berry III is an associate professor of mathematics education at the University of Virginia in the Curry School of Education, with an appointment in the Curriculum Instruction and Special Education Department, in which he serves as the Coordinator of the Elementary Education Program. Dr. Berry teaches elementary and special education mathematics methods courses in the Teacher Education Program. His research focuses on equity issues in mathematics education, with a particular focus on African American boys. In addition, Dr. Berry does research on mathematical instructional quality and children's engineering.

Fred A. Bonner II is the Samuel DeWitt Proctor Chair in the Graduate School of Education at Rutgers University. He is a former professor of higher education administration in the Educational Administration and Human Resource Development Department at Texas A&M University. Dr. Bonner has been the recipient of the American Association for Higher Education Black Caucus Dissertation Award and the Educational Leadership, Counseling, and Foundation's Dissertation of the Year Award from the College of Education at the University of Arkansas. He recently completed the book, *Academically Gifted African American Male College Students*, which highlights the experiences of post-secondary gifted African American male undergraduates in predominantly White and historically Black college contexts. With coauthors Aretha Faye Marbley and Mary F. Howard-Hamilton, he is anticipating the publication of *Diverse Millennial Students in College: Implications for Faculty and Student Affairs* by Stylus Publications. During the 2005–2006 academic year, Dr. Bonner served as an American Council on Education Fellow in the Office of the President at Old Dominion University in Norfolk, Virginia. In addition, he has been awarded a $1 million National Science Foundation grant that focuses on factors influencing the success of high-achieving African American students in science, technology, engineering, and mathematics at historically Black colleges and universities.

Beverly Booker is an assistant professor of school counseling in the College of Education at the California State University, Long Beach. Dr. Booker's research focuses on the impact of international service learning on students' leadership development and level of community engagement; collaborative practices among school leaders that impact students' achievement and opportunity gaps; the use of empowerment and activity theories to address systemic issues in K–12 schools; and school counselors' use of participatory action research to develop collaborative solutions to school issues. In addition, Dr. Booker works as a consultant on diverse topics, such as ethics and advocacy among school counselors; solution focused brief counseling; and school-wide program development in K–12 schools. She has over 12 years of experience as a teacher, school counselor, director of high school counseling, and counselor educator.

Nikol V. Bowen is an assistant professor in the Department of Counseling and Higher Education at Ohio University. Dr. Bowen is also a licensed professional counselor, with experience working in K–12 schools, community agencies, and partial hospitalization programs. Her research interests focus on multicultural issues within counseling and counselor education, self-care and career development for counselors and counselor educators, and the impact of communication skills on mental health. At the current time, Dr. Bowen is the President of both the Ohio Mental Health Counselors Association and Central Ohio Counseling Association. In addition to her work at Ohio University, Dr. Bowen also serves as a consultant for the Kirwan Institute for the Study of Race and Ethnicity at The Ohio State University. In this capacity, she leads focus groups, working groups, and town hall meetings with communities and school districts in various regions of the country to inform public policies on integration and diversity.

Bryan A. Brown is an assistant professor of teacher education in the School of Education at Stanford University. He received his PhD and MA in science education from University of California, Santa Barbara, and his BS in biology from Hampton University. Dr. Brown's research explores the relationship between student identity, discourse, classroom culture, and academic achievement in science education. It also focuses on the social connotations and cultural politics of science discourse in small-group and whole-group interactions. In addition, his research work in science education examines how teacher and student discourse serve to shape learning opportunities for students in science classrooms. Dr. Brown's work over the years has expanded beyond science education to include issues of college access in urban communities.

Bettie Ray Butler is an assistant professor of urban education in the Department of Middle, Secondary, and K–12 Education at the University of North Carolina, Charlotte. Dr. Butler's research interests focus primarily on education policy with specific attention to issues of equity, representation, and achievement among underrepresented student populations.

Gwendolyn Cartledge is a professor in special education at The Ohio State University. Dr. Cartledge earned her bachelor's and master's degrees from the University of Pittsburgh and her doctorate from The Ohio State University. She documents an extensive teaching career in both the public schools and higher education. A faculty member at The Ohio State University since 1986, her professional teaching, research, and writings have focused on students with mild disabilities, the development of social skills, and early intervention and prevention of learning and behavior problems through effective instruction. At the current time, Dr. Cartledge's research and writing interests concentrate on reducing disproportionate representations through behavioral and reading interventions, with a particular emphasis on urban and culturally/linguistically diverse learners. Her work is documented in writings that include four coauthored books, two social skills curricula, and numerous articles in professional journals.

Terah Venzant Chambers received her PhD in educational policy studies from the University of Illinois at Urbana-Champaign. At the current time, Dr. Chambers is an assistant professor in the Department of Educational Administration and Human Resource Development at Texas A&M University. She teaches courses on the foundations of education, contemporary issues in African American desegregation, and research methods. Her research interests are broad, ranging between urban education and education policy. More specific, she is interested in the influences African American students' experiences in tracked schools have on their academic achievement and school engagement, as well as the "costs" of school success (i.e., racial opportunity costs) for high-achieving students of color. In 2010, Dr. Chambers was the College of Education and Human Development Outstanding New Faculty Member at Texas A&M University.

Christopher Dunbar Jr. is a professor in the Department of Educational Administration at Michigan State University. He earned his doctorate in educational policy studies from The University of Illinois at Urbana-Champaign. Dr. Dunbar has published several scholarly articles in journals, including *Theory Into Practice* and *Peabody Journal of Education*. He has also written a book about children expelled from traditional public schools and subsequently placed in alternative school environments. Over the years, Dr. Dunbar has presented his research at the American Education Research Association (AERA), University Council of Educational Administrators (UCEA), and the American Education Studies Association (AESA). His research interests include urban school leadership; alternative education and zero tolerance policies; and the intersection between schools, families, and communities. At Michigan State University, he coordinates the urban specialization sequence of courses developed for PhD students who have an interest in teaching or conducting research in urban school environments.

Edward C. Fletcher Jr. is an assistant professor in the Career and Workforce Education Program at the University of South Florida. Dr. Fletcher currently serves as coordinator for the master's degree program in career and technical education. His primary research interest is studying the longitudinal effects of high school curriculum tracking in regard to postsecondary and labor market outcomes in adulthood. Dr. Fletcher earned his bachelor's degree in business and marketing education and his master's degree in career and technical education from University of Missouri, and his doctorate in workforce development and education from The Ohio State University.

Lamont A. Flowers is the Distinguished Professor of Educational Leadership in the Department of Leadership, Counselor Education, Human and Organizational Development and the Executive Director of the Charles H. Houston Center for the Study of the Black Experience in Education in the Eugene T. Moore School of Education at Clemson University. Dr. Flowers received a bachelor of science degree in accounting from Virginia Commonwealth University. He received a master of arts degree in social studies education and a doctorate in higher education from the

University of Iowa. Dr. Flowers also received a master of industrial statistics degree from the University of South Carolina.

Donna Y. Ford is a professor in both the Department of Special Education and Department of Teaching and Learning at Vanderbilt University. Her work focuses on minority student achievement and underachievement; recruiting and retaining culturally diverse students in gifted education; multicultural and urban education; and family involvement. Dr. Ford is cofounder of the Scholar Identity Institute for Black Males. She is the author of several books and more than 100 articles and chapters, and she makes presentations nationally at professional conferences and school districts.

Lenwood Gibson Jr. is an assistant professor of special education at City University of New York. He received his MS in applied behavior analysis from Northeastern University and his PhD in special education from The Ohio State University. Dr. Gibson's expertise is the identification and treatment of behavioral deficits for high-risk student populations. His current research interests include the use and effectiveness of computer-assisted instruction as a supplemental tool for students at risk for academic failure, particularly in urban schools; closing the academic achievement gap between minority and nonminority students; and closing the research-to-practice gap in special education.

J. Bryan Henderson is a PhD candidate at Stanford University, studying science education. His main interest is in the utilization of educational technology to put students more in charge of their own learning via effective formative assessment. He also sees educational technology as an asset in controlling for teacher fidelity in empirical classroom-based research studies. As a founder and research director of the 501(c)(3) non-profit NorCal EdTech, Mr. Henderson is working with Northern California teachers to make expensive educational technology applications freely accessible over the Internet. His scientific background is in astrophysics, with research stints at major observatories in Arizona, Chile, and The Netherlands. He has taught statistics and physics at both the university and community college level. Mr. Henderson has three bachelor's degrees in physics, astronomy, and philosophy (with distinction) from the University of Washington and two master's degrees in physics and postsecondary education from Portland State University.

Erik M. Hines is an assistant professor and coordinator of the School Counseling Program in the Department of Counseling and Educational Development at University of North Carolina at Greensboro. He is also an affiliate faculty member in the Department of African American Studies at University of North Carolina at Greensboro. Dr. Hines's research focuses on African American male academic achievement and college readiness; parental involvement and its impact on academic achievement for students of color; and improving and increasing postsecondary opportunities for first-generation, low-income, and minority students, particularly African American males.

Cheryl Holcomb-McCoy is Vice Dean of Academic Affairs and a professor in the Department of Counseling and Human Services at Johns Hopkins University's School of Education. She is the author of more than 50 refereed journal articles on topics related to urban school counseling, multicultural counseling competence, and school–family–community partnerships. Dr. Holcomb-McCoy is also the author of the book, *School Counseling to Close the Achievement Gap: A Framework for Success*, and is the recipient of the 2009 Mary Smith Arnold Anti-Oppression Award from the Counselors for Social Justice Division of the American Counseling Association.

LaTrelle D. Jackson is a licensed clinical psychologist and certified forensic counselor. Dr. Jackson is an associate professor in the School of Psychology and Counseling, Special Assistant to the Executive Vice President, and Director of the Psychological Services Center at Regent University. She earned her BA, MA, and PhD from the University of Georgia. After completing her American Psychological Association-accredited internship at Michigan State University, she secured professional appointments at Pennsylvania State University and the University of Florida, before joining the faculty at Regent University. Committed to community empowerment and culturally competent education, Dr. Jackson has engaged in a variety of academic, business, political, and community-based endeavors. Her current research interests include consultation/supervision, mentorship, moral leadership, and diversity issues.

Starr E. Keyes is an assistant professor in special education at Bowling Green State University. She has taught undergraduate and graduate courses on literacy, classroom management, diversity, research methods, and special education. She earned her BA in psychology at The Ohio State University, MEd in special education from the University of Toledo, and PhD in special education and applied behavior analysis from The Ohio State University. Prior to obtaining her doctorate, Dr. Keyes taught general and special education students in kindergarten through eighth grade. She has co-authored several articles. Her teaching and research interests include computer-assisted instruction, literacy, early intervention/prevention of disabilities, disproportionality, and urban education.

Matthew Kloser is currently a postdoctoral scholar at Stanford University's Center to Support Excellence in Teaching. His work is focused on science-specific core teaching practices and the training and professional development necessary for teachers to effectively execute these core practices. Dr. Kloser received his MS in biology and his PhD in science education at Stanford University, where his research focused on teaching and learning in biology classrooms, including issues of climate change in middle and high school settings; the impact of various types of science texts on student interest, learning, and epistemology in high school biology classrooms; and the impact of authentic research lab experiences on undergraduate biology students. Prior to beginning his doctoral studies (after earning his MEd from the University of Notre Dame), Dr. Kloser spent four years teaching high school science and math.

Gilda Martinez-Alba received her EdD in teacher development and leadership from the Johns Hopkins University. She is an associate professor in the Department of Educational Technology and Literacy at Towson University. Dr. Martinez's primary research and teaching interests are literacy development among pre-K English Speakers of Other Languages (ESOL), adolescent literacy in urban contexts, and school–community collaboration, with a particular focus on school–library partnerships. Two of her most recent articles are published in the *TESOL Journal* and the *Journal of Adolescent & Adult Literacy*. She is currently conducting research on the in-school and out-of-school experiences of college students from urban areas in the United States.

Carlos R. McCray is an associate professor at Fordham University where he teaches a seminar on ethics and social justice. His research interests include multicultural education and building level leadership. He has also done extensive research on issues surrounding urban education. His work has appeared in journals, such as the *Journal of School Leadership*, *Journal of Cases in Educational Leadership*, *Urban Education*, and *International Journal of Education Policy and Leadership*. Dr. McCray is also co-author of the book titled *Cultural Collision and Collusion: Reflections on Hip-Hop Culture, Values, and Schools*.

Laura McNeal is a fellow in the Charles Hamilton Houston Institute for Race and Justice at Harvard Law School. Dr. McNeal holds a JD in law from Washington University, St. Louis, and a PhD in education administration from Illinois State University. She has held faculty positions in the College of Education at both Georgia State University and Michigan State University; at the latter, she taught education law, policy and leadership courses. Dr. McNeal believes that urban youth and education policy require an interdisciplinary approach that is refreshingly new, theoretically rich, and methodologically rigorous. More specifically, her research interests involve examining how law and policy impact urban student achievement and effective school leadership. Dr. McNeal is a published author and has presented her research at numerous national conferences.

H. Richard (Rich) Milner IV is an associate professor in the Department of Teaching and Learning at Vanderbilt University. He also has a secondary appointment in the Department of Leadership, Policy, and Organizations. Dr. Milner earned a doctor of philosophy degree and master of arts degree in educational policy and leadership from The Ohio State University. He also earned a master of arts degree in teaching and a bachelor of arts degree in English from South Carolina State University. During his doctoral studies, he worked as an adjunct instructor at Columbus State Community College, where he taught reading and writing courses in the Department of Developmental Studies. Dr. Milner's research, teaching, and policy interests focus on urban education, teacher education, African American literature, and the sociology of education. During the summer of 2010, he was honored with a visiting scholar fellowship at York University in Toronto, Canada, where he taught in the Language, Literacy, and Culture Program. During the summers of 2010 and 2011, he served as a visiting faculty member in the Department of Policy and Leadership at the University of Texas at Austin, where he taught aspiring principals. At the current time, Dr. Milner is chair of the Language, Literacy, and Culture Program and Founding Chair of a new master's program in learning, diversity, and urban studies at Vanderbilt University. He is also the editor of *Urban Education*. Over the years, he has published more than 70 journal articles and book chapters and has published five books. His most recent book, published in 2010 by Harvard Education Press, is *Start Where You Are but Don't Stay There: Understanding Diversity, Opportunity Gaps, and Teaching in Today's Classrooms*.

John W. Murry Jr. is an associate professor of higher education and program coordinator in the College of Education and Health Professions at the University of Arkansas. Over the years, he has held numerous administrative positions, including associate dean for administration, department head, and graduate coordinator. He holds a BS and BA in finance, an MBA in marketing and management, a JD in law, and an EdD in higher education administration from the University of Arkansas. His research interests focus on minority student access to higher education and legal issues related to faculty and academic administration. Dr. Murry is the coauthor with Chritopher J. Lucas of a guidebook for faculty, now in its third edition, titled *New Faculty: A Practical Guide for Academic Beginners*.

Barbara O'Neal is an assistant professor in the School Administration Program in the School of Education at North Carolina A&T State University. She received her bachelor's degree in early childhood education from Winston-Salem State University, her master's degree in educational administration from North Carolina A&T State University, and her doctoral degree in educational administration from Virginia Polytechnic Institute and State University. Dr. O'Neal previously served as the project director and principal investigator for a six-year, $6.7 million U.S. Department of Education teacher quality enhancement partnership grant at South Carolina State University and assistant professor in Educational Leadership. She is the coauthor with Earline Simms and Cash Kowalski and editor of *Perspectives in Teacher Education Reform: Unique Partnership Initiatives*. Dr. O'Neal is currently working on several research projects. Her scholarly foci and interests are in the area of leadership and student achievement for low-performing schools.

W. Max Parker is a licensed mental health counselor in the Counseling and Wellness Center at the University of Florida. Dr. Parker received his BS in English and Spanish from Stillman College and an MS in counselor education from the University of South Florida. He also holds a PhD in counselor education and educational administration from the University of Florida. His areas of specialty include multicultural counseling, group counseling, and psychotherapy. He is the coauthor of three books, including *Becoming Multiculturally Responsible on Campus: From Awareness to Action* (with Jennifer Sager); *Consciousness-Raising: A Primer for Multicultural Counseling* (with Mary Fukuyama)*; and Images of Me: A Guide to Group Work With African-American Women* (with Sherlon Pack-Brown and Linda Whittington-Clark). His current interests include developing self-confidence among college students and enhancing academic achievement among African American males on campus.

Mavis G. Sanders received her PhD in education from Stanford University. Dr. Sanders is a professor of education at the University of Maryland, Baltimore County (UMBC) and Senior Adviser to the National Network of Partnership Schools at Johns Hopkins University. She is the author of many publications on how schools and districts develop their partnership programs and effects of partnerships on African American adolescents' school success. Her most recent book, *Principals Matter: A Guide to School, Family, and Community Partnerships* (with Steven Sheldon), focuses on principals' leadership for developing effective partnership programs. At the current time, Dr. Sanders is conducting a multiple case study on principal, teacher, and parent roles in community schools offering integrated services. This study is a grant-funded project sponsored by the Spencer Foundation.

Alfred W. Tatum is an associate professor in the Department of Literacy, Language, & Culture at the University of Illinois at Chicago. Before joining the faculty, Dr. Tatum was a reading clinic director and senior program associate for the North Central Regional Education Lab and an assistant professor of curriculum and instruction at the University of Maryland. Dr. Tatum currently serves on the National Advisory Reading Committee of the National Assessment of Educational Progress. He has published his work in numerous journals, including *Reading Research*

Quarterly, The Reading Teacher, Journal of Adolescent & Adult Literacy, Educational Leadership, Journal of College Reading and Learning, and *Principal Leadership.*

Temple A. Walkowiak is an assistant professor of mathematics education in the Department of Elementary Education at North Carolina State University (NCSU). She holds a PhD in mathematics education from the University of Virginia and an MEd in middle education and BS in mathematics from James Madison University. At NCSU, Dr. Walkowiak teaches mathematics methods courses to preservice elementary teachers and graduate courses in mathematics education for practicing elementary teachers. Her research focuses on mathematics instructional quality in elementary classrooms. Through this study, she examines factors that influence quality, with a special interest in how teacher education or professional development programs should be structured to increase teachers' mathematical knowledge and to promote high-quality mathematics teaching. Dr. Walkowiak also studies the quality of mathematics instruction received by students of varying socioeconomic backgrounds. As a former classroom teacher, mathematics specialist, and assistant principal, her experiences and interactions with students are the foundation for her understanding of mathematics teaching and learning.

Michelle D. White received her MS in educational leadership from Towson University. She is currently a doctoral student, concentrating on community schools and integrated services in the Department of Teacher Development and Leadership in the School of Education at Johns Hopkins University. Ms. White has brought to her doctoral studies over eight years of experience teaching middle and high school students at various academic levels (e.g., magnet, honors, standard, and special needs). As a master's student, she assisted faculty in conducting qualitative research on adolescents' school experiences. At the current time, she is assisting in research on the implementation and sustainability of school–family–community partnerships that increase student achievement.

Desireé Vega is currently a school psychologist with the Omaha Public Schools District in Omaha, Nebraska. She earned her BA in psychology at Binghamton University and her MA and PhD in school psychology at The Ohio State University. Dr. Vega's research interests focus on the relationship between psychological, social, and school factors and academic outcomes among African American and Latina/o youth; African American and Latina/o parental involvement in urban public schools; access to higher education among first-generation urban and undocumented Latina/o youth; and access to gifted and college-preparatory curricula for African American and Latina/o youth. While pursuing both her undergraduate and graduate education, she received numerous honors and recognitions. As a doctoral candidate, she was selected as a Bell Fellow for her scholastic achievements and strong interests in becoming a college professor.